Forensic Laboratory Management

Applying Business Principles

Forensic Laboratory Management

Applying Business Principles

W. Mark Dale, MBA, ASQ-CQA
Director, New York State Police Forensic Investigation Center - Retired

Wendy S. Becker, PhD
Shippensburg University
Pennsylvania, USA

CRC Press
Taylor & Francis Group
Boca Raton London New York

CRC Press is an imprint of the
Taylor & Francis Group, an **informa** business

CRC Press
Taylor & Francis Group
6000 Broken Sound Parkway NW, Suite 300
Boca Raton, FL 33487-2742

First issued in paperback 2021

© 2015 by Taylor & Francis Group, LLC
CRC Press is an imprint of Taylor & Francis Group, an Informa business

No claim to original U.S. Government works

ISBN 13: 978-0-367-77892-7 (pbk)
ISBN-13: 978-1-4665-5671-3 (hbk)

Library of Congress Cataloging-in-Publication Data

Dale, W. Mark.
    Forensic laboratory management : applying business principles / W. Mark Dale, Wendy S. Becker.
        pages cm
    Includes bibliographical references and index.
    ISBN 978-1-4665-5671-3 (hardback)
    1. Forensic sciences. 2. Criminal investigation. 3. Management. I. Becker, Wendy S. II. Title.

HV8073.D25293 2014
363.25068--dc23   2014027285

Visit the Taylor & Francis Web site at
http://www.taylorandfrancis.com

and the CRC Press Web site at
http://www.crcpress.com

Contents

5   ISO Accreditation Implementation : A Framework to Implement a Quality Service   281

HAROLD PEEL AND MURRAY MALCOLM

Supplementary Resources Disclaimer

Additional resources were previously made available for this title on DVD. However, as DVD have become a less accessible format, all resources have been moved to a more convenient online download option.

You can find these resources available here: https://www.routledge.com/9781466556713

Please note: Where this title mentions the associated disc, please use the downloadable resources instead.

Preface

The beginning ideas for this text all centered on several central questions:

"What is the "So What" or "Return on Investment (ROI)" of Forensic Science?"

"What does a "Right" lab look like?"

"How can forensic managers use proven business concepts to develop a forensic Cost–Benefit Analysis for fiscal policy makers that will provide good data enabling top management to properly resource forensic laboratories and be good stewards of the tax dollar?"

All forensic scientists and managers have seen firsthand the results of their efforts when the court system delivers a "rightful conviction." There are thousands or perhaps hundreds of thousands of these successful forensic analyses that include and exclude suspects resulting in rightful convictions that never make the nightly news. Few other careers can afford the opportunity to have such an impact on survivors of violent crime and the safety of our communities. The efforts of the forensic scientists and managers are multiplied in untold ways when the convicted offender is a recidivist and is no longer at large preying on future victims. The application of new technologies, most significantly DNA, and the application of digital databases (Combined DNA Index System—CODIS, National Integrated Ballistic Imaging Network—NIBIN, Automated Fingerprint Identification System —AFIS, and Biometrics) that continually compare known and question exemplars has transformed forensic science and greatly impacted the efficiency and effectiveness of the investigative processes. However, obtaining proper resources to provide quality and timely forensic services has been and remains a challenge for forensic managers. We propose the application of proven business principles and key metrics, which clearly show how forensic science adds efficiency and effectiveness to the investigative processes, good stewardship of tax dollars, and safety for our communities. The application of these business concepts shall add needed data and outcomes to recommendations for top forensic management and agency policy makers to request adequate resources to deliver the best forensic services.

Our text answers these questions and more with chapters on Leadership, Key Business Metrics, and Cost–Benefit Analyses, Ethics, Training Education and Institutes, ISO/IEC 17025 Accreditation Implementation, and Writing Policies and Procedures.

We have also included select references as a DVD insert that can be used by students, a refresher for experienced forensic scientists, attorneys, and managers:

- Two DNA mock trial transcripts from DNA students in training
- Case files supporting the two DNA mock trials
- Dr. George Carmody's transcribed 1-week workshop on Forensic DNA Statistics
- Dr. George Carmody's Statistics PowerPoint slides
- Dr. Doug Lucas's Ethics PowerPoint slides
- Larger versions of Tables 2.8, 2.17, and 2.21
- Master Excel File

We have included the Master Excel Sheet, used to generate a number of the tables within the book, on the DVD. In doing so, we want to provide readers with the access and ability to take the principles presented in the book to analyze their own data and generate performance measures for use in their laboratories.

This work would not have been possible without the efforts of several forensic champions. Doug Lucas provided a much needed chapter on ethics with an introduction by Joseph Peterson. Harold Peel and Murray Malcolm provided an excellent chapter on the practical implementation of the ISO/IEC 17025 Standard. Doctoral student, Jamie Belrose, contributed a very technical transcription of both DNA mock trials by Taryn Mead and Kimberly Sylvester, and Dr. George Carmody's Forensic Statistics lectures, in addition to her duties as a full-time doctoral student. We thank Taryn and Kimberly for allowing us to use the transcript from their mock trials for this text. They were chosen due to their excellent performance well beyond their years of experience. Our thanks also go to Chi Carmody, son and executor of Dr. George Carmody's estate, for providing his father's forensic statistics work for our text. A portion of our royalties will be dedicated to Carleton University in the name of George Carmody.

Last, I would like to thank my wife Kathy and coauthor Wendy Becker for the constant encouragement to get this "donedone."

Authors

W. Mark Dale, MBA University at Albany, BS biology Florida State University, American Society of Quality Certified Quality Auditor (ASQ-CQA) is currently coprinciple of Becker_Dale Consulting and most recently the former program manager for Forensic Education and Training at the U.S. Army Criminal Investigation Laboratory (USACIL). Previously, Dale was the director of the Northeast Regional Forensics Institute (NERFI) at the University at Albany, State University of New York, providing educa- tion primarily in forensics biology. Before  his position at NERFI, he was the director (inspector in charge) of the New York State Police Laboratory System, Washington State Laboratory System, and the New York City Police Department Laboratory. Dale has also been the presi- dent of the American Society of Crime Laboratory Directors (Emeritus mem- ber), chairman on the New York State Crime Laboratory Advisory Committee, and member of the New York State Commission on Forensic Science. Dale is also an ASCLD/LAB Legacy and International ISO/IEC 17025 trained auditor, ASQ Green Belt Six Sigma certified, and has participated in many ASCLD/LAB Legacy inspections. Dale has coauthored several forensic science management publications with Dr. Wendy Becker.

Wendy S. Becker is assistant to the asso- ciate provost and graduate dean and pro- fessor of management at Shippensburg University. She teaches in undergraduate, Master's, Ph.D., and executive programs in the United States, Austria, Portugal, Spain, and the United Kingdom. Becker received the 2011 Research Excellence Award from the Academy of Human Resource Development. Her research appears in *Organizational Research Methods, Academy*

of Management Learning and Education, Organizational Dynamics, People and Strategy, Research in Organizational Behavior, Human Resource Development Review, Organization Management Journal, Team Performance Management, and *Personnel Psychology,* among others. Becker earned her Ph.D. in industrial-organizational psychology from Pennsylvania State University. Previously, she was the editor of the *Industrial-Organizational Psychologist.*

List of Figures

List of Tables

Leadership in Forensic Science Laboratories

1

Forensic managers face difficult leadership challenges given laboratory resource limitations and constraints. Throughout the text, we address strategies to help forensic managers with difficult leadership challenges. In this chapter, we introduce a performance model with seven recommendations for increasing laboratory efficiency and effectiveness and show how leaders can implement these recommendations. The leadership team must articulate the vision and priorities for laboratory operations. Laboratory priorities have significant short-term and long-term consequences. Leadership is needed at all levels in the forensic science laboratory to provide quality and timely forensic service for the criminal justice community.

Origins and Rationale

Forensic science laboratories provide state-of-the-art services to the criminal justice community. The interdisciplinary and scientific nature of laboratories requires strong leadership ability to manage complex issues, often in adversarial settings ("Editorial: Science in Court," 2010). Many laboratory professional standards contain specific language about the authority and resources that forensic leaders need to perform their job (ISO/IEC 17025: 2005 Second Edition 2005-5-15). Yet there are serious obstacles to overcome. In times of fiscal constraint, limited resources are available for developing effective and efficient forensic science laboratories (Becker, Dale, and Pavur, 2010).

The purpose of this chapter is to review leadership strategically in scientific laboratories. We highlight a model with seven recommendations for developing laboratory efficiency and effectiveness measures and provide examples from research and practice working with forensic science leaders. Throughout we stress that the key to effective lab management is using data to make strategic decisions.

Description: National Leadership Challenges

The National Academy of Sciences (NAS) study titled *Strengthening Forensic Science in the United States: A Path Forward* has been widely discussed within the forensic community for its recommendations to strengthen the forensic sciences. The report reviews both positive and negative aspects of scientific laboratories. However, the report has not articulated a clear vision on where the path leads or how to get there; nor has it provided a vision of the end state, that is, what a quality forensic lab would look like. Rather, the NAS report provides a gap analysis of what is needed, such as sustained funding, graduate and postgraduate training, multidisciplinary and interagency research, as well as ongoing university and agency collaborations. The NAS report provides references and substantiating interviews that clearly define the problem in the state of forensic science today; a snapshot so to speak, of the industry and its challenges. In many respects, forensic science has been ahead of the curve in recognizing the importance of international collaboration and cooperation in standards setting, policy, and protocol development (Lucas, 2011). Lucas expands more on the critical ethical challenges of forensic leaders in Chapter 3. The challenge is for forensic science leaders to go beyond the recommendations from the NAS report to making the most effective and specific day-to-day decisions in their laboratory.

Risks, Problems, Barriers: Leadership Challenges in the Lab

The modern public sector forensic laboratory is a technology enterprise representative of any private organization or company. As such, the leadership challenges are quite similar to any technology-intensive organization. Forensic science leaders need to address these challenges with a heightened sense of awareness. Annual budgets of large public sector laboratory systems can range between $50 million and $100 million and employ several hundred scientific personnel. To survive, leaders in these labs must continuously monitor policy costs using measures of customer requirements, budget, capability, efficiency/effectiveness, performance, quality, turnover, intellectual capital, customer outreach, and branding.

Identifying Leadership Challenges: Insight from Forensic Leaders

Four 2-day workshops were conducted for 45 leaders representing 37 forensic science laboratories in the United States. The number of years of forensic experience in the leaders ranged from 3 to 39 ($X_\emptyset$ = 44. 32). The number of years in management ranged from less than 1 to 30 ($X_\emptyset$ = 5.29). The number of years in current job ranged from less than 1 to 23 ($X_\emptyset$ = 5.88). Position titles included director, associate director, manager, section chief, quality assurance (QA)/quality control (QC) leader, supervisor, senior scientist, and coordinator. Forensic science fields included DNA, biological sciences, toxicology, drug chemistry, latent prints, trace evidence, crime scene, firearms and tool mark, and questioned documents. Workshop topics included classic leadership theory, job analysis, role and behavioral differences between technical specialists and supervisors, conflict models, and leadership influence tactics. The workshops included class lecture and discussion, role-play exercises, modeling, case studies, and a guided tour of a state forensic science laboratory.

In the workshops forensic managers took part in role-play exercises, in which they identified leadership challenges that they had experienced. Table 1.1 provides specific challenges identified by the participants. These involve both internal and external issues including vertical and horizontal relationships with superiors, peers, and subordinates. For example, public labs of all sizes and scope face financial pressures that limit resource allocation and support. The coordination required of leaders in laboratories to influence successful outcomes is significant.

After learning specific leadership influence tactics, the managers practiced problem-solving using situations that they had previously identified. Additional suggestions and support were provided for using the tactics to influence others on laboratory priorities and issues. Much discussion ensued and in the months following the workshop, participants shared their leader influence success stories via e-mail. Dawley and Munyon (2012) provide additional support for enhancing leadership influence and positive work relationships in the laboratory, such as worker autonomy and job embeddedness.

Table 1.1 Typical Leadership Challenges in Forensic Science

• Managing problems associated with less effective employees	• Identifying qualified candidates for key positions
• Balancing backlog reduction while supervising new employees	• Increased workloads
• Managing within a command-and-control type organization	• Providing for lab succession planning
• Maintaining competitive salaries for key disciplines	• Motivating employees
• Cost cutting/staff reduction	• Providing incentives for top performers
• Finding support for sending lab personnel to training programs, especially those off-site or out of state	• Retaining key personnel
• Funding new technology and systems	• Managing a sense of entitlement among employees
• Managing generational differences of personnel	• Managing despite sworn versus civilian cultural differences
• Having time for scientific research	• Using performance appraisals effectively
	• Dealing with workforce freeze or reduction
	• Working with multiple labor representatives

Behavioral Costing of Human Resources

The first organizational attempt to measure the cost of human resources was the R.G. Barry Corp. in Columbus, Ohio, in 1967 (Cascio, 1991). Department managers were asked to measure five *costs* of department personnel: recruitment, acquisition, formal training, informal training, and development. Today's popular notion that *people are assets* involves examining such factors as the organization's historical cost of acquisition of personnel, replacement cost of personnel, the present value of future earnings or benefits of personnel, and the value to the organization of personnel (Cascio, 1991). As an alternative, *behavioral costing* considers the value of employee output, as well as direct employee cost. In this regard, behavioral costing takes into account that effective measurement must include variability of output and cost by individual and group.

However, in the forensic laboratory, many managers do not measure and are not accountable for how well they manage people. Using the expanded view of behavioral costing, all managers need to focus on the dollar value of the behavioral outcomes in their organization. Thus, the focus is not on the value of the individual per se but on the economic consequences of employee behavior (Cascio, 1991). In a sense, the behavioral costing model takes all organizational expenses into consideration.

Lessons Learned and Recommendations: Measures of Efficiency and Effectiveness

Forensic laboratories can provide a continuous learning environment that promotes positive employee outcomes using the best practices of forensic and technology management. Functional partnerships between the academic community (the sciences, business, law, and medicine), practitioner laboratories, and criminal justice community stakeholders provide a learning environment to develop forensic employees.

In order to influence key stakeholders, it is important for leaders to have measures of the efficiency and effectiveness of their initiatives. Measures are needed to ensure, for example, continuous improvement of the lab, retention of intellectual capital of the lab, productivity, efficiencies, and corrective actions or non-conformances (Becker and Dale, 2007; Becker, Dale, and Pavur, 2010).

The question is how to determine the impact of these forensic service measures or the *so what* factor? Which metrics should be used to measure and monitor quality of laboratory services? Measures that are objective and tangible, such as cost and cycle time, are less complex than measures that are more subjective and intangible, such as community safety, quality of life, and reduced recidivism. Yet the subjective factors may be more significant to criminal justice stakeholders than the objective factors. How do forensic leaders decide the most effective policies when resources are fixed? More specifically, how are decisions made to test one submitted item with a particular technology and not test other items? There are limits to resources and they will continue to be further restrained in the future. The consequences of making the wrong decisions can have high consequences for forensic leaders and all of the lab's stakeholders. Table 1.2 provides a list of the types of measures needed in public sector labs.

Components of a forensic laboratory must be in alignment to provide high-quality, effective, and efficient forensic service. For example, facilities, instrumentation/information technologies, human resources, and organizational culture all must be aligned. The NAS report does not provide

Table 1.2 Recommended Measures for Forensic Science Laboratories

Recommendation 1—Identify common laboratory outcomes, both tangible and intangible, in terms that are quantifiable. For example, number of reports, number of testimonies, number of analyses, number of opinions, number of submissions, number of source attributions between unknown items in known controls, and number of exclusions between unknown items in known controls can all be considered as outcome measures.

Recommendation 2—Identify common laboratory outcomes for quality that are both tangible and intangible in terms that are quantifiable. For example, number of task or procedure outcomes that are not acceptable, the total cost of rework, customer surveys that subjectively measure customer satisfaction, and laboratory reputation are examples of quality outcome measures.

Recommendation 3—Benchmark metrics for productivity, efficiency, cost, and quality with similar-sized laboratories in scope of services and customer demographics.

Recommendation 4—Collaborate with similar-sized laboratories to define best practices, comparing metrics for productivity, efficiency, and quality. For example, two or more similar laboratories in size, scope, and customer demographics that exhibit a wide variety of productivity, efficiency, and quality metrics would be matched for best practices.

Recommendation 5—Continually monitor these metrics at least monthly (more than annually) using statistical analysis tools. Continuous monitoring will increase productivity, efficiency, quality, and customer satisfaction. Laboratory managers must also deal with fixed resources in a variety of "production" non-conformances that require solutions.

Recommendation 6—Use cost–benefit analyses and cost-effectiveness analyses as part of the decision tree to solve problems. For example, solutions to problems usually require internal or contracted human resources, such as salary, benefits, expenses, and lost productivity from solution teams. Smart decisions need to be made concerning where resources should be applied that will have the largest effect overall in the lab. For example, systemic reporting errors, contamination, inclusionary and exclusionary false positives, and false negatives are high-risk non-conformances that are categorically unacceptable, requiring resources to continually monitor effectively and efficiently.

specific detail on facility and instrumentation/information technology needs. However, issues regarding scientific human resources and a scientific organizational culture to sustain forensic science education and research are a common thread throughout the NAS report. For example, the NAS report provides a specific recommendation to remove forensic laboratories from the control (and culture) of police departments. To address these needs, seven categories of forensic lab management need to be considered.

The laboratory management performance model (LMPM) in Figure 1.1 consists of seven major categories:

1. *Law enforcement requirements*—The leadership team must predict, to the extent possible, local law enforcement's need for forensic services. For example, community crime rates can be used to estimate future crime rate scenarios. In this regard, forensic science faces a unique challenge in that the customer (the community) is often the same as the supplier. Forensic leaders must view this as an opportunity (rather than an impediment) to maximize efficiency and effectiveness. For example, forensic leaders can determine what type of metrics for local law enforcement requirements can be standardized and used to make good decisions on an ongoing basis. For example, Peterson, Sommers, Baskin, and Johnson (2010) suggest specific metrics for the strategic evaluation of the forensic laboratory system within the context of the criminal justice community.
2. *Laboratory costs*—The leadership team must determine the true cost of laboratory services. For example, laboratory functions can be evaluated and rank ordered to determine the most costly functions.

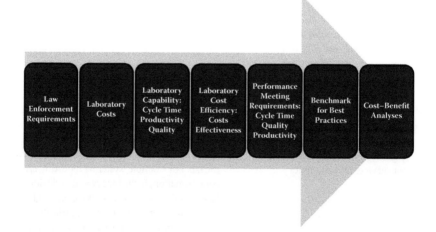

Figure 1.1 Laboratory management performance model.

The rank order will make it clear to all stakeholders that the leadership team cannot accept customer demands if laboratory resources are not adequate to meet these demands. Without managing laboratory cost, public sector laboratories face unfunded mandates if resources are not sufficiently allocated. Low performance leads to crisis management, backlogs, low quality, long cycle time, long queue times, minimal quality, and poor employee morale. Forensic leaders are faced with making decisions at a time when resources or budgets may be inadequate, decreased, or even increased. It is up to the leadership team to determine the true cost of laboratory quality, employee turnover, and training, and to manage these costs by involving laboratory stakeholders.

3. *Capabilities*—The forensic leadership team must define overall laboratory capability, that is, the services that the laboratory is *capable* of providing in a timely, productive, and quality manner. Are the capabilities adequate to meet customer requirements? To the extent possible, metrics for productivity, cycle time, and quality must be defined and standardized for each lab.

4. *Cost-benefit*—Cost-benefit helps determine laboratory efficiency and effectiveness. Metrics for efficiency (for example, return on investment or ROI) are monitored to ensure good stewardship of taxpayer dollars. Effectiveness is the ability of management keeping the eye on the ball and making effective policy decisions that support agency mission, goals, and customer requirements. These metrics help determine the *so what* or impact of laboratory forensic services for continual improvement and benchmarking for best practices. The leadership team must determine which services provide the most and least *so what* metrics.

5. *Performance*—The laboratory leadership team must be cognizant of the laboratory's capacity for fulfilling customer requirements. For example, productivity, cycle time, and quality must be determined to be adequate for all case submissions. Customer satisfaction can be determined on an ongoing basis for cycle times, backlogs, productivity, and quality. Managers analyze the strengths, weaknesses, opportunities, and threats that the lab faced. Managers then generate strategies based on future scenarios using every possible combination. Return on investment of implementing key strategies resulted in a 51% decrease in median turnaround time required to complete toxicology analyses, a 6.6% increase in number of cases per person, and an 87% increase in the number of tests per person (Newman, Dawley, and Speaker, 2011).

6. *Benchmarking*—What metrics can be used to compare with other similar-sized laboratories serving law enforcement agencies within the same scope and geopolitical service area? Are costs, capabilities, cost benefits, and performance approximately the same for two or more similar laboratories? Are law enforcement requirements similar for the same size geopolitical area? Best practices may be identified if there is a significant difference in metrics.

7. *Cost–benefit analyses*—Managers are often challenged with making significant policy decisions or recommendations to top management that change capabilities and reallocate resources responding to ever-changing customer requirements. They must choose the best alternative from several courses of action using a framework of a fixed amount of funding, time, and scope. Cost–benefit analysis (CBA) depends upon cost efficiency/effectiveness metrics and key business ratios used to compare alternatives and recommend the best course of action. Our laboratory management performance model provides the critical cost efficiency and effectiveness metrics essential to perform CBA analyses for top management and legislative bodies.

The laboratory performance management model shown in Figure 1.1 can be used to provide guidance to forensic leaders to operate a state-of-the-art lab that delivers high-quality services in a timely manner to a specific geopolitical region (city, county, state, or federal agency). For example, every laboratory leadership team must determine the best combination of laboratory facility, instrumentation/information technologies, human resources, and organizational culture needed to provide high-quality and timely set services for its population. Included must be measures of what it costs to start the laboratory and what it costs to sustain the laboratory into the future. Leaders must measure and sustain the scientific intellectual capital responsible for providing high-quality forensic services. Key ratios or intellectual capital metrics must be determined that will produce high-quality forensic services. For a laboratory serving a city of 1 million, for example, the forensic leadership team can examine the intellectual capital (Ph.D., master's, and bachelor's degrees, professional organizational memberships, scientific publications, texts, and college classes, etc.) needed to provide the highest quality forensic service. For example, the NAS report cites such multipliers as research (429X), education (223X), and training (241X). Similarly, Moorehead (2011) reports that Orange County saved $4 million through the strategic use of 1,400 interns who donated 191,000 hours of service to the forensic laboratory. A state-of-the-art lab requires scientific leadership working with all stakeholders to provide the best forensic services to the criminal justice community.

Forensic science operates in a performance measurement system that tolerates no errors. The application of new identification technologies such as DNA have forced the traditional crime lab out of the basement and back rooms of the police departments and into state-of-the-art facilities, instrumentation, and information management systems. These new labs are a significant step in the right direction and they require leaders with postgraduate degrees, skills, and business tools to apply the concepts such as economy of scale, high-throughput technology, cost–benefit analysis, cost-effectiveness analysis, efficiency, and effectiveness metrics that will routinely measure continuous improvement.

However, the cultural or *people* factor of scientific intellectual capital is the intangible factor that is the ultimate key to success. A small number of universities have tried to customize undergraduate and graduate science degree programs using elective credits specializing in forensic disciplines. These new forensic academic programs are showing success in specialized areas but do not possess the capacity needed for our nation.

National forensic science leaders need to design, develop, and implement individual laboratory solutions that will resolve the core competency human resource needs for the forensic community. A strategic forensic science performance model designed to provide quality and timely forensic services for small, medium, and large forensic service areas helps day-to-day decision making for top management and budget directors in the criminal justice community. Traditional undergraduate and graduate science academic programs do not address the specific leadership and business tools needed by the forensic community. Forensic science needs a new graduate curriculum designed specifically to address the unique needs of the forensic community. New collaboration between science, law, medicine, information technology, and business schools are needed to select individual core curricula and design innovative new curricula specifically for the forensic scientist, supervisors, managers, and top-level executives. National forensic leadership is essential as the only alternative to bring together a fragmented system consisting of thousands of forensic scientists working within a fragmented system of city, state, and federal laboratories.

References

Becker, W. S., and Dale, W. M. (2007). Critical human resource issues: Scientists under pressure. *Forensic Science Community* 9(2).

Becker, W. S., Dale, W. M., and Pavur, E. J. Jr. (2010). Forensic science in transition: Critical leadership challenges. *Forensic Science Policy & Management* 1(4):214–223.

Cascio, W. F. (1991). *Costing Human Resources: The Financial Impact of Behavior in Organizations*. Boston: PWS-Kent.

Dawley, D. D., and Munyon, T. P. (2012). Enhancing employee outcomes in crime labs: Test of a model. *Forensic Science Policy & Management* 3:105–112.

International Standard 17025:2005 Second Edition 2005-50-15, General Requirements for the Competence of Testing and Calibration in Laboratories.

Lucas, D. M. (2011). Global forensic science collaboration: Standards and research. *Forensic Science Policy & Management* 2:148–152.

Moorehead, W. (2011). Forensic interns: Force multipliers in the crime lab. *Forensic Science Policy & Management* 2:118–134.

National Academy of Sciences (NAS). (2009). *Strengthening Forensic Science in the United States: A Path Forward*. Washington, D.C.: National Academies Press.

Peterson, J. I., Sommers, D., Baskin, D., and Johnson, D. (2010). The role and impact of forensic evidence in the criminal justice process. Washington, DC: U.S. Department of Justice, National Institute of Justice.

Editorial: Science in court. (2010). *Nature* 46:325.

Forensic Laboratory Key Business Metrics and Cost–Benefit Analyses

2

Introduction

Forensic top management needs objective metrics defining law enforcement requirements and the associated forensic service costs, capabilities, cost benefits, and performance to make good decisions. Traditional forensic laboratory organizational culture is reactive adverse risk management requiring a transformational change to proactive leadership. Law enforcement forensic laboratory service requirements have lacked definition for quantity and type of evidentiary analyses. Forensic service requirements are essential for design and resourcing adequate laboratory capability and managing for acceptable performance. Case submissions are generally received by the laboratory with no advance notice and laboratory management reacts with hopefully enough available resources to provide timely, productive, and quality service. Law enforcement may respond that they cannot predict what types of crimes will occur and what types of evidence require analyses. However, prior data and crime trends can allow us to predict with high certainty the number and types of crimes that will require forensic service annually. No private-sector laboratory could survive without customer service requirements. Valid requirements allow top management to define, measure, and monitor all laboratory costs for efficiency and effectiveness of policies and procedures. How else could management be good stewards of the taxpayer's dollar? Are the laboratory's capabilities defined and are they adequate to meet law enforcement's requirements in productivity, timeliness, and quality? A key set of metrics must be developed, standardized, used, monitored, and benchmarked for best practices. Benchmarking compares laboratories with similar size and scope of services using standardized key metrics for customer requirements, costs, capabilities, cost benefits, and performance. Significant differences in key metric ratios may require further investigation to determine if one laboratory's procedure(s) provides better productivity, timeliness, and quality. If so, then other laboratories can benefit from adopting that procedure and enjoy increased performance. Most important, all employees (customer, law enforcement, and laboratory) must know their role and impact upon key metrics working toward continual improvement and high performance and meeting mission requirements directly to Deming's point #1 for management: constancy of purpose (Deming, 1986b).

Our goal is to initiate a discussion and provide the forensic community a foundation to standardize metrics for a quality management system that can be continually monitored for improvement and benchmarking for best practices following guidance in ISO 9004 (ISO 9004, 2000). Our laboratory management performance model (LMPM) provides top management a starting point for what the "Right Laboratory Looks Like." Standardized and institutionalized metrics are essential to audit processes within a quality management system. The American Society of Crime Laboratory Directors (ASCLD) has recognized the importance of fiscal, operational metrics and benchmarking:

> ASCLD Position #5—Standardization and Best Practices. ASCLD believes laboratory managers and parent organizations need to develop, share and support the best practices of technological and fiscal efficiency in order to achieve standardization within the forensic disciplines. The development of standardized methods and procedures, the development of common language in benchmarking performance studies, and the careful analysis of fiscal and operational metrics will provide improved accountability to the justice community and standardization between all forensic science laboratories and operations. (ASCLD, 2008)

We will define key categories for our LMPM as customer requirements, costs, capability, cost–benefit efficiency and effectiveness, and performance. Our LMPM is a large laboratory or perhaps a laboratory system serving 8,000,000 people with a budget of $52,530,000 with a total staff of 265 handling 59,526 cases per year. This is typical of large cities or states, and can be scaled down for smaller laboratories. The key is to find the most efficient and effective model that meets customer requirements. The principles of good management using the structure of our LMPM are applicable to most any size laboratory. The old business adage "if you can measure it, then you can manage and monitor it for continual improvement" holds true for a small and large individual processes or total quality management systems. Large laboratories gain in economies of scale; however, gains may be lost with the development of a "large factory" organizational culture with staff feeling they cannot make a difference. We hope our LMPM provides the foundation of a high-performance quality culture that meets customer requirements in a proactive, productive, timely, and quality manner. Deming's true "constancy of purpose" can be obtained when key metrics are transparent and all employees know their role in the quality system.

Metrics and key ratios are essential components of a cost–benefit analysis (CBA). A CBA is a decision tool for top management that compares two or more courses of action (COAs) and selects the best COA that meets customer requirements. Basic assumptions are required to develop the CBA (Assistant Secretary of the Army Financial Management and Comptroller, 2009):

1. Develop a problem statement or opportunity
2. Formulate assumptions and identify constraints
3. Document the current state
4. Define the course of action (COA) with costs
5. Identify quantifiable and nonquantifiable benefits
6. Define COA selection criteria
7. Compare COAs
8. Report results and recommendations

We first design an LMPM that provides a set of standardized metrics and key ratios for use in cost–benefit analyses. Second, we use LMPM metrics to analyze the efficiency, effectiveness, and return on investment (ROI) of specific forensic disciplines (e.g., DNA, latent prints) that have the ability to include or exclude suspects and significantly aid investigations of violent crimes. And last, we develop a cost–benefit analysis comparing two COAs for increasing the cycle time for DNA analyses.

Laboratory Management Performance Model

Our LMPM (Figure 2.1) consists of seven major categories:

1. *Law enforcement requirements*—Is there a way for law enforcement to accurately predict demand for forensic services? No case is the same, but previous crime rates and resulting evidence can be used to predict future requirements. Forensic science is unique in that the customer is the same as the supplier. Business views this type of business relationship as an opportunity to gain increased efficiency and effectiveness. In the private sector, a contract is established defining exactly what analyses will be applied to specific quantities and types of evidence and costs before items are submitted for analyses. What type of metrics for law enforcement requirements can be standardized and used for laboratory managers to make good decisions?
2. *Costs*—What are the true costs or budget for the total laboratory operations? What functions are most costly? The laboratory should not accept customer requirements if resources are not adequate to meet demand (ISO/IEC 17025, 2005). Why or how could any

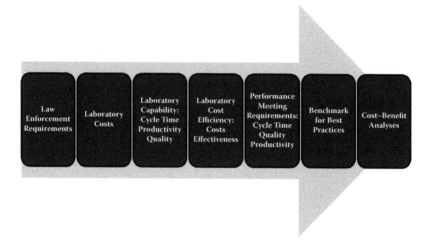

Figure 2.1 Laboratory management performance model (LMPM).

manager accept inadequate funding or an underfunded mandate? Inadequate resources leads to crisis management, backlogs, low quality, long cycle time, long queue times, minimal quality, and poor morale. How can management make decisions when resources or budgets are inadequate or decreased? What are the costs of quality, employee turnover, and training?

3. *Capabilities*—How can management define capability? What type and amount of forensic services is your laboratory capable of providing in a timely, productive, and quality manner? Are the capabilities adequate to meet customer requirements? Can we define and standardize metrics for productivity, cycle time, and quality?

4. *Cost-benefit (efficiency and effectiveness)*—What metrics can be developed to measure the cost-benefit efficiency and effectiveness of management decisions? Metrics for efficiency are monitored to ensure good stewardship of taxpayer dollars. Effectiveness is the ability of management keeping the eye on the ball meeting customer requirements and making effective policy decisions that support laboratory and customer mission, goals and customer requirements. Effectiveness is the *so what* or impact metrics of laboratory forensic services we can monitor for continual improvement and benchmarking for best practices. What services provide the most and least *so what* metrics?

5. *Performance*—How well is the laboratory's capability fulfilling customer requirements? Are capabilities (productivity, cycle time, and quality) adequate for all case submissions? Is the customer satisfied with cycle times, backlogs, productivity, and quality?

6. *Benchmarking*—What metrics can be designed to compare with other similar-sized laboratories serving similar law enforcement agencies in scope and geopolitical service area? Are costs, capabilities, cost benefits, and performance approximately the same for two or more similar laboratories? Are law enforcement requirements similar for the same size geopolitical area? Best practices may be identified if there is a significant difference in metrics.

7. *Cost-benefit analyses*—Top management makes policy decisions daily that affect the efficiency and effectiveness of the laboratory. How can they be assured that they have the best data to make the best decision? Cost–benefit analyses is a tool that compares two or more courses of action using the same costs, scope, and time parameters. We will use metrics from our LMPM in a simple but scalable cost–benefit analysis.

Law Enforcement Requirements

The metrics for the LMPM were developed to simulate a large laboratory with 265 full-time employees (FTEs) with a total budget of $52,530,000 serving a population of 8,000,000. The model is similar to a large state or city laboratory, and is designed to be flexible or scalable for use by the reader. All metrics and key ratios are developed from a basic Excel spreadsheet that is available at no charge from: www.beckerdaleconsulting.com. Standardization of terms and metrics has been a challenge for forensic science for years and we hope this work assists managers to measure their metrics for continual improvement, benchmarking, and cost–benefit analyses.

Law enforcement is the main customer of forensic laboratories. The criminal justice stakeholders (court, prosecution, and defense) and our communities are the ultimate benefactors or receivers of the outcomes of the law enforcement–laboratory relationship. Law enforcement has a relentless need for more timely, productive, and quality forensic services. Regardless of significant improvement in technology and current capabilities, the laboratory is always asked to perform more with higher productivity and shorter cycle times (Chelko, 2012). One does not have to look far to find a myriad of reports and surveys documenting the strong demand and short supply of forensic services (Becker, Dale, and Pavur Jr., 2010; Durose, 2005, 2009; Hickman and Peterson, 2002; Horvath, Messig, and Lee, 2001; NAS, 2009). Laboratories lack adequate resources and inadequate capabilities to meet customer requirements are a constant theme throughout all of these publications. Lack of capabilities results in repressive backlogs, crisis management, poor morale, and a slide toward poor quality.

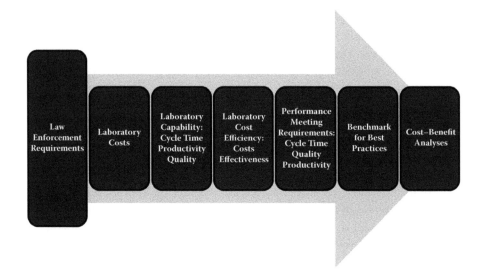

Figure 2.2 Law enforcement requirements.

Laboratories can only define needed resources and capabilities after law enforcement has defined forensic service requirements (Figure 2.2). How can laboratories be expected to provide adequate services with no guidance on customer requirements?

Questions for law enforcement top management:

What are your requirements for forensic services?
How many cases from what type of crimes will be submitted to the laboratory for analyses?
How many items will be submitted for each case?
What forensic analyses (e.g., DNA, latent prints) are required for which items?
What is an acceptable cycle time?
What is an acceptable level of quality?

ISO 9000 (ISO Guide 2, 2004) defines *requirement* as follows: "need or expectation that is stated, generally implied or obligatory."

The traditional business relationship consists of a supplier of raw materials or components, the business enterprise applies processes to the raw materials adding value, and markets the products or services to the customer (Figure 2.3) with an adequate level of profit. In an ISO-based quality management system (ISO, 2013; ISO 9001, 2000; ISO 9004, 2000), key business metrics derived from policies and procedures are managed and audited for continual improvement. Audits are continually performed to measure product or service capabilities with customer requirements. First-party audits

Figure 2.3 Traditional business relationship.

are applied internally by the enterprise. Second-party audits are applied to the supplier and third-party audits are performed by external regulatory or accrediting bodies (Russell, 2005). Forensic laboratories operate in a somewhat unique relationship in which the supplier (law enforcement) of evidence is the same as the primary customer (Figure 2.4). The business community values this type of relationship as it affords many opportunities to improve quality, efficiency, and effectiveness for all operations. Paul Kirk (1953) recognized many years ago the obvious benefits from the laboratory working as a team with law enforcement enabling the wise use of resources: "The efficiency of the laboratory usually bears a direct relationship to the willingness of the police officer to keep the laboratory workers informed of all pertinent facts."

A National Academy of Sciences (NAS) report on forensic science (2009) recommends that forensic laboratories be removed from the command and control of law enforcement, thereby eliminating any bias in performing scientific analyses. We disagree. Forensic laboratories that are accredited and operating in accordance with ISO 17025: 2005 operating with an effective quality management system supplemented with mandatory first-, second-, and third-party audits *and adequately resourced to meet customer requirements* provide excellent service for the criminal justice community. It is very challenging and perhaps unrealistic to perform forensic analyses in a vacuum with no perception of pressure from victims, law enforcement, or the community in general to identify a suspect or solve a case. Policies and procedures are mandated by the ISO standard to acknowledge, manage, and

Figure 2.4 Law enforcement is both the supplier and customer.

monitor any outside influences that may affect laboratory services (ISO/IEC 17025, 2005).

4.1.4 If the laboratory is part of an organization performing activities other than testing and/or calibration, the responsibilities of key personnel in the organization that have an involvement or influence on the testing and/or calibration activities of the laboratory shall be defined in order to identify potential conflicts of interest.

NOTE 1   Where a laboratory is part of a larger organization, the organizational arrangements should be such that departments having conflicting interests, such as production, commercial marketing, or financing do not adversely influence the laboratory's compliance with the requirements of this International Standard.

NOTE 2   If the laboratory wishes to be recognized as a third-party laboratory, it should be able to demonstrate that it is impartial and that it and its personnel are free from any undue commercial, financial, and other pressures which might influence their technical judgment. The third-party testing or calibration laboratory should not engage in any activities that may endanger the trust in its independence of judgment and integrity in relation to its testing or calibration activities.

A major difference between the public agency laboratories and private industry is the sustainability of the private enterprise with profit or adequate margin. Public agencies are not designed or intended to make profits or maximize revenue similar to the business community. If a contract is established between law enforcement and a private forensic laboratory, the private laboratory compares the scope of services required or quantity and types of analyses needed to laboratory capabilities to ensure customer requirements can be met before contracts are pursued and costs are established. Well-established fiscal procedures for sole source or competitive bid contracts for services are designed to ensure good stewardship of taxpayer dollars. Public service forensic laboratories, although not profit oriented, must also align customer requirements with laboratory capabilities and resources efficiently and effectively. Speaker (2009) compares the fiscal objectives of three types of organizations:

- Not-for-profits, maximize revenue
- Government entities, minimize cost
- For-profit organizations, maximize the difference between revenue and cost

Public agency forensic laboratories are clearly the second category minimizing cost for efficiency and good stewardship; however, the other major factors are missing: timeliness, productivity, quality, effectiveness, and performance. Are public laboratories meeting law enforcement requirements and therefore working with high effectiveness? Or, have laboratory

Table 2.1 Surveys

	Hickman and Peterson, 2002	Durose, 2005	Durose, 2009
Cases received	1,204,922	2,003,544	4,120,000
Cases completed	1,051,302	1,820,475	3,905,000
Not completed	153,620*	183,069*	215,000*
Not completed/cases received ratio	.12	.09	.05
Cumulative backlog	270,307	435,879	1,193,000
Backlog/completion ratio	.26	.23*	.30*
Budget		$1.155 billion	$1.562 billion
Costs per case*		$634	$400

* These calculations or data were added by the author for further discussion and not provided by the cited reports.

services drifted away from mission requirements with untimely, low quality, and perhaps unneeded forensic services?

There have been several surveys and projects funded to identify work-load metrics for forensic laboratories. Unfortunately, these surveys have for the most part focused only upon internal measures. These studies were well intended but destined to provide little guidance, as there were no standard terms or lexicon and no metrics and key ratios for benchmarking. The Bureau of Justice Statistics (BJS) and the National Institute of Justice (NIJ) performed three major surveys (Table 2.1) of forensic laboratories collecting and analyzing limited resource and capability data (Durose, 2005, 2009; Hickman and Peterson, 2002).

A nonstatistical analysis of the limited data from these three reports indicates the surveyed laboratories continue to have inadequate resources to meet customer requirements. The cumulative backlog has significantly increased in amount but decreased in percentage of total cases received (12%, 270,307; 9%, 435,879; and 5%, 1,193,000). Laboratory capabilities continue to be inadequate to meet customer requirements resulting in persistent backlogs. Thus starts the relentless cycle of cumulative backlogs, innovative crisis management triage procedures to expedite analyses, long cycle times, minimal quality, and low morale. Laboratory managers become crisis managers accepting an organizational culture controlled by external factors. Managers become risk-adverse, reactive fire fighters (Figure 2.5), sometimes very skilled, trying to control daily crisis instead of breaking this negative reactive cycle and becoming proactive LMPM managers (Figure 2.6) meeting customer requirements in a timely and quality manner. The NAS (2009) also confirms laboratories lack adequate resources; and suffer from relentless backlogs, long cycle times, and minimal quality.

The 2002 NIJ survey (Hickman and Peterson, 2002) included a "backlog/completion" ratio. This ratio was not included in the other surveys, which

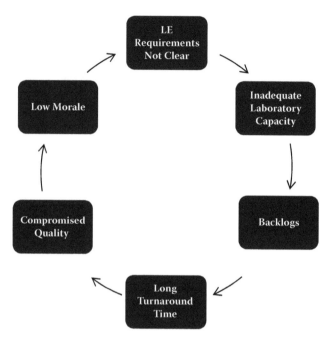

Figure 2.5 Reactive, adverse risk, crisis management.

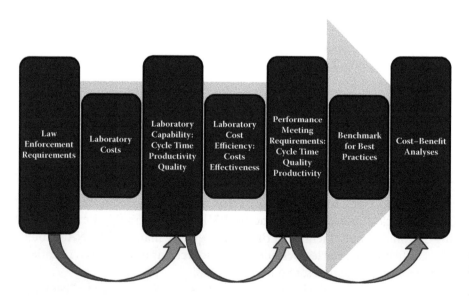

Figure 2.6 LMPM proactive leadership.

prevented any further benchmarking or analyses. Ratios are much more meaningful than discrete numbers. Ratios give the number meaning and context in correlation with other data categories. We calculated the backlog/completion ratio for the two subsequent surveys and the backlog has increased from 270,000 to 1,193,000 with a corresponding backlog/completion ratio from .26 to .30. Further analysis of cost ratios (costs/case) indicates a decrease in costs per case ($400 per case decreased from $634 per case). Does the cost figures derived from the survey include only personnel or all costs including facilities? Do personnel cost figures include support services such as legal, information technology, human resources, fiscal, evidence stores, or security? The lack of standardized business metrics for requirements, costs, capabilities, cost benefits, and performance significantly limits the usefulness of the survey data.

The United Kingdom privatized all forensic services in 2012. The high costs of technology and high risk with a constrained fiscal environment prompted the United Kingdom Forensic Science Service (FSS) and law enforcement agencies to review forensic service cost–benefit efficiency and effectiveness. The FSS and police agencies were challenged to provide a clear description of the forensic market and customer requirements. Unfortunately, the resulting lack of clearly defined metrics for requirements, and high costs of forensic services and resulting uncertainties are two of several factors contributing to the lack of support for the FSS remaining a public service agency funded by taxpayer dollars leading to privatization.

42. Given that the Government expected private forensic science providers (FSPs) to pick up the FSS's 60% share of the external forensics market, it is disappointing that the Government does not appear to have gathered any market intelligence on the capacity and commercial willingness of private forensic science providers to take on the FSS's work.

43. The apparent lack of transparency over the size of the forensics market is unacceptable and we see no reason why the FSS and other forensic science providers should have been unaware of police forensic expenditure figures. The levels of police expenditure on internal and external forensics should have been published, and we recommend that they are published in detail in future. If the Government expects the private sector to pick up the FSS's market share, it must be clear with private forensic science providers about the size of the market and anticipated future trends. (House of Commons, Science and Technology Committee 2010–12, 2011)

FBI Uniform Crime Reports (UCRs) and Incident Based Reporting (Federal Bureau of Investigation, 2010–2011) provide our LMPM with an excellent foundation for law enforcement requirements with standardized mature crime data metrics for analyses and monitoring of crime in specific

Police Department
City of New York

Michael R. Bloomberg
Mayor

Raymond W. Kelly
Police Commissioner

| Volume 20 Number 4 | | | | | | *CompStat* | | | | | *Citywide* |

Report Covering the Week 1/21/2013 through 1/27/2013

Crime Complaints

	Week to Date			28 Day			Year to Date*			2 Year	12 Year	20
			Year									
	2013	2012	% Chg	2013	2012	% Chg	2013	2012	% Chg	% Chg	% Chg (2001)	% Chg (1993)
Murder	3	6	-50.0	23	32	-28.1	23	29	-20.7	-8.0	-58.2	-86.4
Rape	24	32	-25.0	103	115	-10.4	102	111	-8.1	0.0	-30.6	-51.7
Robbery	323	424	-23.8	1,536	1,563	-1.7	1,454	1,485	-2.1	3.8	-32.8	-78.8
Fel. Assault	280	286	-2.1	1,307	1,236	5.7	1,257	1,155	8.8	-0.6	-21.3	-53.8
Burglary	302	377	-19.9	1,303	1,488	-12.4	1,250	1,440	-13.2	-1.3	-51.1	-84.3
Gr. Larceny	717	756	-5.2	3,092	2,898	6.7	2,964	2,758	7.5	19.6	-8.5	-50.0
G.L.A.	135	138	-2.2	552	558	-1.1	526	539	-2.4	-20.2	-75.5	-94.2
TOTAL	1,784	2,019	-11.64	7,916	7,890	0.33	7,574	7,517	0.76	5.27	-36.39	-77.04

Figure 2.7 NYPD CompStat 88 Pct report (note the lack of forensic service requirements).

geopolitical areas (cities, counties, and states). Our LMPM will use these definitions and crime data in lieu of establishing a new set of terms and metrics for forensic service requirements. The synchronization of these data and terms with laboratory capabilities is critical for successful management of the laboratory. Unfortunately, FBI and other similar law enforcement crime type data, such as NYPD CompStat crime data (New York Police Department, 2013) (Figure 2.7), do not incorporate forensic service requirement metrics associated with the crime data. Our LMPM will correlate crime data with subsequent laboratory service requirements.

Our first and perhaps most important LMPM key ratio for requirements is the number of laboratory submissions per UCR crime data. For example, the State of Virginia Department with a population of 8,096,604 (U.S. Census Bureau, 2013) reported 479,582 incident-based reports for Group A incidents (Federal Bureau of Investigation, 2010–2011) and the Virginia Department of Forensic Science (VDFS) received 59,556 case submissions (Virginia Department of Forensic Science, 2013). These standardized crime data related to the number of case submissions to the VDFS results in a forensic service requirements key ratio of 12% (59,556/479,582). A second key metric is Group A incidents per capita equaling 6% (479,582/8,096,604) (U.S. Census Bureau, 2013). LMPM integrates laboratory case the submissions and crime data creating key ratios used to develop law enforcement's forensic service requirements. Laboratory management shall then develop a laboratory team with the capacity and performance to meet customer requirements. Our LMPM is now beginning to develop forensic service requirements based upon crime data.

Defining law enforcement requirements is critical for the establishment of adequate resources. It is our goal to design our LMPM first with the identification of law enforcement requirements for forensic services. The identification of requirements is the first step in delivering quality forensic services in a timely and quality manner using basic quality management business principles.

If a laboratory manager individually interviewed each law enforcement agency submitting cases for analyses and asked "What are your forensic service requirements?" the answers would vary from "I cannot determine what will happen" or "Just use our numbers from last year as a best guess." The question "What are your forensic service requirements?" is arguably the most critical and perhaps the least discussed. Requirements must be defined with knowledge that there are limits on laboratory capabilities. Laboratory managers must also play the role of scientific adviser for the customer. The answer "just use our numbers from last year" is not acceptable but a good starting point for next year's requirements. Requirements must correlate with capabilities to maintain satisfactory performance (productivity: no backlog; timeliness: 30-day cycle time; quality: no non-conformances).

Our LMPM operates with the following requirements assumptions:

1. Requirements (case submissions) are developed from 12% of FBI UCR Group A incidents result in laboratory submissions.
2. 100% of homicides are submitted requiring 30 items per case including controls.
3. 12% of the remaining cases are submitted requiring 10 items per case including controls.
4. LMPM does not include toxicology or pathology.
5. A certain number of cases are expedited due to exigent circumstances.

Using the FBI incident data and the above assumptions we can now estimate the exact number of cases and items requiring a specific type of analyses (Table 2.2 using Virginia data [Virginia State Police, 2011]). There will not be an equal distribution of case submissions from each crime category (e.g., 12% of UCR crime types resulting in laboratory submissions from each category) and we acknowledge some crime types will result in greater than 12% and some will result in less. The 12% rate will allow us to design reasonable capabilities with planned reassessments adjusting to expected changes in requirements.

LMPM customer requirements metrics:
CR_{CS}/Year, Case submissions per year: 57,550 case submissions per year

Table 2.2   Law Enforcement Forensic Service Requirements—Virginia

Category	Crime	Total Incidents	Case Submissions	Item Submissions
Crimes against a person	Homicide, Murder, Manslaughter	305	305	9,150
	Kidnapping	1,475	177	1,770
	Forcible Sex Offenses	5,104	612	6,125
	Assault	108,386	13,006	130,063
	Nonforcible Sex Offenses	211	25	253
Subtotal		**115,481**	**14,126**	**141,261**
Crimes against society	Drug Offenses	50,650	6,078	60,780
	Pornography	683	82	820
	Gambling	156	19	187
	Prostitution	950	114	1,140
	Weapons	9,062	1,087	10,874
Subtotal		**61,501**	**7,380**	**73,801**
Crimes against property	Robbery	5,451	654	6,541
	Arson	1,167	140	1,400
	Extortion	113	14	136
	Burglary	30,438	3,653	36,526
	Larceny	144,491	17,339	173,389
	Motor Vehicle Theft	9,616	1,154	11,539
	Counterfeiting	7,074	849	8,489
	Fraud	26,040	3,125	31,248
	Embezzlement	2,838	341	3,406
	Stolen Property	1,454	174	1,745
	Destruction, Damage, Vandalism	73,893	8,867	88,672
	Bribery	25	3	30
Subtotal		**302,600**	**36,312**	**363,120**
Requirement Total	**Total**	**479,582**	**57,550**	**799,345**

CR_{CS}/Capita, Case submissions/Capita: case submissions per total population of service area

- Case submissions = 57,550 case submissions per year
- Population = 8,000,00
- = 57,550/8,000,000
- = .75%

$CR_{FBI/UCR}$/Capita
- For example, 2011 Virginia
- 500,000/8,000,000 = 6.25%

CR_{CS}/$CR_{FBI/UCR}$
- Case submissions = 59,778 case submissions per year
- Group A incidents = 500,000
- 59,778/500,000
- = 12%

Costs

The LMPM cost (Table 2.3 and Figure 2.8) is the total budget for all laboratory operations. How many public service agency laboratory managers actually control and manage their budget? Or, is the laboratory budget managed by the fiscal unit of the agency with little input from laboratory management? Forensic laboratories are high-cost technology enterprises that develop serious consequences if the budget is not efficiently and effectively managed. Very few laboratories can provide all forensic services with adequate productivity, timeliness, and quality. Limit your laboratory services for services you have the capability to do in a timely, quality, and productive fashion. Six ISO/IEC 17025 standard clauses, now being used to accredit many laboratories, mandate necessary resources be in place before accepting the responsibility to provide service (see Table 2.4) (ISO/IEC 17025, 2005). If you are a new laboratory manager or have many years' experience, this is your first and major responsibility. The lack of adequate resources to meet customer requirements jeopardizes accreditation of the laboratory, productivity, timeliness, quality, and reputation. External laboratory mandates requiring operations in accordance with the ISO standard(s) and all associated legislation, rules, and regulations must be followed or the consequences may be loss of accreditation and risk of litigation. Too often, the basic business concepts of adequate resources are overlooked resulting in excessive backlogs, case triage systems expedited by court calendars, and an unacceptable organizational culture accepting reactive crisis management.

We recommend laboratory managers acquire professional development including mandatory education (e.g., master's in business administration or a certificate program) specializing in fiscal management for public service agencies. Fiscal training and education should include both internal budget management and external management of vendor contracts and grants. How can a laboratory manager be successful with no control over customer requirements, budget, and the associated laboratory capabilities needed to meet customer requirements? Measurement, management, and monitoring key business metric ratios for fiscal management are essential for transformation of reactive management to proactive leadership.

Laboratory top management is responsible to deliver adequate laboratory capabilities (productivity, timeliness, and quality); however, does management also have the authority to carry out responsibilities and the necessary resources? ISO 17025 clearly defines these basic tenants of business operations required for the proper management of any private or public enterprise. Lack of policies clearly establishing management responsibilities, authorities,

Table 2.3   LMPM Budget

BUDGET CATEGORY	FTE	Salary & Benefits	TOTAL COSTS
PUBLIC FUNDS - PARENT AGENCY			$48,626,000
PUBLIC FUNDS - PARTNER AGENCY(S)			$2,000,000
GRANTS - PUBLIC AGENCY(S)			$1,000,000
GRANTS - PRIVATE SECTOR			$1,000,000
SUBTOTAL			**$52,530,000**
EXPENDITURES			
PERSONNEL - SALARY AND BENEFITS		Salary & Benefits per FTE	Salary & Benefits Total
TOP MANAGEMENT			
Director	1	$200,000	$200,000
Executive Officer	1	$175,000	$175,000
CHIEF Quality Operations	1	$165,000	$165,000
CHIEF Digital Evidence	1	$165,000	$165,000
CHIEF DNA	1	$165,000	$165,000
CHIEF Drug Chemistry	1	$165,000	$165,000
CHIEF Firearms and Toolmarks	1	$165,000	$165,000
CHIEF Latent Fingerprints	1	$165,000	$165,000
CHIEF Questioned Documents	1	$165,000	$165,000
CHIEF Trace Evidence	1	$165,000	$165,000
CHIEF Human Resource Officer	1	$165,000	$165,000
CHIEF Legal Officer	1	$165,000	$165,000
CHIEF Research Operations	1	$165,000	$165,000
CHIEF Training, Prof Development	1	$165,000	$165,000
CHIEF Finance	1	$165,000	$165,000
CHIEF Quality Operations	1	$165,000	$165,000
MANAGEMENT SUBTOTAL	16		**$2,685,000**
SUPPORT SERVICES			
Engineer	2	$150,000	$300,000
Finance	2	$150,000	$300,000
Human Resource	2	$150,000	$300,000
Security	3	$150,000	$450,000
Information Technology	4	$150,000	$600,000
Training, Prof Development	3	$150,000	$450,000
Quality Assurance Audit Team	3	$150,000	$450,000
SUPPPORT SUBTOTAL	19		**$2,550,000**
SCIENCE OPERATIONS	FTE	Salary & Benefits	Salary & Benefits Total
Digital Evidence	10	$150,000	$1,500,000
DNA	100	$150,000	$15,000,000
Controlled Substances	40	$150,000	$6,000,000
Firearms and Toolmarks	4	$150,000	$600,000
Latent Fingerprints	50	$150,000	$7,500,000
Questioned Documents	6	$150,000	$900,000
Trace Evidence	20	$150,000	$3,000,000
Total FS Costs		$150,000	$34,500,000
SCIENCE OPERATIONS SUBTOTAL	230		
NONPERSONNEL			
CONTRACTS			$4,000,000
PROFESSIONAL DEVELOPMENT	265	$3,000	$795,000
EQUIPMENT			$2,000,000
Facilities			**$3,000,000**
CONSUMABLES			$2,000,000
TRAVEL			$1,000,000
NONPERSONNEL SUBTOTAL			**$12,795,000**
TOTAL BUDGET			**$52,530,000**

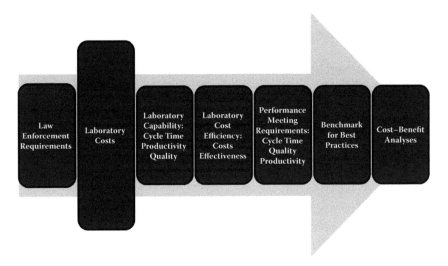

Figure 2.8 LMPM costs.

Table 2.4   ISO Mandates for Adequate Resources

Clause	Requirement
4.1.5	The laboratory *shall* (a) have managerial and technical personnel who, irrespective of other responsibilities, have the *authority* and *resources* needed to carry out their duties;
4.1.5	The laboratory *shall* (h) have technical management which has overall responsibility for the technical operations and the provision of the *resources* needed to ensure the required quality of laboratory operations;
4.1.5	The laboratory *shall* (i) … the quality manager *shall* have direct access to the highest level of management at which decisions are made on laboratory policy or *resources*.
4.4.1	The laboratory *shall* establish and maintain procedures for the review of requests, tenders and contracts. The policies and procedures for these reviews leading to a contract for testing or calibration shall ensure that (b) the laboratory has the capability and *resources* to meet the requirements … Any differences between the request or tender and the contract *shall* be resolved before any work commences. Each contract shall be acceptable both to the laboratory and the customer.
4.4.1 (not mandatory)	Note 2: The review of capability *should* establish that the laboratory possesses the necessary physical, personnel and information resources, and that the laboratory's personnel have the skills and expertise necessary for the performance of the tests and calibrations in question.
4.1.5.1	Management Reviews: In accordance with a predetermined schedule and procedure, the laboratory's top management *shall* periodically conduct a review of the laboratory's management system … other relevant factors, such as quality control activities, *resources* and staff training.
5.4.3	Laboratory-developed methods: The introduction of test and calibration methods developed by the laboratory for its own use *shall* be a planned activity and *shall* be assigned to qualified personnel equipped with adequate *resources*.

and resources jeopardizes the laboratory accreditation and ultimately leads to unsatisfactory laboratory performance.

LMPM Costs and Metrics

Costs (C) = Total budget (personnel costs are salary and benefits)
- $C = \$51,735,000$

Costs for Management (C_M) = Personnel costs for all management positions
- $C_M = \$2,685,000$

Costs for Support (C_S) = Personnel costs for support personnel
- $C_S = \$2,550,000$

Costs for Forensic Scientists (C_{FS}) = Personnel costs for forensic scientists
- $C_{FS} = \$34,500,000$

Costs for Non-Personnel (C_{NP}) = Costs for contracts, facilities, equipment, consumables and travel
- $C_{NP} = \$12,000,000$

Costs of Quality (CQ)

If a manager asked most any member of the organization what is their role in quality and what does it cost I would suspect there would be a wide spectrum of answers from "I really don't know" and "we review all cases to make sure there are no errors" to "everything we do relates to quality." Some individuals may reflect upon what they have done in the past (Corrective Action) to prevent errors, such as administrative and technical review and proficiency tests. Some may discuss how they will prevent future (Preventive Action) errors with the use of controls and internal audits. A more probing question is: What are you doing right now (Present Action)? What is the difference between quality control, quality assurance, and a quality management system? Last, and perhaps most important is the question: What is the cost of quality? There is no perfect answer, however, there have been several highly regarded experts and organizations in the profession of quality management that have studied these questions and developed excellent business frameworks we can apply to forensic laboratories.

Russell defines the costs of quality from two major categories (Russell, 2005):

1. Cost of good quality
   - Prevention of non-conformance to requirements
     - New product review
     - Quality planning
     - Supplier surveys

- Process capability evaluations
- Quality meetings, education, and training
- Appraising a product or service for conformance to requirements
  - Measure performance
  - Incoming material inspection
  - In-process inspection
  - Audits
  - Calibrations
  - Supplies and materials

2. Cost of bad quality
   - Failure to meet requirements
     - Internal
       - Costs of scrap, rework, reinspection
     - External
       - Complaints, returns, recalls

Our LMPM applies two assumptions and develops two quality costs metrics.

1. Costs of good quality (C_{GQ}) assumes 50% of management and scientist supplemented with support (100% support services) personnel costs are expended to operating in compliance to ISO/IEC mandatory ISO/IEC 17025 clauses (see Chapter 5). These activities are for the most part *pre*-report (e.g., quality control, corrective actions, technical review).
2. Costs of bad quality (C_{BQ}) assumes 10% of management, forensic scientist, and support (100% support services) personnel costs are expended to operating in compliance to ISO/IEC mandatory ISO/IEC 17025 clauses (see Chapter 5). These activities are for the most part *post*-report (e.g., case recalls, reanalyses, litigation):

Costs of good quality (CQ_G)
- LMPM = $17,250,000
Costs of bad quality (C_{BQ})
- LMPM = $3,450,000
Total costs of quality (C_{QTotal})
- $C_{GQ} + C_{BQ}$
- LMPM = $20,700,000

A traditional simplistic LMPM costs chart (Figure 2.9) does not reveal true costs of quality, provides data, and has limited value for assessment of the effectiveness and efficiency of management's policies.

CFS—Costs of forensic scientists
CNP—Costs of nonpersonnel

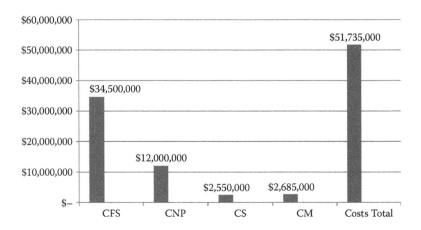

Figure 2.9 Simple costs.

CS—Cost of support personnel
CM—Costs of management

A more useful visual of the costs data is depicted in the quality costs in the Pareto chart (Figure 2.10), which identifies costs of quality (good and bad) and human resource turnover. Management can then target specific categories in an effort to reduce costs and increase efficiencies. Management now can see what exact costs are expended toward costs of good quality, bad quality, and human resource turnover. Deming's (1986b) management point #3 (build quality in and do it right the first time) and Shewart's (1980) principles of statistical process control (redirect quality resources from processes

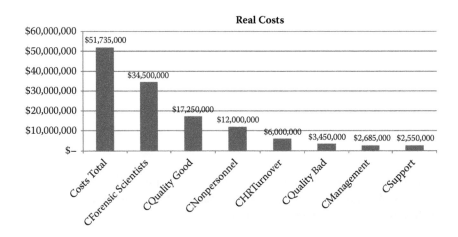

Figure 2.10 Real costs.

under control to processes not under control) can now be applied, managed, and monitored for continual improvements. Why should all cases be 100% administratively and technically reviewed if a specific analyses procedure is properly controlled, exhibits acceptable variance in precision and accuracy, and meets customer requirements? Quality resources should be reallocated from processes under control to processes not under control freeing up quality processes for higher productivity and decreased cycle times. Also included in Figure 2.10 is the costs incurred for employee voluntary and involuntary turnover.

Human Resource Turnover (C_{HRTO})

Human resources are a major part of the budget and should be treated as an investment in the enterprise and not expenditures (Cascio and Boudreau, 2008). Turnover (TO) costs are greater for high-technology industries, such as information management and laboratories, as compared to lower-technology retail services. An accepted standard for cost of turnover in the high-technology industry is 2 years pay with benefits (Dale and Becker, 2004). A strategic human capital management program manages a cradle-to-grave process to recruit, select, train to competency, professional development, and retention of the best people for the organization. Efficient and effective recruitment, selection, training, and retention processes are critical to overall laboratory stewardship of taxpayer funds and quality of services. Voluntary turnover is defined by the number of individuals that self-select out of the organization or left on their own volition. The earlier a candidate or employee voluntarily terminates from the selection process or from employment, the higher the cost savings to the organization. Unplanned voluntary or involuntary turnover or termination of employee(s) is very costly. Involuntary turnover usually includes accusations of low performance or misconduct requiring intensive support from human resources and legal staff. The resulting vacancies may also not be authorized for replacement, leaving the laboratory with unfilled positions resulting in increased backlogs and cycle times.

For the purpose of our LMPM, we will designate 15 voluntary and 5 involuntary turnover of personnel per year multiplied by two times the salary and benefits. Human resource turnover metrics are:

HR turnover% of budget ($C_{HRTO\%}$): $\$6,000,000/\$51,735,000 = 11.6\%$
HR turnover voluntary ($C_{HRTOVol}$): #FTE ToVol $\times$ (2 $\times$ salary and benefits)
   $= 15 \times \$150,000 \times 2 = \$4,500,000$
HR turnover involuntary ($C_{HRTOInVol}$): #FTEToInVol $\times$ (2 $\times$ salary and benefits) $= 5 \times \$150,000 \times 2 = \$1,500,000$

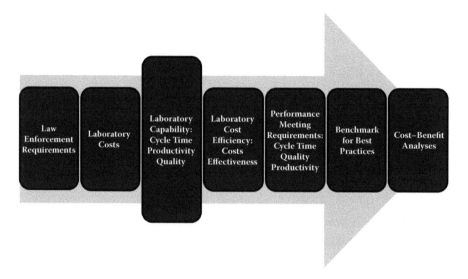

Figure 2.11 LMPM capability.

Capability

According to *ISO Guide 2* (ISO, 2004), *capability* is the ability of an organization, system, or process to realize a product that will fulfill the requirements for that product. We define capabilities with productivity, cycle time, and quality metrics (Figure 2.11). How many, how timely, and what quality forensic services are provided by the laboratory?

Productivity

LMPM total case productivity per year ($P_{TotalCases}$) = 59,926 cases
LMPM total item productivity per year ($P_{TotalItems}$) = 753,260 items
Productivity digital evidence total cases per forensic scientist per year ($P_{DECases/FS}$) = 52
Productivity digital evidence unit total cases per year ($P_{DECases}$) = 520
Productivity digital evidence unit total items per year ($P_{DEItems}$) = 5,200
Productivity DNA total cases per forensic scientist per year ($P_{DNACases/FS}$) = 77
Productivity DNA total cases per year ($P_{DNACases}$) = 7,700
Productivity DNA total items per year ($P_{DNAItems}$) = 231,000
Productivity controlled substances total cases per forensic scientist per year ($P_{CSCases/FS}$) = 752
Productivity controlled substances total per year ($P_{CSCases}$) = 30,800

Productivity controlled substances per forensic scientist per year $(P_{CSItems}) = 308,000$

Productivity firearms and tool marks total cases per forensic scientist per year $(P_{FATMCases/FS}) = 193$

Productivity firearms and tool marks total per year $(P_{FATMCases}) = 772$

Productivity firearms and tool marks per forensic scientist per year $(P_{FATMItems}) = 7,720$

Productivity latent fingerprints total cases per forensic scientist per year $(P_{LPCases/FS}) = 375$

Productivity latent fingerprints total per year $(P_{LPCases}) = 18,750$

Productivity latent fingerprints per forensic scientist per year $(P_{LPItems}) = 187,500$

Productivity questioned documents total cases per forensic scientist per year $(P_{QDCases/FS}) = 74$

Productivity questioned documents total per year $(P_{QDCases}) = 444$

Productivity questioned documents per forensic scientist per year $(P_{QDFItems}) = 4,440$

Productivity trace evidence total cases per forensic scientist per year $(P_{TECases/FS}) = 83$

Productivity trace evidence total per year $(P_{TECases}) = 1,660$

Productivity trace evidence per forensic scientist per year $(P_{TEItems}) = 16,600$

Our LMPM productivity per case per discipline was derived from a National Institute of Justice survey (Table 2.5) (Durose, 2005). Productivity can vary depending upon case complexity, teamwork, batching of case analyses tasks, and automation technologies. Our model also assumes 10

Table 2.5   LMPM Productivity

SCIENCE OPERATIONS	FTE	CASE PRODUCTIVITY PER FTE/YEAR	ITEMS ANALYZED PER CASE	CASE PRODUCTIVITY TOTAL/YEAR	ITEM PRODUCTIVITY TOTAL/YEAR
Digital Evidence	10	52	10	520	5,200
DNA	100	77	30	7,700	231,000
Controlled Substances	40	752	10	30,080	300,800
Firearms and Toolmarks	4	193	10	772	7,720
Latent Fingerprints	50	375	10	18,750	187,500
Questioned Documents	6	74	10	444	4,440
Trace Evidence	20	83	10	1,660	16,600
Total				59,926	753,260

items per case were included as a minimum for analyses (2 known exemplars, 2 blanks, 6 unknowns). DNA cases were allotted 30 items per case.

Cycle Time

Cycle Time (CT) = 30 days

Cycle time is the total time (days) from the date of submission to the issuance of a report.

Cycle time also includes queue time (QT). QT is the time from case submission to the date analyses starts. For example, a case may be submitted to the laboratory on 1 Jan 13, analyses begin 1 Feb 13, and is completed 1 Mar 13. Cycle time (CT) is 60 days, and queue time (QT) is 30 days. Excessive QT resulting from inadequate capability leads to unacceptable backlogs and poor laboratory performance. Our LMPM consisting of 265 forensic scientists analyzes 59,926 cases consisting of 753,260 items per year with a 30-day cycle time with no discernible queue time.

Quality

Quality (Q): Our LMPM goal is no non-conformances provided to the customer.

ISO 9000 (ISO Guide 2, 2004) defines *quality* as the degree to which a set of inherent characteristics fulfills requirements. We have previously defined quality with terms of Costs—Good Quality and Costs—Bad Quality and realized a significant amount of personnel resources are expended with tasks to ensure that the highest quality forensic services are provided to the customer. Our LMPM expends or invests the majority of our scientific operations resources toward quality processes. The LMPM quality goal is a continual decrease in quality costs and no non-conformance(s) of forensic services provided to the customer requirements.

The American Society of Quality (ASQ) and a selection of ISO standards provide externally recognized certifications for individuals who are responsible for quality control and quality management systems. The establishment of a quality program staffed with professional quality managers and audit teams add significantly to the cost effectiveness and cost efficiency of all services provided to the customer. ASQ is one of the few or only international organizations dedicated to quality management systems in the public and private sector (ASQ, 2013). Training and certification programs are provided for:

- Biomedical Auditor, CBA
- Calibration Technician, CCT*
- HACCP Auditor, CHA

- Lean Certification (SME/AME/Shingo Prize/ASQ Partnership)*
- Manager of Quality/Organizational Excellence, CMQ/OE*
- Master Black Belt, CMBB*
- Pharmaceutical GMP Professional, CPGP
- Quality Auditor, CQA*
- Quality Engineer, CQE
- Quality Improvement Associate, CQIA*
- Quality Inspector, CQI*
- Quality Process Analyst, CQPA*
- Quality Technician, CQT*
- Reliability Engineer, CRE
- Six Sigma Black Belt, CSSBB*
- Six Sigma Green Belt, CSSGB*
- Software Quality Engineer, CSQE

Several of the certifications (*) are directly applicable for application within forensic quality management systems. A further advantage of certification with professional organizations such as ASQ is external recognition with certifications that operate incorporating the principles of ISO international standards.

At a minimum, our LMPM follows guidance for operation of a quality management system in accordance with the following ISO standards:

- ISO 9000: 2005 International Standard, Quality Management Systems, Fundamentals and vocabulary (*ISO Guide 2*, 2004)
- ISO 9001: 2000 International Standard, Quality Management Systems, Requirements (ISO 9001, 2000)
- ISO 9004: 2000 International Standard, Quality Management Systems, Guidelines for performance improvements (ISO 9004, 2000)
- ISO 19011: 2002 International Standard, Guidelines for quality and/ or environmental management system auditing (ISO 19011, 2002)
- ILAC Guide 19, Guidelines for forensic science laboratories (International Laboratory Accreditation Cooperation, 2002)
- ISO/IEC 17025: 2005 International Standard, General requirements for the competence of testing and calibration laboratories (ISO/IEC 17025, 2005)

Forensic science management education and certification programs should actively participate in ASQ's highly respected certification programs. Graduate level MBA and postgraduate management certificate programs using ISO standards and statistical process control methodology (Value Stream Mapping, Green Belt, Black Belt, Lean Six Sigma) would greatly increase the quality of forensic services. ASQ and the ISO programs have established the lexicon of standardized terms and, more important, the organizational culture that institutionalizes continual improvement of quality.

W. Edward Deming is one of the pioneers of quality management and statistical process control. "Views not backed by data are more likely to include personal opinions, exaggeration and mistaken impressions ... Data without context or incorrect data are not only invalid but sometimes harmful as well" (Deming, 1986a).

Deming's work with the Japanese after World War II is legendary and transformed Japanese manufacturing from very poor quality to an envied present status of the highest quality products in the world. Before the maturity of the International Organization of Standards and development of quality management system standards (ISO, 2004), Deming developed 14 points for management that are very similar to ISO principles of a quality management system (Table 2.6). All of Deming's 14 points for management are directly applicable to the current high-technology laboratory environment. It

Table 2.6 Deming's 14 Points and LMPM

Point	Deming	LMPM Metrics and Organizational Culture*
1	Create constancy of purpose	LMPM: Customer Requirements—All employees know their role in how law enforcement requirements, laboratory costs, capabilities and cost benefits, and laboratory performance supports the agency's mission goals and objectives.
2	Adopt a new philosophy of leadership for change	Organizational Culture: Transform organizational culture from adverse risk and control by external forces to proactive leadership.
3	Cease dependence upon inspection, build in quality in the first place	LMPM: Costs of Good and Bad Quality—Remove reliance upon 100% administrative and technical review. Do the job right the first time. Reduce the cost of quality.
4	Minimize cost and move toward a long-term relationship with a single supplier	LMPM: Customer Requirements—All employees know their role in how law enforcement requirements, laboratory costs, capabilities and cost benefits, and laboratory performance supports the agency's mission goals and objectives.
5	Improve constantly production and service to improve quality and productivity and decrease costs	LMPM: Continually improve cost–benefit efficiency and effectiveness metrics.
6	Institute training on the job	LMPM: Develop a dedicated full-time training team.
7	Institute leadership	Organizational Culture: Transform organizational culture from adverse risk and control by external forces to proactive leadership.

(Continued)

Table 2.6 Deming's 14 Points and LMPM (*Continued*)

Point	Deming	LMPM Metrics and Organizational Culture*
8	Drive out fear, so that everyone may work effectively for the company	Organizational Culture: Transform organizational culture from adverse risk and control by external forces to proactive leadership.
9	Break down barriers between departments	Organizational Culture: What policies and procedures are linked between units, particularly with multidisciplinary cases? Who is responsible and how are multisection cases managed?
10	Eliminate slogans and targets for productivity as they only develop adversarial relationships	Organizational Culture: Transform organizational culture from adverse risk and control by external forces to proactive leadership.
11	Eliminate quotas and substitute leadership	Organizational Culture: Transform organizational culture from adverse risk and control by external forces to proactive leadership.
12	Remove barriers that rob people of their pride in workmanship	Organizational Culture: Transform organizational culture from adverse risk and control by external forces to proactive leadership.
13	Institute a vigorous program of education and self-improvement	Organizational Culture: Transform organizational culture from adverse risk and control by external forces to proactive leadership.
14	Put everybody in the company to work to accomplish the transformation	Organizational Culture: Transform organizational culture from adverse risk and control by external forces to proactive leadership.

* Added by author to correlate with text.

is revealing to note that Deming's goals for management are primarily subjective relating to organizational culture as compared to his objective analytical statistical process controls. The manager who can develop and institutionalize a quality organizational culture will have to be a successful manager and perhaps a leader. For example, point #1 (constancy of purpose) may be the most important and is listed as such by Deming. Do all employees know their role in how their daily work affects fulfilling law enforcement requirements for forensic services? Do all employees know how their daily work affects costs, capabilities, cost benefits, and performance? Do all employees know how their daily work benchmarks with similar laboratories? Last, do all employees know how they contribute to the accomplishment of the agency's mission, goals, and objectives? The alternative is employees drifting aimlessly from case to case with no pride of accomplishment or knowledge on how they contribute to the success of law enforcement and the laboratory. Point #3 (cease dependence upon inspection, build quality in the first place) also deserves further discussion. Note Deming's use of the word *inspection*. Many forensic laboratories incorrectly define "administrative review, technical review, and audits" as "quality" whereas these tasks are reactive inspections instead of a proactive total quality management system. Forensic laboratories dedicate excessive resources to inspection and should develop policies and procedures to "design quality in the front of the process" (Deming, 1986b). Why not do the job right the first time and reallocate inspection resources to units with high non-conformances continually improving laboratory capability and performance (productivity, timeliness, and quality)? Laboratory managers that can transform the organizational culture of the laboratory from reactive, risk adverse, and relentless inspection to proactive leadership by applying principles of a quality management system (ISO, 2004) are the hope and future of forensic science.

Shewart's classic work *Economic Control of Quality of Manufactured Product* examines how statistical analyses of non-conformances and the identification and elimination of causative factors brings a process under control. Under control is defined as a process that exhibits acceptable variation of quality within predictable limits. Quality control costs or personnel time can then be reallocated to increase productivity.

The major benefits of managing a process under control are:

1. Reduction in the cost of inspection
2. Reduction in the cost of rejection
3. Attainment of maximum benefits from quantity production
4. Attainment of uniform quality even though the inspection test is destructive
5. Reduction in tolerance limits where quality measurement is indirect (Shewart, 1980)

Quality control identifies non-conformances and eliminates causative factors with corrective actions. If your employees are asked to define all or one non-conformance from their daily work, how would they respond? When they perform administrative and technical quality control activities for others' work, how are the non-conformities defined in policies and procedures? Are non-conformances clearly differentiated between remediation (not requiring corrective action) and recurring non-conformances requiring corrective actions (ISO/IEC 17025, 2005)? Personnel must develop their own quality constancy of purpose (Deming, 1986b) through awareness of all non-conformances possible within a process and subsequent *personal and present action* eliminating causative factors. Let's build in quality up front in the process and drive out the cost of quality control.

After extensive training, professional development, and career development programs we now ask the question to all of our employees once again: What is your constancy of purpose or role in the quality management system?

Top management should strive for an organizational culture that would support the following answers: My role in quality is manyfold:

1. My goal is to have no remediation or non-conformances identified in my work.
2. Non-conformances are objectively defined by customer requirements and our quality management system.
3. I am aware of all possible causes of non-conformances defined in my procedures used daily.
4. Upon becoming aware of a non-conformance in my work or others', I will do my best to remediate the non-conformance immediately or notify my supervisor of the possibility of recurrence and request a corrective action. I will call these OFIs (opportunities for improvement).
5. In high risk (high frequency and significant consequences from non-conformance), I will suggest a preventive action be initiated to monitor the process.
6. I continually monitor how my actions affect LMPM metrics and strive for continual improvement.
7. I am aware of how my actions affect quality management system metrics applying Pareto diagrams, control charts, and fishbone causative analyses quality control tools.
8. I continually monitor and decrease the number, mean, standard deviation, and special causes of non-conformances in my daily work.
9. My quality work costs 50% of my time (salary and benefits) for good quality and 10% of my time for bad quality, which equals $110,000 × .6 = $66,000. I strive to reduce the costs of quality.
10. My quality goal is to identify, control, and continually decrease all causes of variation and non-conformances in my daily work procedures resulting in increased productivity and releasing quality control resources for other procedures.

Quality control Pareto diagrams, control charts, and fishbone causative analyses tools (Table 2.7; Figures 2.12, 2.13, and 2.14) are very effective visual tools to be monitored by all employees for continual improvement and feedback for quality efforts. Following are some examples used for DNA analyses.

Quality system (Figure 2.15) process audit teams focus upon meeting laboratory mission and goals, customer requirements, increasing capabilities, cost–benefit efficiency/effectiveness, and performance. Most important, all customers (law enforcement, prosecutors, and the court) are surveyed to verify forensic service requirements are up to date. LMPM metrics for all categories are reviewed for continual improvement. Recall in Figure 2.10 the highest cost category is cost of good quality (33%). Cost of good quality is primarily the result of quality control activities (Figure 2.16). The applications of Deming's

Table 2.7   DNA Quality Control Worksheet

DNA TECHNICAL REVIEW QUALITY CONTROL CHECKLIST			
Sample/Sim Set #		Trainee	
1st Tech Reviewer		Date	
2nd Tech Reviewer		Date	

	General (Reviewer enters Y, N, or NA)		**Amplification**
		22	Lot numbers recorded
1	Case file in correct order	23	Worksheet(s) filled out completely
2	All pages marked with case #, initials, date	24	Results from plate map entered correctly
3	Pages numbered correctly with 1 of x	25	Dilution calculations correct
	number of total pages on first page of data	26	Amp setup calculations correct
4	All cross outs with single-line/initials	27	Controls (9947A/kit neg/reagent blank(s)) included
5	Work performed in accordance with SOP		
			STRs / GMID
Case Notes		28	Lot numbers recorded
6	Notes complete	29	Worksheet filled out completely
7	Portion(s) consumed/remaining noted	30	2 ladders in each run, at least 1 of which is acceptable
8	Adequate description of items provided	31	Expected typing results for 9947A/RFUs/morphology
		32	No peaks above threshold in kit neg/reagent blank(s)
Extraction Worksheet(s)		33	SQO "X" present on all EPGs
9	Lot numbers recorded	34	Checkmarks on each pane are present
10	Reagent blank(s) included	35	Redundant EPGs appropriately marked
11	Times in/out recorded/addressed	36	Unacceptable profiles crossed out/initialed/with
12	Worksheet(s) filled out completely		annotations as appropriate
		37	EPG data corresponds to quant data (e.g., partial
Quant			profiles have low quant values)
13	Lot numbers recorded	38	Artifacts properly addressed
14	Quant setup calculations correct	39	Single source peak height ratio imbalance addressed
15	Omitted standard crossed out, annotated as	40	D3, D7, & Amelogenin checked for concordance
	"standard omitted," initialed by supervisor		
16	Worksheet(s) filled out completely		**Frequency Calculations**
17	Slope acceptable (–2.92 to –3.27) or	41	Source of profile and correct alleles entered/listed
	initialed as acceptable for training	42	Correct statistical calculation(s) performed
18	R2 acceptable (>0.98) or initialed as		
	acceptable for training		**Report**
19	Intercept acceptable (28.06 to 29.33) or	43	Allele table complete/concordant with answer key
	initialed as acceptable for training	44	Allele assignments accurately transcribed
20	Kit neg is lower than 0.023 ng/uL	45	Conclusion statements present for all testing results
21	Plate map has no unexplained neg results	46	Conclusion statement(s) identify(ies) potential
			donor(s) of profiles
		47	Frequency(ies) of profile(s) given / accurately
			transcribed
		48	Profile(s) to CODIS in report/statement(s) correct
		49	Disposition of evidence/biobag statements present
		50	Each page of report marked Page X of Y

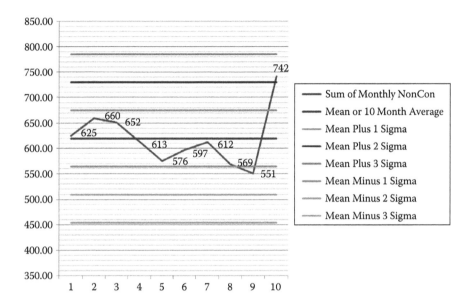

Figure 2.12 DNA non-conformance control chart.

and Shewart's principles of quality are arguably the most effective method of increasing the overall performance of the LMPM quality system metrics.

The quality control and quality system auditors require training and preferably certification by professional bodies such as the American Society of Quality (ASQ, 2013). The quality control and quality system audits shall also provide an ROI >1, meaning the resulting audits should develop cost benefits equal to or more than the costs of the audit program. A quality control and quality system program, staffed with trained auditors with a quality manager reporting directly to top management, is essential.

Cost: Efficiency and Effectiveness

Cost efficiency in the business world is producing a product or service with the lowest costs. Public agencies are not designed to make a profit, however, top management and all employees should be good stewards of taxpayer's funds. Several efficiency metrics are useful for monitoring costs and benchmarking with similar agencies or the private sector (Figure 2.17). For example, if a similar public laboratory can provide a specific analysis for half the costs; perhaps, the costly process is lacking automation technologies or performs redundant or unnecessary processes. The more efficient laboratory may have processes under control and are benefiting from less quality control costs for that specific process. Most public laboratories willingly share best practices for the greater good. Similarly, if a high volume private laboratory

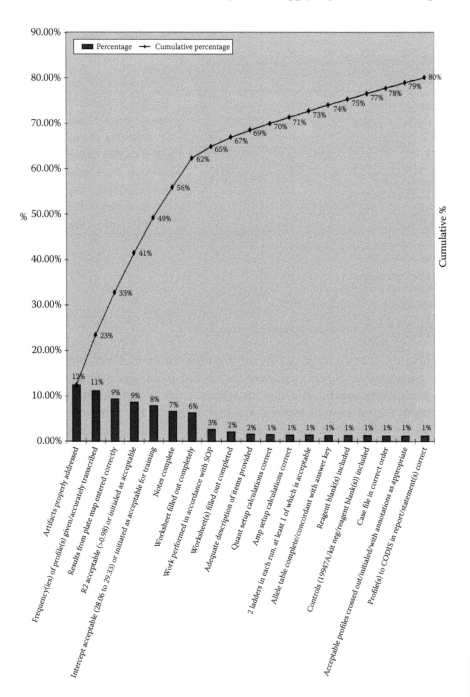

Figure 2.13 DNA non-conformance Pareto chart.

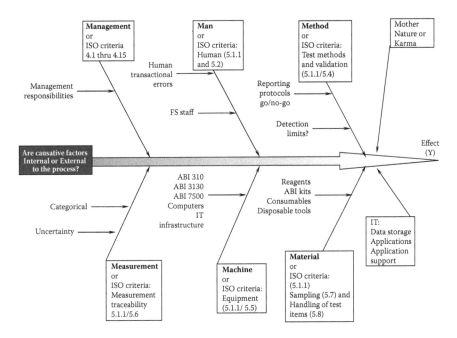

Figure 2.14 Fishbone causative analyses.

can provide routine analyses for one half the costs due to economies of scale, then the public laboratory may consider outsourcing routine analyses and thereby saving resources for more complex analyses.

Cost Efficiency Metrics

The LMPM cost efficiency metrics (Table 2.8) assume salaries are $150,000 including benefits with case productivity rates derived from the NIJ 2006 survey (Durose, 2005). The LMPM assumes 10 items are analyzed per case,

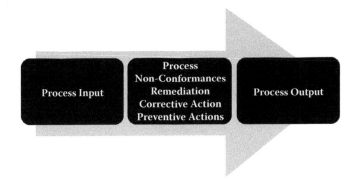

Figure 2.15 Quality control process audits.

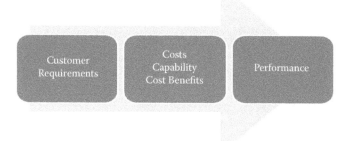

Figure 2.16 Quality management system audit.

except DNA, which analyses 30 items per case. "Lab costs" per case use the total budget as the numerator in the metric (cost/productivity) and "section costs" use only the salary of the respective discipline forensic scientists. Using the higher lab costs metrics assumes the remaining disciplines' contribution in multisection case analyses and use of all support, management, facilities, and nonpersonnel resources. We have chosen total LMPM costs ($52,530,000) divided by the total number of cases equals $877 a case. Similarly, costs per item is $70. These two metrics would be useful for benchmarking, as they include all laboratory costs in the metric. We have also calculated total laboratory costs per case in each discipline and section costs per case per discipline. We recommend the section costs per case and item

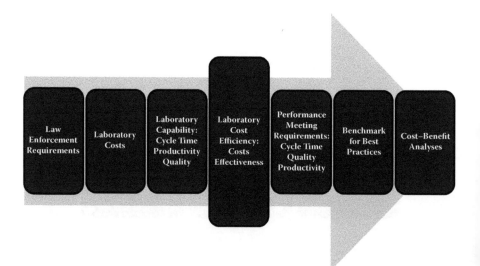

Figure 2.17 Cost efficiency and effectiveness.

Table 2.8   LMPM Cost Efficiency Metrics (Larger version of table included on the supplemental DVD enclosed.)

SCIENCE OPERATIONS	FTE	Salary & Benefits	Salary & Benefits Total	CASE PRODUCTIVITY PER FTE/YEAR	ITEMS ANALYZED PER CASE	CASE PRODUCTIVITY TOTAL/YEAR	ITEM PRODUCTIVITY TOTAL/YEAR	Lab Cost per Case	Lab Cost per Item	Section Cost per Case	Section Cost per Item
Digital Evidence	10	$150,000	$1,500,000	52	10	520	5,200	$101,019.23	$10,102	$2,885	$288
DNA	100	$150,000	$15,000,000	77	30	7,700	231,000	$6,822.08	$227	$1,948	$65
Controlled Substances	40	$150,000	$6,000,000	752	10	30,080	300,800	$1,746.34	$175	$199	$20
Firearms and Toolmarks	4	$150,000	$600,000	193	10	772	7,720	$68,044.04	$6,804	$777	$78
Latent Fingerprints	50	$150,000	$7,500,000	375	10	18,750	187,500	$2,801.60	$280	$400	$40
Questioned Documents	6	$150,000	$900,000	74	10	444	4,440	$118,310.81	$11,831	$2,027	$203
Trace Evidence	20	$150,000	$3,000,000	83	10	1,660	16,600	$31,644.58	$3,164	$1,807	$181
Total FS Costs			$34,500,000								
Average						59,926	753,260	$877	$70		

may be the most useful for internal and external benchmarking. Once significant increases or decreases occur or there are significant differences in benchmarking studies between agencies, then further analysis is needed to determine the causative factors for best business practices. Overall, the best strategy is to select a few metrics that are the best fit for your laboratory, standardize the overall disciplines, and sustain over the long term for a continual increase of improvement of the quality management system.

Cost efficiency metrics (section costs do not reflect support services or multisection cases) are:

Total LMPM cost per case (C_{Case}): Total Lab Costs/Total Productivity (P_{Case}) = \$877

Total LMPM cost per item (C_{Item}): Total Lab Costs/Total Productivity (P_{Item}) = \$70

Cost per case digital evidence (C_{DE})/P_{DECase}) = \$2,885

Cost per item digital evidence (C_{DE})/P_{DEItem}) = \$288

Cost per case DNA ($C_{DNACase}$) = \$1,948

Cost per item DNA ($C_{DNAItem}$) = \$65

Cost per case controlled substances (C_{CSCase}) = \$199

Cost per item controlled substances (C_{CSItem}) = 20

Cost per case firearms and tool marks ($C_{FATMCase}$) = \$777

Cost per item firearms and tool marks ($C_{FATMItem}$) = \$78

Cost per case latent prints (C_{LPCase}) = \$400

Cost per item latent prints (C_{LPItem}) = \$40

Cost per case questioned documents (C_{QDCase}) = \$2,207

Cost per item questioned documents (C_{QDItem}) = \$23

Cost per case trace evidence (C_{TECase}) = \$1,807

Cost per item trace evidence (C_{TEItem}) = \$181

Cost Effectiveness (*So What*)

The cost–benefit effectiveness metrics are both objective and subjective metrics that are very challenging to develop and monitor for continual improvement. Effectiveness measures are the *so what* or impact of the forensic services provided to law enforcement. What is the effect of the forensic services provided to the criminal justice community, our community, and victims? Top management must keep services focused upon the mission and goals of the laboratory, which should in turn meet law enforcement requirements. We will focus upon the impact of two major forensic disciplines for cost-effectiveness metrics: DNA and latent prints (LP). DNA and LP are two forensic disciplines that result in the identification or exclusion of suspects, and provide significant leads for criminal investigations. The significance, impact, or effect increases significantly when a recidivist is identified as a suspect and convicted for a violent crime. The identification, arrest, conviction, and incarceration of a violent crime recidivist prevents the victimization of at least one individual and perhaps countless victims when serial offenders are stopped.

Forensic science has undergone a technology revolution and is continuing to benefit from application of new techniques in forensic molecular biology and digital imaging technologies. Forensic molecular biology and imaging technologies has allowed the development of computer databases that can search and compare DNA profiles and fingerprint images with source attributions to individuals. Specifically, probative DNA profiles derived from physiological fluids and tissues, and latent fingerprints developed from evidence or crime scenes are compared to DNA profiles and LP record prints from known suspects and convicted offenders. Similar database comparisons are made with ballistic digital images for comparisons of known weapons, projectiles, and cartridges. These three main databases (Combined DNA Index System [CODIS], Automated Fingerprint Identification System [AFIS], and National Integrated Ballistic Identification Network [NIBIN]) have been refined and expanded allowing local and national law enforcement investigations near instant and continual comparison of unknown and known profiles and images. Before the development of forensic databases an investigator would deliver an individual latent print or cartridge/weapon to the laboratory and ask for one specific comparison of the unknown to the known record. If an individual or weapon was excluded, then the investigator would continue to deliver individual items for comparison until, hopefully, identification was made and the suspect or murder weapon was identified. The success of the databases relies on recidivism (Langan and Levin, 2002) and the correlation between lesser offenses and violent crime (Dale, Pizzola, McCarthy, and Faber, 2005; Virginia Department of Forensic Science, 2013).

The first area of cost–benefit effectiveness is fulfilling the internal mission and goals of the laboratory. Does the laboratory have a strategic plan with outcomes using objective metrics for performance? Does the strategic plan link with all employees' performance programs and professional development training objectives? For example, a mission statement for a forensic laboratory could be: "The Metro Forensic Laboratory provides forensic services for the Metro criminal justice community through application of the best science to the best evidence in a productive, timely, quality, efficient, effective and ethical manner."

The next step is to define the scope for goals and objectives with outcome metrics:

- Metro criminal justice community
- Best science
  - Facilities
  - Equipment
  - Personnel
- Best evidence
  - Crime type
  - Evidence probativity
- Productivity
- Timeliness
- Quality
- Efficiency
- Effectiveness
- Ethics

As we have discussed earlier with the development of a quality management system the laboratory mission and goals shall be linked to the customer requirements. Ideally, forensic and law enforcement management expect the use of forensic services to decrease crime rates (Table 2.9 and Table 2.10).

Does the laboratory mission, goals, and objectives provide a cost–benefit effectiveness for the customer or what is the *so what* of the forensic services? Can we measure and then monetize the impact of forensic services? Crime costs are tangible and intangible. Tangible costs are made up of responding agencies' personnel and nonpersonnel costs from law enforcement, laboratories, emergency response personnel, and medical costs. Intangible costs are quality of life for victims and a sense of safety for citizens in their home and community. Miller, Cohen, and Rossman (1993) classifies crime costs in three major areas:

1. Direct losses, such as medical, mental health, emergency response, and insurance
2. Productivity losses, wages, benefits, and housework
3. Nonmonetary losses in pain, suffering, and lost quality of life

Table 2.9   Virginia FBI UCR Crime Data

Category	Crime	Total Incidents	Crime Rate
Crimes against a person	Homicide, Murder, Manslaughter	305	0.0636%
	Kidnapping	1,475	0.3076%
	Forcible Sex Offenses	5,104	1.0643%
	Assault	108,386	22.6001%
	Nonforcible Sex Offenses	211	0.0440%
Subtotal		115,481	24.0795%
Crimes against society	Drug Offenses	50,650	10.5613%
	Pornography	683	0.1424%
	Gambling	156	0.0325%
	Prostitution	950	0.1981%
	Weapons	9,062	1.8896%
Subtotal		61,501	12.8239%
Crimes against property	Robbery	5,451	1.1366%
	Arson	1,167	0.2433%
	Extortion	113	0.0236%
	Burglary	30,438	6.3468%
	Larceny	144,491	30.1285%
	Motor Vehicle Theft	9,616	2.0051%
	Counterfeiting	7,074	1.4750%
	Fraud	26,040	5.4297%
	Embezzlement	2,838	0.5918%
	Stolen Property	1,454	0.3032%
	Destruction, Damage, Vandalism	73,893	15.4078%
	Bribery	25	0.0052%
Subtotal		302,600	63.0966%
Requirement Total	Total	479,582	100.0000%

Source: Virgina State Police, 2011, Crime in Virginia, retrieved January 8, 2013, from http://www.vsp.state.va.us/Crime_in_Virginia.shtm.

Other researchers have made varied attempts to determine the costs of crime directly to the victim, subsequent later effects (victimization), and to society as a whole (Cohen, 2000; Dhiri and Brand, 1999; Doleac, 2012; Horvath, Messig, and Lee, 2001; Miller, Cohen, and Rossman, 1993; NAS, 2009; Zedlewski, 2009, 2010).

Following are a sampling of crime cost metrics identified in the literature:

Total U.S. crime costs: $178 billion (Cohen, 2000)
Total U.S. forensic costs: 1.6 billion (Durose, 2009)
Total U.S. forensic scientist: 13,100 (Durose, 2009)
Average offender costs: $430,000 (Zedlewski, 2010)
Incarceration ROI: $430,000/$25,000 = 17 (Zedlewski, 2010)

Table 2.10 NYPD 88 Pct CompStat Report

Police Department
City of New York

Michael R. Bloomberg
Mayor

Raymond W. Kelly
Police Commissioner

Volume 20 Number 4   *CompStat*   *Citywide*

Report Covering the Week 1/21/2013 through 1/27/2013

Crime Complaints

	Week to Date			28 Day			Year to Date*			2 Year	12 Year	20
		Year										
	2013	2012	% Chg	2013	2012	% Chg	2013	2012	% Chg	% Chg	% Chg (2001)	% Chg (1993)
Murder	3	6	-50.0	23	32	-28.1	23	29	-20.7	-8.0	-58.2	-86.4
Rape	24	32	-25.0	103	115	-10.4	102	111	-8.1	0.0	-30.6	-51.7
Robbery	323	424	-23.8	1,536	1,563	-1.7	1,454	1,485	-2.1	3.8	-32.8	-78.8
Fel. Assault	280	286	-2.1	1,307	1,236	5.7	1,257	1,155	8.8	-0.6	-21.3	-53.8
Burglary	302	377	-19.9	1,303	1,488	-12.4	1,250	1,440	-13.2	-1.3	-51.1	-84.3
Gr. Larceny	717	756	-5.2	3,092	2,898	6.7	2,964	2,758	7.5	19.6	-8.5	-50.0
G.L.A.	135	138	-2.2	552	558	-1.1	526	539	-2.4	-20.2	-75.5	-94.2
TOTAL	1,784	2,019	-11.64	7,916	7,890	0.33	7,574	7,517	0.76	5.27	-36.39	-77.04

Source: New York Police Department, 2013, January, CompStat 88 Pct 12/31/21–01/06/13, retrieved January 20, 2013, from http://www.nyc.gov/html/nypd/downloads/pdf/crime_statistics/cscity.pdf.

Cost–benefit effect of DNA database sample increase: .57 decrease in crime rates (Doleac, 2012)
Individual crime costs (Cohen, 2000)
  Fatal crime: $2,940,000
  Child abuse: $60,000
  Rape and sexual abuse: $87,000
  Robbery: $8,000
  DWI: $18,000
  Larceny: $370
  Burglary: $1,400
Vehicle theft: $3,500

In the private sector a return on investment greater than one (ROI >1) is necessary to remain in business. The enterprise applies resources to raw materials supplied and the manufacturing or service process must add value greater than the resources used to provide the product or service for the customer. Obviously, if not, the enterprise will fail to exist and will go out of business. Tables 2.11, 2.12, 2.13, and 2.14 (Dale and Becker, 2007) show ROI calculations for DNA and LP analyses, total LMPM costs, and Laura Lake homicide analyses costs, respectively. The main assumption being

Table 2.11   Cost Effectiveness of Rightful Conviction with DNA Analyses

DNA ANALYSES	Crime Costs	LMPM DNA Case Analyses Costs	Investment / Return (IoR)	Return / Investment — ROI (DNA analyses)	Ratio Description: ROI = Return / Investment	Ratio Description: IOR = Investment / Return
Fatal Crime	$2,940,000	$6,822	0.23%	431.0	ROI = 431 for DNA analyses preventing one fatal crime	IOR is .23% for DNA analyses preventing one fatal crime
Rape	$87,000	$6,822	7.8%	12.8	ROI = 1 for 12.8 DNA analyses preventing one rape	IOR is 7.8% for DNA analyses preventing one rape
Child Abuse	$60,000	$6,822	0.113701299	8.8		
DWI	$18,000	$6,822	0.379004329	2.6		
Robbery	$8,000	$6,822	0.85275974	1.2		
Vehicle Theft	$3,500	$6,822	1.949165121	0.5		
Burglary	$1,400	$6,822	4.872912801	0.2		
Larceny	$370	$6,822	18.43804844			

Table 2.12   Cost Effectiveness of Rightful Conviction with Latent Print Analyses

LATENT PRINT ANALYSES	RETURN (Crime Costs)	INVESTMENT (LMPM Latent print case analyses costs)	Investment / Return (IoR)	Return / Investment — ROI	Ratio Description: ROI = Return / Investment	Ratio Description: IOR = Investment / Return
Fatal Crime	$2,940,000	$2,802	0.1%	1049.40	ROI = 1049 for LP analyses preventing one fatal crime	IOR is .1% for LP analyses preventing one fatal crime
Rape	$87,000	$2,802	3.2%	31.05	ROI = 1 for 31 LP analyses preventing one rape	IOR is 3.2% for LP analyses preventing one rape
Child Abuse	$60,000	$2,802	4.7%	21.42		
DWI	$18,000	$2,802	15.6%	6.42		
Robbery	$8,000	$2,802	35.0%	2.86		
Vehicle Theft	$3,500	$2,802	80.0%	1.25		
Burglary	$1,400	$2,802	200.1%	0.50		
Larceny	$370	$2,802	757.2%	0.13		

Table 2.13   Cost Effectiveness of Rightful Conviction with Total LMPM Costs

TOTAL LMPM COSTS	RETURN (Crime Costs) or Cost Avoidance	INVESTMENT (Total LMPM Costs)	Investment / Return (IoR)	Return / Investment — ROI	Ratio Description: ROI = Return / Investment	Ratio Description: IOR = Investment / Return
Fatal Crime	$2,940,000	$52,530,000	18	5.597%	ROI = 18 for total LMPM costs preventing one fatal crime	IOR is 5.5% for LP analyses preventing one fatal crime
Rape	$87,000	$52,530,000	604	0.166%	ROI = 1 for 604 for total LMPM costs preventing one rape	IOR is .16% for total LMPM costs preventing one rape
Child Abuse	$60,000	$52,530,000	876	0.114%		
DWI	$18,000	$52,530,000	2,918	0.034%		
Robbery	$8,000	$52,530,000	6,566	0.015%		
Vehicle Theft	$3,500	$52,530,000	15,009	0.007%		
Burglary	$1,400	$52,530,000	37,521	0.003%		
Larceny	$370	$52,530,000	14,1973	0.001%		

that the DNA and LP analyses identified and contributed to the conviction and incarceration of a recidivist violent offender preventing at least one violent crime. Recidivism rate studies in the United States reported 67% of prisoners released will be arrested for a new crime within 3 years (Langan and Levin, 2002). Identification of serial or recidivistic offenders, exclusion of suspects, and the resultant incarceration of a *rightful recidivist offender* prevent future crime and victimization costs. Although the ROI for DNA analyses of burglary cases is low (.2), in fact the impact is much more due to high hit rates in data banks from these lesser offenses. Lesser offenses or nonviolent offenses contribute to the majority (5,487/8,245) of investigations aided in Virginia and other jurisdictions (Virginia Department of Forensic Science, 2013). The identification and subsequent incarceration of a recidivist prevents, through the use of DNA or latent print forensic case

Table 2.14   Cost Effectiveness of Laura Lake Homicide

Crime	RETURN (Crime Costs)	INVESTMENT (Lake Homicide Total Lab Costs)	Return / Investment	Investment / Return	Ratio Description: ROI = Return / Investment	Ratio Description: IOR = Investment / Return
Laura Lake Homicide	$2,940,000	$199,961	14.70	6.8%	ROI = 14.7 for total LMPM costs for Laura Lake homicide analyses	IOR is 6.8% for total LMPM costs for Laura Lake homicide analyses

Source: Dale, W. M., and Becker, W. S., 2007, *The Crime Scene: How Forensic Science Works*, New York: Kaplan.

analyses, *at a minimum at least one future crime*. Using Cohen's data for crime costs and our LMPM data for case analyses costs (DNA and LP) we develop the cost–benefit effectiveness or ROI for *rightful conviction of one recidivist* (Tables 2.11, 2.12, 2.13, and 2.14).

In summary, the ROI for one DNA case analyses solving one homicide and convicting one serial offender is .23% or 431 similar analyses. In summary, the ROI for a conviction of a serial offender through the use of DNA, LP, total LMPM costs and Laura Lake homicide total LMPM costs are shown in Table 2.15.

These ROIs are compelling and are metrics that can be used by policy makers to verify the effectiveness of quality forensic analyses. A similar and perhaps more effective description of the ROI would be "credits" to criminal justice funding:

- The cost avoidance of one homicide ($2,940,000) by a serial offender by DNA would fund 431 additional DNA analyses.
- The cost avoidance of one rape ($87,000) by a serial offender by DNA would fund 12 additional DNA analyses.
- The cost avoidance of one burglary by a serial offender by DNA would fund .2 DNA analyses.

We propose the cost benefits of rightful conviction of recidivist and the associated prevention of one violent crime are real resource *credits* for the criminal justice community decreasing crime and associated costs. Perhaps the most significant metrics are the intangible and immeasurable benefits derived from prevention of victimization pain and suffering costs not incurred on many potential victims of violent crimes or wrongful convictions.

We have also analyzed the negative cost benefit of wrongful convictions (Better Government Association, 2011) depicted in Table 2.16. The total costs incurred from 85 wrongful convictions and 14 rapes and 11 child abuse cases by perpetrators not caught multiplied by the forensic error/misconduct factor (11%) × ($28,504,316)/85 wrongful convictions equals $335,345. The litigation ($335,345) *debit* incurred upon the criminal justice community paid by tax dollars per wrongful conviction due to poor forensic service is a worst

Table 2.15   Cost Effectiveness Summary

	ROI		
	Homicide	Rape	Burglary
DNA analyses costs	421	12	.2
Latent print analyses costs	1,049	31	.5
Total LMPM costs	5.9%	.16%	.003%
Laura Lake homicide analyses costs	14		

Table 2.16 Wrongful Conviction Costs: Costs Ineffective and Inefficient

Wrongful Conviction (WC) Costs				
	Costs	# of Wrongful Convictions	Average Costs per Wrongful Conviction	Forensic Factor = .11
Total Cost of Wrongful Conviction, 1989–2010	$ 214,000,000	85	$ 2,517,647	$276,941
Settlements and judgements	$ 156,000,000	85	$ 1,835,294	$201,882
Lawyers Fees	$ 31,500,000	85	$ 370,588	$40,765
Incarceration Costs	$ 18,500,000	85	$ 217,647	$23,941
Court of Claims Costs	$ 8,000,000	85	$ 94,118	$10,353
Fatal Crime	$2,940,000	# Additional Crimes by Actual Perpetrator Not Caught	Total Costs of Additional Crimes	Costs of Forensic Errors or Misconduct (11%)
Rape	$87,000	14	$41,160,000	$4,527,600
Child Abuse	$60,000	11	$957,000	$105,270
DWI	$18,000			
Robbery	$8,000			
Vehicle Theft	$3,500			
Burglary	$1,400			
Larceny	$370			
Kidnappings				
Felonies				
GRAND TOTAL: 85 Wrongful Convictions Additional Crimes Costs by Perps Not Caught			$ 256,117,000	$ 28,172,870
Average Total Costs of 85 Wrongful Convictions Additional Crimes Costs by Perps Not Caught			$ 3,013,141	$331,446
GRAND TOTAL FORENSIC CAUSES (11%)				$28,504,316
COSTS PER WRONGFUL CONVICTION FORENSIC CAUSES (total costs x .11)/ 85				$335,345
Causes of Wrongful Convictions	Number	Percentage		
Police Misconduct and Errors	66	24%		
Erroneous Eyewitness Identification	46	17%		
Alleged Prosecutorial Misconduct or Error	44	16%		
False Confession	33	12%		
Incentivized Witness Testimony	30	11%		
Questionable Forensic Evidence or Testimony	29	11%		
Alleged Ineffective Assistance or Counsel	23	8%		
TOTAL	271	100%		

case scenario for the forensic community, the wrongfully convicted, and the untold number of future victims of recidivists not originally caught and stopped.

Recommendations for Management: Cost–Benefit Efficiency and Effectiveness

- Efficiency
  - Provide relentless excellent stewardship of taxpayer dollars, continually monitor all processes for cost savings strategies.
- Effectiveness
  - Target the most effective forensic services (e.g., DNA, LP) to reduce most serious law enforcement investigations (e.g., FBI UCR violent crimes).
  - Identify and locate all recidivists in a geopolitical region.
  - Ensure all convicted offenders contribute a sample to the databases before release.
  - Ensure all database and casework samples are analyzed in a timely manner (30 days).
  - A majority of leads from databases emanate from lesser offenses such as burglaries, establish a high throughput analyses center for all lesser offenses targeting LP and DNA analyses.
- Last, critique old/cold case hits resulting from database technologies. Why was the case not solved in the first place when it was "hot?" A causative analyses critique of cold cases solved by database technologies will add continual improvement to the efficiency and effectiveness of the investigative processes.

Performance

Performance (Pf) = Total LMPM Capability (P, CT, Q)/Customer Requirements (P, CT, Q)

Performance is the ability of the laboratory to meet customer requirements (Figure 2.18). Productivity: If all LMPM customer agencies submit a total of 59,926 cases per year, is the LMPM productivity capable of analyzing 59,926 cases per year? If the laboratories productivity is 50,000 cases per year, then productivity performance equals 83% (50,000/59,926) with a backlog of 9,926 cases. Cycle time: If the average cycle time for all cases is 45 days, the cycle time performance is 66% (30/45). If 100 non-conformances are delivered to the customer (reports with errors), then quality performance is 99.83% (59,826/59,926).

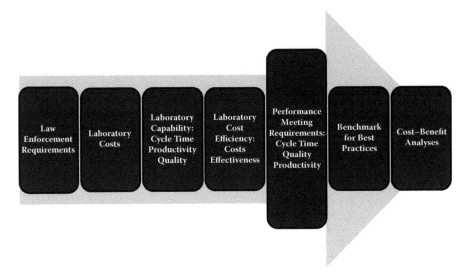

Figure 2.18 Performance.

For the sake of our discussion, the LMPM is designed to have a total performance of 100% with no backlog. Although not normally the case or an exceedingly rare event, the laboratory may also have excess capability overall or in specific disciplines. In that case, performance would exceed customer requirements resulting in decreased cycle times, and increased productivity and quality.

Productivity (PReq)/(P$_{Real}$): 100%
Cycle Time (CTReq)/(CT$_{Real}$): 100%
QReq/Q($_{Real}$) = 100%

The key to performance management is continual monitoring of LMPM requirements, capability, and performance metrics. If LMPM performance for a specific discipline begins to lag requirements, then capabilities and costs are inadequate. Poor capability and performance lead to increased cycle/queue times and backlogs, which require management to make adjustments with available resources. Cost–benefit efficiency and effectiveness metrics are the primary metrics for targeting potential internal resource shifts or real-location to other areas. Specifically, *high cost inefficiency and low effectiveness* should be the first areas to review. If these types of analyses are unnecessarily costly with no impact, then these services should be reduced or terminated and resources reallocated to other areas. Similarly, perhaps the most significant step is to bring processes under control resulting in more resources expended toward production and less efforts expended on quality control as discussed in the quality section.

Table 2.17 Performance versus Capabilities Scorecard (Larger version of table included on the supplemental DVD enclosed.)

Category	Crime	Total Incidents	Case Submissions	Item Submissions	Monthly Requirements	DE	DNA	CS	FATM	LP	QD	TE
	Performance vs. Capabilities Scorecard — Month 6											
PERFORMANCE = REQUIREMENTS (Annual Submissions per Crime — 12% except homicides)						CAPABILITIES (Items analyzed per discipline)						
Crimes against a person	Homicide, Murder, Manslaughter	305	305	9,150	763	3,050	3,050			4,543		3,432
	Kidnapping	1,475	177	1,770	148							
	Forcible Sex Offenses	5,104	612	6,125	510		6,125			3,256		3,344
	Assault	108,386	13,006	130,063	10,839		70,243					
	Nonforcible Sex Offenses	211	25	253	21	253				154		253
Subtotal		115,481	14,126	141,261	11,772							
Crimes against society	Drug Offenses	50,650	30,390	303,900	25,325		178,000			23,321		
	Pornography	683	82	820	68							
	Gambling	156	19	187	15							
	Prostitution	114	114	1,140	95							
	Weapons	9,062	1,087	10,874	906				5,556			
Subtotal		61,501	31,692	316,921	26,410							
Crimes against property	Robbery	5,451	654	6,541	545		3,654					2,223
	Arson	1,167	140	1,400	117							543
	Extortion	113	14	136	11						136	
	Burglary	30,438	3,653	36,526	3,044		19,876			15,432		
	Larceny	144,491	17,339	173,389	14,449					77,654		
	Motor Vehicle Theft	9,616	1,154	11,539	962							
	Counterfeiting	7,074	849	8,489	707							
	Fraud	26,040	3,125	31,248	2,604						2,221	
	Embezzlement	2,838	341	3,406	284						22	
	Stolen Property	1,454	174	1,745	145							
	Destruction, Damage, Vandalism	73,893	8,867	88,672	7,389							
	Bribery	25	3	30	3							
Subtotal		302,600										
Requirement Total	Total	479,582	57,550	1,285,585	107,132		178,000					
Productivity CS			30,080	300,800	25,067			178,000				
Productivity DE			520	5,200	433	3,050						
Productivity DNA			7,700	231,000	19,250		103,201					
Productivity FATM			772	7,720	643				5,556			
Productivity LP			18,750	187,500	15,625					124,360		
Productivity QD			444	4,440	370						2,566	
Productivity TE			1,660	16,600	1,383							9,795
Productivity Total			59,926	753,260	62,772							
Projected Performance												
Performance Productivity (Preq/Preall)						50%	50%	50%	50%	50%	50%	50%
Performance Cycle Time (CTreq/CTreall)						59%	45%	59%	72%	66%	58%	59%
Performance Quality (Qreq/CTreall)						100%	100%	100%	100%	100%	100%	100%
						100%	100%	100%	100%	100%	100%	100%
						DE	DNA	CS	FATM	LP	QD	TE
Total Capability	Population	8,000,000										
Total Requirements	Case Submission Rate		0.12	100% for Homicides	60% for Drugs							
Capabilities	Items per case		10	30 Items for DNA								

LMPM and law enforcement's continual use of a performance scorecard (Table 2.17) provides top management data to monitor LMPM performance. Are the case submissions (law enforcement requirements) and laboratory capabilities (case/item analyzed) correlated for excellent performance?

Table 2.17 is an example of how managers can measure and monitor the LMPM performance by correlating requirements to capabilities. This scorecard should be developed by the laboratory information management system (LIMS) monthly or weekly for the total laboratory and the customers (law enforcement). Ever-changing requirements or capabilities that affect performance should be monitored closely to provide data for reallocating resources between units or developing data for next year's funding requests. The number and types of investigations worked by law enforcement must be monitored for the number of cases and items submitted for what types of analyses. We have made a few assumptions in the earlier example:

1. The case evidence submission rate is 12%. This means 12% of the criminal cases result in evidence being submitted to the laboratory. There are some exceptions, for example, 100% of homicides and 60% of drug cases result in evidence being submitted to the laboratory.
2. Total annual requirements for analyses are divided by 12 to develop a monthly rate.

3. The number and types of analyses for each discipline was projected by previous years' average number of submissions and customer surveys and interviews.
4. LMPM capabilities should be at 50% at month 6 in Table 2.17.
5. FATM (firearms and tool marks) and LP are above 50% and should be monitored closely, as inadequate capability will lead to backlogs and unacceptable cycle times.

A second method to measure the effectiveness of forensic services is the impact upon crime rates and associated evidence submissions per type of crime using the customer FBI UCR crime rate data as shown in Table 2.18. Albeit there are many other factors affecting crime rates in addition to the impact of forensic services, forensic managers should work with law enforcement to channel forensic technologies efficiently and effectively. Forensic services may be very effective in high crime rate areas or when applied to crimes that are trending upward at an unacceptable rate.

Benchmarks for Best Practices

Metrics are also used to benchmark or compare to metrics between similar laboratories. The American Productivity and Quality Center (APQC) Benchmarking Portal (APQC, 2013) (Figure 2.19 and Figure 2.20) provides an open portal for the manufacturing industry that compares key business metrics. The following metrics are used for the APQC benchmarking studies:

Cost effectiveness—Total cost to manufacture per $1,000 in revenue
Process efficiency—Value of plant shipments per employee
Process efficiency—Unplanned machine downtime as a percentage of scheduled run time
Cycle time—Manufacturing cycle time in hours

We suggest benchmarking metrics for the LMPM five major categories for the identification and sharing of best practices. Further analyses and benchmarking of Group A offenses provides information for tactical responses to specific offenses. For example, if similar agencies benchmarked the number of sexual assault investigations and revealed a significant difference in the amount of evidence, then the benchmarking agencies should share more efficient and effective procedures for recognition, collection, and protection of sexual assault evidence.

Tables 2.19, 2.20, and 2.21 are examples of benchmarking using CODIS and population data for best efficiency and effectiveness. There are many

Table 2.18   Performance Effectiveness: Crime Rate Reduction

PERFORMANCE = REQUIREMENTS / CAPABILITIES					
Category	Crime	Total Incidents	Crime Rate	Case Submissions	Item Submissions
Crimes against a person	Homicide, Murder, Manslaughter	305	0.0636%	305	9,150
	Kidnapping	1,475	0.3076%	177	1,770
	Forcible Sex Offenses	5,104	1.0643%	612	6,125
	Assault	108,386	22.6001%	13,006	130,063
	Nonforcible Sex Offenses	211	0.0440%	25	253
Subtotal		115,481	24.0795%	14,126	141,261
Crimes against society	Drug Offenses	50,650	10.5613%	6,078	60,780
	Pornography	683	0.1424%	82	820
	Gambling	156	0.0325%	19	187
	Prostitution	950	0.1981%	114	1,140
	Weapons	9,062	1.8896%	1,087	10,874
Subtotal		61,501	12.8239%	7,380	73,801
Crimes against property	Robbery	5,451	1.1366%	654	6,541
	Arson	1,167	0.2433%	140	1,400
	Extortion	113	0.0236%	14	136
	Burglary	30,438	6.3468%	3,653	36,526
	Larceny	144,491	30.1285%	17,339	173,389
	Motor Vehicle Theft	9,616	2.0051%	1,154	11,539
	Counterfeiting	7,074	1.4750%	849	8,489
	Fraud	26,040	5.4297%	3,125	31,248
	Embezzlement	2,838	0.5918%	341	3,406
	Stolen Property	1,454	0.3032%	174	1,745
	Destruction, Damage, Vandalism	73,893	15.4078%	8,867	88,672
	Bribery	25	0.0052%	3	30
Subtotal		302,600	63.0966%		
Requirement Total	Total	479,582	100.0000%	57,550	799,345
Productivity CS				30,080	300,800
Productivity DE				520	5,200
Productivity DNA				7,700	77,000
Productivity FATM				772	7,720
Productivity LP				18,750	187,500
Productivity QD				444	4,440
Productivity TE				1,660	16,600
Productivity Total				59,926	599,260
Performance Productivity (Preq/Preal)					
Performance Cycle Time (CTreq/CTreal)					
Performance Quality (Qreq/Qreal)					

other factors that may affect the number of investigations aided per capita or investigations aided per forensic sample such as the maturity/size of the database. These types of benchmarking provide management an indicator of efficiency and effectiveness of performance when compared to similar agencies. LMPM cost data allow cost–benefit efficiency and effectiveness analyses. Top management of agencies responsible for agencies serving geopolitical areas similar in size and scope can use these types of benchmarking tools

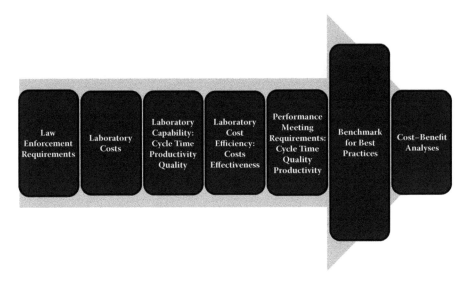

Figure 2.19 Benchmarking for best practices.

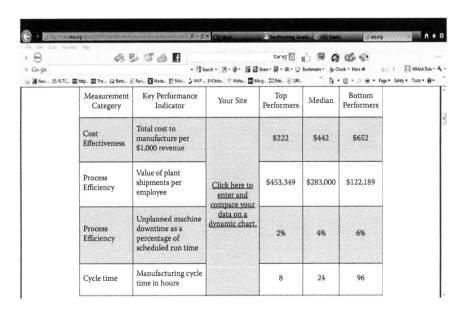

Measurement Category	Key Performance Indicator	Your Site	Top Performers	Median	Bottom Performers
Cost Effectiveness	Total cost to manufacture per $1,000 revenue		$222	$442	$652
Process Efficiency	Value of plant shipments per employee	Click here to enter and compare your data on a dynamic chart.	$453,349	$283,000	$122,189
Process Efficiency	Unplanned machine downtime as a percentage of scheduled run time		2%	4%	6%
Cycle time	Manufacturing cycle time in hours		8	24	96

Figure 2.20 APQC benchmark survey. (From the American Productivity and Quality Center [APQC], 2013, Retrieved February 14, 2013, from Benchmark Portal, http://rube.asq.org/apqc/2012/04/benchmarking/manufacturing-diagnostic.pdf?WT.dcsvid = MTA5NzYyNDI3ODIS1&WT.mc_id = EM119807. With permission.)

Table 2.19   CODIS Effectiveness Benchmark: Investigations Aided per Capita

State	Offender Profiles	Arrestee	Forensic Samples	Investigations Aided	Population	Investigation Aided per Capita
Missouri	239,462	14,922	15,176	7,348	5,704,484	0.001288
Florida	859,788	24,773	41,856	21,020	17,019,068	0.001235
Illinois	449,017	23	28,043	15,387	12,653,544	0.001216
Oregon	157,756		8,728	4,054	3,559,596	0.001139
Alabama	208,746	4,227	9,882	4,791	4,500,752	0.001064
Virginia	351,831	4,583	15,793	7,791	7,386,330	0.001055
Arizona	252,468	20,665	13,177	5,705	5,580,811	0.001022
South Carolina	171,799		9,783	4,239	4,147,152	0.001022
Nevada	76,136		4,605	2,183	2,241,154	0.000974
New Mexico	58,125	22,840	3,953	1,654	1,874,614	0.000882
Arkansas	131,521	644	6,244	2,398	2,725,714	0.000880
Louisiana	121,679	277,119	8,450	3,756	4,496,334	0.000835
New York	425,208		39,719	14,982	19,190,115	0.000781
FBI	719,351	92,961	2,697	697	897,934	0.000776
Wisconsin	165,039		11,234	3,929	5,472,299	0.000718
New Jersey	251,840		14,040	6,145	8,638,396	0.000711
Colorado	155,608	76,404	7,956	3,168	4,550,688	0.000696
California	1,423,121	569,586	46,738	24,553	35,484,453	0.000692
Alaska	22,200	17,679	1,149	429	648,818	0.000661

Table 2.20   CODIS Benchmarking: Investigations per Forensic Sample

State	Offender Profiles	Arrestee	Forensic Samples	Investigations Aided	Population	Investigations Aided per Forensic Sample
Puerto Rico	19,613	459	42	32	3,725,789	0.761905
Illinois	449,017	23	28,043	15,387	12,653,544	0.548693
California	1,423,121	569,586	46,738	24,553	35,484,43	0.525333
Florida	859,788	24,773	41,856	21,020	17,019,068	0.502198
Virginia	351,831	4,583	15,793	7,791	7,386,330	0.493320
Alabama	208,746	4,227	9,882	4,791	4,500,752	0.484821
Missouri	239,462	14,922	15,176	7,348	5,704,484	0.484186
Nevada	76,136		4,605	2,183	2,241,154	0.474050
Oregon	157,756		8,728	4,054	3,559,596	0.464482
Michigan	319,815	8,845	13,591	6,103	10,079,985	0.449047
Pennsylvania	283,048		10,215	4,567	12,365,455	0.447088
Louisiana	121,679	277,119	8,450	3,756	4,496,334	0.444497
Hawaii	26,687		718	317	1,257,608	0.441504
New Jersey	251,840		14,040	6,145	8,638,396	0.437678
South Carolina	171,799		9,783	4,239	4,147,152	0.433303
Arizona	252,468	20,665	13,177	5,705	5,580,811	0.432951
Washington	221,661		4,326	1,848	6,131,445	0427184
New Mexico	58,125	22,840	3,953	1,654	1,874,614	0.418416
Colorado	155,608	76,404	7,956	3,168	4,550,688	0.398190

Table 2.21 CODIS Cost–Benefit Effectiveness: Costs Investigations Aided (Larger version of table included on the supplemental DVD enclosed.)

State	Offender Profiles	Arrestee	Forensic Samples	Investigations Aided	Population	DNA Cost Offender Samples @ $40	LMPM DNA Costs per Case @ $5,911	Total Costs	Cost per Investigation Aided
Illinois	449,017	23	28,043	15,387	12,653,544	$ 17,960,680	$ 165,762,173	$183,722,853	$11,940
Florida	859,788	24,773	41,856	21,020	17,019,068	$ 34,391,520	$ 247,410,816	$281,802,336	$13,406
Missouri	239,462	14,922	15,176	7,348	5,704,484	$ 9,578,480	$ 89,705,336	$99,283,816	$13,512
California	1,423,121	569,586	46,738	24,553	35,484,453	$ 56,924,840	$ 276,268,318	$333,193,158	$13,570
Virginia	351,831	4,583	15,793	7,791	7,386,330	$ 14,073,240	$ 93,352,423	$107,425,663	$13,788
Nevada	76,136		4,605	2,183	2,241,154	$ 3,045,440	$ 27,220,155	$30,265,595	$13,864
Alabama	208,746	4,227	9,882	4,791	4,500,752	$ 8,349,840	$ 58,412,502	$66,762,342	$13,935
Oregon	157,756		8,728	4,054	3,559,596	$ 6,310,240	$ 51,591,208	$57,901,448	$14,283
Louisiana	121,679	277,119	8,450	3,756	4,496,334	$ 4,867,160	$ 49,947,950	$54,815,110	$14,594
New Jersey	251,840		14,040	6,145	8,638,396	$ 10,073,600	$ 82,990,440	$93,064,040	$15,145
Michigan	319,815	8,845	13,591	6,103	10,079,985	$ 12,792,600	$ 80,336,401	$93,129,001	$15,260
South Carolina	171,799		9,783	4,239	4,147,152	$ 6,871,960	$ 57,827,313	$64,699,273	$15,263
Arizona	252,468	20,665	13,177	5,705	5,580,811	$ 10,098,720	$ 77,889,247	$87,987,967	$15,423
New Mexico	58,125	22,840	3,953	1,654	1,874,614	$ 2,325,000	$ 23,366,183	$25,691,183	$15,533
Pennsylvania	283,048		10,215	4,567	12,365,455	$ 11,321,920	$ 60,380,865	$71,702,785	$15,700
Hawaii	26,687		718	317	1,257,608	$ 1,067,480	$ 4,244,098	$5,311,578	$16,756
New York	425,208		39,719	14,982	19,190,115	$ 17,008,320	$ 234,779,009	$251,787,329	$16,806
Colorado	155,608	76,404	7,956	3,168	4,550,688	$ 6,224,320	$ 47,027,916	$53,252,236	$16,809
Arkansas	131,521	644	6,244	2,398	2,725,714	$ 5,260,840	$ 36,908,284	$42,169,124	$17,585

to identify best practices thereby providing the customer better service and good stewardship of the tax dollar.

Table 2.22 provides an overview of all LMPM metrics that are measured, managed, and monitored in the LMPM quality management system for continual improvements. Benchmarking allows laboratories statistical comparisons of data allowing the development of Pareto diagrams and control charts that can serve as management tools for contributors. Individual laboratories can request contact to best practice agencies facilitating further discussions. The key to benchmarking is to form trusting relationships to share confidential data and keep the metrics useful and easy to monitor.

Basics of Cost–Benefit Analyses

We now have developed the metrics needed to perform a cost–benefit analysis (CBA) (Figure 2.21). The CBA should be performed before any major changes in scope of forensic services are recommended to top management. Some organizations require a CBA when a new program exceeds a specific dollar amount as a single one-time expense, an increase or decrease in the base budget, or reallocation of funds from one operational unit to another. CBAs are relatively simple analyses that should be practiced by middle managers on smaller projects in preparation for CBAs with larger scope. As a part of a career development tool the CBA is excellent preparation for making decisions and instituting policies with increased authorities and responsibilities. Top management relies upon good data and recommendations to make policy decisions affecting the costs, capabilities, efficiency, effectiveness, and perfor-

Table 2.22 LMPM Benchmark Metrics

LMPM Metric Category	LMPM Metric	Your Laboratory	Mean	Median	Range	Standard Deviation	n
LE Requirements	FBI UCR Part 1 Crimes/# Laboratory Submissions = 12% UCR Part 1 lead to evidence submissions						
Costs	Costs per Capita $51,735,000/8,000,000 = $6.47						
Capabilities	Average cases per Forensic Scientists 59,926 cases/230 Forensic Scientists = 260 cases per scientist FS/Capita = 230/8,000,000 1/34,782						
Cost efficiency	Total Budget/Total number of cases $51,735,000/59,926 = $863.31 per case $51,735,000/753,260 = $68.68 per item						
Cost effectiveness	# Homicides solved # Sexual assaults solved						
Performance	Capabilities/Requirements = Performance (Productivity, Timeliness, Quality) LMPM = 100%						

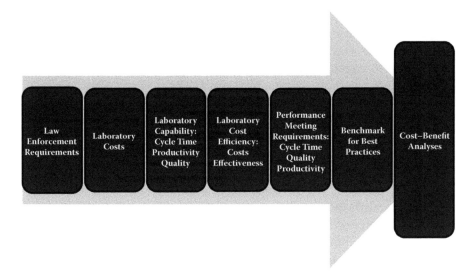

Figure 2.21 Cost–benefit analyses.

mance of the laboratory. We will use the following "Forensic Express Pilot Project" service as an example for a cost–benefit analysis.

There are several steps in the CBA process (Assistant Secretary of the Army Financial Management and Comptroller, 2009):

1. Define the problem statement, define the objective and the scope
   a. Customer (law enforcement and the court) would like a "Forensic Express" service to expedite analyses for violent crimes and burglary increasing the timeliness of results from 30 days to 15 days. The first 15 days of an investigation are often the most critical for success. A 15-day cycle time would allow law enforcement to identify and exclude suspects and reconstruct crime scenes sooner, increasing the efficiency of the investigation. Prosecutors would be able to develop fact patterns and proper criminal law charges against more probable suspects in a much more timely manner.
   b. The LMPM is constantly reacting to expedited cases, which disrupt the work flow of the DNA unit. Maximum efficiency can only be achieved when DNA sample preparation is synchronized with instrument throughput. Injecting an expedited case in the complex work flow sets back normal cases under analyses and lengthens cycle times.
   c. Legislature has increased the LMPM base budget $1,000,000 from $46,406,000 to $47,406,000 for the Forensic Express Pilot project.

2. Formulate assumptions and identify constraints
   a. Formulate assumptions
      i. The Forensic Express Pilot project will be limited to a 10-county region. Using the Deming (1986b) Plan, Do, Check, Act method, the pilot program will be evaluated after 2 years. If the project met law enforcement and court requirements to expedite violent crime DNA case analyses with a 15-day cycle time, the program will be expanded to other geopolitical areas.
      ii. Customers were surveyed for what type of cases to be targeted for the Forensic Express 15-day cycle time requirements for expedited case analyses. It was decided to limit the Forensic Express analyses to homicides, rapes, and burglary. Law enforcement and the court would like violent crimes (homicides and rapes) to be expedited in an effort to reduce recidivist offenders and therefore prevent further crimes. Burglary-convicted offenders entered into the DNA databank results in the highest number of hits or investigations aided for violent crimes (Dale, Pizzola, McCarthy, and Faber, 2005; Langan and Levin, 2002; Virginia Department of Forensic Science, 2013). The customer would therefore encourage the analyses of burglary evidence to maximize the efficiency and effectiveness of the DNA databank and resulting convictions of recidivistic violent offenders.
      iii. Law enforcement and the court estimated that 36 homicides, 60 rapes, and 1,800 burglaries would require express service annually. Homicides and rapes require 30 items for analyses including controls and burglary require 5 items for analyses:
          1. 36 homicides × 30 items = 1,080 items
          2. 60 rapes × 30 items = 1,800 items
          3. 1,800 burglaries × 5 items = 9,000 items
          4. Grant total expedite items = 11,880 items
   b. Identify constraints
      i. Labor management agreements need to be considered for any movement of personnel between disciplines. Experienced DNA scientists can be selected from the traditional DNA unit for assignment to the Forensic Express project. This would allow implementation within 12 months (6 months instrument acquisition followed by 6 months validation and

training). The traditional DNA unit would be negatively impacted until new hires could be hired and trained to competency. This would increase cycle time in the traditional unit but may be offset by cases completed by Forensic Express.

ii. Instrument contract and acquisition requires approximately 6 months.

iii. New instrument throughput is estimated at 100 items per day, 3 days per week equaling 300 items per week.

iv. New high-throughput DNA analyzers and software need validation before use on casework samples. Forensic Express team members should preferably perform the validation. The instrument validation project would also serve as a process validation, training, and competency exercise for team members.

v. Time: 2 years. If experienced new hires can be internally recruited, then time from recruitment, instrument acquisition, validation, and training to casework competency can be decreased to 12 months. Year 2 is dedicated to implementing the Forensic Express project.

3. Document the current state
   a. Current state capability "Normal Analyses Cycle Time = 30 Days"
      i. 100 forensic scientists
      ii. Forensic scientists average 77 case analyses per year
      iii. Each homicide case averages 30 items per case including blanks, exemplars from victims and suspects, and unknown crime scene or investigative samples.
      iv. Total productivity is 7,700 cases including 231,000 items.
      v. Cycle time is 30 days.
      vi. DNA total LMPM unit cost efficiency per case equals $6,822 per case, $227 per item, and includes total LMPM support and facilities. DNA unit only costs $1,948 per case and $65 per item.

4. Define alternatives with cost estimates with metrics and key ratios for analyses. (See Table 2.23.)

5. Define Forensic Express selection criteria
   a. Requirements
      i. 15-day cycle time
      ii. 36 homicides
      iii. 60 rapes
      iv. 1,800 burglaries

Table 2.23   Define Alternatives

	COA #1 Forensic Express Team (Add 4 FTE and High Throughput Instrument) dedicated for expedited cases requiring 15-day cycle time	COA #2 (Add 6 FTE to Current State DNA Unit) for expedited cases requiring 15-day cycle time
Customer DNA Requirements (Law Enforcement and Court)	36 homicides × 30 items = 1,080 items 60 rapes × 30 items = 1,800 items 1,800 burglaries × 5 items = 9,000 items Grand total cases = 1,896 cases Grand total expedite items = 11,880 items	
Costs	3 forensic scientists @ $110,000 salary + $50,000 benefits = $480,000 1 technician @ $60,000 salary + $30,000 benefits = $90,000 1 new high throughput instrument @ $440,000 High performance teamwork training at $20,000 Total personnel: $570,000 Total nonpersonnel: Instrument $460,000 Grand total: $1,000,000	6 forensic scientists @ $110,000 salary + $50,000 benefits = $960,000
Capabilities	Instrumental Throughput: 3 forensic scientists 1 technician 300 items per week with dedicated instrument throughput 15,600 items per year 15-day cycle time	6 DNA scientists expediting items in queue with all other cases: 1 forensic scientist = 77 cases per year 1 forensic scientist = 2,310 items per year 6 forensic scientists = 13,860 items 15-day cycle time
Cost efficiency: Good stewardship of taxpayer funds	$1,000,000/15,600 items $64.10 per item Does not include support costs	$1,000,000/ 13,860 items $72.15 per item Does not include support costs

Cost effectiveness: Meeting customer Requirements for expediting violent crime and burglary cases with a 15-day cycle time	36 homicides + 60 rapes + 1,800 burglaries = 1,896 cases $1,000,000/1,896 = $527 per case 2,489 × 10% suspect inclusions = 249 potential recidivists charged in a criminal action $1,000,000/249 = $4,016 per inclusion 2,489 × 20% exclusions = 498 potential suspects excluded $1,000,000/498 = $2,008 per exclusion Cost prevention for one recidivist homicide = $2,400,000 Cost prevention for one recidivist rape = $87,000 Intangibles: Forensic Express team "constancy of purpose" dedicated to violent crimes and burglary or "ownership" of a specific geopolitical area providing a 15-day cycle time. Intangibles: Forensic Express team dedicated to support and operation or "ownership" of one high-throughput instrument dedicated to the project. Management is proactive for analyses of violent crime and burglary cases instead of reactive to expedited cases.	36 homicides + 60 rapes + 1,800 burglaries = 1,896 cases × 117% Performance = 2,226 cases $1,000,000/2,226 = $449 per case 2,226 x 10% suspect inclusions = 222 potential recidivists charged in a criminal action $1,000,000/222 = $4,504 per inclusion 2,226 × 20% exclusions = 445 potential suspects excluded $1,000,000/445 = $2,247 per exclusion Cost prevention for one recidivist homicide = $2,400,000 Cost prevention for one recidivist rape = $87,000
Performance	15-day cycle time: 100% Productivity: 15,600/11,880 = 131% Quality: 100% no non-conformances	15-day cycle time: 100% Productivity: 13,860/11,800 = 117% Quality: 100% no non-conformances

      b. Costs
         i. $1,000,000
      c. Capabilities
         i. Items analyzed per year
      d. Cost efficiency
         i. Costs per item
      e. Cost effectiveness
         i. Costs per inclusion
        ii. Costs per exclusion
       iii. Intangibles
           1. Teamwork
           2. Dedicated geographical service area
           3. Dedicated instrumentation
      f. Performance
         i. Productivity
        ii. Cycle time
       iii. Quality
    6. Compare alternatives (Table 2.24)
    7. Report results and recommendations

Table 2.24 Compare Metrics

	COA #1: Forensic Express Team	COA #2: Add staff to current state
Requirements	36 homicides × 30 items = 1,080 items	36 homicides × 30 items = 1,080 items
	60 rapes × 30 items = 1,800 items	60 rapes × 30 items = 1,800 items
	1,800 burglaries × 5 items = 9,000 items	1,800 burglaries × 5 items = 9,000 items
	Grand total cases = 1,896 cases	Grand total cases = 1,896 cases
	Grand total expedite items = 11,880 items	Grand total expedite items = 11,880 items
Costs	$1,000,000	$1,000,000
Capability	15,600 items	13,860 items
Cost efficiency	$64.10 per item	$72.15 per item
Cost effectiveness	$4,016 per suspect inclusion	$4,504 per suspect inclusion
	$2,008 per suspect exclusion	$2,252 per suspect exclusion
Performance	Cycle time 15 days = 100%	Cycle time 15 days = 100%
	Productivity = 131%	Productivity = 117%
	Quality = 100%	Quality = 100%

MEMORANDUM

FROM: Forensic Cost–Benefit Analyses Unit
To: Forensic Executive Committee
SUBJECT: Cost–Benefit Analyses for Forensic Express 15-day cycle time
COA #1: Forensic Express Team, COA#2: Add staff to Current State

Executive Overview: Law enforcement and prosecutors have requested a 15-day cycle time to expedite violent crime investigations such as homicide and rape. They have also requested lesser offenses, such as burglary, be included in the project as lesser offenses significantly increase the effectiveness of the DNA data bank. The current state capabilities are 100 forensic scientists with a productivity of 7,700 cases consisting of 231,000 items analyzed per year with a 30-day cycle time. The DNA unit cost is $18,000,000 excluding non-personnel costs.

It is recommended a pilot Forensic Express Team (COA#1) be selected as the best alternative to provide a 15-day cycle time to expedite violent crimes and burglaries in a specific geographical service area. COA#1 has a higher productivity, lower cost efficiency, lower cost effectiveness, and greater performance than COA#2. Projected intangible effectiveness factors (dedicated team for specific geographic service area, dedicated instrument, and no disruption from other cases in the queue) may prove to be the most important. Team members working together with a constancy of purpose with a specific set of law enforcement agencies should provide professional relationships, which act as a force multiplier for efficiency and effectiveness.

	COA #1: Forensic Express Team	COA#2: Enhance Current State
Requirements	36 homicides 60 rapes 1,600 burglaries	36 homicides 60 rapes 1,600 burglaries
Costs	$1,000,000	$1,000,000
Capability	Productivity: 15,600 items Cycle time: 15 days Quality: No non-conformances	Productivity: 13,860 items Cycle time: 15 days Quality: No non-conformances
Cost Efficiency	$64.10 per item	$72.15 per item
Cost Effectiveness	$4,016 per suspect inclusion $2,008 per suspect exclusion Intangibles: Teamwork and dedicated constancy of purpose	$4,504 per suspect inclusion $2,252 per suspect exclusion
Performance	100%	100%

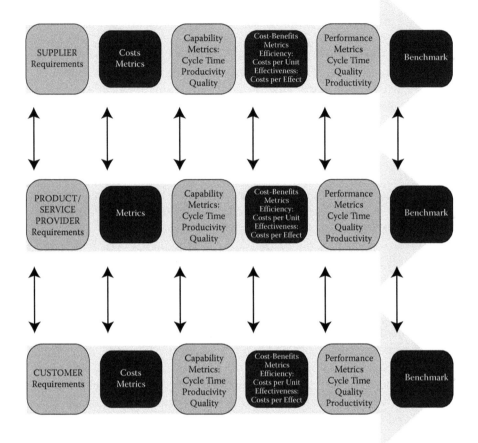

Figure 2.22 Supplier—forensic service provider—customer metric linkage.

One could propose a limitless variety of business categories, metrics, and key ratios to measure and manage for continued improvement of laboratory processes. Limitless scenarios could provide higher or lower values for our LMPM metric values. The actual value of the metric is actually inconsequential to the fact that top management has institutionalized a process to develop reliable and verifiable data used to make good decisions. Our LMPM is for a large laboratory or laboratory system that serves a population of 8,000,000 and is scalable to smaller laboratories. Most forensic laboratories are much smaller and serve cities and counties throughout the United States. Laboratory facilities and equipment

Table 2.25 LMPM Metrics

R_{CS}/Year	Case submissions per year	59,926
R_{CS}/Capita	Case submissions per capita	59,556/8,000,000 =.75%
$R_{FBI/UCR}$/Capita	FBI/UCR/IBR Group A incidents per capita	479,582/8,000,00 = 6%
$R_{CS}/R_{FBI/UCR}$	Case submissions per FBI/UCR/IBR Group A incidents	59,926/479,582 = 12%

Costs

C	Total budget	$51,735,000
C_M	Costs for management personnel	$2,685,000
C_S	Costs for support	$2,550,000
C_{FS}	Costs for forensic scientists	$34,500,000
C_{NP}	Costs for nonpersonnel	$12,000,000

Hidden Costs

C_{QTotal}	Total costs for bad and good quality	$20,700,00
C_{GG}	Costs for good quality	$17,250,000
C_{BQ}	Costs for bad quality	$3,450,000
C_{HRTO}	HR turnover costs total	$6,000,000
$C_{HRTOInvol}$	HR turnover costs involuntary (5) × 2	$1,500,000
$C_{HRTOVol}$	HR turnover costs voluntary (15) × 2	$4,500,000

Capability

P	Productivity (total for all disciplines)	59,926 cases
CT	Cycle time in days (average for all disciplines)	30 days
Q	Quality good (NonCom before report issued) and bad (NonCom after report issued)	0

Cost–Benefit Efficiency

$CEffic_{Case}$	Cost per case	$863.31
$CEffic_{Item}$	Cost per item	$68.68
$CEffic_{DEcase}$	Cost per case DE	$2,884.62
$CEffic_{DEitem}$	Cost per item DE	$288,46
$CEffic_{DNAcase}$	Cost per case DNA	$1,948.05
$CEffic_{DNAitem}$	Cost per item DNA	$64.94
$CEffic_{CScase}$	Cost per case CS	$199.47
$CEffic_{CSitem}$	Cost per item CS	$19.95
$CEffic_{FATMitem}$	Cost per case FATM	$777.20
$CEffic_{FATMitem}$	Cost per item FATM	$77.72
$CEffic_{LPitem}$	Cost per case LP	$400.00
$CEffic_{LPitem}$	Cost per item LP	$40.00
$CEffic_{QDcase}$	Cost per case QD	$2,027.03
$CEffic_{QDitem}$	Cost per item QD	$202.70
$CEffic_{TEcase}$	Cost per case TE	$1,807.23

(Continued)

Table 2.25   LMPM Metrics (*Continued*)

$CEffic_{Capita}$	Cost per capita	$6.47
$CEffic_{TEitem}$	Cost per item TE	$180.72
	Cost–Benefit Effectiveness "So What?"	
	DNA case suspect inclusions per case (10%)	770
	DNA unit costs per suspect inclusion	$19,481
	Total LMPM costs per DNA inclusion	$67,188
	DNA case suspect exclusions (20%)	1,440
	DNA case suspect exclusions per case (20%)	$9,740
	Total LMPM costs per DNA exclusion	$33,594
	Latent print suspect inclusions (10%)	1,875
	Latent print costs per suspect inclusion	$4,000
	Total LMPM costs per latent print suspect inclusion	$27,592
	Latent print suspect exclusions (20%)	3,750
	Latent print costs per suspect exclusion	$2,000
	Total LMPM costs per latent print suspect exclusion	$13,796
DNA	Crime	Effectiveness ROI
	Fatal crime	437.6
	Rape	12.9
	Child abuse	8.9
	DWI	2.7
	Robbery	1.2
	Vehicle theft	.5
	Burglary	.2
	Larceny	.1
Latent Print	Crime	Effectiveness ROI
	Fatal crime	1065.53
	Rape	31.53
	Child abuse	21.75
	DWI	6.52
	Robbery	2.90
	Vehicle theft	1.27
	Burglary	.51
	Larceny	.13
Total LMPM	Crime	Effectiveness ROI
	Fatal Crime	18
	Rape	595
	Child Abuse	862
	DWI	2,874
	Robbery	6,467
	Vehicle Theft	14,781

Table 2.25 LMPM Metrics (*Continued*)

	Burglary	36,954
	Larceny	139,824
Performance		
PERF$_{CT}$	Performance Productivity (Req/Actual)	100%
PERF$_P$	Performance Quality (Req/Actual)	99.81%
PERF$_Q$	Performance Quality (Req/Actual)	99.81%
Additional Metrics Useful for Benchmarking		
LMPM		
	FTE per capita	0.0033%
	FS per capita (FSc)	0.0029%
	Cost per capita	$6.47
	Cases per capita	0.75%
	Group A incidents per capita	5.9%
	Cases per FBI UCR Group A Incidents	12%
	Management Efficiency_FS	5.2%
	Support Efficiency_FS	4.9%
	QA good costs% of budget	33.34%
	QA bad costs% of budget	6.67%
	Digital evidence% of budget	2.90%
	DNA% of budget	28.99%
	Controlled substances% of budget	11.60%
	Firearms and tool marks % of budget	1.16%
	Latent fingerprints% of budget	14.50%
	Questioned documents% of budget	1.74%
	Trace evidence% of budget	5.80%
National		
	Number of FS nationally	13,100
	National forensic budget	$1,600,000,000
	US population	311,591,917
	# FS per capita US	0.0042%
	Costs per capita	$5.13

are high-cost technology enterprises that may be difficult to sustain for smaller departments. Smaller laboratories may also not have the customer requirements necessary to justify service in all forensic disciplines. Less required services may best be forwarded to larger laboratories, either public or private, that benefit from economies of scale with larger case loads. We have assumed the majority of facilities, infrastructure, and equipment are sunk costs with depreciation and replacement funds not included in the calculations.

Commitment from top management and getting started are essential for implementation of the LMPM. Inaccurate or unknown customer requirements will lead to unacceptable costs, capabilities, cost benefits, and performance. The old adage "if you can measure it, you can manage it" is simple, yet directly applicable to managing public sector forensic laboratories using proven business strategies. The most important category in the model is the accurate description and continual updates of customer and supplier requirements.

Establishment and linkage of LMPM with customer quality system (CMPM) and supplier (SMPM) metrics provides a synergistic transformational quality management system enterprise in which all three components of the business model (supplier, service/product provider, customer) work together driving down costs, increasing effectiveness and efficiency, and increasing capability and performance metrics with benchmarking for best practices (Figure 2.22 and Table 2.25).

Criminal Case Cost Vignette: Laura Lake Homicide

Source: W. M. Dale and W. S. Becker, 2007, The Crime Scene: How Forensic Science Works, New York: Kaplan.

Crime Scene: Laura Lake Residence, 159 Walnut Street, Metroland, New York

Local businesswoman Laura Lake has operated a successful jewelry business in Metroland, New York, with her family for over 20 years. Laura wants to open new stores and expand Lake Jewelry to neighboring communities to provide more opportunities for family members. Laura was recently given a Small Business Award by the area Chamber of Commerce because of Lake Jewelry's generous support for local charities. As part of the award ceremony, Metroland News interviewed Laura, providing recognition for her very successful family business.

Laura lives in the suburbs, just outside Metroland. Most residents leave for work early in the morning and the suburban neighborhood is relatively deserted during the day. Laura is a hard worker and would normally be at work, but today she is meeting with a new landscaper who left a flyer on her door. She usually researches contractors thoroughly but was desperate to get some yard work done.

Lake's neighbor, Betty Smith, is outside picking up the paper from her driveway when she hears loud, unusual noises coming from Lake's home. She calls 911, and Emergency Technician Mary Marcel is the first one on the scene. Mary arrives driving the ambulance. Patrolman Barry Lasker is the next to arrive in his patrol car. First responders establish the scene as safe and provide care for any victims found at the scene.

Both Barry and Mary have little experience with criminal cases and no experience with a homicide. Mary's mission is to provide life-saving support to victims as soon as possible at the risk of compromising or destroying any evidence. She goes right to Laura Lake, administers CPR, and uses a portable defibrillator. In her rush she accidentally steps in some blood. Mary knows that she could destroy some of the evidence but she also knows that a live victim is better than a dead one.

The Case Triage Team (CTT) for the Laura Lake homicide is now assembling for the third time in 4 weeks. The team has been working together nonstop since the first day of the Laura Lake investigation, including:

- First Responder—Patrolman Barry Lasker
- Crime Scene Technician—John Goodspeed
- Forensic Science Supervisor—Olivia Johns
- Medical Examiner—Dr. Ali Kumar
- Laboratory Quality Assurance Supervisor—Carol Lent
- Forensic Scientist 3, Latents—Larry Poler
- Forensic Scientist 3, DNA—Sara Herbst
- Forensic Scientist 3, Drugs—Sanjay Predeep
- Detective Lieutenant—Daniel Escobar
- Detective, Homicide Squad—Louis Muscato

The team has gone over all of the statements from neighborhood interviews, family members, and phone and computer messages to no avail. The laboratory results all seem to be routine. No drugs or medications have been found in the toxicology analyses of all bodily fluids and tissues. There is also no evidence of a sexual assault exhibited by the injuries, and no sperm or seminal fluid was detected on the victim's clothing or swabs collected during the autopsy.

Sam Livingston, the main suspect, has not been totally excluded, but he does appear to have an alibi for the day the homicide occurred. Sam adamantly denies any involvement in the killing. But he was found to have injuries to his hands that appear to be deep scratches. These could have been caused by the victim in the struggle for her life. Sam states that he has a landscaping job at an estate in the same neighborhood and that he injured his hands while trimming brush with power tools. The owner of the estate confirms that Sam has been working hard on the property over the past several weeks. However, the owner was not present at the estate on the day of the homicide. Therefore, he cannot confirm Sam's presence on that day, nor can he confirm the cause of Sam's injuries.

Laboratory forensic scientists processed all items of evidence looking for any fingerprints or blood from Sam at the crime scene. None were found. Sam's clothing and vehicle were processed for any blood from Laura Lake, with negative results. The laboratory had dedicated several scientists to work this case and they had analyzed over 100 items of evidence attempting to identify either Sam's fingerprints or blood found at the crime scene or known samples from the victim, Laura Lake, in Sam's vehicle.

EMT Mary Marcel is particularly distraught, knowing that she may have compromised the significant blood spatter evidence at the scene. When she arrived at the scene, Mary was concerned that victim Laura Lake was still alive. Mary rushed to apply compresses to stop the bleeding from the deep stab wounds. Since the victim was still warm, Mary thought that there may be a chance to save the victim. Her job is to save lives. Even though she has been trained in the preservation of evidence, Mary unknowingly stepped in and destroyed several bloody footprints next to the body of the victim. These may have been made by the perpetrator.

The shoes confiscated from the suspect have several bloody smears and blood drops. One particular blood drop came from the top of the shoe. It is consistent with a low velocity, vertical droplet. This could have been from the suspect's hand wounds, allegedly caused by working as a landscaper. The DNA lab works quickly to process the blood drops from the top of the shoe. They are from suspect Sam Livingston. Sam's alibi is holding up.

Carol Lent, quality assurance supervisor, is a serologist with the laboratory for 25 years. Recently, Carol was promoted to a newly created supervisor position. She has seen the biology section progress from the old ABO blood typing to the new technology of DNA. Polymerase chain reaction (PCR) obtains DNA profiles from trace or invisible amounts of blood, semen, or saliva. As a serologist, Carol has worked many homicides over the course of her career. The lab had needed one person to take charge of quality assurance in order to prepare the laboratory for the new ISO/IEC 17025:2005 accreditation program. Carol decided that it was time to move into an administrative position in order to contribute to the overall quality of laboratory operations. Carol has the right background for her new supervisory duties as she has attended many accreditation courses and has successfully prepared the lab for several International Standards Organization (ISO) accreditation inspections in the past. It appears that the new forensic scientists in the lab are skilled in DNA since they possess advanced degrees in molecular biology.

But Carol misses casework so she tries to attend Case Triage Team meetings when her schedule permits. Sitting next to EMT Mary Marcel, Carol thinks about the footprints found next to the victim and wishes that they had not been obliterated. The photos of the floor at the scene clearly show the presence of another set of shoes, but the imprints in blood could only be matched to Mary Marcel's shoes. The other set of shoe prints do not have enough detail remaining to match to the shoes of suspect Sam Livingston.

Carol asks Detective Lieutenant Daniel Escobar for the photo file. The team has taken over 500 photos of the scene and all items in evidence. Carol wants to see the shoes. Mary's shoes are covered with blood and the imprints are clearly caused by her tread design. Carol next focuses on Sam Livingston's shoes. The round blood drop on the top of the right shoe is very noticeable on the lightly colored shoelaces and insole. However, the sides of Sam's shoes and soles are black. Carol asks to have Sam's shoes sent to the clean room in the DNA lab so that she can inspect them more closely.

The next week Carol comes back to the Case Triage Team meeting and announces: "Sam's your guy!" Carol works with the new scientists to show them how to use an alternate light source to identify blood on dark surfaces. While the new scientists are proficient in DNA analysis, they had not been trained to recognize and collect possible DNA evidence. The horizontal blood spatter on both sides of Sam's shoes could not have been caused by vertical drops from his hands. The horizontal blood spatter was caused by the multiple knife wounds to the victim while she was on the floor. The DNA lab quickly analyzes the horizontal blood spatter and confirms that the source of blood on the side of Sam's shoes is from victim Laura Lake. Presented with the new findings, Sam Livingston fully confesses to the killing of Laura Lake.

The combination of an experienced quality assurance manager, new technology from an alternate light source, and DNA ultimately solved the case. Sam's early alibi of an injury from yard work on the estate could not be eliminated, but it also could not be confirmed. Later analysis of the horizontal blood spatter on Sam's shoes puts him at the scene and excludes his alibi. The blood drop on the top of his shoe is blood from Sam's own injuries, but the injuries were not from clearing brush, they were caused when the victim, Laura Lake, fought for her life. The horizontal blood spatter on Sam's shoes was caused by the violent struggle on the floor. The blood spatter is at the same level as Sam's shoes. Laura Lake fought for her life and lost, but her struggle transferred evidence that resulted in the identification and prosecution of the defendant, Sam Livingston.

Using case costs from the LMPM cost metrics we can provide an estimate of laboratory costs and ROI for the Laura Lake homicide assuming, at a minimum, 10 items analyzed per discipline with controls and blanks (Table 2.26).

Table 2.26 Laura Lake Homicide Costs (Assume Toxicology Costs Similar to Controlled Substances)

Item Description	Item #	Location	Serology	Nuclear DNA	Firearms & Tool Marks	Latent Prints	Toxicology	Trace Hair Fiber Impressions	Questioned Documents	Drugs	Forensic Scientist	Report Date	Total Costs
LMPM Case Section Costs			$1,429		$570	$293	$146	$1,325	$1,486	$146			$5,395
LMPM Lab Costs per Case			$5,911		$58,597	$2,497	$1,513	$27,419	$102,511	$1,513			$199,961
Known Controls													
Vic Control Blood	K1	CS											
Vic Control Prints	K2	CS											
Susp Control Blood	K1	CS											
Susp Control													
Prints	K4	CS											
Victim 10 Prints	K8	CS											
Suspect 10 Prints	K9	CS											
EMT Shoes	K10	CS											
Susp Shoes													
AUTOPSY													
Blood	K11	A											
Urine	K12	A											
Liver	K13	A											
Bile	K14	A											
Vitreous Humor	K15	A											

Stomach Contents	K16	A
Prescription Drugs	K17	A
Other Standards	K18..n	A
QUESTIONED		
Blood on Floor	Q1..n	CS
Latent Print	Q2..n	CS
Shoe Prints	Q5..n	CS
Blood on Knife	Q6..n	CS
VEHICLE		
Latent Prints	Q7..n	V
Blood	Q8..n	V

Source: Dale, W. M., and Becker, W. S., 2007, *The Crime Scene: How Forensic Science Works*, New York: Kaplan.

References

American Productivity and Quality Center (APQC). (2013). Retrieved February 14, 2013, from Benchmark Portal: http://rube.asq.org/apqc/2012/04/benchmarking/manufacturing-diagnostic.pdf?WT.dcsvid=MTA5NzYyNDI3ODIS1&WT.mc_id = EM119807.

American Society for Training and Development. (2012). *2012 State of the Industry*. Retrieved May 28, 2013, from http://www.astd.org/Publications/Research-Reports/2012/2012-State-of-the-Industry.

American Society of Laboratory Directors (ASCLD). (2008, December). ASCLD Position Statements. Retrieved January 9, 2013, from http://www.ascld.org/about-ascld/ascld-position-statements/.

American Society of Quality (ASQ). (2013, February 25). ASQ certifications. Retrieved February 25, 2013, from http://www.asq.org.

Assistant Secretary of the Army Financial Management and Comptroller. (2009, December 30). U.S. Army Cost Benefit Analyses Guide ver. 1.0. Retrieved January 10, 2013, from http://asafm.army.mil/Default.aspx?aspxerrorpath =/offices/LinksDocsOffice.aspx.

Becker, W. S., Dale, W., and Pavur Jr., E. J. (2010). Forensic science in transition: Critical leadership challenges. *Forensic Science Policy and Management* 1(4), 214–223.

Better Government Association (BGA). (2011, June). High costs of wrongful convictions. Retrieved July 6, 2013, from http://www.bettergov.org/investigations/wrongful_convictions_1.aspx.

Better Government Association. (n.d.). Better government, wrongful convictions. Retrieved July 5, 2013, from http://www.bettergov.org/investigations/wrongful_convictions_1.aspx.

Cascio, W. F., and Boudreau, John W. (2008). *Investing in People: Financial Impact of Human Resource Initiatives*. Upper Saddle River, NJ: Society for Human Resource Management.

Chelko, L. (2012, August). Director, U.S. Army Criminal Investigation Laboratory. (W. M. Dale, Interviewer).

Cohen, M. A. (2000). Measuring the costs and benefits of crime and justice. In *Measurement and Analysis of Crime and Justice*, vol. 4, edited by David Duffee, p. 263–315. Washington, D.C.: Government Printing Office.

Dale, W. M., and Becker, W. S. (2004). A case of forensic science turnover. *Forensic Science Communications* 6(3).

Dale, W. M., and Becker, W. S. (2007). *The Crime Scene: How Forensic Science Works*. New York: Kaplan.

Dale, W. M., Pizzola, P., McCarthy, D., and Faber, L. (2005, May 31). NYPD BioTracks. Retrieved January 19, 2013, from Harvard Kennedy School, Ash Center for Democratic Governance and Innovation, http://www.innovations.harvard.edu/showdoc.html?id = 6902.

Deming, W. E. (1986a). "Doing it with data." In M. Walton, *The Deming Management Method*, chapter 20, p. 96. New York: Berkley Publishing Company.

Deming, W. E. (1986b). *Out of Crisis*. Cambridge, MA: Massachussetts Institute of Technology.

Dhiri, S., and Brand, S. (1999). *Crime Reduction Program, Analyses of Costs and Benefits: Guidance for Evalutators*. London: Research, Development and Statistics Directorate, Home Office.

Doleac, J. L. (2012, December 2). DNA Databases. Retrieved January 14, 2013, from University of Virginia, http://www.batten.virginia.edu/sites/default/files/fwpapers/Doleac_DNADatabases_0.pdf.

Durose, M. R. (2005). *Census of Publicly Funded Forensic Crime Laboratories*. Washington, D.C.: National Institute of Justice.

Durose, M. R. (2009). *Census of Publicly Funded Forensic Crime Laboratories*. Washington, D.C.: National Institute of Justice.

Federal Bureau of Investigation (FBI). (2010–2011). FBI Facts and Figures. Retrieved January 14, 2013, from http://www.fbi.gov/stats-services/publications/facts-and-figures 2010-2011/facts-and-figures 2010-2011-pdf.

Hickman, M. J., and Peterson, J. L. (2002). *50 Largest Crime Labs in the US 2002*. Washington, D.C.: Bureau of Justice Statistics.

Horvath, F., Messig, R. T., and Lee, Y. (2001). *A National Survey of Police Policies and Practices Regarding the Criminal Investigation Process: 25 Years After Rand*. East Lansing, MI: Michigan State University, School of Criminal Justice.

House of Commons, Science and Technology Committee. (2011). *Forensic Science Service: Seventh Report of Session 2010–12*. London: The Stationery Office Limited.

International Laboratory Accreditation Cooperation (ILAC). (2002). *Guidelines for Forensic Laboratories*. Australia: ILAC.

International Organization for Standardization (ISO). (2004). *ISO Guide 2*. Retrieved 2013 from http://www.iso.org.

International Organization of Standardization (ISO). (2013). ISO 9000: 2005 Quality Management Systems—Fundamentals and Vocabulary. Retrieved from http://www.iso.org.

ISO 19011. (2002, October 1). *Guidelines for Quality and/or Environmental Management Systems Auditing*. Switzerland: ISO.

ISO 9001. (2000, December 15). *Quality Management Systems Requirements*. Switzerland.

ISO 9004. (2000, December 15). *Quality Management Systems—Guidelines for Performance Improvements*. Switzerland.

ISO/IEC 17025. (2005). General requirements for the competence of testing and calibration laboratories. Switzerland: ISO.

Kirk, P. L. (1953). *Crime Investigation, Physical Evidence and the Police Laboratory*. New York: Interscience Publishers.

Langan, P. A., and Levin, D. J. (2002). *Recidivism of Prisoners Released in 1994*. Washington, D.C.: Bureau of Justice Statistics.

Miller, T. R., Cohen, M. A., and Rossman, S. B. (1993). Victim costs of violent crime and resulting injuries. *Health Affairs* 12(4), 186–197.

National Academy of Sciences (NAS). (2009). *Strengthening Forensic Science in the United States: A Path Forward*. Washington, D.C.: National Academies Press.

New York Police Department. (2013, January). CompStat 88 Pct 12/31/21–01/06/13. Retrieved January 20, 2013, from http://www.nyc.gov/html/nypd/downloads/pdf/crime_statistics/cscity.pdf.

Russell, J. P. (2005). *The ASQ Auditing Handbook* (3rd ed.). Milwaukee, WI: ASQ Quality Press.

Shewart, W. A. (1980). *Economic Control of Quality of Manufactured Product, 50th Anniversary Commemorative Issue.* New York: American Society for Quality.

Speaker, P. J. (2009). Key performance indicators and managerial analyses of forensic laboratories. *Forensic Science Policy and Management* 1(1), 32–42.

U.S. Census Bureau. (2013, January 10). U.S. Census. Retrieved January 10, 2013, from http://www.census.gov.

Virginia Department of Forensic Science. (2013, March 7). DNA Databank Statistics. Retrieved March 7, 2013, from http://www.dfs.virginia.gov/statistics/index.cfm.

Virginia State Police. (2011). Crime in Virginia. Retrieved January 8, 2013, from http://www.vsp.state.va.us/Crime_in_Virginia.shtm.

Zedlewski, E. W. (2009). Conducting cost benefit analyses in criminal justice evaluations: Do we dare? *European Journal on Criminal Policy & Research*, 15(4), 355–364.

Zedlewski, E. W. (2010). *Adding Value to Justice Outcomes Evaluations.* Washington, D.C.: National Institute of Justice.

Laboratory Excellence and Ethics

3

An Essential Association*

DOUGLAS LUCAS

There is no person more qualified to discuss the critical importance of ethics in building an excellent laboratory organization than Douglas Lucas. He has had a distinguished career as a forensic scientist, laboratory director, and leader of professional associations, and has been a member of several teams investigating laboratory management problems. The recent ethical lapses of some criminalists have done staggering damage to the justice system and to laboratories' reputations. In this chapter, Lucas has reviewed many of these incidents, why he believes the problems occurred, the possible motives of the scientists involved, and how the problems might have been prevented. This chapter should be required reading of all new forensic examiners and newly appointed supervisors and laboratory directors.

The chapter details why criminalists need to be concerned about ethics, the content of various codes, and whom they govern. Criminalistics laboratories must acknowledge that the *process* of scientific inquiry is key to optimal performance, and many violations are the result of that process breaking down, and on the part of supervisors who failed to ensure proper procedures were being followed. The U.S. Supreme Court's *Daubert* decision and the 2009 National Academy of Sciences (NAS) report emphasize the importance of the scientific process in judging the admissibility of forensic evidence. Lucas notes that following proper scientific procedure and doing things right is a simple but essential professional duty. He discusses the special problems facing scientists working within law enforcement systems and how ethical duties of criminalists are often different from those of legal personnel. He notes, too, the dilemmas sometimes faced by scientists operating within an adversarial legal system. Such problems may be the thorniest of all those facing a criminalist and how scientific truth does not always coincide with legal truth.

---

* This chapter is based on an article written by Douglas Lucas published in the *Journal of Forensic Sciences* in 1989. The material has been updated, supplemented, and modified to reflect the reality of forensic science in 2012. Lucas, M.Sc., D.Sc. (Hon), is the retired director of The Centre of Forensic Sciences, Toronto, Ontario, Canada.

Lucas sums up by reminding the reader that a criminalist is a scientist first and a forensic scientist second. This is a very important chapter and places ethics front and center to those building and improving forensic science laboratories.

Joseph Peterson
California State University, Los Angeles

Introduction

Although the description of a linkage between excellence and ethics as "essential" may not be one that many forensic science laboratory managers (or their staff) have previously considered, it will be the objective of this chapter to convince them that it is so. This will be attempted by a description of the author's view of what ethics are, using a definition appropriate to the context; how ethics relate to morals; and a discussion of what codes of ethics are and who they are for. Examples from the author's experience of behavior that has been found to be unethical will be presented as will—almost of equal importance—action that has been deemed not to be unethical. A description of some of the sources of the occasional ethical dilemmas that confront forensic scientists will be included, accompanied by some speculation about the motivation for ethical misconduct.

But before proceeding to the what and the who, we should first consider the why. Why devote a chapter in this book to ethics when there are so many other challenging topics to be covered relevant to forensic laboratory management?

Why Is Ethical Conduct Important to Forensic Laboratory Management and Staff?

The simple—but admittedly not very compelling—reason ethical conduct is important in the forensic laboratory is because our professional associations (both national and regional), laboratory accreditation bodies, and even the National Academy of Sciences (NAS) tell us so.

Professional Association Mandates

The American Academy of Forensic Sciences (AAFS, 2012) requires its members to reaffirm annually that they endorse the Academy's Code of Ethics and Conduct.

The American Society of Crime Laboratory Directors (ASCLD, 2005) requires its members to confirm that "as members of ASCLD, we will strive to foster an atmosphere within our laboratories which will *actively encourage* [my emphasis] our employees to understand and follow ethical practices."

The rationale provided for this requirement is: "We are holders of a public trust because a portion of the *vital affairs of other people* [my emphasis] has been placed into our hands by virtue of the role of our laboratories in the criminal justice system" (ASCLD, 1994).

It is important that forensic scientists be reminded occasionally that the items they regularly examine in their laboratories are indeed vital to someone (e.g., a victim or a suspect) and are not simply things because they are the routine samples they examine every day.

The principal forensic science laboratory accrediting body in the United States, the American Society of Crime Laboratory Directors Laboratory Accreditation Board (ASCLD/LAB), has since 2008 included in its accreditation requirements for staff training: "Training must also include a substantial knowledge of forensic science across its wide spectrum, the *application of ethical practices in forensic science* [my emphasis], and of criminal and civil law and procedures."

Finally, the National Research Council in its 2009 report *Strengthening Forensic Science in the United States: A Path Forward* recommended that:

> The National Institute of Forensic Science (NIFS) in consultation with its advisory board, should establish a national code of ethics for all forensic science disciplines and encourage individual societies to incorporate this national code as part of their professional code of ethics. Additionally, NIFS should explore mechanisms of enforcement for those forensic scientists who commit serious ethical violations. Such a code could be enforced through a certification process for forensic scientists. (Recommendation 9)

Public Interest

A more compelling reason for emphasizing the importance of ethical conduct in our laboratories is the enormously enhanced interest in ethics on the part of the general public created by highly publicized examples of ethical misconduct. We have been inundated with descriptions of ethically challenged behavior by senior executives of corporations such as Enron, Martha Stewart Omnimedia, the Murdoch media empire, and blatant misconduct by "financial advisers" such as Bernard Madoff.

Ethics (or lack thereof) in sport is another area that has captured public attention. There have been shocking examples such as the use of drugs for performance enhancement by athletes in several sports, "creative: judging in Olympic figure skating," and "sweetheart" exams for college athletes. The prevailing attitude for some seemed to be the one attributed to former

Chicago Cub Mark Grace: "If you're not cheating, you're not trying" (Levitt and Dubner, 2006).

The relevance of these examples to the current discussion is that ethical misconduct has not been restricted to corporate boardrooms or athletic playing fields. There have also been some highly publicized problems in forensic laboratories as exemplified by newspaper headlines such as: "S.F. Police Lab Worker Accused of Drug Testing," "More Wrongdoing Found at FBI Crime Lab," "HPD Appetite for Evidence Assailed," "Error-Prone Detroit Police Crime Lab Shut Down," and "SF Crime Lab Scandal Strains Justice System." The relevance of such headlines is that many, if not most, of them were initiated by a lapse in ethical conduct on the part of one or just a few individuals in those labs. For example, one of those headlines relates to an investigation in 1996/97 by the Department of Justice (DOJ) Office of Inspector General (OIG) of allegations of wrongdoing in the Federal Bureau of Investigation (FBI) Lab (Bromwich 1997). The OIG reported that although most of the allegations were unfounded, there were a few that had merit. Those few involved instances of overstating the significance of findings, providing testimony beyond the examiner's expertise, and improper preparation of laboratory reports. As a result of unethical conduct by a very few lab staff members in a relatively small number of cases, over 3,000 major criminal cases were cast into doubt and the otherwise well-deserved excellent reputation of a fine forensic laboratory was tarnished.

Another example is provided by the report of an independent investigator (coincidentally the person who had been the DOJ inspector general) appointed by the City of Houston to investigate problems in the Houston Police Department Laboratory. The 350-page final report of that 2-year investigation (Bromwich, 2007) revealed what were described as "major issues" in almost one quarter of the 1,155 cases reviewed in the serology/DNA section. These issues included failure to examine critical evidence, such as known samples from one or more of the parties in an investigation; failure to perform potentially probative examinations, such as genetic marker grouping; failure to report potentially exculpatory results, such as complainant and suspect having the same genetic markers in sexual assault cases; and misreporting the statistical significance of DNA profiles. The lab staff members were not performing as forensic scientists but rather as technicians for the investigators! Of particular interest to readers of a book on laboratory management, the report attributed these problems to a lack of scientific leadership, incompetent supervision, poorly trained staff and, of course, serious underfunding.

Academic Studies

In addition to the media reports, bad cases involving forensic science lead to critical academic studies that present great concern. For example, in March

2009, Brandon Garrett and Peter Neufeld published a devastating paper in the *Virginia Law Review* titled "Invalid Forensic Science Testimony and Wrongful Convictions." In it they described testimony in 156 of 232 DNA exoneration cases that had some form of what they referred to as "forensic" testimony in the original trial. Citations to the actual trial transcripts in 137 of the cases were provided and in 82 (60%) of these there was what the authors described as "invalid testimony."

Although one might challenge their categorization of some of the examinations they identified as "forensic science" and their assessment of some of the testimony as "invalid," the fact is that in many of the cases the scientific/technical testimony was disturbing. And these cases were not just from the Zains, Gilchrists, and Melnikoffs who are the usual suspects in these horror stories, they were much more widespread involving 72 examiners in 52 labs from 25 states.

Not surprisingly, many of these cases were sexual assaults from the early 1980s that involved ABO blood group types or phosphoglucomutase (PGM) analyses or microscopic hair comparisons, that is they involved examinations that had minimal discrimination capability and were the types of cases that would have the potential DNA evidence that could lead to an eventual exoneration. They also predated accreditation requirements (ASCLD/LAB was established in 1982) that would have at the very least informed the examiners of the requirements of acceptable performance and were before more complete disclosure requirements were implemented in many jurisdictions.

Nevertheless, the criticism of the testimony was not based simply on any misunderstanding by the article's authors of the limited discrimination capabilities of this type of evidence but rather on the improper significance the witnesses attributed to it. The most common, but not the only, problems were, as they were in Houston, failure to present evidence about the complainant's blood type when it was the same as that of the suspect, and presenting population distribution statistics based on the suspect's blood type rather than the type found in the actual evidence.

One concern for forensic scientists arising from such reports is that they produce an enormous amount of negative publicity and are damaging to the entire profession. In Houston, for example, the lab has been under almost constant critical observation since November 2002 when a local television station aired the results of its investigation of seven cases from the DNA/serology section. Since then, there have been well over 225 articles published in the *Houston Chronicle* about the lab's shortcomings. Even though the lab has since improved significantly, the staff continues to be subject to intense scrutiny and enormous pressure.

Such publicity and widespread public interest generates grave concern about the credibility and integrity of not just the individuals directly involved but of the entire laboratory. This has a traumatic impact on morale and is extremely agonizing for all members of the staff. Although recovery is possible, it is unbelievably difficult and takes months or years of enormous effort by the entire organization. Even when rehabilitation is successful, the lab staff will be constantly reminded that the headlines remain in the media files, because they will be resurrected every time attention is again focused on the lab—even for a positive story.

If there is any consolation to be found in the headlines, it is in the very fact that the incidents are considered newsworthy. Although all would agree that even one such case is one too many, these events are actually relatively rare, sufficiently so that they merit the headline treatment. The day that a newspaper has a headline blaring "Crime Lab Does a Good Job," will be the day when forensic science laboratories will know they have truly gone under!

The reason for the lengthy preamble to this chapter is that, often, the headline cases begin simply with one examiner one day deciding to cut a corner, perhaps even a small corner, and for what at the time may seem a good reason, such as expediting the arrest of a dangerous person. Their rationale is "Well, it's a gray area!" or "Who's to know?" When they get away with it, as they may well do, the corners may become sharper and the incidents more frequent until a disaster inevitably occurs. As Professor John Thornton (1983), formerly of the University of California at Berkley, has written: "The key to sound science is sound process, which cannot be disregarded for long without regrettable consequences."

We must therefore be leery of granting favors. As Peter Barnett (2001) advised in his book on ethics (and attributed to his wife): "There should be no quarter given to those who would ask anyone to violate a professional obligation in favor of some temporary convenience or popular movement."

With every case worked, we must remind themselves that although there will always be another case, there may not always be another chance to repair our integrity. No one wants to be the spark that ignites one of these conflagrations. An excellent way to avoid doing so is to ensure that our performance is always guided by a commitment to ethical conduct.

Other Reasons

Beyond the aforementioned, there are other good reasons for performing ethically. When we do, we can have confidence in our results and be more comfortable in coping with any challenges to them. In Management 101, we were taught to focus on doing the right things. Although this is clearly good advice, we must also never forget the importance of doing things right. Many members of ASCLD will remember the sage advice provided at one of their meetings by Judge Gerald Scheindlin of the New York Supreme Court. He tried the *Castro* case, one of the first significant challenges to DNA evidence, in 1989. In that case, he rejected the DNA evidence because of a failure by the laboratory to use precise methodologies; but, in so doing, he gave us some critical yet simple counsel: "If you are going to do it, do it right."

Finally, to complete this section on the why, if none of the aforementioned reasons for ethical conduct are persuasive, there is one more, a more selfish one. Simply, it is much easier to behave ethically than it is to cheat! We do not have to remember all the stories and excuses we used to explain what or why something was done. Martha Stewart is a good example; she was not convicted of insider trading, she was not even charged with it. She was convicted for not telling the truth about what she actually did. She forgot that you should never trust the people you cheat with. She ignored Benjamin Franklin's (1735) famous advice: "Three can keep a secret—if two of them are dead!"

Ethics: What Are They?

The word *ethics* is derived from the Latin *ethos*, which means "customary behavior." Ethics deal with the ability to distinguish right from wrong; good from evil; and the commitment to do what is right, good, and proper. That sounds simple enough, but things can get complicated.

Morals versus Ethics

Webster's (1988) defines *ethics* as: "The moral principles which determine the rightness or wrongness of particular acts or activities." Note the use of the word *moral*. Morals and ethics deal with similar principles. One way (for me at least) to distinguish between them is ethics relate to our professional activities and morals to our personal behavior.

Although the influence of our education in science has a profound effect on our concept of professional responsibility, we cannot ignore the influence of our evolution as a human being. The late Professor Oliver Schroeder (1984) of Case Western Reserve University, a former president of AAFS, provided a scholarly analysis of this relationship:

> To consider the relationship of ethics and morality to the forensic sciences, professionals must be measured against a standard which begins with the individual as a person not as a forensic scientist. *Within each individual's moral fiber rests the professional's ethical performance.* Without a consciously developed sense of individual morality, neither personal morals nor professional ethics is attainable. *The cornerstone of all ethical thinking, including professional ethics, is private morality* [my emphasis].

We begin developing our personal moral standards at an early age, primarily through the influence of our parents but also that of our schoolteachers and our spiritual advisors. For example, to lie, cheat, steal, or kill is behavior we come to instinctively reject. By the time we arrive at a university, the basis for our ethical character has already been quite firmly established.

Ethics versus Duties

My preferred definition of ethics (and there are many to choose from) is from the *Oxford Dictionary* (1956): "the science of human *duty* [my emphasis] in its widest context including besides ethics, the science of law whether civil, political or international." If we substitute the word *professional* for *human* in the Oxford definition, we have a definition that can work well for any profession. By linking *ethics* with *duty* in a professional context, we have the basis for specific conduct being considered quite ethical for one profession but patently unethical for another. The duties (and associated privileges) of each profession are different. Nowhere is this enigma more apparent (and sometimes confusing) than in forensic science because of its close association with three professions: science, law, and law enforcement.

For example, forensic scientists often complain about the "unethical" conduct of aggressive lawyers. However, when counsel vigorously challenge our opinions, they are doing nothing more than fulfilling the duty imposed upon them by their profession—to forcefully represent the interests of their clients. Similarly, lawyers sometimes complain about the unethical conduct of scientists who may provide different opinions in the same case; but these scientists, through their differing interpretations of the same data, may be doing nothing more than confirming the tenuous nature of so-called scientific laws and facts. An explanation for this was provided by James Osterburg (1968), another former AAFS president and one-time member of the New York City Police Department laboratory, who wrote many years ago: "The essence of science is a willingness to change beliefs in the light of evidence. Indeed, *scientists hold in high regard the idea of constant critical inquiry* [my emphasis] of any and all ideas."

Some Examples

Forensic science and law enforcement are distinct professions with complementary but different duties and thus different ethical standards. During the OIG investigation of the FBI Lab in 1996–1997, we observed several examples of the conflict between the duties and thus ethics of the forensic scientist and those of the investigator. For the first 50 or 60 years of the existence of the FBI Lab, all examiners were required to be sworn special agents. Regardless of their academic background, before being assigned to the laboratory they had to spend several years as field agents. Although such experience can be invaluable to the forensic scientist to help develop an appreciation of the needs and challenges of the investigator, it is essential, however, that, once assigned to the lab, the investigator's standards be left behind and those of the scientist adopted. The conclusions of the examiner in the laboratory must be based solely on the *demonstrable* scientific evidence and not on collateral field investigative information.

Two of the agents criticized in the OIG report were unable to distinguish between these separate roles and in fact confused them. In one international terrorism case, an agent/examiner testified that he had identified the explosive PETN on some tools belonging to a suspect. The identification was based on only a liquid chromatography analysis. When challenged in court about the absence of any confirmatory analysis, he replied that his confirmation came from a field agent who told him that he knew it was PETN because some stripped detonating cord had been found in the suspect's trash. The judge recognized the fallacy of this "confirmation," rejected the evidence, the charge was dismissed, and an accused terrorist went free. The white powder probably was PETN, but the *scientific* evidence developed by the examiner was inadequate to establish this.

For a law enforcement officer, acting on information received from another officer is quite proper. For a scientist, however, arriving at a conclusion in the absence of proper scientific data is quite unethical. This distinction is particularly important—and sometimes difficult—for scientists who are part of a law enforcement agency, and especially for those who are also sworn officers.

In a trial resulting from the first World Trade Center attack in 1993, another FBI agent/examiner testified that the bomb consisted of about 1,200 pounds of urea nitrate. He had no analytical data from the bomb scene with which to identify urea nitrate and his estimate of the amount was more precise than the enormous damage would permit anyone to make. During his interview with the OIG, he acknowledged this but claimed he could testify as he did because he knew that field agents had found receipts showing that the defendants had purchased large quantities of urea and nitric acid. The difference between the amounts purchased and the amounts subsequently recovered from the suspects' property was sufficient to make about 1,200 pounds of urea nitrate. His circular reasoning seemed to be that the defendants had the capacity to manufacture 1,200 pounds of urea nitrate, the defendants had planted the bomb, therefore the bomb had to consist of 1,200 pounds of urea nitrate. His conclusion may well have been correct, but it was not based on any valid *scientific* data and was therefore a breach of his scientific ethics. This same examiner did very much the same thing in the Oklahoma City bombing in 1995.

These examples of less than excellent scientific testimony serve as a useful reminder of the astute observation I have heard presented by Professor Peter De Forest of the John Jay College of Criminal Justice at several scientific meetings: "There is a need to recognize the difference between the 'opinion of a scientist' and a 'scientific opinion.' The former may have no scientific basis and, if so, is out of place in any scientific report or testimony."

Codes of Ethics: What Are They? Who Needs Them?

In the foreword to Peter Barnett's book on ethics in forensic science, the editors of the series answered the question: *What are codes of ethics?*

> Several aspects of self-government define a profession: accreditation of agencies, certification of individuals, a minimum program of education and training and a *set of rules by which the profession operates*. This set of rules usually takes the form of a code of ethics, a standard *by which members of the profession agree to abide* [my emphasis]. (Rudin and Inman 2001)

A code of ethics should represent a "distillation of a profession's collective experience and wisdom." As such it "can offer guidance towards excellence for individual professionals who find themselves uncertain about the proper course of action" in a particular situation. A code of ethics can also be used to support members against "unwarranted erosion of their autonomy" or "improper demands upon them." It may also strengthen an individual's hand in resisting "unduly intrusive incursions on professional autonomy by employers" (Frenkel, 1989).

In addition to being of assistance to its practitioners, the code of ethics of a profession can also be informative for the public. If people perceive that a profession has a reasonable code of ethics and—of equal importance—a process for enforcing it, the credibility of that profession is enhanced. Conversely, as Peter Barnett (2001) observed, if a profession is not seen as reacting swiftly and appropriately when unethical conduct is alleged, the public may conclude that such behavior is condoned or even endorsed. This public reaction became very apparent in Houston in the plethora of articles in the *Houston Chronicle*. Some of these described the police department's totally inadequate response when, for example, two drug chemists were caught "drylabbing," not once but twice. No significant disciplinary action was taken against them.

The Research Council report recommendation, referred to earlier, recognized the current reality that most forensic science professional associations—national, regional, and discipline specific—have (and for many for some considerable time have had) codes of ethics. Its recommendation referred to the establishment of a national code of ethics for all disciplines and incorporation of such a code into the codes of all associations. Whether such a broad universal code is necessary, desirable, or even possible is a discussion for another occasion.

Codes of Ethics Formats

The California Association of Criminalists (CAC) in 1957 was the first forensic science association (in North America at least) to adopt a code of ethics for its members; it is still one of the most comprehensive and detailed available. The AAFS has had a code of ethics and conduct since 1976, the Association of Firearms and Tool Mark Examiners (AFTE) since 1980, ASCLD since 1987, and there are many other associations that have their own codes. (Although codes of ethics are most often associated with professional associations, there is no reason for an organization or institution not to have their own, and many in fact do.) ASCLD/LAB adopted its code in 2008 thus putting a national code of ethics into effect in almost 400 forensic laboratories comprising the vast majority of forensic scientists in the United States.

The set of rules manifested in a code of ethics may be quite generic, such as that of AAFS, which consists of only four provisions:

a. Every member of the Academy shall refrain from exercising professional or personal conduct adverse to the best interests and objectives of the Academy.

(For this to be helpful to the membership, they must be aware of the objectives of the AAFS, which include "promoting education for and research in the forensic sciences, encouraging the study, improving the practice, *elevating the standards and advancing the cause* [my emphasis] of the forensic sciences." The emphasized portion can cover a wide range of conduct.)

b. No member shall materially misrepresent his or her education, training experience, area of expertise, or membership status within the Academy.
c. No member shall materially misrepresent data or scientific principles upon which his or her professional opinion is based.

One other provision from the original AAFS bylaws, although not strictly an ethical matter, was included in its Code of Ethics:

d. No member shall issue public statements that appear to represent the position of the Academy without specific authority first obtained from the Board of Directors. (AAFS, 2012)

Alternatively, a code may be long and detailed, such as that of the CAC, which contains about 40 provisions (CAC, 2010). These are divided into five sections:

I. Ethics relating to the scientific method—For example, "The criminalist has a truly scientific spirit and should be inquiring, progressive, logical and unbiased."

II. Ethics relating to opinions and conclusions—For example, "Tests are designed to disclose true facts and all interpretations shall be consistent with that purpose and will not be knowingly distorted."

III. Ethical aspects of court presentation—For example, "The ethical expert does not take advantage of his privilege to express opinions by offering opinions on matters within his field of qualification which he has not given formal consideration."

IV. Ethics relating to the general practice of criminalistics—For example, "Where the criminalist engages in private practice, it is appropriate that he set a reasonable fee for his services."

V. Ethical responsibilities to the profession—For example, "The criminalist shall discourage the association of his name with developments, publications, or organizations in which he has played no significant part, merely as a means of gaining personal publicity or prestige."

The CAC code includes matters that relate not so much to ethics but rather to good laboratory practice. Nevertheless they are appropriate in the code as guidelines since to knowingly not follow good laboratory practices would be a breach of the criminalist's duty and thus unethical.

Both formats (AAFS and CAC) are valid and can assist their members on their path to excellence. The former is more appropriate for a multidisciplinary body such as the AAFS and the latter for an organization of more limited disciplinary makeup. Some of the disciplines represented in the AAFS such as law, medicine, dentistry, and engineering have their own professional codes that apply only to those professions. For these, the AAFS code is a supplement relating to the forensic aspects of their practices.

The AAFS code of ethics was originally developed by an ad hoc committee that established four criteria for inclusion of a provision in the code:

It must be desirable.
It must be feasible.
It must be enforceable.
It must be enforced.

Many potential provisions suggested by the membership were not included in the code because, although perfectly reasonable, they either did not meet all four criteria or they dealt with standards of professional practice appropriate to a code of conduct for a specific discipline rather than to a code of ethics for a multi-disciplinary organization.

The last criterion on the list is essential if a code is to be effective; it also requires that the enforcement procedures in any code must provide for due process.

Regardless of format, no code can possibly deal with all the complexities of real situations. They at best can serve only as guidelines. To provide guidance to its members, the AAFS code requires knowledge of decisions by its Ethics Committee in specific cases, that is, a collection of Ethics Committee "jurisprudence." Unfortunately, such a collection is not available at present. The more detailed type of code such as that of the CAC is undoubtedly more helpful to the individual member in a specific case.

Typical Code of Ethics Provisions

As already noted, there are many forensic science associations that have codes of ethics with differing formats and specific provisions. They all, however, tend to cover much the same ethical landscape. Most advise their members in some way to:

- Be objective, unbiased, rigidly impartial, logical, progressive
- Perform adequate examinations; no bolstering of conclusions with unwarranted or superfluous tests
- Use no unreliable, unproven, secret, or discredited procedures
- Maintain skills and currency
- Ensure no distortion of tests or interpretations
- Ensure no confusion of scientific fact with investigative theory
- Ensure no going beyond one's competence
- Testify in clear, concise, comprehensive, understandable language avoiding jargon unless required for accuracy
- Disclose exculpatory findings to the court
- Ensure no misrepresentation of qualifications
- Avoid conflicts of interest and disclose any that arise
- Alert the association to anyone who has committed serious or frequent infractions

All of these should be quite obvious as we strive for excellence; none should be controversial. This is not rocket science! An Australian judge who conducted an inquiry into the Chamberlain (the dingo–baby) case succinctly summed up these fundamental requirements in 1987:

> In criminal cases where the standard of proof is proof beyond a reasonable doubt, it is highly desirable that complex scientific evidence called by the prosecution should be *so carefully prepared and expressed* [my emphasis] that the necessity for the defence to challenge it is reduced as much as possible. (Morling, 1987)

Most would agree that these mandates are all included in forensic scientists' professional duty and therefore their ethical standards. Nonetheless, adopting them into a formal code of ethics serves as a helpful reminder to an organization's members of their professional responsibilities.

So, who needs a code of ethics? We all do.

Examples of Some Ethical Problems

Although the provisions of most codes of ethics are quite straightforward and uncomplicated, and the vast majority of forensic scientists have no difficulty abiding by them; nevertheless, complaints of ethical misconduct do come before association ethics committees. A few examples will be described derived from my 17 years of service on the AAFS Ethics Committee, 12 as the committee chair.

Many of the cases we considered were quite simple. For example, claiming a degree not earned or a professional appointment not held is so flagrant and so easily confirmed or refuted, it is difficult to understand why anyone would be so foolish as to do so. I could not help but wonder if someone was prepared to cheat about something so simple, what else might they be willing to try? Indeed, the first complaint received about one former member was that he had testified that he had a master's degree from a particular institution, which we subsequently confirmed, he did not possess. This same person went on to become quite notorious for providing incriminating testimony in capital murder cases without the bother of making any examinations. Incredibly, after he was found out in one state, he went on to do (or actually not do) exactly the same thing in another.

Misrepresentation of data, such as issuing a report without benefit of any examinations, is also usually easy to prove and is clearly unethical. In one such case, the committee received a copy of a decision of a state supreme court that said about a member's conduct: "The matters brought before this court are shocking and represent egregious violations of the right of a defendant to a fair trial. They stain our judicial system and mock the ideal of justice under the law." Not only do they stain the judicial system, they bring disrepute to forensic science as well.

Another complaint involved a member who, incredibly, provided autopsy reports in three different jurisdictions in cases in which it was later found that no autopsy had been performed. (He presumably had some sort of sweetheart agreement with the local funeral directors for whom his neglect must have been abundantly apparent!) It is impossible to conceive of a more flagrant example of misrepresentation of data than claiming data that does not actually exist. *Drylabbing* really does occur; in an accredited lab it is much more difficult, but not impossible, for it to go undetected. As already noted, there were flagrant examples of drylabbing in Houston although the lab was not accredited at the time.

The AAFS Ethics Committee also has decided that misrepresentation of data is not limited to case reports or sworn testimony; it can also occur in publications and oral presentations. It is not the medium but the message that is important. In one case, the misrepresentation was of photographs published in a paper in the *Journal of Forensic Sciences*. What was purported to be a comparison photograph of two images was found to actually be mirror images of a single item.

Some allegations are more complex and require detailed and lengthy investigation. For example, an odontologist frequently testified that a particular weapon had "indeed and without doubt" caused a particular wound. His conclusions were based not on any standard of reasonable scientific certainty; indeed he stated that he did not believe in reasonable scientific certainty as an appropriate standard. He asserted that his opinions were based simply on gut instinct. Many transcripts, reports, photographs, and interviews had to be reviewed over approximately 2 years to bring this matter to a conclusion.

In addition to conduct that has been found to be unethical, it is also of importance to appreciate the types of conduct that have been found not to be unethical. Of these, the most common is professional disagreement between two members. These complaints usually amounts to simply: "His conduct must be unethical because his opinion is different from mine." Such differences of opinion not only are not unethical but, in many instances, are quite reasonable. As an example, in one case the Ethics Committee concluded that: "The majority of the specifics of the complaint represent differences of opinion between two well-qualified professionals. Such differences of opinion are inevitable in any professional endeavor and do not constitute unethical conduct."

An explanation for this was provided in 1996 by the internationally respected physicist and science philosopher Professor Thomas Kuhn of University of California–Berkeley: "Philosophers of science have repeatedly demonstrated that more than one theoretical construction can always be placed upon a given collection of data."

In 1870, Thomas Huxley had provided the explanation: "The great tragedy of Science—the slaying of a beautiful hypothesis by an ugly fact."

Why Do People Do Such Things?

Most ethical challenges are not really close calls and are easily identified. It is interesting to speculate on the reasons why otherwise intelligent people do some ethically stupid things. As described by Professor Marianne Jennings (2005) of Arizona State University: "They underestimate the likelihood that the truth will eventually come out, they overestimate their ability to manage the situation, or they succumb to pressure—budget, time, peer, superior or political."

But what motivates them in the first place? The most obvious potential motivator is money and sometimes this may be so, but perhaps not as often as one might think. I'm convinced there is a more powerful motive: ego. When we are constantly referred to as "experts" there is a risk that we may begin to believe it. The kudos we receive from investigators, prosecutors, and sometimes even judges enhance this feeling. We can be tempted to believe that we are smarter than everyone else and therefore can say anything we like. We are, after all, with the good guys on the side of the angels. This is a temptation that all forensic scientists must be alert to.

The *New York Times* described this motivator in an article about the Enron trial in 2006 (Eichenwald, 2006): "Management deteriorated as arrogance overrode careful judgment." The article continued:

> It was not simply that the ethics of the corporate world changed overnight; the ever-rising bubble of market prices created a sense of invincibility among corporate executives, who read market delusions as proof of their own genius. Arrogance gave way to recklessness, which in turn opened the door to criminality.

Remember what happened to the economy 2 years later.

Another subtler motivator is one I refer to as the "adrenaline factor." In the heat of a rigorous cross-examination we may have difficulty controlling our competitive instincts. The adrenaline flows and we may be tempted to defend what we have said beyond that which can be defended. A former member of the FBI Lab admitted this—too late—and was convicted of perjury. She was an expert in the analysis of lead in bullets who became upset at being frequently challenged in court by a former colleague and went a bit too far in her defense to his challenge. All of us must constantly be conscious of this hazard and recognize it before it is too late.

A less obvious motive in some cases is spite. Someone becomes so upset with their laboratory or its management that they decide to do something that will damage the reputation of the organization, completely ignoring the fact that it will also impact on them even more severely. This was the case with an examiner in a lab in California. All she wanted to do was DNA analysis, but because of a court-imposed timely reporting requirement, all members of the lab staff sometimes had to work weekends working drug cases. There she was, alone in the lab on sunny California Saturday afternoons, unhappy with her lot, angry with her superiors, and so she wrote her reports without bothering to perform any analyses. She was eventually found out when coworkers thought it strange that no reagents were being used up on the weekends she worked and a hidden camera was installed to observe her.

It must be recognized that once an unethical (or even illegal) act has been committed, fear of discovery can be a powerful motivator for secondary and tertiary misbehavior. There have been too many instances of forensic scientists "robbing Peter's drug locker to repay Paul's" to avert discovery of their initial misuse of the drugs in their own cases.

There may be one more cause for improper conduct: ignorance of one's level of incompetence. This was a factor in the problems of a former director of a state crime laboratory in one of the western states in the United States, which resulted in at least three wrongful convictions. He believed that the chance of a wrongful "match" of hairs (microscopically) was about 1/100 so if he had a "match" of a head hair and of a pubic hair in a case, the chance of a wrongful "match" was $1/100 \times 1/100$ or 1/10,000. He later explained that he did not understand that in order to multiply two frequencies it had to be known that they were independently variable. It cost the state \$3.5 million to settle just one of the cases.

Another example of problems caused by a forensic scientist's ignorance (or denial) of his lack of competence occurred in Canada in the late 1990s to early 2000s. A pathologist, who was well-qualified in pediatric clinical pathology in a world-renowned children's hospital, agreed to perform forensic autopsies on children at the request of the coroner's office because of his location and expertise. He was totally unqualified in forensic pathology. Although he initially provided his services as a form of public service in cooperation with his colleagues in the hospital, he found that he enjoyed the satisfaction he derived from working with the police and the apparent respect he received in the courts. He therefore gradually took over all the forensic pediatric work from his colleagues who were more than happy to surrender it. Without a mentor in forensic pathology to guide and counsel him, he began to exaggerate his range of expertise and qualifications. The fact that he was rarely challenged only added to his sense of infallibility. Eventually, he was found out and, in 2005, a panel of outside experts reviewed all of his work and found that in at least 20 child autopsies he had made major scientific errors, leading to baseless charges of murder or manslaughter and 13 subsequent criminal convictions, many of which, thankfully, have since been overturned. A judicial inquiry in 2008 (Goudge, 2008) found, among other things, that: "Dr— lacked basic knowledge about forensic pathology, he violated a cardinal rule of scientific expertise *that the expert must be aware of the limits of his or her expertise* [my emphasis]." That excellent advice for all forensic scientists was also enunciated by E. J. Wagner. In 2006, in his book *The Science of Sherlock Holmes*, he wrote about a famous forensic pathologist in England: "There are few figures as dangerous as that of an expert witness who is brilliant, persuasive, famous, obstinate, and absolutely wrong."

Some Ethical Challenges and Dilemmas

With ethical challenges, the generalizations are simple; most of us believe in ethical conduct and are convinced we practice it. In fact, most of us believe our ethical standards are higher than those of our colleagues and we therefore achieve excellent results. It is when we come to the specifics of any issue that difficulties may arise. When the choice is clearly between good and bad, the decision is easy. The difficulties arise when the choice is not between good and bad but rather between good and better or, even more challenging, between not so good and bad.

As scientists, we are expected to be scrupulously honest, totally objective, technically competent, and openly communicative of the results and significance of our work. The reality is, however, that forensic scientists are required to function within an adversarial system and that system places a premium on winning. There is an inherent tension between the goals and methods of science and the goals and methods of litigation, even though each makes sense and serves vital social purposes in its own domain.

In addition to the adversary system, there are other conflicting factors that can present challenges: investigative requirements (we need it now!), scientific methodology (the GC/MS is down), political reality (the war on drugs), managerial policy (report all cases within 30 days), legal mandate (no work for the defense), and professional ethics (What is my duty here?) (Barnett, 2001).

Helpful guidelines may be found in statutes, jurisprudence, agency policies, and professional codes of ethics, but they are just guidelines. Actual decisions in specific cases will usually be dependent on the particular facts and context. These, in turn, may be influenced by pressures from four distinct sources: (1) the police, who are usually our clients; (2) the adversary system, which will receive our data; (3) the science, on which our data is based; and sometimes (4) our personal sense of ethics and morals.

Pressures from Law Enforcement

Forensic scientists bring to their work a concept of professional ethics determined by their education and training in science. However, for most of us, our constant contact with law enforcement, which has its own unique duties and thus a different set of professional ethics, can exert subtle pressure to broaden this concept. (Sometimes the pressure is not so subtle, for example, "Well, if you won't do it I'm sure someone else will" or "Well, that's the way it has always been done around here.")

The police are, quite properly, a partisan unit in the criminal justice system. Forensic science, on the other hand, is supposed to be an impartial component of the system and, I would argue, our value to the system is significantly enhanced when we are, and are seen to be, nonpartisan. A challenge for forensic scientists, particularly those whose employer is a law enforcement agency, is to ensure that based on their performance they are genuinely accepted as objective scientists and not simply as another element of the agency.

This issue was also discussed in the NAS Report (2009). Recommendation 4 stated:

> To improve the scientific bases of forensic science examinations and to maximize independence from or autonomy within the law enforcement community, Congress should authorize and appropriate incentive funds to the National Institute of Forensic Science (NIFS) for allocation to state and local jurisdictions for the purpose of *removing all forensic laboratories and facilities from the administrative control of law enforcement agencies or prosecutor's offices* [my emphasis].

This recommendation was not well received by many of the interested parties, and there are arguments that can be made that the issue is one of perception rather than reality. There are also many practical reasons for retention of the status quo. The NRC recommendation was neither new nor original. For example, the late Lowell Bradford, a well-respected criminalist in California, called in 1976 for "forensic science systems that are independent of the executive control of public protection agencies."

For purposes of this discussion of ethics, the question raised is: Is it ethical for the forensic scientist to accept cases from only one side in a two-sided system? As long as forensic scientists remain under the administrative control of one of the parties in the criminal justice system and are thus restrained from providing services to both sides, they will be confronted by this ethical dilemma for which there is no easy answer.

The police generally control the input to the forensic laboratory. They decide which events will be investigated, what items will be collected, which will be submitted for examination, and, in some jurisdictions, what examinations will be requested. An ethical challenge is presented to the forensic scientist if relevant significant items known to exist are either not collected or not submitted, if significant examinations are not requested, or, even worse, instructions are issued not to perform certain examinations. These can create tension between the professional standards of the police and those of the scientist.

For the forensic scientist operating under the direct control of the police, and even more so for the scientist who is also a sworn officer, the sometimes conflicting ethics of science and law enforcement can present a major dilemma. As scientists, we strive to achieve excellence and the "right" answer from our examinations. For the police investigator, the right answer is usually the one that supports his view of the investigation. Scientific validity is not a significant issue for him unless the evidence fails to meet a challenge in court. As long as the scientist keeps coming up with the right answers, investigators and prosecutors are usually content. There have been some very disturbing examples of this in wrongful conviction cases in several jurisdictions.

I believe this type of conflict contributed in large part to the well-publicized problems of a serologist/hair examiner in a city lab in Oklahoma in the 1980s and early 1990s. At the time, it was a small lab, managed by non-scientist, career-sworn officers. She received inadequate training and had no scientist mentor. Her superiors in the police department and the prosecutors were pleased with her performance because she always produced what for them was the right answer. She was rarely challenged and reveled in the nickname "Black Magic" given to her by investigators, because she had the ability to see things no one else could. She was convinced, for example, that she had never seen hairs from two individuals that she could not differentiate (or so she testified.) She may not have appreciated her level of incompetence. Unfortunately, several tragic miscarriages of justice resulted from her work including cases in which a young man served 18 years in prison and another 19 years for rapes they did not commit. One of these cases cost the city $4 million and the other $16.5 million. Good quality work (excellence) is expensive; poor quality work even more so!

Pressures from the Adversary System

The most significant pressures presenting ethical dilemmas to forensic scientists result from our association with the adversary process where we confront the clash of two cultures: science and law. As described by Cavers (1996): "The process of drawing on scientific knowledge in adjudication reveals that our adversary system of litigation and the scientific method and the temperament of scientists are incompatible."

Although some might argue that "incompatible" is a bit harsh, litigation and science certainly can be "uncomfortable" with each other. Having stepped into the witness box, forensic scientists must remind themselves that they really have not stepped through the looking glass. They must accept that the judicial process is not a search for truth in the scientific sense, but rather a search for truth as defined by one adversary or the other. Shades of gray, so familiar in scientific endeavor, are not recognized; indeed in the criminal justice system all shades of gray are defined as white. The U.S. Supreme Court (1993) recognized this in its decision in *Daubert*: "There are important differences between the quest for truth in the courtroom and the quest for truth in the laboratory. Scientific conclusions are subject to perpetual revision. Law, on the other hand, must resolve disputes finally and quickly."

Conflicts can readily arise between the scientist and the lawyer. It is the scientist's duty to describe the evidence as it actually is; it is the duty of the attorney to describe it in the most favorable light for his client. As a result, in the courtroom the science may sometimes be abused; this abuse of science can be subtle, but it may not be trivial (Thornton, 1983). Although it is conceded that the adversary process may be poorly suited to objective presentation and evaluation of scientific data, it must be remembered that this is not the essential purpose of the process. The system has evolved over many years as an effective and usually fair process for resolution of conflict, which, although easy to criticize, is difficult to improve upon.

Although there are many ethical conflicts confronting us in the adversary system, perhaps the most difficult relates to confidentiality. Disagreements in science are resolved by experimentation, publication, and peer review. It is an open process; the natural inclination of the scientist is to discuss data openly and in its entirety. The natural inclination of the attorney is to control the distribution of information. As forensic scientists, our reports are typically issued to police investigators, to prosecutors, or to other attorneys. Control of their subsequent handling passes to these participants who do not always share the scientist's professional attachment to the merits of open discussion.

Some examples of ethical challenges for the forensic scientist that may arise from this situation are:

1. A request by the client to remove irrelevant or unfavorable material from a report. Since reports should always be carefully written with due attention to contextual relevance and scientific validity, they should only rarely need to be rewritten.
2. Having reported verbally, the scientist is instructed not to prepare a written report. Should not a written report always be prepared, if only for the scientist's protection?
3. The client decides not to use the report because it contains material helpful to the other side. In most jurisdictions, the defendant in a criminal trial has a right to be informed of the facts including those favorable to him. If the prosecutor should fail to disclose such facts, does the forensic scientist not have an ethical responsibility to do so lest he become an accessory to the deprivation of the defendant's rights? (Starrs, 1971)

It would be easy for us—and tempting—to simply abdicate all disclosure decisions to the attorneys; it is, after all, their province. However, as forensic scientists we must be conscious of the legal requirements for discovery and make decisions based not only on the scientific aspects of an issue but also on at least some of the relevant legal ones. We cannot ignore our role in the discovery process. Our responsibilities do not begin at the laboratory door nor do they end at the courthouse steps. If we fail to properly document our observations and examinations, or to maintain all our data in notes and provide a written report, the discovery process may be thwarted and we have not fulfilled all of our responsibilities. As observed by Mark Frenkel (1989) of the American Association for the Advancement of Science (AAAS): "Forensic scientists must retain professional autonomy over their work and the ethical principles which have traditionally guided their profession."

A less obvious source of pressure from the adversary system is the subtle contagion of winning that accompanies participation in it. As stated by Professor Joe Peterson (1986) of Cal State LA: "The principal objective of the litigants is to win the case, often at the expense of the truth."

The other-sidedness and winning at all costs mind-set of the adversary system can have significant influence on the requirement for impartiality of the scientist. Gamesmanship can be a legitimate function for police and attorneys, and the temptation for the scientist to enter the game may be subtle, but it can be strong. It may even go unnoticed or unappreciated. Legitimate advocacy for a finding or an opinion can with almost imperceptible ease become advocacy for a cause. We must always keep in mind the caution that "impartiality is an elusive virtue" (Cavers, 1966) and the advice by Professor James Starrs (1971) of George Washington University: "The line between legitimate tactics and ethical impropriety is often so dim as to be indistinguishable."

For the forensic scientist working primarily in the criminal justice system there is a tendency to most frequently be called by one side. Whichever side that may be, as a consequence of the frequent and continuing exposure to the thought process of that side, there is a risk of being influenced by it, a risk we must conscientiously strive to avoid. Such influence can produce pressures that may lead to some unfortunate practices. Some examples that, although they were at one time fairly common, are much less so today as a result of certification and accreditation requirements, broader disclosure rules, and a general maturation of the profession:

1. The preparation of reports containing minimal information in order not to give the other side ammunition for cross-examination. Given the well-known propensity of lawyers to leave no nit unpicked, one can understand, if not approve, this practice.
2. The reporting of findings without an interpretation, on the assumption that if one is required it can be provided from the witness box. This ignores the possibility that the scientist may not be called to testify and the interpretation of the scientific data may then be left to laypeople.
3. Omitting a significant point from a report to trap an unsuspecting cross-examiner, thereby teaching him a lesson.

4. During cross-examination, expressing an opinion with greater certainty than the data or the witness's experience may warrant. This can result from inexperience, from a desire to support the team, or simply from the ego trip that accompanies the exhilaration of being the star of the moment.

5. Failure to report or acknowledge any weakness in a finding or opinion. If cross-examination is the only way for a court to discover misleading or inadequate testimony, then too much is being expected from it and not enough from the forensic scientist.

6. Failure to differentiate between opinions that are based on experimental findings and those that are based on study, experience, and judgment.

There are imperfections in the adversary system and forensic scientists must be sensitive to them. Where possible, we should strive to change those that impact on the use of science or on our professional standards (Peterson, 1985), and we must ensure that there is nothing in our personal performance to expand those imperfections.

Pressures from Science

One of the hallmarks of science is thoroughness in the execution of an experiment. Specific sample requirements, appropriate controls, valid standards, proper equipment, and established protocols are fundamental. Yet, in forensic science, often the examiner has little or no control over the quality of the samples; the ones provided are the only ones there are. Appropriate controls and valid standards are occasionally not available, the best equipment cannot be afforded, and procedures must sometimes be extemporized for the one-off cases where, it is argued, the forensic scientist can often provide the greatest help to an investigation. Such limitations do not preclude acceptable results, but the confidence levels of those results must be carefully evaluated and fully expressed. This adds immensely to our responsibility and represents an ethical issue if not acknowledged.

A similar but reverse problem can occur when examinations beyond those required to establish a finding are performed. When does thoroughness evolve through redundancy to gamesmanship? If additional examinations add nothing and are performed only to impress a jury with how thorough we have been, is it not unethical to carry them out? While no one would argue that professional competence is not a critical issue for any scientist, it is not so clear that it is an ethical issue. Some might argue that there is no connection between ethics and competence; if we try to do something we think we can do and it does not turn out well, that is not a breach of our ethics. Others might claim that we do have an ethical responsibility to be technically competent and to not attempt something we are not certain we are competent to do. Still others, including this author, will acknowledge the reality that there are degrees of competence, but that there is nevertheless a certain "baseline level of competence" (Barnett, 2001) in the various disciplines that every forensic scientist must achieve; and there are practices so fundamental (e.g., validation of a procedure and proper record keeping) that any failure to follow them is unethical.

Particularly challenging is the situation of the forensic scientist in a small, isolated (either geographically or philosophically), seriously underfunded police laboratory managed by a nonscientist career officer. (Thankfully, such situations are much less common today than in earlier times, but some still do exist.) For these, the pressure to inappropriately expand their professional capabilities just to help out because that is the culture of the organization may be irresistible. Without resources to attend professional conferences or to keep up with the literature, such individuals may extend their range of incompetence simply because they have no awareness of what is the current state of the art.

Pressure from Within

A few ethical issues for forensic scientists relate directly to individual moral values and may in fact be in conflict with them. For example:

1. A forensic scientist who finds the death penalty morally repugnant or contrary to his religious beliefs may be required to provide a professional opinion that, if accepted, can lead to a death sentence.
2. Outside the courtroom, there are situations in which the scientist may feel on moral grounds that the "whole truth" should be withheld because parts of it are irrelevant to the issue and would be psychologically or culturally devastating to the recipient. For example, a DNA analysis that reveals an unexpected family relationship not relevant to the investigation.
3. Although most codes of ethics require not accepting cases on a contingency basis, what of the indigent defendant who requires professional evidence from a scientist whose sole income is based on fee for service? Can service be denied (morally or ethically) in such a case? Does the situation change if the work is initially performed *pro bono* but subsequently an honorarium is offered? The reason for this code provision may relate more to credibility than to ethics.
4. Whistle-blowing on managers, colleagues, or other professional associates for many if not most of us can be difficult and agonizing. However, would it not be unethical to knowingly conceal unethical actions of others? It might be easy to rationalize the improper conduct

as an isolated incident that won't happen again. That would probably be naive. Unfortunate facts do not get better with the passage of time. As that journalist/curmudgeon the late Andy Rooney of CBS once said: "I've learned that to ignore the facts does not change the facts."

In every laboratory, there is rarely a problem that at least some staff members do not know about. Sometimes they will not say anything because of concern about being ignored, of not having a simple avenue in which to raise the problem, or fear of being disciplined for raising it. These are issues resulting from inadequate or incompetent management and thus ones that good managers can avoid.

The pressures on forensic scientists to expand the range of what we consider ethical are many and from disparate sources. There are, however, boundaries to that range. There are limits that are fundamental to science and, if they are ignored, then we would no longer be practicing science.

Conclusion

The reader who has gotten this far may be frustrated because clear answers to all dilemmas have not been presented. The reason: There may not be clear answers to some or, if there are, I am not certain what they are. Mandatory provisions (must not misrepresent qualifications) in codes of ethics make some proper decisions easy but aspirational provisions (examinations should be objective and use accepted methods) may only be somewhat helpful. Some provisions are based on ideals—organizational, structural, financial, and legal—perhaps unattainable but always worth striving for.

Jennings (2005) has some simple advice about dealing with ethical conflicts:

- Be selfish about your personal and professional reputation.
- Do not make ethics more difficult than they actually are.
- Trust discomfort.

To these I would add:

- Remember what the duties of a forensic scientist are.

And if those do not work, I would suggest one other:

- Ask yourself what your mother would want you to do.

Finally, I firmly believe that if we remember that we are scientists first and forensic scientists second, and if we apply the fundamental standards of science (ethics) and personal integrity (morals), all ethical questions can be answered and excellence achieved to the betterment of the profession and of society.

References

American Academy of Forensic Sciences (AAFS). 2012. Code of Ethics and Conduct. Accessed April 23, 2012. http://www.aafs.org/aafs-bylaws#Art2.

American Society of Crime Laboratory Directors (ASCLD). 1994. Guidelines for forensic laboratory management practices. Accessed April 23, 2012. http://www.ascld.org/files/library/labmgtguide.pdf.

American Society of Crime Laboratory Directors (ASCLD). 2005. Code of Ethics. Accessed April 23, 2012. http://www.ascld.org/files/library/Code%20of%20Ethics.pdf.

American Society of Crime Laboratory Directors/Laboratory Accreditation Board (ASCLD/LAB). 2008. *Laboratory accreditation board manual.* Garner, NC: ASCLD/LAB.

Barnett, P. D. 2001. *Ethics in Forensic Science: Professional Standards for the Practice of Criminalistics.* Boca Raton, FL: CRC Press.

Bradford, L. W. 1976. Problems of ethics and behavior in the forensic sciences. *J Forensic Sci.* 21:763–768.

Bromwich, M. R. 1997. *The FBI Laboratory: An Investigation into Laboratory Practices and Alleged Misconduct in Explosives—Related and Other Cases.* Washington, DC: U.S. Department of Justice, Office of the Inspector General.

Bromwich, M. R. 2007. Final report of the independent investigator for the Houston Police Department crime laboratory and property room. Accessed April 27, 2012. http://www.hpdlabinvestigation.org.

California Association of Criminalists (CAC). 2010. Code of Ethics. Accessed April 23, 2012. http://www.cacnews.org/membership/handbook.shtml.

Castro. 1989. *People v. Castro.* 545 N.Y.S. 2d 985 (Sup. Ct. 1989.)

Cavers, D. V. 1966. In *Law and the Social Role of Science,* edited by H. W. Jones. New York: Rockefeller University Press.

Eichenwald, K. 2006. The Enron verdict: The fallout; verdict on an era. *The New York Times,* May 26.

Franklin, B. 1735. *Poor Richard's Almanac.* Cited in *Bartlett's Familiar Quotations,* 17th ed., p. 319, 2001. Boston: Little, Brown and Co.

Frenkel, M. S. 1989. Ethics and the forensic sciences: Professional autonomy in the criminal justice system. *J Forensic Sci.* 34: 763–771.

Garrett, B. L., and P. J. Neufeld. 2009. Invalid forensic science testimony and wrongful convictions. *Virginia Law Review* 95: 1–97.

Goudge, S. T. 2008. *Report of the Inquiry into Pediatric Pathology in Ontario.* Toronto: Queen's Printer.

Huxley, T. H. 1870. *Biogenesis and Abiogenesis.* Cited in *Bartlett's Familiar Quotations,* 17th ed., p. 537, 2001. Boston: Little, Brown and Co.

Jennings, M. 2005. Presentation at the annual meeting of the American Society of Crime Laboratory Directors, Phoenix, Arizona.

Kuhn, T. S. 1996. *The Structure of Scientific Revolutions*, 3rd ed. Chicago: University of Chicago Press.

Levitt, S. D., and S. J. Dubner. 2006. *Freakonomics*. New York: Harper Perennial.

Lucas, D. M. 1989. The ethical responsibilities of the forensic scientist: Exploring the limits. *J Forensic Sci.* 34: 719–729.

Morling, T. R. 1987. Report of the royal commission of inquiry into Chamberlain convictions. Darwin, Australia: Government Printer.

National Academy of Sciences (NAS). (2009). *Strengthening Forensic Science in the United States: A Path Forward*. Washington, D.C.: National Academies Press.

Osterburg, J. W. 1968. The significance of science and law in the quest for order and justice. *J Forensic Sci.* 13: 503–508.

Oxford. 1956. *The shorter Oxford English Dictionary on Historical Principles*. 3rd ed., rev. Oxford, UK: Clarendon Press.

Peterson, J. L. 1986. Ethical issues in the collection, examination and use of physical evidence. In *Forensic Science*, 2nd ed., edited by G. Davies. Washington, D.C.: American Chemical Society.

Peterson, J. L., S. Mihajlovic, and J. L. Bedrosian. 1985. The capabilities, uses and effects of the nation's criminalistics laboratories. *J Forensic Sci.* 30: 10–23.

Rooney, A. n.d. Accessed April 30, 2012. http://www.funny2.com/rooney.htm.

Rudin, N., and K. Inman, eds. 2001. Forward. In *Ethics in Forensic Science: Professional Standards for the Practice of Criminalistics*, edited by P. D. Barnett. Boca Raton, FL: CRC Press.

Schroeder, O. C. 1984. Ethical and moral dilemmas confronting forensic scientists. *J Forensic Sci.* 29: 966–986.

Starrs, J. E. 1971. The ethical obligations of the forensic scientist in the criminal justice system. *J Assoc Off Anal Chem.* 54: 906–914.

Thornton, J. I. 1983. Uses and abuses of forensic science. *ABA J.* 69: 289–292.

U.S. Supreme Court. 1993. *Daubert v. Merrell Dow Pharmaceuticals*, 509 U.S. 579.

Wagner, E. J. 2006. *The Science of Sherlock Holmes*. Hoboken, NJ: John Wiley & Sons.

Webster's. 1988. *The New Lexicon Webster's Encyclopedic Dictionary of the English Language*. Canadian ed. New York: Lexicon.

Ethics Vignette

Laboratory Director Wilfredo Pareto was alarmed with the development in his laboratory of several ethics violations and was not sure what to do. Pareto transferred a significant amount of human resources to the quality management system in a response to the increased number of nonconformance competency and ethical violations. These reassignments of resources resulted in longer cycle times for casework, less throughput, and cast doubt on the reputation of the laboratory. The cost of quality was continually increasing. Ironically, the increase in quality activities gave the appearance of lower quality with identification of more nonconformances. A few non-conformances also developed into misconduct, ethical, and criminal charges. Although intentional misconduct is very difficult to detect, Pareto felt most all competency and ethical violations could have been prevented with early and timely assessment by the quality management system and disclosure to all affected parties. All ethical investigations resulted in much negative press coverage and dampened staff morale. Competency-based remediation and non-conformances are not acceptable but expected. How are competency non-conformances developing into ethical situations?

Pareto increased the staff's quality training and made sure his key managers were up to date on all the latest quality, accreditation, and audit programs proven to be effective in the laboratory community. His laboratory was also one of the first to be accredited using the new ISO/IEC 17025: 2005 International Standard. He assigned more staff to establish a new audit program. The audit team was trained by quality experts and performed first-party internal horizontal, vertical, and process audits on 6-month intervals. Pareto requested from his parent agency more frequent second-party customer-focused audits to decrease internal bias in the auditing process. Last, third-party audits were performed annually by the independent regulatory accreditation assessment body.

The main customers of the laboratory (court, prosecutors, and defense attorneys) were very concerned that disclosures of errors were not made or untimely, which led to ethical violations. Ethical violations resulted in extraordinary extensive legal consultations between the laboratory and customer legal representatives (parent agency legal counsel, prosecutor, defense, and judges). Pareto obtained support to hire an attorney dedicated to laboratory ethics issues with the goal of increasing effectiveness of communications between the laboratory and the court. The quality management team's resources were overcome reacting to ethics violations, instead of proactively managing laboratory quality. The amount of resources assigned to quality seemed to be directly related to the number of non-conformances and ethical situations instead of decreasing errors. Pareto anticipated a temporary increase when implementing his quality system, however, the ethical situations were very disturbing. Could they be reduced and controlled?

The relationship between the laboratory and criminal justice community is challenging as humans are not perfect and forensic science can suffer no human errors. It is also human nature to resist self-disclosure of errors to all affected parties resulting in negative consequences to one's profession, career, and employer. Errors or a pattern of errors affect an employee's ratings, promotions, and reputation, and may result in termination.

Is there a process that will identify, manage, monitor, and continually reduce errors in a timely fashion before they become ethical violations that affect the "vital affairs of others?" Laboratories should nurture an organizational culture that will encourage staff to recognize the inevitable consequences of human error, identify errors early in the process, and eradicate them with quality tools concurrent with timely disclosure to the customer. If laboratory management encourages the identification of potential errors, then quality will improve.

Metro Forensic Laboratory has an ethics policy answering the question why a laboratory needs ethical conduct but does not have an ethics procedure to answer the question who does what, when, where, and how. Pareto's laboratory and the forensic community would greatly benefit from the development and implementation of a clearly written, understood, used, and effective ethics procedure. Federal regulations result in detailed procedures in high-risk industries such as nuclear, medical, environmental, and pharmaceutical manufacturing, all of which affect the "vital affairs" of others. Forensic science is no different and it is now time to develop an ethics procedure that is clearly written, understood, and used answering the questions: When one becomes aware of a potential ethics violation who does what, when, where, and how?

ETHICS PROCEDURE

4.8 ETHICS VIOLATIONS

(Also see Figure 3.1.)

METRO FORENSIC LABORATORY MISSION STATEMENT

Metro Forensic Laboratory applies the best science to the best evidence in a timely, quality, and ethical manner.

POLICY

Metro Forensic Laboratory adopts the American Society of Crime Laboratory Director's Code of Ethics (http://www.ascld.org/files/library/Code%20of%20Ethics.pdf, 2005).

PROCEDURE

SCOPE

Metro Laboratory staff are aware of their role in the quality management system (QMS) and realize how untimely or no disclosure of wrongful reported test results leads to ethics violations, potential criminal misconduct, and other serious negative consequences for our laboratory, agency, customers, and community. Laboratory errors result in serious negative consequences. Our staff is diligent with timely identification and disclosure of ethics violations resulting from wrongfully reported test results and continually follow up with our customers until all associated issues are resolved.

Our customers, as receivers of our products and services, place trust in us to perform at the highest level for the greatest good. This trust is not

ETHICS PROCEDURE
"Who Does What When?"

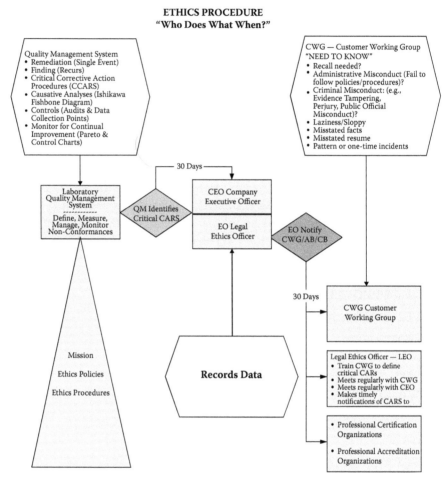

Figure 3.1 Ethics process flow chart.

an entitlement and is a priceless core value of our agency's organizational culture. Once trust is lost it may never be regained. The American Society of Crime Laboratory Directors (ASCLD) states the "vital affairs of other people" has been placed in our trust. "We are holders of a public trust because a portion of the vital affairs of other people has been placed into our hands by virtue of the role of our laboratories in the criminal justice system" (ASCLD 1994).

Additional professional organization ethics policies are listed in Table 3.1 (California Associate of Criminalist, 2012).

There are six basic causative factors of errors or non-conformances classically categorized as human (e.g., competency or intentional misconduct), machines or equipment (e.g., faulty equipment), materials (e.g., evidence contamination, nonhomogeneous, reagents, controls), methods

Table 3.1 Ethics Policies

AAFS	American Academy of Forensic Sciences (Article II: Code of Ethics and Conduct), http://www.aafs.org/aafs-bylaws#Art2
ABC	American Board of Criminalistics (Rules of Professional Conduct), http://www.criminalistics.com/ethics.cfm
ABFDE	American Board of Forensic Document Examiners (Code of Ethics and Standard Practices), http://www.abfde.org/htdocs/AboutABFDE/Ethics.pdf
ABFT	American Board of Forensic Toxicology, http://www.abft.org/index.php?option=com_content&view=article&id=56&Itemid=65
ACSR	Association for Crime Scene Reconstruction (Bylaws, Article 8, Code of Ethics), http://www.acsr.org/code-of-ethics
AFTE	Association of Firearm and Tool Mark Examiners (Code of Ethics, Enforcement of the Code of Ethics), http://www.afte.org/AssociationInfo/a_codeofethics.htm
ANZFSS	Australian and New Zealand Forensic Science Society (The Code of Ethics), http://www.anzfss.org.au/code_of_ethics.htm
ASCLD C	American Society of Crime Lab Directors (Code of Ethics), http://www.ascld.org/files/library/Code%20of%20Ethics.pdf
ASCLD G	American Society of Crime Lab Directors (Guidelines for Forensic Laboratory Management Practices) 2004, http://www.ascld.org/files/library/labmgtguide.pdf
ASCLD/LAB	ASCLD/Laboratory Accreditation Board (Guiding Principles of Professional Responsibility for Crime Laboratories and Forensic Scientists), http://www.ascld-lab.org/about_us/guidingprinciples.html
ASQDE	ASCLD/Laboratory Accreditation Board (Guiding Principles of Professional Responsibility for Crime Laboratories and Forensic Scientists), http://www.ascld-lab.org/about_us/guidingprinciples.html
CAC	California Association of Criminalists (Code of Ethics, Code of Ethics Enforcement), http://www.cacnews.org/membership/handbook.shtml
CIS	Canadian Identification Society, http://www.cis-sci.ca/frame.htm > By-Laws > Rules of Professional Conduct
CSDIAI	California State Division of the IAI, http://www.csdiai.net/documents/Constitution%202009.pdf
CSFS	Canadian Society of Forensic Sciences (Code of Conduct), http://www.csfs.ca/eng/membership/code-of-conduct
ENFSI	European Network of Forensic Science Institutes (Code of Conduct), http://www.enfsi.eu/page.php?uid=191
FSREG	Office of the Regulator, UK, http://www.homeoffice.gov.uk/publications/police/forensic-science-regulator1/codes-conduct-practice?view=Binary
IAAI	International Association of Arson Investigators, http://firearson.com/l_Membership/l_Code-of-Ethics.aspx
NAME	National Association of Medical Examiners, http://thename.org/index.php?option=com_content&task=view&id=134&Itemid=29
FSS UK	Forensic Science Society (United Kingdom) (The Code of Conduct), http://www.forensic-science-society.org.uk/AboutUs/Constitution

(Continued)

Table 3.1   Ethics Policies (*Continued*)

IABPA	International Association of Bloodstain Pattern Analysts (Article III: Code of Ethics), http://www.iabpa.org/Bylaws%2010-09-08.pdf
IAI	International Association for Identification (Code of Ethics and Professional Conduct)
MAAFS	Mid-Atlantic Association of Forensic Scientists (Code of Ethics)
MAFS	Midwestern Association of Forensic Scientists (Code of Ethics), http://www.mafs.net/index.php?id=codeofethics
NEAFS	Northeastern Association of Forensic Scientists (Code of Ethics), http://www.neafs.org/ethics.htm
NJAFS	New Jersey Association of Forensic Scientists, http://www.njafs.org/pdf_files/NJAFS_BY_LAWS.pdf
NWAFS	Northwest Association of Forensic Scientists (proposed Code of Ethics), http://www.nwafs.org/Documents/Code%20of%20Ethics.pdf
RMABPA	Rocky Mountain Association of Bloodstain Pattern Analysts (membership application, p. 2), http://www.rmdiai.org/rmabpa/
SAFS	Southern Association of Forensic Scientists (Bylaws: Ch. I, Section 5.c; Ch. IV, Section 2.a), http://www.southernforensic.org/bylaws.asp
SCAFO	Southern California Association of Fingerprint Officers, http://www.scafo.org/code_of_ethics/default.html
SMANZFL	Senior Managers Australian and New Zealand Forensic Science Laboratories, http://www.nifs.com.au/SMANZFL/SMANZFL.html?index.asp&1
SOFT	Society of Forensic Toxicologists, http://www.soft-tox.org/index.php?option=com_content&view=article&id=104&Itemid=118
SWAFDE	Southwestern Association of Forensic Document Examiners
SWAFS	Southwestern Association of Forensic Scientists (Article 13: Code of Professional Conduct), http://www.swafs.us/pdf/2009/2008bylaws.pdf
SWFS	Society for Wildlife Forensic Science, http://www.wildlifeforensicscience.org/content/code-ethics
TIAFT	The International Association of Forensic Toxicologists, http://www.tiaft.org/node/46

or procedures (e.g., poorly written, not validated), measurement (e.g., no uncertainty budget for procedure), and environment (e.g., facility, organizational culture). Many quality management texts, literature, procedures, applied research, and professional organizations (Deming, Ishikawa, Shewhart, American Society of Quality, www.asq.org) are dedicated to the management of causative factors designed to monitor and manage quality metrics for continual improvement (Shewhart and Deming). Errors or non-conformances can be classified progressively more serious from administrative clerical errors to issued reports with errors that affect test results, were not disclosed, and resulted in catastrophic consequences for all stakeholders. The vast majority of non-conformances are small errors that usually do not recur and are remediated immediately before a report is issued to the customer. These errors are identified and remediated by a myriad of quality control processes before a report is issued, do not normally require disclosure, and continually increase the quality of forensic services. More serious errors recur, cast doubt on test results, and require the initiation of corrective action procedures that identifies and eliminates causative factors before the report(s) are issued to the customer. The majority of competency non-conformances is not misconduct and initially affects only one or a few cases, do not require extensive reanalyses, are remediated in relatively short order before a report is issued, and do not wrongfully affect the customer.

A forensic scientist must be aware of the pressures to solve the most heinous violent crime investigations and not deviate from approved scientific procedures. Misconduct invariably leads to criminal violations against the scientist minimally being charged with issuing false reports, evidence tampering, and perjury. The most egregious ethics violations occur when investigators, scientists, or the court knowingly hinder or through negligence do not disclose a remediation, corrective action, or misconduct that wrongfully affects the investigation, analyses, or prosecution process potentially leading to a wrongful acquittal or conviction. A faulty forensic service could wrongfully exonerate a recidivist, wrongfully convict the innocent, and result in progressively more victimization of innocent citizens.

The distinction between remediation, misconduct, and ethics violations is at times difficult to comprehend. Most errors can be prevented from becoming ethics violations if one uses the old adage "the issue is not the error that was committed, it is what and when you do something about it." The timely disclosure of most errors affecting reported test results significantly reduce the number and frequency of ethics violations. Misconduct errors are rare and normally are caused intentionally by a lazy scientist who succumbs to pressure to complete the case sooner, or seeks recognition for higher productivity or notoriety for providing essential results leading to case closure. Ironically, the recognition or notoriety may not be positive, but upon disclosure may lead to the scientist being terminated or criminally prosecuted.

DEFINITION: ETHICS VIOLATION

"Knowingly or through negligence hindered or delayed the disclosure to the customer of a remediation, corrective action, or misconduct (error) event that affected reported test results wrongfully affecting the customer."

Examples of ethics violations that require immediate notification to supervisors, disclosure to the customer, and continual follow up until resolved:

- Error has potential or resulted in wrongful conviction.
- Error has the potential or resulted in wrongful exclusion.
- Error has potential or resulted in recidivists' continued criminal actions.

- Error has potential or required reanalysis of all work required.
- Error is misstated facts in report thus creating false documents.
- Error is misstated facts in testimony resulted in perjury.
- Error is misstated resume or qualifications in testimony resulted in perjury.
- Error is caused by lazy or sloppy work or was intentional resulted in criminal misconduct.

RESPONSIBILITIES AND AUTHORITIES

ALL STAFF

All staff is responsible to formally notify within 24 hours the quality manager and supervisor when their work is the cause of a potential ethics violation. Staff also similarly report potential ethics violations when becoming aware of coworkers' ethics violations. The quality manager provides updates on 30-day intervals to all affected parties until the ethics violation is resolved.

Staff responsible for the ethics violations and certified by professional certification bodies (CBs) seek guidance from the agency legal officer to formally notify the appropriate CB, and if appropriate, disclose the potential ethical violation within 24 hours and provide updates continually every 30 days until the ethics violation is resolved.

(Note 1: It is recommended that staff seek legal representation during this procedure.)

(Note 2: It is recommended staff seek professional liability insurance through agency programs [e.g., www.fedsprotection.com], professional organizations, or from a well-established insurance provider specializing in professional liability insurance.)

LABORATORY/CHIEF EXECUTIVE OFFICER (CEO)

The chief executive officer (CEO) of the laboratory, upon notification by the quality manager (QM) of an ethics violation, immediately consults with the legal ethics officer (LEO). It is the CEO's responsibility and authority to direct the legal ethics officer to disclose to the customer working group within 24 hours the existence of a founded or potential ethics violation and to continually provide 30-day updates until the matter is resolved.

QUALITY MANAGER

The quality manager (QM) notifies the chief executive officer (CEO) and legal ethics officer (LEO) within 24 hours a potential ethics violation has been identified and immediately initiates an ethics violation investigation. The QM will continually provide ethics violation investigation updates to the CEO/LEO on 30-day intervals until the ethics violation investigation is completed. The QM will complete all ethics violation investigations within 180 days.

LEGAL ETHICS OFFICER

The legal ethics officer (LEO) establishes a customer working group (CWG) consisting of customer representatives and members of the stakeholder community. The LEO develops and implements necessary memoranda of understanding between the agency and the CWG that facilitates proper communication in a timely and effective manner. The LEO provides the CWG training for awareness and working knowledge of the ethics violation investigative processes. The LEO reviews all ethics violation investigations for accuracy, completeness, and satisfaction of all agency and legal policies for disclosure. The LEO and CWG meet quarterly to discuss all ongoing ethics violations.

The LEO, upon direction of the CEO, discloses ethics violations or investigations to the associated accrediting body (AB) within 24 hours and provides continual updates every 30 days until the ethics violation investigation is completed.

The LEO consults with all staff and provides guidance and training on staff disclosure of ethics violations.

CUSTOMER WORKING GROUP (CWG)

The customer working group is comprised of a representative selection of laboratory customers from the criminal justice community. Prosecutors, defense attorneys, judges, law enforcement agencies, and citizens are selected for service on the CWG. The main goal of the CWG is to facilitate effectiveness and efficiency of communication and the timely disclosure of ethics violations to limit or eliminate negative consequences to victims, suspects, defendants or citizens in the community. The CWG develops a mission statement, policies, and procedures that adds efficiencies and effectiveness to the flow of information between the LEO and CWG.

Forensic Training, Education, and Institutes

4

The return on investment (ROI) for structured academic forensic education with dedicated facilities and staff as compared to unstructured training in operational laboratories is

2.74

This chapter is dedicated to the late Dr. George Carmody. Major outcomes for many academic programs are select lectures provided by subject-matter experts. One such expert was Carmody, a professor at Carleton University in Ottawa, Canada. I first became aware of George Carmody's unique professional attributes when assembling the Kinship and Data Analysis Panel (KADAP) in response to the 9/11 World Trade Center tragedy. The New York State Police Forensic Investigation Center (NYSP FIC) provided significant support to the New York City Medical Examiner's Office with ready-to-use software and hardware information management systems and the analyses of victim exemplars for comparison to victim tissue samples. As director of the NYSP FIC, I (Mark Dale) also reached out to the National Institute of Justice, specifically Dr. Lisa Forman, program manager, and Sara Hart, director, for assistance setting up a panel of forensic DNA experts to assist in establishing statistical DNA identification policies and procedures. Carmody was one of the many experts selected to join the KADAP panel. Carmody possessed the priceless attributes of an academic statistics expert: working knowledge of forensic science, a great sense of humor, and the uncanny ability to explain statistics to a layman and forensic experts alike. We lost Carmody several years ago to a tragic accident and miss him greatly. However, we did archive his DNA Statistic Lectures on DVD and had them transcribed to text including reference materials. We are also greatly indebted to Ph.D. student Jamie Belrose for her scientific transcription of Carmody's statistic lectures and several exemplar mock trial audio videos to text. Belrose transformed from an excellent graduate student to a forensic champion, professional scientist, office manager, and mentor to many students in the institute's DNA academies and university graduate programs.

Obituary

George R. Carmody

(New York, New York, March 29, 1938–Ottawa, Ontario, June 13, 2011) Passed away suddenly June 13th, 2011. Born March 29, 1938 in Brooklyn, New York. Educated at the Brooklyn Technical High School and Columbia University (B.Sc. 1960, Ph.D. 1967) and was a Post-Doctoral Fellow at the University of Chicago (1967-69). In 1969 he joined the Department of Biology at Carleton University, Ottawa, where over the next 42 years he taught courses in evolutionary biology, population genetics and forensic science. He also served as Associate Dean of Science (1987–89) and head of Carleton's Integrated Science Program (1983–87, 1991-96, 1997–98).

Later in his career George developed a special interest in forensic DNA and statistical biology. In that capacity he served as a consultant to a number of government agencies, including the Royal Canadian Mounted Police, the Federal Bureau of Investigation, the Home Office (U.K.) and many provincial and state forensic identification offices. He testified on DNA evidence issues at leading criminal trials in Canada in the 1990s and was later called upon to help with statistical modeling and identification questions in a number of modern mass disasters including the Swissair Flight 111 crash off Peggys Cove, Nova Scotia (September 1998), the World Trade Centre disaster in New York (September 2001) and Hurricane Katrina (August 2005). Over time George also lectured internationally in Singapore, Australia, Jamaica and Barbados, and assisted with victim identification efforts in situations of forced disappearance in Chile and Guatemala. At the time of his passing George was an expert adviser on DNA identification to state governments in Virginia and New York.

George had a broad range of interests, including photography, jazz, vintage Cadillacs, railroading, fine dining and ethnic cuisine, and believed strongly in the fusion of arts and science for greater understanding of both. He was an amateur mechanic, and loved solving mathematical problems and playing with his grandchildren.

George is survived by his wife Zoë Chios Carmody of Ottawa, son Chios Carmody of London, Ontario; daughter Daphne Carmody of Ottawa; and son Ian Carmody (Chrissy) of New Orleans; and grandchildren Caroline and Grace Carmody.

A gathering in celebration of his life will take place Tuesday, June 21, 2011 at Beechwood Cemetery, 280 Beechwood Ave., Ottawa at 10 A.M. In lieu of flowers donations to the George Carmody Memorial Award for Forensic Biology, Department of University Advancement, 510 Robertson

Hall, Carleton University, 1125 Colonel By Drive, Ottawa ON K1S 5B6, or on-line at: www.carleton.ca/giving.
Inquiries may be made: Prof. Chi Carmody, Faculty of Law, University of Western Ontario, London, Ontario, Canada N6A 3K7; e-mail: ccarmody@uwo.ca.

We argue the return on investment (ROI) of structured academic education with dedicated facilities and staff is 2.74. This compelling ratio is based upon the following assumptions:

1. Structured academic programs are more efficient and effective than unstructured mentor training (Cascio and Boudreau, 2008).
2. The training of new employees within an operational laboratory is dysfunctional. Trainees that have not reached a semblance of competence cannot be left unattended near evidence or instrumentation without the high risk of data and material transaction errors and contamination. Casework operations take a priority over training, which leads to a competition for instrumentation usage.
3. Mentors often are the most productive casework scientists, which significantly decreases the overall productivity of the laboratory when they assume the responsibility of trainer.
4. Reduction of "time to competency" is the major tangible return.
   a. The time to competency from hiring to independent casework duties for a DNA analysis is approximately 18 months when trained with a mentor in an operational forensic laboratory.
   b. The time to competency in a structured academic training laboratory with dedicated staff and facilities is 6 months.
5. Intangible outcomes are perhaps the most important.
   a. Professional relationships between practitioner forensic scientists, students, academic faculty, and researchers.

The Northeast Regional Forensic Institute (NERFI) at the University at Albany, New York, developed a forensic molecular biology graduate program and 6-month DNA academies for newly hired DNA scientists employed by public service forensic laboratories. The DNA academy students were also enrolled as nonmatriculated students in the forensic molecular biology graduate program, earning 12 graduate credit hours. The academic "champion" providing the academic leadership and management was Dr. Donald Orokos. His everyday guidance and scientific expertise was critical to the success of the NERFI programs.

Following is the NERFI scorecard for resources and deliverables:

University at Albany/Northeast Regional Forensic Institute Scorecard

2002–2008

- 12–16 week DNA Academies, 12 graduate credit hours >100 students attend program
- Students from NYSP, MassSP, NYS local labs, Kansas State Bureau of Investigation, San Francisco
- Supported numerous Graduate Student Assistants and Ph.D. students
- Supported research Raman Technology forensic applications (Dr. Igor Lednev)

Awards

2002	NIJ Crime Laboratory Improvement Program	$1.5 million
2004	Massachusetts State Police DNA Academy I, II	$505,238
2005	Massachusetts State Police DNA Academy III	$318,952
2006	Massachusetts State Police DNA Academy IV	$323,652
2006	New York State Police DNA Academy I, II, III	$2 million
2007	New York State Police DNA Academy IV, V, VI	$2 million
2007	New York State Criminal Justice Services DNA Academy	$369,750
2007	COPS Technology Lab/Prosecutors LIMS	$100,000
2008	Congressional Appropriation (DNA Academies, Prosecutors IT connectivity, Chat Minder, Crime Mapping)	$540,000
2008	NIJ DNA Training Grant	$950,000
2008	San Francisco DNA Academy	$80,000
2008	California Department of Justice ISO Training	$54,000
	Grand Total	$8,741,952

Main Deliverables

- Provided research seed funding for Graduate Forensic Chemistry program (Dr. Igor Lednev).
- Renovated 15,000 square feet of Biology and Chemistry laboratory space.
- Fully equipped DNA and Chemistry laboratories used jointly by academic and forensic academy program.
- Implemented Forensic Molecular Biology and Chemistry Graduate Programs.
  - Approximately 20 students matriculated per year.
  - One of 14 nationally accredited forensic programs (Forensic Education Program Accreditation Commission).
- Graduate placement rate for employment or higher education = 100%.
- 6 Forensic Graduate Student Assistants hired yearly (6 students × 4 years = 24) during academic year to assist in Forensic Program.
- NERFI funds pilot research projects and assists in grant submission and attendance at professional meetings.

DNA Academy Metrics

- >100 students collectively earning 1,080 Graduate Credit hours.
- >100 students were ready for DNA Casework or DNA Data Bank analyses within 6 months of hiring, as compared to 18 months with traditional mentor training.
- NERFI staff and Graduate Student Assistants produced and QC profiled 15,000 DNA training samples.

- >100 students collectively analyzed 11,700 DNA training samples.
- >100 students collectively attended 450 days of Statistics lectures.
- >100 students collectively attended 450 days of Molecular Biology lectures.
- >100 students collectively worked 43,200 hours in a DNA laboratory.
- >100 students collectively prepared and participated in 900 hours of mock trials.

The ROI for the NERFI programs is calculated as follows:

1. The return for investing in one DNA academy trained student versus a mentor/trainee is decrease Time to Competency (18 months to 6 months) measured in the salary and benefits of the mentor and trainee.
   a. 12-month mentor salary = $100,000 + Benefits = $50,000 = Total = $150,000
   b. 12-month Trainee Salary = $60,000 + Benefits = $30,000 = Total = $90,000
   c. 12-month Total Mentor/Trainee = $240,000
   d. Return = $240,000 × 100 NERFI Students = $24,000,000
   e. NERFI Investment = $8,741,952
   f. ROI = $24,000,000/$8,741,952 = 2.74

Our nation requires a competent forensic workforce. Forensic science has transformed to a high-cost, high-technology, and high-risk business that can lead to serious consequences when things go wrong. It is paramount that the managers, technical leaders, bench scientists, and all staff are competent. Quality science and management education are the solution.

There have been a significant number of studies underlining why forensic science needs foundational undergraduate and graduate degrees followed by in-house training and professional development programs (Becker, Dale, and Pavur Jr., 2010; Kirk and Thornton, 1953, 1974; NAS, 2009; NIJ, 2004). In the past, forensic science only applied technologies that were fully vetted for years by research, academic, and private laboratories. In the real world of practitioner forensic service laboratories, most forensic scientists apply proven technologies with well-written procedures and training, and present findings in courts of law. Today, the gap between research in the laboratory to casework perhaps leading to acceptance in court has narrowed significantly. Solid education, experience, and annual professional development activities are essential for all employees to maintain competence and provide the best forensic services for the customer.

Unfortunately, education, training, and professional development are always the first items to be reduced or eliminated when budgets are constrained. Top management must realize that the consequences of inadequate education, reduced training, and professional development activities can lead to marginal quality and even catastrophic errors such as false positives and negatives that can lead to wrongful acquittals or incarcerations of suspects. The consequences of getting it wrong are much more costly than doing it right. What is the cost of a model education, training program, and "what does right look like?" How can we institutionalize education, training, and the resulting competent workforce for the future?

Education, training, and professional development requirements coupled with top management support is even more critical now with new emerging technologies.

> For reasons of *objectivity and efficiency* operations, the criminal justice process must utilize physical evidence to a greater extent, and there should be additional emphasis on the laboratory aspects of the investigative process. Judging from the *present inadequacy of training facilities* for laboratory criminalists, this aspect of the total professional field of criminalistics appears to be the *most deficient*. While many laboratories have achieved great distinction in training their personnel by means of an "on the job training" or apprenticeship system, it is clear that successes have been the product of outstanding individuals who have demonstrated an intelligent devotion to fulfilling the need. The most pressing current need, however, is the establishment of a system of training that does not require this unusual and often absent devotion. *In probably no other profession is standardized and effective training so neglected at this time as in the field of criminalists.* (Kirk & Thornton, 1953, 1974; emphasis added)

Sadly, this statement by John Thornton from the preface of the second edition of Kirk's 1952 classic text *Crime Investigation* is an accurate statement on how training is *today*, 39 years after his comments. How long must forensic science continue with a fragmented, at best, system of training and professional development that is continually reactive to sporadic and at times systemic inadequate performance?

Forensic science is a unique public service in that public agencies are entrusted in providing forensic science services that shall include or exclude defendants as perpetrators of minor and horrific violent crimes. Forensic services, normally in the form of reports explaining facts and expert opinions, support elements of a crime or investigative leads. Errors in forensic services, particularly in serious offenses, can lead to serious consequences in which violent offenders can remain free or innocent suspects may be wrongfully convicted.

The public, taxpayers, criminal justice, and intelligence communities place their trust in forensic laboratories to apply the best science to the best evidence/material in a timely, quality, and ethical manner. Top laboratory management is responsible to recruit, select, hire, train to competency, and retain the best scientists that will sustain the best forensic laboratory services. The best forensic laboratory services require more than facilities and equipment. The most essential expenditure of resources necessary to provide forensic services of excellence is the investment in forensic human capital (Dale and Becker, 2005).

Top management must be dedicated to providing the best forensic basic training, sustainment training, and professional development opportunities for employees that will support high standards and performance incentives for recruitment and retention of the best forensic scientists. Management is also responsible for balancing the costs of these programs with the benefits of high standards, keeping current with developments in science technologies and maintaining solid stewardship of taxpayer dollars.

Forensic Science Manager Job Requirements

Perhaps we should go back to the basics and perform a job analysis to determine skills necessary to perform as a manager in a laboratory. Why not standardize the job duties of a forensic science manager? Efficiencies from economies of scale, effectiveness metrics, and benchmarking would soon follow. Formal education (B.S., M.S., Ph.D.), posthire training to competency, and professional development would then be focused upon the job duties of the forensic manager. An excellent place to start the development of a standardized forensic science manager job description is the U.S. Department of Labor (2013). The Department of Labor established natural sciences manager tasks could be customized for forensic science followed by performance metrics. Standardized training and professional development programs would be designed to address all tasks.

U.S. Department of Labor
Employment and Training Administration
O*NET OnLine–Occupation Report, Natural Science Managers 11-9121.00
Plan, direct, or coordinate activities in such fields as life sciences, physical sciences, mathematics, statistics, and research and development in these fields.

Tasks

Confer with scientists, engineers, regulators, or others to plan or review projects or to provide technical assistance.

Develop client relationships and communicate with clients to explain proposals, present research findings, establish specifications, or discuss project status.

Plan or direct research, development, or production activities.

Prepare project proposals.

Design or coordinate successive phases of problem analysis, solution proposals, or testing.

Review project activities and prepare and review research, testing, or operational reports.

Hire, supervise, or evaluate engineers, technicians, researchers, or other staff.

Determine scientific or technical goals within broad outlines provided by top management and make detailed plans to accomplish these goals.

Develop or implement policies, standards, or procedures for the architectural, scientific, or technical work performed to ensure regulatory compliance or operations enhancement.

Develop innovative technology or train staff for its implementation.

Identifying the Need for Education, Training, and Professional Development

National Academy of Sciences

The National Academy of Sciences (NAS) was formed by Congress to fill the need of a national independent scientific advisor. The Congressional Charter was signed by President Lincoln in 1863. The National Academy of Sciences was expanded with the National Research Council in 1916 to address the ever-increasing role of science in government and private life. In 2005, the Science, State, Justice, Commerce, and Related Agencies Appropriations Act of 2006 became law and Congress authorized the NAS to conduct a study on forensic science. An esteemed group of scientists, academics, and forensic professionals met continually to discuss the status of forensic science and issued a report in 2009 with 13 recommendations to improve forensic science services. Recommendation 6 in part states: "Standards should reflect best practices and serve as accreditations tools for laboratories and as guides for the education, training, and certification of professionals." The NAS cited the need for training, research, and funding repeatedly throughout all sections of the 2009 report.

> The forensic science system, encompassing both research and practice, has serious problems that can only be addressed by a national commitment to overhaul the current structure that supports the forensic science community in this country. This can only be done with effective leadership at the highest levels of both federal and state governments, pursuant to national standards, and with a significant infusion of federal funds. (NAS, 2009)

The NAS report dedicates chapter 8 to education and training (synopsis by author):

Chapter 8: Education and Training in Forensic Science

ENDURING FUNDING NEEDED FOR ACADEMIC AND RESEARCH PROGRAMS

Congress should authorize and appropriate funds to improve and develop partnerships between practitioner laboratories, and academic teaching and research institutions (medical, legal, and science) that will provide accredited graduate multidisciplinary studies and continuing education courses (face-to-face and distance learning) critical to forensic science and the legal community. Scholarships and fellowships are needed not only to attract the best students but to fund the continuing education of established professionals.

Forensic Challenges Remedied by Academics

Forensic deficiencies are best remedied through formal, structured undergraduate, graduate education, and research. Education, training, and research prepare the next generation of forensic practitioners, and provide continuing professional development and training for users in the legal community.

Supply and Demand for Forensic Scientists

The demand for forensic scientists far exceeds supply. The forensic science community is small with 13,000 scientists employed today; however, a projected increase of 31% will be needed by 2016, not including a turn-over rate of at least 10%. To achieve a 30-day turnaround time for DNA cases requires a 73% increase in DNA scientists; remaining disciplines require a 6% increase in scientists.

Forensic Academics Lacking in Breadth and Depth

Academic undergraduate and graduate programs specializing in forensic science are small in number and range in scope from broad criminalistics to specialty programs in chemistry and molecular biology. Trends favor graduate degrees. There are no enduring specialty doctoral programs receiving stable funding for scholarships, fellowships, residencies, or research.

Forensic Laboratories Lack Education Expertise

Public laboratories do not have resources, academic expertise, or dedicated staff and facilities for training or continuing education. Forensic science education challenges cover the spectrum of a rapidly changing technology industry. Funding is inconsistent and insufficient. Forensic science education programs, until recently with the Forensic Science Education Programs Accreditation Committee (FEPAC), have no mandated standards or performance metrics. The lack of fundamental undergraduate and graduate education results in significant resources dedicated for training by public service forensic laboratories, increasing backlogs and cycle times.

Integration of Research, Education, and Training

Research is a critical component of the forensic education program. No sustainable and enduring source of local or federal funding exists for forensic education. Traditional education and research funding mechanisms have never supported forensic science.

The lack of academic and research funding has prevented research universities from developing forensic programs.

EDUCATION FOUNDATION FOR QUALITY

The greatest issue for continuing education is quality. Continuing education programs for all forensic personnel require professional instructors, professional conferences, distributed and Internet distance learning, apprenticeships, residencies, internships, and independent learning to foster a continual and professional learning environment. Curricula lack detailed syllabi, performance goals, periodic assessments, competency tests, and temporal milestones.

EDUCATION AND THE LEGAL SYSTEM

The forensic science community needs to educate those who use forensic services. Law enforcement, judiciary, pathologists, bar, general public, and policy makers' core competencies are not forensic science. Judges have struggled with complex scientific evidence while engaged in sophisticated epidemiology, toxicology, mass tort, econometric models, and antitrust cases. Engineering principles are at the center of patent litigations including decisions using Daubert case law policies and procedures.

The American Society of Crime Laboratory Directors passed a resolution in 2007 recognizing the basic needs of a competent workforce and training:

> The most effective way for a crime laboratory to ensure the continuing competence and effectiveness of its forensic scientists is to provide those scientists with continuing education, job-specific training, and access to products and services that can enhance their overall effectiveness. (ASCLD Resolution 07-0422-02, 2007)

National Institute of Justice

In 2003, as director of the New York State Police Laboratory System, I reached out to Dr. Lisa Forman, program manager at the National Institute of Justice (NIJ), to form a Technical Working Group on Education (TWGED) that would standardize forensic academic curricula, training, and professional development. Too often, managers would interview forensic science applicants with a "forensic major" and the applicant either did not have adequate science credits or had excellent academic grades but failed law enforcement background investigations. The lack of a solid education and or inability to pass law enforcement background integrity investigations was very inefficient and frustrating for applicants and employers. The NIJ TWGED published the first guidelines for forensic education, training, and professional development (NIJ, 2004). This publication developed by the TWGED committee provides excellent guidance on how to design effective and efficient training and professional development programs:

> Training is the formal, structured process through which a forensic scientist reaches a level of scientific knowledge and expertise required to conduct specific forensic analyses. Appropriate training is required before an individual is assigned case analysis responsibilities. Continuing professional development is the mechanism through which a forensic scientist remains current or advances to a higher level of expertise, specialization, or responsibility. All forensic scientists have an ongoing obligation to remain current in their field through continuing education and other developmental activities. Similarly, laboratory management and its parent agency have an ongoing responsibility to provide support and opportunities for this continuing professional development.

Training and continuing professional development based on the model criteria can be implemented in a variety of ways to maximize opportunities, minimize costs, and ensure high standards of professional practice. The following examples offer guidance for implementation.

Approaches

Different disciplines require varying levels and combinations of approaches. The approach depends on the relative degree of academic and experiential learning required to attain and maintain competency. For example, the questioned-document discipline may require more experience-based skill, whereas forensic biology may require more academic knowledge. It is recommended that this guidance be considered when choosing any approach. Some approaches include:

- Instructor led
- Professional conferences/seminars
- Distributed learning
- Apprenticeship
- Residency
- Internship
- Teaching and presentations by trainee/employee
- Independent learning

Administration

It is recommended that forensic laboratories establish a process to oversee, coordinate, and document all training and continuing professional development. Training and continuing professional development programs are expected to undergo external periodic audits.

It is recommended that continuing education and training courses include:

- Qualified instructor(s)
- Written course syllabus/outline
- Written course objectives
- Instructor/course evaluation
- Mechanism for student assessment
- Documentation of student performance
- Quantifiable element, such as continuing education units, academic credits, number of hours, or points

Although seminars, lectures, professional meetings, and in-service classes may be less structured than a formal course, they also add to the professional development of forensic scientists. Content and attendance are expected to be documented and available for external audits.

American Academy of Forensic Science

These efforts led to the development of the American Academy of Forensic Sciences Forensic Education Program Accreditation Commission (AAFS, FEPAC). As the former director of the Northeast Regional Forensic Institute at the University at Albany, I observed the significant effort needed to revise the graduate curricula in forensic molecular biology and chemistry. Course elective curricula were modified to fulfill FEPAC requirements and the forensic practitioners were added as adjunct faculty to teach forensic specialty courses. Laboratory space was renovated with similar instruments used in practitioner laboratories in an effort to reduce training time when students were hired by forensic laboratories.

ISO/IEC 17025: 2005 International Standard

The ISO/IEC 17025: 2005 International Standard clause 5.2 addresses competence of laboratory personnel. Training and quality go hand in hand, in that non-conformances must be clearly identified in policies and procedures to enable data or metrics that define the training program. In other words and as stated earlier, training must address non-conformance in an effort to reduce good and bad quality metrics. Training programs' main goal should be to build quality in up front in all procedures, and reduce or eliminate costly inspection and quality control activities (Deming, 1986).

Training activities should be directly correlated to reducing remediation and non-conformities. Training of personnel in the identification, management, monitoring, and continual decrease of non-conformances as required by the ISO/IEC International Standard is critical and essential. Competency of personnel directly correlates with non-conformances, remediation, corrective action, and resources used for good quality and bad quality as discussed in previous chapters. Untimely actions and lack of disclosure can often lead to ethical and criminal violations against personnel leading to termination. The development of an internal training program customized for one's specific laboratory's policies and procedures with the goal to eliminate non-conformances greatly increase the efficiency and effectiveness of laboratories. All personnel must know what quality looks like and just as important what non-conformance looks like.

5.2 Personnel

5.2.1 The laboratory management shall ensure the competence of all who operate specific equipment, perform tests and/or calibrations, evaluate results, and sign test reports and calibration certificates.

5.2.2 The management of the laboratory shall formulate the goals with respect to the education, training and skills of the laboratory personnel. The laboratory shall have a policy and procedures for identifying training needs and providing training of personnel. The training programme shall be relevant to the present and anticipated tasks of the laboratory. (ISO/IEC 17025, 2005)

Codes of Federal Regulation

One very effective way ahead for the forensic community would be to add all forensic disciplines to the existing DNA regulations for training, education, and technical leader requirements.

It is interesting that the forensic discipline of DNA or forensic biology is the only forensic discipline subject in the Code of Federal Regulation with the consequence of lack of compliance resulting in no access to the DNA index (Cornell University Law School, n.d.). The regulation includes continuing education requirements of 8 hours per year for technical leaders and bench scientists. One could argue that the remaining forensic disciplines are no less important or essential to the forensic or criminal justice community. The expansion of 28 CFR to include all forensic disciplines would level the playing field and apply good lessons learned in the DNA processes. For example, a DNA Commission started the process with a group of experts examining issues for one forensic discipline: DNA. The commission expired in 5 years and led to the Scientific Working Group (SWG) for DNA and FBI Quality Assurance requirements. The concept of a discipline-specific commission, SWG, FBI quality requirements, and federal regulations is continually improving, and has been accepted by the community and assured quality overall in DNA analyses.

> 28 Code of Federal Regulations Judicial Administration, 28 DNA Identification System (28 CFR 28)
> 42 United States Code 14132–Index to facilitate law enforcement exchange of DNA identification information
> (c) Failure to comply
> Access to the index established by this section is subject to cancellation if the quality control and privacy requirements descried in subsections (b) of this section are not met.
> 42 United States Code 14131–Quality assurance and proficiency testing standards FBI Quality Assurance Standards for Forensic DNA Testing Laboratories effective 9-1-2011

> 5. Personnel
>> Standard 5.1 Laboratory personnel shall have the education, training and experience commensurate with the examination and testimony provided. The laboratory shall:
>> 5.1.3.1 Continuing education: The technical leader, casework CODIS administrator, and analyst(s) shall stay abreast of developments within the field of DNA typing by attending seminars, courses, professional meetings or documented training sessions/classes in relevant subject areas at least once each calendar year. A minimum of eight cumulative hours of continuing education are required annually and shall be documented.

American Society for Training and Development

The American Society for Training and Development tracks metrics for trends in the private sector workplace for training, performance, costs, and benchmarks for best practices. The ASTD annually surveys a sampling of Fortune 500 companies to harvest training metrics. The training data is analyzed to identify best practices that support and leverage knowledge management for increased effectiveness and efficiencies (ASTD, 2012). The ASTD annual survey identifies metrics for learning expressed in average expenditure per employee, percentage of payroll, cost per learning hour, and percentage of distance learning. U.S. organizations expend approximately $100 billion annually on learning and development with 75% spent internally and 25% externally (see Table 4.1).

Table 4.1   ASTD Survey

2006 ASTD Survey of Fortune 500 Companies n = 39					
Ave Expenditure per FTE	Ave Hours/ FTE Learning Received	% Expenditure Payroll	% Expenditure External Services	Cost per Hour Received	% Time Distance Learning
$1,672	45	2.57%	30%	$43	39%

Laboratory Management Performance Model
Professional Development Costs

Professional development requires a base budget of at a minimum $3,000 per full-time employee (FTE) or at least 2% of the laboratory budget. At present-day travel and per diem rates this equates to approximately 5 days off-site at a conference event (U.S. General Services Administration, 2013). The lack of dedicating funding in the base budget will result in reduction of basic competence and sustainment skills to stay current with technology, increasing the costs of good and bad quality.

This fiscal environment in public service agencies is cyclical in nature, reliant upon external political realities and the state of the economy. A robust economy traditionally provides budget resources supporting more than essential basic and professional development activities. Fiscal constraints are an ever-present reality in public service agencies and the private sector. We must all strive to be the best stewards of taxpayer dollars and provide the best forensic services in a timely and quality manner. As such, we will practice due diligence to achieve the highest scientific standards in the performance of forensic analyses and continue to stay current with the latest technologies through continuing education, professional development, and career development activities.

At $3,000 professional development costs per FTE the laboratory management performance model (LMPM) budgets $891,000 for professional development activities for all employees ($3,000 × 297 FTE = $891,000). Professional development activities are not the same as basic new employee training for competence (NIJ, 2004). Training activities are focused upon non-conformances and remediation identified by quality control activities (Figure 4.1 and Figure 4.2). Training activities should focus upon the continual decrease of costs for good and bad quality as identified in Chapter 2. All employees should know how their individual activities contribute to the costs of quality and strive to reduce these costs. The major cost factor is time. How much time does each employee expend for good and bad quality efforts? Professional development activities keep employees current on technology and knowledge in their field of expertise and are directly linked to existing and future career development plans and job duties. A major goal of

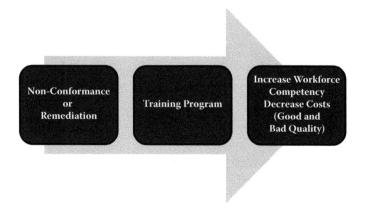

Figure 4.1 Training program goals.

training and professional development programs should be to offset the costs by reductions in good and bad quality costs. What is the ROI of your training and professional development programs? Are they efficient and effective? Have these efforts improved LMPM metrics?

Solution: Academic Institutes for Forensic Science

Essential Components of a Successful Institute

Forensic science has gained much attention in the media resulting in students and academics alike hypothesizing that a new forensic program can ignite renewed interest in a variety of academic programs. Perhaps even a

Figure 4.2 Professional development program.

"center of excellence" or "institute" can be developed within the university that will specialize in one or several of the forensic disciplines. Although this may sound attractive, the academic institution must proceed as if this was a business entrepreneurial venture with a solid business plan. Funding, of course, is critical, and the future institute normally requires startup funds and a finite time period to be self-sustaining.

A business plan requires at a minimum the following (Figure 4.3):

- Customer requirements
- Stakeholder memoranda of understanding or contracts
- Core team and staffing
- Academic
- Forensic practitioner
- Facilities
- Curricula
- Fiscal plan
- Marketing

Forensic Institute Essential Components

Customer requirements
- Market analyses
- Identify clear gap in supply and demand for forensic training and education

Figure 4.3 Forensic institute essential components.

- Measure need for undergrad, grad, and postgrad education training and professional development
- Identify primary customers and requirements, forensic practitioner laboratories, law enforcement, and the court

Institute core team
- Administration
- Faculty
- Adjunct
- Student assistants
- Internships

Institute core competencies addressing customer requirements or the gap
- Academic core curricula
- Graduate programs
- Training and professional development
- Facilities
- Support resources

Marketing
- Web presence
- Professional meetings
- Mailings
- Networking

Financial plan
- Revenue sources
- Contracts
- Grants
- Interagency agreements
- Expenditures
- Budget

Customers and Requirements

Primary customers are forensic laboratories, law enforcement, and the court. Surveys and meetings with primary customers are essential to learn requirements for education, training, and professional development. Are postgraduate degrees (MBA, MPA, MS, Ph.D.) needed for managers and executives? Many agencies select middle managers and top executives for advanced specialized postgraduate education as a capstone professional development program. These degrees or certificates are often funded by labor management contracts and are renewed annually. Projects or theses are directly linked to current job challenges. The DNA forensic discipline mandates graduate degrees and coursework in molecular biology for technical leaders and 8 hours of specialized training for all personnel performing benchwork activities (Federal Bureau of Investigation, 2013). Accreditation programs (ISO/IEC 17025, 2005) mandate training goals and measures for effectiveness.

These mandates can be used as a guide to develop specific customer requirements for education, training, and professional development.

Academic and public agency stakeholders have a direct interest in the program in that many of the services impact their agencies' mission and goals. Stakeholders can also contribute to the curricula with additional areas of expertise. Institute management should reach out to other departments within the university and outside to academic and public agencies. For example, internally there may be an opportunity to partner with several arts and science departments (biology, chemistry, mathematics) and to other schools such as business or information technologies. External to the university, relationships with medical and law schools can provide assistance for autopsy and court procedures. Public agencies such as public defenders, district attorneys, and judges can provide assistance with mock-trial training, often considered the capstone of the programs. Law enforcement agencies are both the supplier of evidence and receiver of scientific laboratory results and as such have a vested interest in training and professional development activities. Last but not least are forensic laboratories. Forensic laboratories are in critical need for training of new employees and professional development training for existing employees.

All stakeholders can assist with grant and congressional funding request with letters of intent or commitments to use services. These types of endorsements from stakeholders are often the difference between being approved for a grant or not. Initially, it is best to develop relationships with all key stakeholders and sign a memorandum of understanding (MOU) between agencies. The MOU can be signed by the top managers of both agencies with a public ceremony covered by the local media. The agencies' employees and local community must know that the leaders of the two or more agencies are fully supportive of the new relationship and resulting education and training initiatives. Media documentation can be used later for other requests. An example of a MOU follows:

Memorandum of Understanding
The University _
and
Law Enforcement Agency _
A partnership between the University _ and the _ Police Department
    Whereas, both the University _ and the _ Police Department have missions which embody the ideal of service to the people of the State of New York; and
    Whereas, the University at _ considers the development of partnerships with academic, business, cultural, and governmental organizations to be an integral component of its educational mission. Likewise, the _ Police Department works to achieve its mission to serve, protect, and defend the people while preserving the rights and dignity of all by creating partnerships with individuals, organizations, and communities throughout the _; and

Whereas, crime exacts a serious toll on society in that it victimizes people of all ages and abilities and economically burdens individuals, government, and private enterprise with billions of dollars worth of losses each year. Accordingly, the reduction of crime–in both residential and business communities and along the technology infrastructure statewide–remains one of _ State's top public policy priorities; and

Whereas, the University _ and the _ Police Department have complementary high technology facilities and intellectual resources:

A leading academic and research institution, the University _ has a number of nationally acclaimed research centers and schools including _.

Recognized as one of the leading law enforcement agencies nationwide, the _ Police Department operates the _ Forensic Science Laboratory. _ Police Department experts at these facilities provide a full spectrum of forensic science; and

Whereas, the University at _ and the _ Police Department have a mutual interest in developing new approaches and leading technologies to improve public protection and strengthen the criminal justice system in _ State. The development of such practical solutions and technological innovations will provide the State's criminal justice agencies with the tools needed to advance their respective missions of public service; and

Whereas, the _ Police Department has a wide range of law enforcement responsibilities including forensic investigative analysis in areas such as _; and

Whereas, the University at _ has a substantial number of degree programs and course offerings which could be used to provide sworn officers, forensic scientists, technicians and other Police Department personnel with invaluable skills and professional development opportunities in criminal justice, biological sciences, computer and information sciences, psychology and sociology; and

Whereas, the President of the University at _ and the Chief of the _ Police Department believe that a formal Memorandum of Understanding will provide the structure and impetus necessary to establish a partnership whereby both the University and the Police Department can cooperatively pursue innovative solutions for the law enforcement challenges of tomorrow; and

Whereas, the _ Police Department will be able to further advance its mission by partnering with the University at _ and gain access to valuable resources including a highly skilled and renowned faculty, a talented and diverse student population, an extensive high-tech infrastructure, state-of-the-art research centers, and a broad array of industrial partners; and

Whereas, the University _ will be able to advance its mission from an alliance with the _ Police Department in that researchers will be able to conduct meaningful research in a practical setting and students—both undergraduate and graduate—will be able to gain invaluable career experience; and

Whereas, the University _ has extensive relationships in the private sector with corporate partners that have research, development and technology deployment expertise and integrated advanced technologies which could be used for public protection and criminal justice applications; and

Whereas, both the University _ and the _ Police Department wish to develop a partnership which provides both organizations an opportunity to maximize their unique resources by engaging in joint public service and research projects, as well as mutually beneficial educational programs;

Therefore be it resolved, that the University _ and the _ Police Department wish to facilitate the aforementioned goals by agreeing to the following:

The University _ and the _ Police Department will explore possible joint ventures consistent with their missions of public service.

The University _ and the _ Police Department will designate appropriate staff to identify potential projects and relevant issues associated with those projects. Upon identifying a viable project, a working group comprised of University _ and _ Police Department personnel will be formed to develop a comprehensive action plan.

The University _ and _ Police Department will pursue external funding opportunities from federal, state, and private sources to advance mutually agreed upon research and development goals. Appropriate staff from the University _ and the _ Police Department will be designated in each instance to coordinate and facilitate the application for such funds.

The University and the Division will work cooperatively to promote joint training, distance learning, and continuing education initiatives which fulfill the program needs of the _ Police Department and utilize the expertise of both the University and the Division. The University _ and the _ Police Department will designate appropriate staff to identify areas of need, and in so doing, work to develop appropriate educational programming.

The University _ and the _ Police Department will explore and work cooperatively to develop technologies for applications in criminal justice and public protection by supporting the research, development, demonstration and deployment of such technologies through the University's technology transfer program.

The University _ and the _ Police Department will work to create student internships (paid and/or unpaid) which will not only benefit the _ Police Department, but will also afford students with practicum experiences and training in a real-life setting. The _ Police Department will identify applicable program areas where internships would be beneficial.

The University _ and the _ Police Department will jointly appoint an advisory committee comprised of a diverse group of individuals with experience in criminal justice policy, applications of technology for law enforcement, government and/or private enterprise. The composition of the advisory board shall be mutually agreed upon by the University _ and _ Police Department. The _ and the _ Police Department will review this Memorandum of Understanding on the anniversary date of its signing to assess whether the goals stated herein are being met or are in need of modification.

Either the University _ or the _ Police Department may elect to terminate this Memorandum of Understanding at anytime without reason or justification.

Therefore be it resolved, this Memorandum of Understanding shall take effect immediately.

Agreed this date,

President

University _

Chief of Police _

Financial Plan

An overall financial plan is needed to support the institute. Most revenue streams, whether they are grants, congressional requests, or contracts require 1 to 2 years lead time. In addition to having the institute be a successful recipient for a grant, the institute can also be included as a contractor or vendor within a customer's (law enforcement agency or laboratory) grant application. Grant solicitations are issued by federal and state agencies perhaps once or twice a year with usually short applications deadlines. It takes a minimum of 3 to 4 months to draft a grant application within the traditional guidelines of the soliciting agencies. Final review of the application following the guidance of the solicitation and electronic submission of the application may take at least 1 to 2 months. Over the next 6 months the soliciting agency will process the application through the agency governess. If approved the funds are usually released per federal budget calendar (October 1). Congressional requests (federal and local) are also potential sources of revenue. Federal, state, and local legislative bodies have access to discretionary funds for their respective localities. Institute management should regularly meet with local representatives to explain the economic impact of the institute programs. Economic spinoff results from local dollars go back to the community in the form of travel and per diem, tuition and fees, salaries and benefits, and ultimately the sustainment of a competent forensic workforce. The ROI of the institute for the local area can be measured and managed showing gains in efficiency and effectiveness for the primary customers and stakeholders. For example, structured academic programs for training or professional development are more efficient than decentralized programs (Cascio and Boudreau, 2008). Increased worker competency and satisfaction will also result in fewer good and bad quality expenditures, less litigation, less turnover, and increased overall efficiency and effectiveness increasing the overall ROI for the total program.

In addition to grants and legislative requests, individual contracts from federal, state, and local agencies or private sector enterprises are also an excellent source of revenue. These contracts are directly related to customer requirements. For example, has there been a legislation to increase support to a local laboratory for a specific discipline to address a backlog or new service? There have been many legislative efforts to increase the size of DNA data bank programs through increasing the scope of designated offenses. Most programs begin with designation of serious felonies as offenses requiring DNA sample collection from convicted offenders. Some states have progressed to all offenses and arrestees. Recent Supreme Court decisions have endorsed this concept paving the way for local agencies to significantly increase the scope and DNA databanks (*Maryland v. King*, 2013). Many laboratories will need to increase staff and facilities to meet these new requirements.

See Table 4.2 for an overall budget for one 16-week DNA academy.

Table 4.2   16-Week DNA Academy Budget for 16 Students

Personnel		
Name	Position	Cost
Manager 1	Director	$46,668
Graduate Assistant 1	Lab Tech	$2,700
Graduate Assistant 2	Lab Tech	$2,700
Subtotal Personnel			**$52,068**

Fringe		
Name	Position	Cost
Manager 1	Director	$17,967
Graduate Assistant 1	Lab Tech	$338
Graduate Assistant 2	Lab Tech	$338
Subtotal Fringe			**$18,642**

Travel		
Total Travel Costs			$0

Equipment		
Item		
16 Laptop PCs	16,000	
16 GenemapperID Licenses	40,000	
Total Equipment		$56,000

Supplies		
DNA Supplies and Reagents	64,000	
Total Supply Costs		$64,000

Construction		
Purpose		
Total Construction Costs		

(*Continued*)

Table 4.2   16-Week DNA Academy Budget for 16 Students (*Continued*)

	Consultant Contracts		
A	12 weeks	$27,000	
B	12 weeks	$27,000	
C	16 weeks	$36,000	
D	5 days	$5,000	
E	5 days	$5,000	
F	5 days	$5,000	
Total Consultant Contracts			**$105,000**
	Consultant Expenses		
A	12 weeks	$16,200	
B	5 days	$1,350	
C	5 days	$1,350	
D	5 days	$1,350	
Total Consultant Expenses			**$20,250**
	Contracts		
Mock Trials		$15,000	
Total Contracts			$15,000
	Other Costs		
Subtotal			$330,960
Indirect Costs			$168,790
Total Costs			$499,750
	Budget Summary		
Personnel			$52,068
Fringe			$18,642
Travel			$0
Equipment			$56,000
Supplies			$64,000
Construction			
Consultants/Contracts			$140,250
Total Direct Costs			$330,960
Indirect Costs			$168,790
Cost per Student			$31,234
Total Costs			$499,750

Institute Core Team

Staffing the institute is arguably the most challenging component of the total program. Institute management must work very closely with the university human resources and finance units to ensure policies, procedures, and even legislated rules and intent are followed. Most forensic experts will not relocate for even a full-time position, as the future of the institute is uncertain.

Very few of the positions are full time as compared to part-time hourly hires and consultants. Managing several revenue streams also can lead to one person being funded by more than one revenue source. Institute management must ensure revenues are used for their intended purpose. For example, if Expert A is hired as a consultant for DNA Academy #6 funded by Agency Y, then only those funded received by Agency Y should be used to compensate Expert A.

One needs to become a scientist before becoming a forensic scientist. Some of the best instructors have no forensic experience and are excellent scientists. Some students in the graduate program become excellent scientists and develop into excellent instructors, having never been in a forensic laboratory.

The decisions to hire an expert as a full- or part-time hourly employee versus a contractor are significant (Internal Revenue Service, 2013). Labor management agreements are very specific about conditions of contract consultants. The resulting decisions will affect the budget. Full-time and part-time employees above a specific number of hours are paid benefits (sick leave, vacation, medical, dental, eye care, all resulting from labor management agreements). These benefits are funded at a rate of approximately 50% of base salary. For example, if an individual's salary is $100,000 then the benefits will be an additional $50,000 for a total of $150,000 expenditure in the institute budget. Contactors, on the other hand, are usually paid an hourly or daily rate for a specific amount of time and scope of duties requiring minimal supervision with no benefits. For example, a contractor is hired to deliver 5 days of lectures at $500 per day equals $2,500 plus expenses. Expenses are air travel, room, and food usually following General Services Administration rates (www.gsa.gov).

One best alternative for instructors is to recruit excellent scientists from the university that are between grant funding and hire them as full-time or part-time instructors. These types of individuals are priceless, in that they are excellent scientists, know how the university works, and can learn forensic procedures relatively quickly. Individual forensic expert contractors can be hired as consultants to fill in the gaps in the curricula for specialty topics such as statistics or instrument software operation and maintenance. Support staff is comprised of student assistants (SAs) from the graduate program. The SAs compete for positions and their time is usually limited to 15 to 20 hours per week. SAs are indispensable in the laboratory performing quality control tasks and maintaining inventory of all consumables and supplies. Good SAs then compete for full-time positions in the institute and practitioner forensic laboratories. It is very fulfilling observing students mature from students, to SAs, to full-time employees and some go on to postgraduate degrees and employment as excellent scientists, technical leaders, and supervisors in many laboratories.

Institute Core Competency: Forensic Curricula

A Model Forensic Graduate Program   An academic "champion" is the first essential ingredient needed to modify an existing excellent graduate program into a forensic graduate program. Professor Donald Orokos, administrator for the University at Albany Graduate Program in Forensic Molecular Biology, was the champion that designed, implemented, and has sustained the program from inception. Orokos' personal involvement and "ownership" for the program is the main factor for success. Many graduates have been placed as forensic scientists in local public or private laboratories or gone on to advanced degrees in law or science (see student comments by Belrose and Hart). A champion such as Orokos is highly respected within the university and knows the academic processes and rigor needed for curricula to meet requirements of academic governess and accrediting bodies. Any modifications or newly designed curricula or courseware will need approval internally by university governess committees and externally by academic accrediting bodies before implementation. These steps establish academic credits, number of class and laboratory hours, learning goals, instructor qualifications, curricula materials, student feedback, and practical competencies with written and oral assessments. The key to development of a forensic molecular biology program is to supplement a strong graduate program with course electives customized for forensic science.

Advice for Students Considering a Forensic Career[*]

How can you tell the difference between a pseudo forensic program and a highly competent forensic program? Here is where the prospective forensic student needs to do their homework and investigate the programs offered at the various colleges and universities. If you are a prospective student, what are some of the questions you need to ask of the various programs?

> First, you need to find out how long the program has been in existence and how many students have graduated from the program?
> Second, are there forensic practitioners who are part of the faculty for the forensic program at that college or university?
> Third, is there a forensic laboratory/agency associated with the existing forensic academic program?

[*] From Dale, W. M., and Becker, W. S., 2007, *The Crime Scene: How Forensic Science Works*, New York: Kaplan.

Fourth, what is an internship and does the program include internships or research projects? Why are they important and are they assigned or part of the student's responsibility to obtain?

Fifth, are students that have graduated from the program hired in an accredited forensic agency?

Sixth, is the university or colleges accredited by an accrediting body recognized by the U.S. Department of Education, for example, the Middle States Commission on Higher Education?

Seventh, what about the facilities? Are students learning up-to-date theory and practicing on state-of-the-art technology?

Eighth, does the program include a natural science core and at the same time require coursework in the various forensic science disciplines?

These are the questions you need to ask, but how do you go about getting answers to these questions? Sometimes it is best to visit the college or university and talk with the program director, faculty, and current students. For example, the University at Albany is an accredited institution, recognized by the U.S. Department of Education. The University at Albany's Forensic Program has been in existence since 2001, and more important became approved by the Forensic Science Education Programs Accreditation Commission (FEPAC) February 2007. Furthermore, as of May 2007, the program graduated 45 students. We have a number of practitioners that take part in the instruction of the forensic program. They are full-time forensic scientists so they are extremely knowledgeable in the most current forensic practices and theories, which they share with the students in the program through lecture and laboratory coursework. Even before the program came into existence, the university collaborated with the forensic community to create, develop, and implement a graduate-level forensic molecular biology program. To date, this partnership with the forensic community continues. The local law enforcement and forensic agencies provide personnel to train our students in the various disciplines in forensic science. The ultimate goal of any forensic program is to produce scientists, not technicians.

An internship is an independent research project. Each student in the University at Albany's program must complete a 6-credit internship project in a laboratory that offers up-to-date training and laboratory expertise in areas that are potentially applicable to forensic biology. In our program there are a number of ways in which students can fulfill their internship/research requirement. Students in the program can satisfy the internship requirements by either completing a basic/applied research project or a comprehensive validation study. Student take the knowledge and skills they obtained in their coursework and apply it to a research project that is potentially applicable to forensic science and will be performed in a laboratory setting. After completion of the project a detailed scientific report must be submitted for review and evaluation. In addition, most programs require students to present the project to their peers.

Students can arrange for their internship in one of two ways. Either they find on their own a laboratory that they are interested in working in, or the program director or faculty will help locate an appropriate laboratory facility. An internship may be paid or unpaid, but is an important avenue in the creation of a mentor relationship with local forensic professionals. Many students also choose to volunteer in local laboratories to continue learning as well as building ties with the forensic community.

To date, all the students that were interested in employment in forensic laboratories have been employed as either forensic scientists or DNA analysts. A very successful program is more than willing to provide answers to all your questions as well as give contact names of recent graduates. A successful program will also have a career placement and career development center. The University at Albany has such a career services program that helps with resume and cover letter reviews, mock interviews, and networking as well as helping with letters of recommendations. Students are also advised to take advantage of the extensive career services provided by the university and the forensic community, such as the American Academy of Forensic Sciences, American Society of Crime Laboratory Directors, and the Northeastern Association of Forensic Scientists.

The University at Albany offers state-of-the-art technology in DNA and serology. For example, students in our program are trained on the most current equipment, software, and standard operating procedures currently used in forensic laboratories. This is through laboratories set up on campus that mirror laboratories at currently operating forensic facilities. Certain natural science courses are required in chemistry, biology, physics, and mathematics.

A program supported by the forensic community should have instruction in communication skills, both written and verbal. In addition, a strong forensic program must also include coursework in the law, ethics and professional practices, evidence identification, collection and processing, and quality assurance as well as courtroom testimony. Much of this information can be covered in lecture, but a program that offers hands-on training is highly desirable. Eventually, a forensic scientist is going to have to testify in court. Not only do they have to have an understanding of the natural sciences, but they also must have an understanding of the courtroom process, a familiarity of the other forensic disciplines (evidence identification, collecting, and processing) and they must give their testimony in an unbiased, ethical manner that supports all quality assurance practices. The University at Albany's Forensic Molecular Biology Program encompasses all these points.

The next question you may ask yourself is what is the difference between an undergraduate program and a graduate program. Why would you choose one type of program over the other?

A graduate program, such as our master's in science in forensic molecular biology, is for those students that are interested in becoming a technical leader, a supervisor, or a director of a smaller forensic laboratory. Students successfully graduating from our program have the education necessary for such positions. However, to apply for these supervisory-level positions they would generally need at least 3 years of bench experience. Today, many laboratory director positions require a doctoral degree from an accredited university or college.

An undergraduate 4-year program is very good for the forensic scientist who wants to be a nonsupervisory practitioner, a scientist who wants to work and be a valuable asset to a lab but not run it. They will testify and perform all nonsupervisory benchwork and laboratory support, like validation studies, quality control, and quality assurance. Most undergraduate programs have an internship/research requirement like graduate school. These internships provide additional benchwork and analytical and interpretive skills necessary for work in the forensic field. In addition, an internship should require students to present their results in a written scientific paper followed by an oral presentation. An internship is a great way of networking with the forensic community and establishing the possibility of a mentor relationship with local forensic professionals.

Now that you know what questions to ask, how do you go about finding which colleges and universities have the desired program you need? You could use the Internet to find a listing of colleges that have forensic programs. You could go to a specific regional forensic Web site like the Northeast Academy of Forensic Scientists (NEAFS) or national Web sites such as the American Academy of Forensic Sciences (AAFS) and the American Society of Crime Laboratory Directors (ASCLD). These Web sites will give a listing of programs that are FEPAC approved and they may also provide scholarship information. You could look at privately run forensic Web sites, such as Reddy's, which gives a listing of all academic programs, both graduate and undergraduate. These listings not only provide information on academic programs, but they give information on forensic science in general, plus employment opportunities. Once you have found a number of programs that you have identified as potential programs you are interested in, you could go to their Web site, read more about their programs, then contact them and request more information (e.g., brochures, program guidelines). The information you are looking to include are the description of the programs, the prerequisites for the program, the course requirements, grading policy, and internship requirements as well as the answers to the other questions we have previously discussed. At this time you may wish to contact the program director and arrange a visit to see the actual facilities and meet with faculty, support staff, and current students.

Now if you have asked all your questions, visited the facilities, and chosen your desired college or university, how do you go about applying to the program? At the University of Albany, all applications, admission and degree-granting requirements, and regulations shall be applied equitably to individual applicants and students regardless of age, sex, race, disability, religion, or national origin. For a master's program at most schools, each prospective graduate student must submit a formal application for admission and receive a formal letter of admission before registering for any courses. Graduate students are expected to hold a bachelor's degree from an accredited college or university. Their preparation must be appropriate to the program they wish to pursue and their academic record should generally be a B or better in coursework that the department considers preparatory for graduate study. Meeting this requirement does not ensure that an application will be admitted, but it sure does help. These students would apply directly to the Office of Graduate Studies.

For a potential student who is seeking to be admitted to a 4-year college or university, you would need to take your ACTs or SATs, obtain at least three personal references, an official high school or 2-year community college transcript, and write a personal essay to be sent along with your completed application to the admissions office of the school of your choice.

For the high school student interested in a career in forensic science, you should contact your guidance office to see which courses your school may offer. Many high schools have college-credit forensic courses (for example, Syracuse University Project Advance, or SUPA) as well as beginning forensic courses that are available. You would then need to decide whether you want to go for the 4-year forensic degree, where you would be potentially hired as a nonadministrative forensic scientist, or get a bachelor's degree in a complimentary field and apply for the master's forensic degree of which has the potential for managerial positions. Suggested bachelor's degrees that would be complimentary to the master's in forensics are those in biology, life sciences, chemistry, physics, criminal justice, or mathematics. Once the bachelor's degree is obtained, you would then apply to the graduate programs as outlined earlier. High school students may also obtain internships at local forensic institutions, but these are noncredit, nonresearch-based volunteer internships. Internships at this level often include clerical and general nontechnical support for the forensic laboratory. However, these internships are extremely useful in allowing the student to get a general overview of the day-to-day operations in a forensic laboratory environment. These internships also provide networking, possibilities for letters of references, and potential future employment opportunities.

Be prepared that most graduates from any forensic program seeking employment as a forensic scientist in an accredited forensic science laboratory will normally have to undergo a background check. Depending on the agency or company, the background check may be quite extensive and include fingerprinting, a lie-detector test, and drug screening. Most background checks take upward of 6 months to complete. Once you have your degree in hand, whether a bachelor's from a 4-year school or a master's degree in a forensic discipline, where do you go for employment and what should you expect once you are hired?

As previously mentioned, a good program has a career placement office. That is always a good place to start. Second, your program director and the school faculty are important sources of employment opportunities. Web sites such as Reddy's, the AAFS, and the ASCLD will have current listings posted. Word-of-mouth from past graduates as well as practitioners is key to finding new employment opportunities. Your mentors that were formed by either volunteer lab work or during your internship will also be valuable instruments in finding a job. Steps to help you with employment are keep an updated curriculum vitae; have official transcripts available upon request; and at least three letters of recommendation either from professors, internship advisors, the program director, or mentors.

Once you are hired, forget *CSI*—this is the real world! Crimes are not solved in 60 minutes, with time for commercials. The degree that you have from your college or university only provides a very solid foundation in the forensic sciences. Once you are hired by a forensic agency, you are required to successfully complete an intensive training program. Depending on where you get hired will depend on the forensic discipline that you will work with most. The first 6 months to 2 years you will be going through additional training and competency testing. Upon successful completion of that training, you will be given more responsibilities in regard to casework. Currently, most labs do a one-on-one training with new hires. If done this way, it can take at least 12 to 18 months of training. During this time period you will be expected to perform all standard operating procedures of your laboratory, and learn basic usage and troubleshooting of all equipment, various software programs, proper documentation, chain of custody, quality assurance, and proper testimony procedures. Recently, forensic laboratories have been using training facilities such as the one provided by the Northeast Regional Forensic Institute (NERFI) to eliminate the one-on-one mentor system. At NERFI there are small classes; intense, concise benchwork; and a shorter time investment for training than the traditional one-on-one mentor system. Most newly hired forensic scientists going through the training program at NERFI will be required to spend 12 to 16 weeks at the training facility. However, an additional 3 months of training is required back at the parent forensic laboratory. Once this training is complete, there are still continuous training opportunities that are required in most accredited forensic laboratories. Some forensic disciplines, for example DNA, require their forensic scientists to complete at least 8 hours of continuing education each year. This requirement is usually completed through national meetings, regional meetings, and workforce development programs such as the ones provided by NERFI.

Other continuing education opportunities include certification programs provided by the American Board of Criminalistics (ABC). Passing the examinations provided by ABC (i.e., FSAT) demonstrates a level of competency supported by the forensic community. Some of the examinations currently provided by ABC include forensic biology, trace evidence, fire debris analysis, and drug chemistry. It is highly recommended that all new hires and senior-level scientists achieve these certifications and continue their education in the forensic sciences because the technology is rapidly changing every day.

Curricula: Biology Master of Science in Forensic Biology   The University at Albany graduate degree program involves a unique collaboration between the New York State Police Forensic Investigation Center and the Department of Biological Sciences in training scientists with state-of-the-art knowledge and laboratory expertise in forensics (University at Albany, 2013a).

General Requirements   A minimum of 40 graduate credits is required for the master's degree.

Biology (29 credits):
  Required courses (17 credits): Bio 515a (1 credit) Responsible Conduct and Skills in Research and Bio 515b (1 credit) Responsible Conduct and Skills in Scientific Communication; Bio 517a (1 credit) Current Literature in Forensic Biology I; Bio 519/Ant 519 (3 credits) Human Population Genetics; Bio 524 (3 credits) Advanced Molecular Biology; Bio 514 (2 credits) Biotechnology Laboratory; Bio 650 (0 credits) Graduate Research Seminar, for two semesters; Bio 627 (1 credit) Courtroom Testimony for Forensic Scientists; Bio 575 (3 credits) Forensic Biology Laboratory; and Bio 577 (2 credits) Techniques in Forensic Science. Students who have not had an undergraduate course in Genetics, Molecular Biology, Biochemistry and Immunology will be required to make up the deficiency by taking the appropriate undergraduate or graduate courses.
  Internship: Bio 698 (6 credits): Satisfactory completion of an internship in forensic biology laboratory for which 6 credits will be awarded. The results obtained during the internship will be the subject of a substantial written report, which will be examined by a committee of three members, approved by the Graduate Examinations Committee.

Biology electives: (6 credits) Two chosen from the following: Bio 504 Cell Biology I (3 credits); Bio 505 Cell Biology II (3 credits); Bio 513 Modern Use of Light Microscopy (3 credits); Bio 521 Cell and Molecular Developmental Neurobiology (3 credits); Bio 523 Biochemisty and Molecular Structure (3 credits); Bio 531 Comparative and Evolutionary Immunology (3 credits); Bio 540 Principles of Bioinformatics (3 credits); Bio 541 Molecular Neurobiology (3 credits); Bio 563 Integrative Principles of Evolution (3 credits); and Bio 617 Molecular Evolution (3 credits).

Supporting courses (8-12 credits). Required courses: Sta 552 Principles of Statistical Inference or Mat 565 Applied Statistics, Crj 626 Law and Science in Criminal Justice, and other courses in mathematics or statistics, business, biology, chemistry, psychology, and criminal justice as advised; courses in other fields with the formal consent of the advisor.

Satisfactory completion of core and final examinations in Biology. The written internship report will serve as the final examination.

Admission for Masters of Science Programs   Applicants must have a bachelor's degree from an accredited university or college, and are required to submit a standard graduate application, three letters of recommendation, all undergraduate transcripts, and scores from the Graduate Record Exam General Test. Students applying for the forensic biology sequence must have completed, with a grade of C or better, the following courses: genetics, biochemistry, immunology, and molecular biology; and have received a baccalaureate in a natural science.

Core and Final Examinations in Biology   The graduate training program in the department is divided into two core areas: (1) ecology and evolutionary biology (EEB); and (2) molecular, cellular, developmental, and neural biology (MCDN). Students lacking undergraduate courses in any of the four core areas may be required, at the discretion of their master's committees, to make up these deficiencies.

Students are expected to acquire and demonstrate by means of an examination a comprehensive insight into the current state of knowledge and the current problems in one of these core areas. They will choose this area in consultation with their advisor.

To assist in preparation for the core examination, the appropriate faculty groups will provide a reading list of textbooks and original papers directed to the more significant aspects of the field.

Core area examinations will be administered at the end of the spring session of the student's first full year of study. Based on the student's performance, the appropriate core area faculty will recommend that the student: (1) pass; (2) be dropped from the departmental graduate program; or (3) be allowed to continue and retake the examination at the next offering. Failure of this examination a second time necessarily will result in the academic dismissal from the master's program.

A final written or oral examination in the student's area of specialization (for students not registered for Bio 699), or an oral defense of the thesis (for those registered in Bio 699) must be passed prior to the receipt of the degree.

Curricula

Standardized and centralized core curricula with dedicated laboratory facilities and staff are more efficient and effective than traditional mentor training programs (Cascio & Boudreau, 2008). Mentors are usually selected from a pool of the best bench forensic scientists and are trained in casework laboratories. This arrangement immediately reduces productivity of the forensic unit as the mentor is taken off casework duties to act as a trainer. Training provided in an operational laboratory is also very problematic as competition for instrumentation and the risk of students causing contamination or loss of evidence is high. In a training environment you want the students to make mistakes and learn from them. In an operational laboratory you want no errors. Dedicated facilities and dedicated trained instructors are critical for the success of a training program. The best scientists may not be the best trainers, as additional skills are needed to be an effective instructor. Presentation skills and the design and delivery of curricula with learning objectives, course materials, readings, and competency assessments linked to objectives are essential for all instructors and directly related to the success of the program. A temporal aspect adds a finite timeline that starts and ends the program with an assessment with passing grade metrics. There is a schedule that must be maintained with little room for adjustments for individual students. Accommodations can be made for students requiring more time, however, the students must be made aware of the program completion requirements and the timeline to be "DoneDone."

Example: 16-Week DNA Academy

Module 1: Molecular Biology and Forensic DNA Typing

Starting	Ending	Course Title	Instructors	Comments
Sept 8th	Sept 17th	Molecular Biology and Forensic DNA Typing	Institute staff	Lectures prepared from Watson et al., *Molecular Biology of the Gene*, 5th edition, Butler Second Edition, and primary scientific literature.

Module 1

Course Instruction and Description:

Primary Instructors: Institute teaching staff and experts from the field of Forensic DNA Typing

Description: Topics in Molecular Biology and Forensic DNA Typing Discussion of nucleic acid structure and organization, chromatin and chromosome structures, mechanisms of replication and recombination, mechanisms of gene expression, regulation, and repair in eukaryotic cells. Emphasis is placed on unique features of eukaryotic systems with examples given from higher and lower eukaryotes. Where appropriate, Forensic DNA Typing applications based on principles from molecular biology are stressed in this course.

Lectures: Daily lectures on the theory and practice of Forensic Molecular Biology will be given from 8:30 am to 10:15 am and 12:30 pm to 2:30 pm. Assignments: Each day during module 1, trainees will do assigned readings and homework from 10:30 am to noon and from 2:45 pm to 4:00 pm.

Primary Resources: Watson, JD. 2004. *Molecular Biology of the Gene*. 5th ed. Benjamin Cummings, CA, and primary scientific literature.

Additional Resources: Butler J. 2005. *Forensic DNA Typing*, 2nd edition. Elsevier Academic Press. Burlington, MA (ISBN 0121479528) and scientific literature required by SWGDAM.

Attendance: Mandatory—unexcused absences on the trainee's part will result in a failing grade for all assignments that day.

Academic Integrity: See Graduate Bulletin for details. Deviations will be treated according to university regulations.

Final Grade for Module 1	
Exam	50 pts
Assignments	25 pts
Participation	10 pts
Performance (Weekly Assessment Memo, Attitude, etc.)	15 pts
Total Points	100 pts

Note: Each trainee must earn at least 80 points to pass Module 1: Topics in Molecular Biology and Forensic DNA Typing.

Notes

Trainees are expected to work on Sim Set and Sample Set reports as time allows during the day—while samples are centrifuging, quanting, amping, or being analyzed, and so forth—and at home as necessary to complete a total of 20 reports by the conclusion of the academy.

For the Competency Test, trainees must make their own master mixes and must not discuss techniques or results with other trainees. *For comp tests, all work must be done independently, including master mixes, quantitation standards, and so forth. No batching of samples!*

Module 3 (Weeks 2, 3, 4, and 6–14):
Forensic DNA Analysis Laboratory

Important points:

Software: GeneMapper ID 3.2 and Data Collection 3.0

Platforms: ABI 7500, ABI 9700 & 9600, ABI 310 and ABI 3130XL

Kits: Human & Y Quantifiler, Profiler Plus, COfiler and Identifiler

2. SWGDAM Guidelines—as they apply to the 50-sample recommendation:

Section 5.5 of the Training Guidelines (Jan. 01) states the following: A new DNA laboratory trainee must complete a training notebook documenting his/her own experiences performing evidentiary or known sample analysis. The type of samples included must vary, reflecting the range, type, and complexity of casework or database analyses routinely handled by his/her laboratory duties. To assist in ensuring basic competency, this training notebook must document analysis of a minimum of 50 samples for nuclear DNA analysis.

3. SWGDAM Guidelines—as they apply to the 20-data set recommendation:

Section 6.4.2 of the Training Guidelines (Jan. 01) states the following: The trainee will review 20 sets of data representative of casework and provide a written interpretation of the data according to the laboratory policy. The trainer will review and assess the reports for accuracy. These data sets can be samples representative of typical casework or actual casework data. The laboratory can maintain a standard file of data sets or share sets with other laboratories.

Course Instruction and Description:

Primary Instructors: Institute teaching staff and experts from the field of forensic science

Description: Trainees in Forensic DNA Analysis Laboratory will learn how to perform molecular analytical procedures that include organic DNA extraction, DNA quantification, PCR-based methods, multiplex amplification of STR loci, capillary electrophoresis of amplified products, and data analysis, interpretation, reporting of single source and mixture data samples and courtroom presentation.

Textbook: John Butler, *Forensic DNA Typing*, 2nd ed. (ISBN 0121479528), and all pertinent literature required by SWGDAM.

NRC II Report, David J. Balding, *Weight-of-Evidence for Forensic DNA Profiles*, *ABI User's Manuals* as reference materials, and other readings from primary resources.

Attendance: Mandatory—unexcused absences on the trainee's part will result in a failing grade for all assignments that day.

Academic Integrity: See Graduate Bulletin for details. Deviations will be treated according to university regulations.

Final Grade for Module 3: Each trainee must earn at least 80 points to pass Forensic DNA Analysis Laboratory.

Final Exam	30 pts
Competency Exam	35 pts
Quizzes (2.5 pts each × 4)	10 pts
Performance (Weekly Assessment Memos, Attitude, etc.)	15 pts
Moot Court	10 pts
Total Points	**100 pts**

Assessment Memos: Each trainee must submit, via e-mail, a weekly Assessment Memo to Institute instructors. Assessment Memos are due every Monday at 8:00 am unless a holiday falls on Monday. In that case, it is due the following instruction day.

All Assessment Memos submitted must contain the following information:

1. Total number of samples extracted to date.
2. Total number of independent setups and operations on the ABI 7500, ABI 9700, 9600, ABI 310, and ABI 3130XL.
3. Any comments, concerns, and mistakes made during the week. In the "mistake" section students must include a description of what was done to correct each mistake and how to prevent the same mistake from reoccurring in the future. In addition, include specific comments about lessons learned, what they think they still need help with, what they feel they are improving on, what they feel proficient at, etc. In this section the trainee may also include suggestions for the Institute to improve the DNA academies.

Competency Exams: There will be one final competency exam that will be graded pass/fail. Those trainees failing this exam on the first try will be issued another exam and allowed only one additional attempt to pass. Failure to pass the second competency exam will result in a failure for that exam.

Laboratory Attire: All trainees must wear all appropriate personal protective equipment (PPE) when working in the DNA Laboratory. Eating and drinking are prohibited in these areas.

Performance Metrics: At the end of each week, Institute staff will update each trainee's performance metric and send that report, via e-mail, to their home laboratory. The performance metric along with a copy of the assessment memo each week will allow the home lab's supervisors a window into each trainee's progress during the academy.

Week 1: Molecular Biology and Forensic DNA Typing Schedule: Lectures via Video or On-Site

Homework and Assessment Memos submitted via e-mail	Day 1	Day 2	Day 3	Day 4	Day 5
		Homework Due	Homework Due	Homework Due	Homework Due
8:30–10:15 am	Institute Welcome Basic Genetics Central Dogma	Structure of DNA & RNA The Replication of DNA in Eukaryotes	Mechanisms of Transcription	DNA Damage & Repair DNA Quantitation	Homologous Recombination
10:30–12:00	Assigned Readings and Assignments	Assigned Readings and Assignments	Assigned Readings and Assignments	Assigned Readings and Assignments	Assigned Readings, Assignments and Review
12:30–2:30 pm	DNA Isolation	PCR DNA Amplification	History of Forensic DNA testing Quality Assurance & Quality Control	Repetitive DNA & other DNA Polymorphisms used as Genetic Markers	Electrophoresis & Fluorescent DNA Detection
2:45–4:00 pm	Assigned Readings and assignments	Assigned readings and assignments	Assigned readings and assignments	Assigned Readings and assignments	Assigned readings and assignments

Lecture times and lecturers may change.

Week 2: Molecular Biology and Forensic DNA Typing (cont'd.), Final Exam and Laboratory Demos

Date	Time	Morning	Time	Afternoon	Comments
Day 1	8:00	8:00—Assessment Memo 1 due 8:30—Mechanisms of Translation 4:00—Last homework due	12:30	Last homework from Module 1 returned to trainees. Study time for final exam	During the 16-week on-site training, all trainees must submit weekly Assessment Memos (via e-mail) to the instructors
Day 2	8:00	Question & Answer session for final exam University Biological Hazards Safety Training (1 hr)	12:30	Study time for final exam	Assessment Memos are due every Monday
Day 3	8:00	Final Exam for Module 1— (8:00 am–12:00 pm)	12:30	Pizza Party for trainees and staff	Required Readings: Organic DNA Extraction DNA Quantitation
Day 4	8:00	8:30—7500 Q-PCR Instrumentation Lecture 10:30—310/3130xl Instrumentation Lecture	12:30	AFTERNOON OFF	DNA Amplification Setting up the 310 Setting up the 3130xl
Day 5	8:00	DAY OFF	12:30	DAY OFF	Staffing:

Week 3: Forensic DNA Analysis Laboratory

Date	Morning	Time	Afternoon	Comments
Day 1	8:00—Assessment Memo 2 due Organic extraction demo	12:30	Quantitation demo—Q-PCR 7500	Instructors will be in the laboratory during the first 2 Sample Set analyses to assist trainees with techniques and evaluate their skills
Day 2	Amplification demo (CO/Pro/Ident)	12:30	CE 310 demo	
Day 3	CE 3130xl demo	12:30	Extra time to bring all trainees to the same point.	Required Readings: Quantifiler Manual
Day 4	SAMPLE SET 1: Sample prep, organic extraction	12:30	SAMPLE SET 1: Organic extraction	Pro/CO/Ident. Manual DNA Training Bibliography
Day 5	SAMPLE SET 1: Quantitation—setup	12:30	SAMPLE SET 1: Quantitation—results interpretation & amp calculations Day 5 meeting	Sample Set 1 consists of blood serial dilutions. Staffing:

Week 4: Forensic DNA Analysis Laboratory

Date	Morning	Time	Afternoon	Comments
Day 1	8:00—Assessment Memo 3 due SAMPLE SET 1: Amplification—setup Sim Sets 1 & 2 assigned	12:30	SAMPLE SET 1: Amplification Work on Sample Set 1 case file Order of the case file lecture	Instructors will be in the laboratory during the first 2 Sample Set analyses to assist trainees with techniques and evaluate their skills
Day 2	SAMPLE SET 1: 3130xl CE—setup 10:00—Introduction to GeneMapper & individual data analysis assistance GeneMapper ID Lecture	12:30	12:30—Introduction to GeneMapper & individual data analysis assistance GeneMapper ID lecture	Oral quizzes will be worked in to impact lab work as minimally as possible
Day 3	SAMPLE SET 2: Setup differential ext	12:30	Work on Sample Set 1 case file 4:00—Sample Set 1 case file due	Sample Sets 1 and 2, DO NOT write analytical reports, but do put together case file with allele chart only
Day 4	SAMPLE SET 2: Finish differential ext	12:30	SAMPLE SET 2: Quantification—setup	
Day 5	SAMPLE SET 2: Amplification—setup Quiz 1: Oral quiz on laboratory procedures, extraction, quantitation, & QA	12:30	SAMPLE SET 2: CE 3130xl—setup Day 5 meeting Quiz 1: Oral quiz on laboratory procedures, extraction, quantitation, & QA	Sample Set 2 consists of semen serial dilutions Staffing:

Module 2 (Week 5): Forensic Statistics

Date	Morning	Time	Afternoon	Comments

Day 1	8:00—Assessment Memo 4 due
	Probability, Statistics, and Population
	  Genetics
	Estimating the frequency of a DNA
	  profile, Hardy-Weinberg Equilibrium
	Accuracy vs precision of statistical
	  estimates
	Suspect population and relevance of
	  defendant racial group
	Distribution of human genetic variation
	Probability axioms; frequentist vs
	  Bayesian probability
		12:30	Heterozygosity as a measure of
			  genetic discrimination
			Conditional probability; odds;
			  likelihood ratio
			Sample size; hypothesis testing;
			  goodness-of-fit tests
			Bootstrap, jackknife, permutation
			  test, exact tests
			Permutation test for HWE
			  exercise
				Instructor:

Day 2	Applications to Transfer Evidence,
	  Minimum allele frequency; database
	  searches and calculations
	Calculations of relatives' genotypes;
	  calculation of putative sibs
	Source attribution approaches
	  (uniqueness)
		12:30	NRC II recommendations; theta
			  values; laboratory error
			Conditional DNA profile formulas
			Comparisons of formulas for
			  profile frequency
			Counting method;
			  Misinterpretation of random
			  match probability	

Day 3	Paternity and Missing Persons
	Likelihood ratio evidence; exclusion
	  probability
	Applying theta to paternity calculations
	Simple two-person kinship calculations
		12:30	Calculations for more extended
			  pedigree data
			Errors of interpretation;
			  transposed conditional
			Prosecutor's fallacy, Defense
			  attorney's fallacy
			Example paternity calculation
			  exercises	

Day 4	Mixtures and Presenting Statistics in
	  Court
	Quantifying mixture interpretation
	Exclusion probability; likelihood ratio
	  approach to mixture
	Example mixture calculation exercises
		12:30	1-hour exam
			Review and discussion of exam
			Presenting quantitative evidence
			  in court
			Defense issues and attacks	

Day 5	DAY OFF	12:30	DAY OFF	

Week 6: Forensic DNA Analysis Laboratory

Date	Time	Morning	Time	Afternoon	Comments
Day 1	8:00	DAY OFF—Holiday	12:30	DAY OFF—Holiday	

Day 2	8:00	8:00—Assessment Memo
		  5 due
		8:30—Mixture
		  Interpretation Lecture
			12:30	12:30—Population Genetics &
				  Stats Lecture
					Sim Sets
					submitted with:

Day 3	8:00	8:00—CODIS Lecture
		SAMPLE SET 2: GMID
		  Analysis & Report Writing
			12:30	SAMPLE SET 2: GMID
				  Analysis & Report Writing
					Case report
					CODIS Upload
					Request

Day 4	8:00	SAMPLE SET 2: GMID Analysis & Report Writing	12:30	SAMPLE SET 2	Staffing:
Day 5	8:00	SAMPLE SET 2	12:30	SAMPLE SET 2 Day 5 meeting 4:00—Sample Set 2 case file due	

Week 7: Forensic DNA Analysis Laboratory

Date	Time	Morning	Time	Afternoon	Comments
Day 1	8:00	8:00—Assessment Memo 6 due SAMPLE SET 3	12:30	SAMPLE SET 3	Starting with the 3rd sample set, the trainees will start dividing their analysis between the 3130xl and the 310
Day 2	8:00	SAMPLE SET 3	12:30	SAMPLE SET 3	
Day 3	8:00	Sim Sets 1 & 2 reports due Sim Sets 6 & 7 assigned SAMPLE SET 3	12:30	SAMPLE SET 3	Trainees continue to work on Sim Sets
Day 4	8:00	Work on Sample Set 3 case file	12:30	12:30—Quiz 2—Written (diff extraction, quant, PCR) Work on Sample Set 3 case file Day 5 meeting	Sample Set 3 consists of several high concentration samples as well as blanks to test for carry-over contamination
Day 5	8:00	DAY OFF	12:30	DAY OFF	Staffing:

Week 8: Forensic DNA Analysis Laboratory

Date	Time	Morning	Time	Afternoon	Comments
Day 1	8:00	8:00—Assessment Memo 7 due SAMPLE SET 3	12:30	SAMPLE SET 3	Trainees continue to work on Sim Sets
Day 2	8:00	SAMPLE SET 3	12:30	SAMPLE SET 3	
Day 3	8:00	SAMPLE SET 3	12:30	SAMPLE SET 3 Sim Sets 6 & 7 reports due Sim Sets 8 & 11 assigned Sample Set 3 report due	Sample Set 4 consists of challenging samples such as: gum, cig butt, feces, etc.
Day 4	8:00	SAMPLE SET 4	12:30	SAMPLE SET 4	Staffing:
Day 5	8:00	SAMPLE SET 4	12:30	SAMPLE SET 4 Day 5 meeting	

Week 9: Forensic DNA Analysis Laboratory

Date	Time	Morning	Time	Afternoon	Comments
Day 1	8:00	8:00—Assessment Memo 8 due SAMPLE SET 4	12:30	SAMPLE SET 4	Trainees continue to work on Sim Sets
Day 2	8:00	SAMPLE SET 4	12:30	SAMPLE SET 4	
Day 3	8:00	SAMPLE SET 4	12:30	SAMPLE SET 4	
Day 4	8:00	SAMPLE SET 4	12:30	Sim Sets 8 & 11 reports due Sim Sets 3 & 4 assigned Day 5 meeting Sample Set 4 report due	Staffing:
Day 5	8:00	DAY OFF	12:30	DAY OFF	

WEEK 10: Forensic DNA Analysis Laboratory

Date	Time	Morning	Time	Afternoon	Comments
Day 1	8:00	DAY OFF	12:30	DAY OFF	
Day 2	8:00	DAY OFF—Holiday	12:30	DAY OFF—Holiday	
Day 3	8:00	8:00—Assessment Memo 9 due Sim Sets 3 & 4 reports due Sim Sets 9 & 10 assigned SAMPLE SET 5	12:30	SAMPLE SET 5	Trainees continue to work on Sim Sets; time in the evenings may have to be used to complete the Sim Sets
Day 4	8:00	SAMPLE SET 5 Study time for quiz	12:30	SAMPLE SET 5	Sample Sets 5, 6 and the Comp Exam are mock cases, with scenarios, that include partial profiles and mixtures
Day 5	8:00	Quiz 3—Oral (CE, troubleshooting) SAMPLE SET 5	12:30	Quiz 3—Oral (CE, troubleshooting) Day 5 meeting SAMPLE SET 5	Staffing:

Week 11: Forensic DNA Analysis Laboratory

Date	Time	Morning	Time	Afternoon	Comments
Day 1	8:00	8:00—Assessment Memo 10—due SAMPLE SET 5	12:30	SAMPLE SET 5	
Day 2	8:00	SAMPLE SET 5	12:30	SAMPLE SET 5	Trainees continue to work on Sim Sets; time in the evenings may have to be used to complete the Sim Sets
Day 3	8:00	SAMPLE SET 5 Sample Set 5 report due Sim Sets 9 & 10 reports due Sim Sets12 & 13 assigned	12:30	SAMPLE SET 5	
Day 4	8:00	SAMPLE SET 6	12:30	SAMPLE SET 6	Staffing:
Day 5	8:00	SAMPLE SET 6	12:30	SAMPLE SET 6 Day 5 meeting	

WEEK 12: Forensic DNA Analysis Laboratory

Date	Time	Morning	Time	Afternoon	Comments
Day 1	8:00	8:00—Assessment Memo 11 due SAMPLE SET 6	12:30	SAMPLE SET 6	
Day 2	8:00	SAMPLE SET 6	12:30	SAMPLE SET 6	
Day 3	8:00	SAMPLE SET 6	12:30	SAMPLE SET 6	Staffing:
Day 4	8:00	SAMPLE SET 6		Sample Set 6 report due Day 5 meeting Sim Sets 12 & 13 reports due Sim Sets 5 & 15 assigned	
Day 5	8:00	DAY OFF	12:30	DAY OFF	

Week 13: Forensic DNA Analysis Laboratory

Date	Time	Morning	Time	Afternoon	Comments
Day 1	8:00	8:00—Assessment Memo 12 due COMPETENCY TEST	12:30	COMPETENCY TEST	The 7th Sample Set is the final Competency Exam. It will be analyzed from Extraction through the entire process. All procedures must be done independently by each trainee without assistance from any source. Two full weeks are allotted for the competency exam for this reason. Up until this point, the trainees often work together and batch their samples on the instruments, taking turns with independent setup. Staffing:
Day 2	8:00	COMPETENCY TEST	12:30	COMPETENCY TEST	
Day 3	8:00	COMPETENCY TEST Sim Sets 5 & 15 reports due Sim Sets X assigned	12:30	COMPETENCY TEST	
Day 4	8:00	COMPETENCY TEST		COMPETENCY TEST	
Day5	8:00	COMPETENCY TEST	12:30	COMPETENCY TEST Day 5 meeting	

Week 14: Forensic DNA Analysis Laboratory

Date	Time	Morning	Time	Afternoon	Comments
Day 1	8:00	8:00—Assessment Memo 13 due COMPETENCY TEST	12:30	COMPETENCY TEST	
Day 2	8:00	COMPETENCY TEST	12:30	COMPETENCY TEST	
Day 3	8:00	COMPETENCY TEST	12:30	COMPETENCY TEST	
Day 4	8:00	COMPETENCY TEST	12:30	Sim Set X report due COMPETENCY TEST report due	
Day 5	8:00	Oral Quiz—Stats, QC/QA	12:30	Oral Quiz—Stats, QC/QA Day 5 meeting	

Week 15: Forensic DNA Analysis Laboratory

Date	Time	Morning	Time	Afternoon	Comments
Day 1	8:00	8:00—Assessment Memo 14 due Sample/Sim Set completion and review	12:30	Sample/Sim Set completion and review	During this week the trainees are given time to wrap up all of their case file corrections and study for the final exam. Past trainees have expressed that this scheduling arrangement lessens their stress and allows them to focus on the upcoming moot court testimony.
Day 2	8:00	Sample/Sim Set completion and review	12:30	Sample/Sim Set completion and review	
Day 3	8:00	Study time for final exam	12:30	Study time for final exam	
Day 4	8:00	Questions & answers for final exam	12:30	Study time for final exam	
Day 5	8:00	Study time for final exam	12:30	Final Exam (12:00–4:00) Day 5 meeting	

Module 4 (Week 16): Moot Court Prep

Date	Time	Morning	Time	Afternoon	Comments
Day 1	8:00	8:00—Assessment Memo 15 due	12:30	Moot Court Case File review	
		Moot Court Preparation Lecture: Part 1			
Day 2	8:00	Lab cleanup	12:30	Practice session for Moot Court	
		Study Moot Court case file			
Day 3	8:00	Moot Court preparation discussion	12:30	Study Moot Court case file	Staffing:
		Study Moot Court case file			
Day 4	8:00	Pre-Trials	12:30	Pre-Trials	
Day 5	8:00	Pre-Trials	12:30	Pre-Trials	
				Day 5 meeting	

Week 17: Moot Court

Date	Time	Morning	Time	Afternoon	Comments
Day 1	8:00	DAY OFF—Holiday	12:30	DAY OFF—Holiday	
Day 2	8:00	8:00—Assessment Memo 16 due	12:30	Moot Court	
		Moot Court			
Day 3	8:00	Moot Court	12:30	Moot Court	
Day 4	8:00	Moot Court	12:30	Moot Court	Staffing:
Day 5	8:00	Completion of Training Binder including Institute staff signatures, completion certificates, receive moot court feedback & final exam grades. Class photo. Final meeting and farewells.	12:30	AFTERNOON OFF	

DNA Academy Student Metrics

Performance Metrics for Week

Sample Sets		
Sample Set #	Sample ID	Sample Name
	06TR00001	Bloodstain
	06TR00002	Bloodstain
	06TR00003	Bloodstain
1	06TR00004	Bloodstain
	06TR00005	Vaginal Swab
	06TR00006	Vaginal Swab
	06TR00007	Vaginal Swab
2	06TR00008	Vaginal Swab
	06TR00009	Vaginal Swab
	06TR00010	Vaginal Swab
	06TR00011	Vaginal Swab
3	06TR00012	Vaginal Swab
	06TR00013	Chewing gum

Performance Metrics for Week

	Sample Sets	
Sample Set #	Sample ID	Sample Name
	06TR00014	Fecal swab
	06TR00015	Licked envelopes
	06TR00016	Pulled hair root
4	06TR00017	Fingernail scrapings
	06TR00018	Suspect
	06TR00019	Victim
	06TR00020	Vaginal Swab
5	06TR00021	External Genital
	06TR00022	Victim
	06TR00023	Suspect
	06TR00024	Stain from Wall #1
6	06TR00025	Stain from Wall #2
	06TR00038	Suspect
	06TR00039	Victim
	06TR00040	Vaginal Swab—epi
10 Pre- extracted	06TR00041	Vaginal Swab—sperm
	06TR00042	External Genital—epi
	06TR00043	External Genital—sperm
	06TR00044	Victim
	06TR00045	Suspect
	06TR00046	Stain from wall #1
11 Pre- extracted	06TR00047	Stain from wall #2
	06TR00048	Suspect
	06TR00049	Victim
	06TR00050	Stain from victim shirt #1
12 Pre- extracted	06TR00051	Stain from victim shirt #2
	06TR00052	Victim
	06TR00053	Suspect
	06TR00054	Swab from stain on floor
13 Pre-extracted	06TR00055	Cig butt from ash tray
		Blood standard
		Blood standard
		Bloodstain from shirt
Competency Exam		Bloodstain from shirt

Instrument Usage

Real Time PCR	ABI 7500 usage
Amplification	ABI 9600/9700 usage
Capillary Electrophoresis	ABI 310 usage
	ABI 3130 usage

Simulated Case Files

Electronic case 1
Electronic case 2
Electronic case 3
Electronic case 4
Electronic case 5
Electronic case 6
Electronic case 7
Electronic case 8
Electronic case 9
Electronic case 10
Electronic case 11
Electronic case 12
Electronic case 13
Electronic case 14
Electronic case 15
Electronic case X EPG data is the same data used for moot court case file.
Electronic Cases Reports Completed and Reviewed (need 15)
Sample Set Reports Completed and Reviewed (includes comp exam)
Total Case Reports Completed and Reviewed

Institute Grading Metrics

Description	Points
Bio501	Molecular Biology and Forensic DNA Typing
Exam	50
HW Day 1	5
HW Day 2	5
HW Day 3	5
HW Day 4	5
HW Day 5	5
Participation	10
Memos/Attitude	15
Total	100
Bio 522	Forensic DNA Analysis Laboratory
Final Exam	25
Competency	35
Quiz I	2.5
Quiz II	2.5
Quiz III	2.5
Quiz IV	2.5

Memos/Attitude	10
Stats test	15
Moot Court	5
Total	100

Instrumentation Lectures

Students	Lecture
Student A	Biological Health & Safety
Student B	Biological Health & Safety
Student C	Biological Health & Safety
Student D	Biological Health &Safety
Student E	Biological Health & Safety
Student A	Real-Time PCR 7500
Student B	Real-Time PCR 7500
Student C	Real-Time PCR 7500
Student D	Real-Time PCR 7500
Student E	Real-Time PCR 7500
Student A	310 & 3130
Student B	310 & 3130
Student C	310 & 3130
Student D	310 & 3130
Student E	310 & 3130
Student A	CODIS & PopStats
Student B	CODIS & PopStats
Student C	CODIS & PopStats
Student D	CODIS & PopStats
Student E	CODIS & PopStats
Student A	GeneMapper v 3.2.1
Student B	GeneMapper v 3.2.1
Student C	GeneMapper v 3.2.1
Student D	GeneMapper v 3.2.1
Student E	GeneMapper v 3.2.1
Student A	Mixtures & Interpretation
Student B	Mixtures & Interpretation
Student C	Mixtures & Interpretation
Student D	Mixtures & Interpretation
Student E	Mixtures & Interpretation

Student A	Moot Court Prep
Student B	Moot Court Prep
Student C	Moot Court Prep
Student D	Moot Court Prep
Student E	Moot Court Prep

Dedicated Facilities

Dedicated laboratory training facilities are essential and critical components of a successful program. Training laboratories can also be the largest expenditure of the program or even be a showstopper preventing the program altogether. The best and least expensive alternative is to renovate existing laboratory space. The Northeast Regional Forensic Institute located several laboratories that were used by researchers that have been relocated to new facilities. Although outdated and in need of renovation, the space was collocated with lecture and administrative areas providing a one-stop shop for all students. Renovations included electrical, water, storage, and replacing bench tops with Formica instead of expensive traditional soapstone. The institute laboratories were also shared with graduate students from the Forensic molecular biology graduate program and the traditional molecular biology graduate program. Instrumentation, supplies, and competency/validation materials were also shared among forensic and non-forensic students and university researchers. The chemistry department also developed an undergraduate and graduate program in the same vision as the institute biology program. A chemistry instrumentation laboratory was fully equipped with instruments that were being upgraded and replaced at the NYSP Forensic Investigation Center. These types of collaborations between the academic community and practitioner public service forensic laboratories would not have been possible without joint agency commitment, leadership, and memorandums of understanding between all associated agencies.

The major outcomes of the program are student graduates. Graduates go on to careers in forensic laboratories or pursue advanced degrees in science or law. Following are two student self-proclamations on their experience obtained from the University at Albany Graduate Program in Forensic Molecular Biology and the Northeast Regional Forensic Institute.

Two Student Cameos

Ashley Hart, Law

While in my senior year at Vassar College, I was looking to enhance my bachelor's degree in biochemistry with a master's degree. Unsure of my future career path but knowing I enjoyed learning about forensic science and forensic anthropology while in high school, I applied to master's degree programs in forensic science. The focus on molecular biology, real lab work on simulated forensic samples, and the opportunity to work in the field in an internship were factors that attracted me to the University at Albany Forensic Molecular Biology program.

Entrance into the Forensic Molecular Biology program (or as graduates fondly call it, the FMB program) was straightforward but competitive. The application consisted of having a competitive undergraduate GPA in biological science with prerequisite courses, a competitive GRE score, and an essay explaining an interest in forensics in general and the FMB program in particular. When I was accepted into the program, and decided to attend, I was warmly greeted by Dr. Don Orokos, director of the FMB program. Dr. Orokos took me on a tour of the campus and forensic facilities and was very welcoming as he introduced me to current FMB students.

I wanted to increase my involvement in the university through a work-study program so Dr. Orokos introduced me to Mark Dale, director of the Northeast Regional Forensic Institute (NERFI). They informed me of an opening for a student assistant at NERFI and I began working in an administrative assistant role. Because I had a little experience extracting DNA in undergraduate labs, I soon entered the NERFI lab to get hands-on experience analyzing mock forensic samples and the DNA profiles from those samples.

As a student assistant at NERFI, I prepared mock forensic samples and observed the training of Police Department Forensic Investigation Center forensic analysts. Later, after graduating from the FMB program, I became a lecturer in laboratory procedures and techniques, and had firsthand experience actually teaching the forensic analysts. Later still, while continuing my education, I continued to work as a senior research support specialist, performing analysis and quality control of the mock forensic samples used in various testing scenarios for a variety of scientists. I cannot think of a place other than NERFI where I could have gained that much thorough, hands-on, and real-world experience in a forensic lab.

While in my first semester of the FMB program, I took a course that changed my life and helped shape the direction of my career. Law and Science in Criminal Justice, taught by two skilled attorneys—Jim Acker and Steve Hogan—was my introduction to law and a glimpse of what it would be like to be a first-year law student, drafting briefs and being put on the hot seat. In this class, I could see a future where I combined my knowledge of science and law—potentially criminal law—and I started investigating law schools. The FMB class in Expert Witness Testimony intersected neatly with the training program at NERFI and continued to spark my interest in what I could do with my background in a law career. As part of their final exam, the NERFI trainees were put on the witness stand and examined as expert witnesses in forensic DNA analysis. As a NERFI employee, I was in the audience for a few mock testimonies, learning from the trainees, which helped me perform in the FMB program when we were asked to be mock expert witnesses ourselves. Moreover, NERFI and the FMB program introduced me to practicing attorneys who mentored the trainees and with whom I was able to network.

Fast-forward to today: I am currently an attorney working as a technology transfer professional. The skills I learned and connections I made while at the University at Albany and NERFI helped prepare me for my career. My technical background and lab work has helped instill confidence in the researchers with whom I work to commercialize their inventions. My connections to the legal community while at NERFI continue to be strong and support my development as an attorney. I am forever thankful and grateful for Mark Dale, Dr. Orokos, Steve Hogan, Jim Acker, and other professors and NERFI staff who initiated me into the world of forensics and were instrumental in supporting me and helping me get where I am today.

Jamie Belrose, Ph.D. Biology Student

After earning a bachelor's in forensic science, I possessed a basic understanding of several of the disciplines often utilized in casework: crime scene processing, fingerprint analysis, ballistics, drug chemistry, trace, biology, and criminal law. I also gained a solid foundation in the sciences, with courses such as histology, cell biology, physics, biochemistry, immunology, genetics, molecular biology, statistics, and analytical and instrumental chemistry. These courses facilitated my acceptance into SUNY Albany's forensic biology graduate program. It was here that I first met Dr. Donald Orokos, associate director of the forensic biology graduate program. Unbeknownst to him, he would serve as my supervisor, mentor, and friend long after I graduated.

After graduating with a master's of forensic science, a colleague mentioned that Mark Dale had recently established a forensic training facility at SUNY Albany named the Northeast Regional Forensic Institute (NERFI). NERFI was designed with one objective in mind: transform newly hired scientists into forensic DNA analysts in record time, using advanced techniques and state-of-the-art equipment. I had previously met Mr. Dale as an undergraduate intern at the New York State Police Forensic Investigation Center. I reached out to him and inquired about employment opportunities. He responded, and during our meeting Mr. Dale graciously offered me a position. Coincidentally, Dr. Orokos was now the associate director of NERFI as well.

NERFI afforded me the opportunity to meet a wide range of professionals from academia as well as the law enforcement community. NERFI had a continuous stream of renowned professionals, including Dr. Doug Lucas, Dr. George Carmody, Steve Hogan, Attorney Robert Prosecutori, Attorney Paul Kline, Attorney Patricia DeAngelis, Judge John Bailey, Lucy Davis, Karolyn Tontarski,

Andrew Wist, Dr. Carl Selavka, Joanne Sgueglia, Dr. Charlotte Word, Jacki Higgins, Margaret Terrill, NYSP Sr. Investigator Ron Stevens, and NYSP Sr. Investigator John Carey. We interacted with forensic professionals nationwide at a number of crime labs. We had exhibit booths at annual conferences and traveled to a number of crime labs offering on-site training and workshops. While at NERFI, I wore a number of proverbial hats: teaching, management, finance, and marketing. The professional experiences afforded to me while at NERFI are immeasurable.

I enjoyed learning the science and teaching a great deal, always meeting new people, watching academy group dynamics unfold, accommodating different styles of learning, taking in different cultures (i.e., East Coast versus West Coast and North versus South). The staff at NERFI was a tight-knit group; always working together as a team to accomplish a myriad of tasks. But, I enjoyed teaching the most. The students at NERFI were very enthusiastic and gifted. It is very gratifying to help people help themselves and achieve goals they once thought unattainable. I enjoyed motivating people and giving them confidence in themselves. But, sadly, all good things must come to an end. For some time I had been considering pursuing a Ph.D. in biology.

I am currently a third-year doctorate student in the molecular, cellular, developmental and neural biology program at SUNY Albany (where Dr. Orokos is still my friend and mentor 10 years later). Having reached this point, I'm confident that I am capable of much more. By joining the doctorate program, I hope to acquire an enhanced sense of self, strengthen my research abilities, refine my teaching style, and broaden my area of expertise. I am grateful to have had encouraging friends, colleagues, and mentors at NERFI. The relationships I built while there instilled in me confidence in my ability to move upward and overcome any challenge presented to me.

The Capstone: Testimony[*]

> fo·ren·sic (fə-rĕn'sĭk, -zĭk) Relating to, used in, or appropriate for courts of law or for public discussion or argumentation ... Relating to the use of science or technology in the investigation and establishment of facts or evidence in a court of law: *a forensic laboratory.* (*The American Heritage Dictionary of the English Language*, 4th ed.)

[*] From Dale, W. M., and Becker, W. S., 2007, *The Crime Scene: How Forensic Science Works.* New York: Kaplan.

This definition highlights two major roles of the forensic scientist. First, forensic scientists collect and analyze evidence in support of legal, primarily criminal investigations. Second, forensic scientists frequently appear as witnesses in court to present the conclusions derived from their analysis of that evidence. This chapter discusses aspects of both roles.

Legal Issues in the Gathering of Forensic Evidence

For the most part, determinations of the legality of searches that lead to forensic evidence lie outside the expertise of the forensic scientist. That said, in many jurisdictions forensic scientists directly engaged in the collection of evidence must have a thorough grounding in the legal requirements for conducting those searches. This section is not intended to represent a complete description of any area of law. Forensic scientists must discuss legal issues with local prosecutors or police officers trained in the collection of evidence.

The Fourth Amendment to the U.S. Constitution provides: "The right of the people to be secure in their persons, houses, papers, and effects, against unreasonable searches and seizures, shall not be violated, and no Warrants shall issue, but upon probable cause, supported by Oath or affirmation, and particularly describing the place to be searched, and the persons or things to be seized."

Over the years, the courts have intertwined the Amendment's two clauses. As a result, American courts presumptively require the issuance of a search warrant or some other form of court order prior to the seizure of evidence. In general, search of a suspect's home may only occur following the issuance of a search warrant.

The courts have recognized a number of exceptions to the requirement for a search warrant. These exceptions often come into play in criminal investigations, resulting in the seizure of evidence subject to forensic analysis. Exceptions include:

Search incident to arrest. Police may search lawfully arrested subjects and seize any evidence recovered from them or from their immediate area.

Consent. Authorities may search areas for which the owner has voluntarily consented to a search. The scope of the search is limited to the extent of the consent. Note that consent is very frequently the means by which evidence is secured from victims or cooperative witnesses.

Automobiles. Given the mobility of automobiles and the consequent likelihood of the destruction of evidence when a vehicle is allowed to leave a location, the courts have recognized a limited authority for law enforcement to search vehicles. An officer who has probable cause to believe that a vehicle contains evidence may search that vehicle as long as there is some likelihood that the vehicle may be removed during the delay necessary to obtain a search warrant. The timeframe for an automobile search is limited. Once a vehicle is reduced to police custody for any appreciable amount of time, law enforcement's ability to conduct a warrantless search evaporates.

Inventory. Containers that come into police possession may be inventoried pursuant to specific police department regulations. The purpose of the inventory is to protect the owner's property against loss, to protect the police against lawsuits resulting from the loss of that property, and protect the police against dangers, such as concealed bombs. An inventory may not be used as an excuse to conduct a search for evidence.

Exigent circumstances. If evidence may be destroyed due to an exigency, authorities may seize it without securing a warrant. Fleeing suspects who may destroy evidence in their possession may be pursued and that evidence may be secured, even in areas that would otherwise not be subject to search. The exigent circumstances exception frequently allows for the seizure of a suspect's blood, since biological processes may destroy evidence of crime, such as alcohol intoxication.

Plain view. Evidence inadvertently observed from a location where an investigator has a lawful presence may be seized. Investigators executing a search warrant for illegal drugs may seize weapons discovered in plain view, even though those weapons are not specified in the search warrant.

Courtroom Presentation

The courtroom represents the greatest difference between the forensic scientist and scientists in other fields. Whether the trier of fact is a jury or a trial judge sitting without a jury, the goal of the forensic scientist is to present the results of forensic analysis in a clear and accurate manner that does not imply bias in favor of either side. To that end, the forensic scientist must keep several things in mind.

Documentation. The rules concerning preservation of documentation and its disclosure among the parties to the case will vary by jurisdiction and by the nature of the case. Whatever those rules might be, the forensic scientist should keep thorough and accurate documentation and should preserve that documentation. Inaccurate or incomplete documentation is often the subject of cross-examination. In addition, lost or destroyed documentation may cause the trier of fact to speculate about what that documentation said.

Preparation. Prior to trial, the forensic scientist should thoroughly review all documentation concerning the scientific analysis that will be the subject of testimony. During that review, mental note should be taken of problems with the documentation, such as missing documentation, inaccuracies in the documentation, or anomalies in the analysis. The forensic scientist should exercise care in taking additional written notes on those issues, since in some jurisdictions the additional written notes may be subject to disclosure.

Before trial, the forensic scientist should meet with the prosecutor. Although many prosecutors strive to educate themselves, the forensic scientist is always in a better position to understand scientific material. As a result, the forensic scientist should prepare to educate the prosecutor about the analysis and results of forensic testing. The forensic scientist should highlight any discrepancies, errors, omissions, or testing anomalies shown in her documentation.

Testimony. The difference between the forensic scientist and other scientists is testimony. Critical issues related to courtroom testimony are discussed next.

Qualifications. The forensic scientist should prepare and regularly update her curriculum vitae. In addition, since expert credentials separate the forensic scientist from other witnesses, the forensic scientist should be thoroughly conversant in her own qualifications. Discussion of qualifications should be the forensic scientist's moment to shine, not an occasion for lapses of memory on the witness stand. The young forensic scientist should not be embarrassed by sparse qualifications but should emphasize her strong points. Areas of expert qualifications include education, employment history, publications, and previous testimony in court or before grand juries.

Conversational language. The goal of the forensic scientist is to convince the jury of the accuracy of scientific analysis. A jury is much more likely to believe testimony if it is presented in a conversational style. Scientific terms should be discarded in favor of equivalent, nonscientific explanations. For example, rather than the word "analysis" the forensic scientist could choose "testing." Instead of the word "reagents" the scientist can say "chemicals." Rather than the word "migrate" to describe electrophoresis, the scientist could use "travel" or "move."

During a mock trial exercise, a student forensic scientist described a process in which chemicals "get happy." While certainly conversational, this language does not accurately convey the nature of the analysis. Such inaccuracies should be avoided.

Reducing scientific terminology to conversational language can be difficult. The forensic scientist should consider how to describe the work to a friend or relative who is not involved in science. Conversational language does not mean inaccurate language. The forensic scientist should choose language that correctly conveys the nature and results of scientific testing.

Conversational analogies designed to illustrate the nature of scientific testing in layman's terms should be developed and rehearsed.

Simple analogies can be used to describe complex phenomena. For example, a conversational analogy could include boxcars to describe simple repeat sequences of STR loci. A tennis ball and a beach ball can illustrate the relative strengths of the walls of a sperm cell and an epithelial cell in a differential extraction.

Eye contact. Since the forensic scientist's goal is to convince the jury, she should look at the jury. Eye contact conveys sincerity. The experienced prosecutor will often help by positioning himself in the courtroom so that the forensic scientist witness is forced to look toward the jury. There is a happy medium between looking at the jury in response to every question and looking robotic. Thus, turning the head toward the jury to give a one-word answer can look stilted and should be reserved for longer explanations.

Direct and cross-examination. The party calling a witness conducts direct examination. Then the opposing party conducts cross-examination. The calling party may then ask questions on redirect examination, followed by re-cross-examination, and the process may continue in that fashion until both parties have completed examining the witness. There is a fundamental difference between the nature of direct examination, that is, examination conducted by the party calling a witness, and cross-examination conducted by the opposing party. Television courtroom dramas often show attorneys objecting that "counsel is leading the witness," without describing the concept of a leading question. A leading question is one that suggests the answer and may generally not be used by the party calling a witness. On the other hand, the party cross-examining a witness is permitted to use leading questions, and good cross-examiners will use them almost completely. Thus, for example, the question "What color was the traffic light?" is nonleading since it suggests no answer and the witness is free to provide the requested information. On the other hand, the question "The traffic light was red, right?" is leading since it clearly suggests the answer the examiner seeks. Leading questions must still be answered accurately, and the forensic scientist should not be taken in by the phrasing of the question. Note that nonleading does not necessarily mean broadly phrased. Questioners can ask nonleading questions that focus on specific facts. Some prosecutors will ask forensic scientists narrow questions, moving them through a direct examination in baby steps. Some prosecutors will ask very broad questions, and expect the forensic scientist to provide all the details. The forensic scientist should be prepared for both types of direct examination.

Refreshing recollection. No witness is required to completely remember every detail of the facts they are to testify about. Given the complexity of forensic science, it is likely that the forensic scientist witness will forget some detail of her analysis. If that happens, the forensic scientist may simply ask the court for permission to review her notes so that she can provide accurate testimony. Courts will frequently dispense with the requirement of asking for permission, but the forensic scientist should at first defer to the court for guidance. Of course, forensic scientists should thoroughly review the case before testifying to minimize the number of times needed to refresh her memory.

The 1993 United States Supreme Court decision in *Daubert vs. Dow Pharmaceuticals,* Inc. established new standards regarding scientific legitimacy and the limitations of professional scope with respect to the court system. The following are considered:

Has the scientific theory or technique been subjected to peer review and publication?

What is the known or potential error rate?

What is the expert's qualifications and stature in the scientific community?

Can the technique and its results be explained with sufficient clarity and simplicity so that the court and the jury can understand its plain meaning?

Visual aids. The forensic scientist may be called upon to prepare visual aids for the prosecutor. These visual aids include charts that illustrate the results of forensic testing. Presentation software, such as Microsoft PowerPoint, is often used to present material in court. Many forensic laboratories will have the facilities to prepare such courtroom presentations. The forensic scientist should be conversant in the various technologies in order to assist in the preparation of those visual aids.

Cross-examination with literature. Defense attorneys frequently use published writings as sources for cross-examination questions. Before an attorney can quote from a published writing, the expert witness must admit that the writing is authoritative. Once that admission is made, the expert witness may be cross-examined with any material in the writing. The forensic scientist should avoid admitting that a specific source is authoritative. At a minimum, the forensic scientist should be thoroughly conversant in the writing before making that admission.

Calculations. Forensic work often requires detailed numerical calculations. Attorneys often ask the forensic scientist to perform calculations on the witness stand. This should be avoided, since an inaccuracy can undermine the witness's credibility. If asked to perform calculations, the witness should defer, asking the court for a recess to perform calculations outside the jury's presence, using other resource material if available.

Q: Is there a minimum amount of experience the forensic scientist must have before she may testify in court?

A: No. The forensic scientist may be called to testify about the first case that she handled. She must be prepared to testify from the beginning of her career.

Q: Will the forensic scientist ever be called upon to prepare a search warrant?

A: Probably not. In general, prosecutors and police are trained to prepare search warrants, and the forensic scientist will not be required to do so. The forensic scientist may, however, be called upon to sign a sworn statement in support of a search warrant.

Q: Is there a minimum qualification level before a forensic scientist may testify?

A: Legally, no. As long as the forensic scientist is qualified to discuss the area, she may testify about it. There may be standards within the particular scientific field that must be met before the forensic scientist performs the work, but failure to meet those standards would not alone preclude the forensic scientist from testifying.

Major Academic and Institute Outcomes

Testimony

As we have emphasized many times, a forensic scientist must be a scientist before becoming a forensic scientist. However, one of the main differences between the two occupations is the forensic scientist must testify in courts of law the outcomes of their analyses and expert opinions. The ability to explain scientific terms and concepts to juries comprised of a varied academic and occupational backgrounds is a challenging and essential skill. Forensic scientists must practice and master the communication and understanding of their findings to the layman jury as it is the most unique and critical component of their professional occupation. We have selected two mock trial videos from over 100 mock trial videos as excellent examples of forensic scientists qualifying themselves as expert witnesses and undergoing direct and cross-examination questioning when presenting their scientific findings in a mock trial scenario. We provide the full DVD video recording, a transcribed text of the audio, and the mock trial scientific case file supporting the forensic report and testimony. We commend the students for a job well done and appreciate their willingness to share these mock trial exercises with our readers.

Mock Trial #1

Prosecutor: Ms. Forensic Science Student let me ask you to keep your voice up, okay, the jurors way down on this end have to be able to hear what you say, alright?

Forensic Science Student: OK.

Prosecutor: What do you do for a living?

Forensic Science Student: I'm a Criminalist at the ____ Police Dept.

Prosecutor: You're going to have to keep your voice up, I can barely hear you.

Forensic Science Student: I'm sorry. I'm a Criminalist at the ____ Police Dept.

Prosecutor: How long have you been doing that?

Forensic Science Student: Approximately one year.

Prosecutor: Can you describe for the members of the jury your education that qualifies you to be a Criminalist at the ____ Police Dept.?

Forensic Science Student: Yes, I have earned a Bachelor's of Science degree from the University of ____ in Chemistry, with a Biochemistry emphasis.

Prosecutor: Do you have any specific course work that's related to your role as a Criminalist at the ____ Police Dept.?

Forensic Science Student: Yes, I have taken a biochemical genetics class, also a molecular biology course was covered at my training at NERFI—that's the Northeast Regional Forensic Institute in Albany, NY, which was a 17-week DNA Academy. I have also taken biological statistics.

Prosecutor: You mentioned that you worked at the ____. How long have you been there?

Forensic Science Student: I have been there since November of 2007 as a Criminalist. Prior to that, I was an intern at the same lab.

Prosecutor: Do you have any other continuing education over and above your Bachelors of Science from USF?

Forensic Science Student: Yes, I have received extensive training in the laboratory of the ____ Police Dept. I have also completed several courses at the California Criminalists Institute, Applied Biosystems ... and, as I already mentioned, the 17-week DNA academy at NERFI.

Prosecutor: What is NERFI?

Forensic Science Student: NERFI is the Northeast Regional Forensic Institute in Albany, New York.

Prosecutor: So, what kind of training is that?

Forensic Science Student: It's an extensive DNA academy that covers ... it's specific to DNA analysis and includes laboratory work, lecture, and statistics courses.

Prosecutor: Do you have any other professional activities or any awards that are relevant to your role as a Criminalist at ___?

Forensic Science Student: I am currently an applicant for the American Academy of Forensic Sciences as well as the California Association of Criminalist.

Prosecutor: At this stage Your Honor I will offer Ms. Forensic Science Student's testimony as that of an expert in the area of forensic DNA analysis.

Judge: Defense Attorney, do you wish to object or voir dire the witness on her qualifications?

Defense Attorney: No judge, no objections.

Judge: Alright then, I will advise the jury that Ms. Forensic Science Student is to be treated as an expert witness.

Prosecutor: Ms. Forensic Science Student the ___ Police Dept. Laboratory, is that an accredited laboratory?

Forensic Science Student: Yes, it is, the lab ...

Prosecutor: What does it mean to be accredited?

Forensic Science Student: It means that the laboratory has been reviewed by the American Society of Crime Laboratory Directors, Laboratory Accreditation Board, and has met the federal standards and guidelines for a forensic laboratory.

Prosecutor: Are you familiar with the term proficiency testing?

Forensic Science Student: Yes, I am.

Prosecutor: What's that?

Forensic Science Student: A proficiency test is something that is required by the federal standards of quality assurance to be completed by the analyst, twice a year and it shows that the analyst is competent and is able to perform the DNA analysis and the test are of ... the test results are known and that they receive the correct results.

Prosecutor: Now, have you had proficiency testing?

Forensic Science Student: I have successfully completed a proficiency test for biochemical fluid identification.

Prosecutor: Are you familiar with the term competency testing?

Forensic Science Student: Yes, I have also successfully completed a competency test in the area of DNA analysis while at NERFI. A competency test is completed by an analyst at the completion of training or whenever a new method is used in a laboratory.

Prosecutor: Okay, tell us if you would please, what DNA is?

Forensic Science Student: DNA is a chemical found in the body, in every cell expect for red blood cells, because the DNA is located in the nucleus of a cell, and red blood cells don't have a nucleus. You inherit your DNA half from your mom and half from your dad making every individual's DNA unique—expect for identical twins. And DNA remains the same throughout one's entire life, so the day you were born, your DNA is the same today.

Prosecutor: Okay, you told us that DNA is unique between people except identical twins.

Forensic Science Student: Yes, that is correct.

Prosecutor: How does DNA compare from one cell in one person's body to another cell in the same person's body?

Forensic Science Student: DNA in all cells is the same, so if I received a skin sample, which is an epithelial cell sample, the DNA in that cell will be the same as a blood sample from someone.

Prosecutor: Have you ever heard the phrase forensic DNA analysis?

Forensic Science Student: Yes, I have.

Prosecutor: What's that?

Forensic Science Student: In forensics, it's the analysis of the DNA at 16 different fragments … excuse me, 16 different areas of the DNA that vary between individuals.

Prosecutor: OK, what are you doing, what are you doing with those 16 different areas?

Forensic Science Student: We are looking for variations between individuals at those areas.

Prosecutor: Are you familiar with the phrase short tandem repeat?

Forensic Science Student: Yes, I am.

Prosecutor: What does that mean?

Forensic Science Student: STRs …

Prosecutor: STR, I take it, is the abbreviation, right?

Forensic Science Student: Yes it is, short tandem repeats, which we refer to as STRs, are the repeats that we see at these locations and they vary between individuals.

Prosecutor: OK, is there an easy way for you to describe to us what an STR might look like?

Forensic Science Student: Yes, when we are analyzing the DNA, we are looking at the different number of repeats—as I said—so, to visualize it you can imagine a train and a train has a number of cars and they, are identical in length, so, the repeats that we are looking at are four bases long, so …

Prosecutor: A base? What's a base?

Forensic Science Student: The bases that we're looking at, are adenine, guanine, thymine, and cytosine … and abbreviated A, T, C, and G.

Prosecutor: OK, I take it from your description that a base is a chemical on the DNA molecule. Is that right?

Forensic Science Student: Yes, it is.

Prosecutor: Go ahead, I interrupted you.

Forensic Science Student: So we're looking at these bases and the number of repeats they have of these bases—so, AATG AATG—someone might have seven of those repeats and then another repeat of ten. So, if this was the train, you might have seven cars and ten cars and you're able to see the difference in the lengths of the segments, like the length of a train.

Prosecutor: Are all of the 16 different locations that you're looking at, are all of them these short tandem repeats that you've just described for us?

Forensic Science Student: No they're not.

Prosecutor: OK, which ones aren't, and what are they?

Forensic Science Student: The sex chromosome we're looking at is not a short tandem repeat.

Prosecutor: Okay, what is that?

Forensic Science Student: On the sex chromosome, it's the sex determining factor. So it tells us if the sample originated from a male or a female.

Prosecutor: That doesn't line up in this boxcar fashion that you've mentioned—that's a different portion of the DNA molecule that doesn't work that way. Is that right?

Forensic Science Student: Yes.

Prosecutor: Can you describe for us what the process is by which you perform DNA analyses?

Forensic Science Student: DNA analysis is performed in four steps. The first step is extraction, in order to analyze the DNA we first must expose it, so we need to open up the cell and the nucleus, and separate out the DNA from the rest of the cellular material. Once we've done that, we then quantitate it, which is the second step …

Prosecutor: OK, let me stop you there. What's the name of that process called, that you just mentioned?

Forensic Science Student: Extraction.

Prosecutor: There are different types of extractions, aren't there?

Forensic Science Student: Yes there are.

Prosecutor: Are you familiar with something known as a differential extraction?

Forensic Science Student: Yes, I am.

Prosecutor: What's that?

Forensic Science Student: A differential extraction is something that we perform in the lab when you have a mixture of two different cells; epithelial cells are commonly mixed with sperm cells when we receive a vaginal swab. So, in order to analyze it, our goal is to separate the sperm cells from the rest of the epithelial cells in that sample. So, during a differential extraction we end up with two separate tubes.

Prosecutor: One with sperm and one without ... Is that right?

Forensic Science Student: Yes, that is the goal.

Prosecutor: And you were going to go on to this a ... quantitation step that I cut you off on ... what's that?

Forensic Science Student: Quantitation is the second step and we are required to measure the amount of DNA in our sample. It's also very useful because we are targeting a specific amount in the next steps that we are going to use in the DNA analysis process. We need to know if we have enough DNA in our sample, or if we have a lot so we can use the amount of DNA that will help us analyze the sample clearly.

Prosecutor: What's the next step after extraction and quantification?

Forensic Science Student: The third step is amplification. We use a method called PCR, the polymerase chain reaction. This method makes many, many copies of the DNA fragments we have in our samples, of the areas that we are looking at, that vary between individuals.

Prosecutor: And then what's the next ... is there another step after the amplification?

Forensic Science Student: Yes, there is the fourth step. It is the final step, this is called capillary electrophoresis, it is a method used to separate and detect the DNA fragments. We are able to separate them based on size using an instrument called the 3130, and the samples are detected by a camera-like device, and the data is transferred into a graph that we analyze called an electropherogram, and this produces the DNA profile.

Prosecutor: Are there any controls that you use in your process at the ____ lab when performing this type of analysis?

Forensic Science Student: Yes, we use several controls.

Prosecutor: Such as?

Forensic Science Student: We use a positive amplification control, a negative amplification control, also a reagent blank from the extraction process.

Prosecutor: OK, let's take them one at a time. What's a positive control?

Forensic Science Student: A positive control is used during the amplification process, PCR, to ensure that the reaction is occurring successfully. It shows us that the thermal cycler—the instrument that we use to amplify the DNA—is working properly, that all the reagents were added, and that we had a successful amplification.

Prosecutor: OK, what is a negative control?

Forensic Science Student: A negative control for the amplification process is ensuring us that the reagents we're using are free of any human DNA.

Prosecutor: And you mentioned a third, a reagent blank ... what's that do?

Forensic Science Student: A reagent blank is used as a … starting from the extraction process is carried all the way through, just like all the samples, and it also ensures that all the reagents used from the extraction step on are free of any human DNA.

Prosecutor: Any other controls?

Forensic Science Student: No.

Prosecutor: Is there a review process in your lab, by which supervisors, or your superiors, check the accuracy of your work?

Forensic Science Student: Yes.

Prosecutor: How does that work?

Forensic Science Student: A technical review is performed on my casework before it is released. It is a review of the complete case file, including the notes, data, and report by another qualified analyst, or my Technical Leader … to ensure that all protocols and methods were used in the laboratory and were up to their standards.

Prosecutor: Alright, let's talk about this case. Now did there come a time when you received some samples in this case on which you performed forensic DNA analyses?

Forensic Science Student: Yes.

Prosecutor: What samples did you receive?

Forensic Science Student: Your Honor, may I refer to my case file?

Judge: Do you have any objections Mr. Defense Attorney of the witness referring to her file?

Defense Attorney: No, Your Honor.

Judge: Then you may refer.

Forensic Science Student: Thank you.

Forensic Science Student: I received item 62, which was a buccal swab from Monica Thompson, item 63 a buccal swab from Adam Jones, item 64 a vaginal swab collected from Monica Thompson, and a cutting from a T-shirt found in Adam Jones's apartment was item 65.

Prosecutor: OK, let me show you what we have labeled here as People's exhibit 97. Can you tell us what 97 is please?

Forensic Science Student: Yes, this is the item I received in the laboratory labeled item #65. It contains the shirt obtained from Adam Jones's apartment.

Prosecutor: OK, just looking at the envelope, can you tell … how did that envelope look when you received it?

Forensic Science Student: When I received it, it looked very similar to this minus the marking I made on the front, including the item number, date, and my initials, and case number. As well as this seal, I put there.

Prosecutor: Why did you put that seal there?

Forensic Science Student: After I opened it, I had to close the envelope.

Prosecutor: OK, so that end of the envelope, well the right-end as we look at it here, the right-end of the back, that was the original seal when you received that item—item 97?

Forensic Science Student: That is correct.

Prosecutor: And otherwise, as you are looking at it today, does it appear to be in the same condition, otherwise, as it was when you received it?

Forensic Science Student: Yes.

Prosecutor: Now if you would open up the envelope for us please. Now you've got a pair of rubber gloves up there, right?

Forensic Science Student: Yes, I do.

Prosecutor: She brought a knife too. So prepared …

Prosecutor: OK, you've got it open.

Forensic Science Student: Yes, I do.

Prosecutor: Can you take the contents out for us please?

Prosecutor: OK, what's inside?

Forensic Science Student: This is the T-shirt that I examined, item 65, and it also contains the extracts that I had made during my analysis.

Prosecutor: OK, now, you took some cuttings from that T-shirt, didn't you?

Forensic Science Student: Yes, I did.

Prosecutor: Are those on the T-shirt?

Forensic Science Student: Those are contained here in the envelopes along with the DNA extracts.

Prosecutor: But the T-shirt itself has those places cut, correct?

Forensic Science Student: Yes.

Prosecutor: The extract envelope is also sealed now, it that right?

Forensic Science Student: Yes, it is.

Prosecutor: How did it get in that condition?

Forensic Science Student: I sealed it, initialed and dated.

Prosecutor: Those items inside, the T-shirt, the extracts, that we've been discussing, do those appear to be the same as they were after you completed your analysis in this case?

Forensic Science Student: Yes they do.

Prosecutor: Anything appear different about them, from the way that they were back when you completed your analysis.

Forensic Science Student: Nope. They're the same.

Prosecutor: At this point Your Honor, I will offer People's number 97 into evidence please.

Judge: Any objections?

Defense Attorney: No, Your Honor.

Prosecutor: Now the analysis you performed on the items in exhibit 97, is that the same DNA analysis that you described a little while ago?

Forensic Science Student: Yes, except for the extraction process, I did not perform a differential as we had spoke about, but a simple organic extraction.

Prosecutor: OK. Did you use the same controls as you described a few minutes ago?

Forensic Science Student: Yes, I did.

Prosecutor: And was your work reviewed in the lab in connection with item 97, in the same manner that you described in general for the review process?

Forensic Science Student: Yes, it was.

Prosecutor: OK. Now there came a time after your analysis that you got some results, is that right?

Forensic Science Student: Yes.

Prosecutor: If you would for us, please, take a look at the chart there, People's exhibit number 98. Do you recognize 98?

Forensic Science Student: Yes, I do.

Prosecutor: What is it?

Forensic Science Student: It is the table I generated of my results.

Prosecutor: That's a blown up version of a table that's in your report—is that right?

Forensic Science Student: Yes.

Prosecutor: If you wouldn't mind, come on down off the stand a little bit for us.

Prosecutor: You've reviewed that chart before we came to court today, right?

Forensic Science Student: Yes, I have.

Prosecutor: And as you look at the chart can you tell the members of our jury, does it accurately reflect the results of your analysis in this case?

Forensic Science Student: It does.

Prosecutor: And would it help you in testifying before this jury and describing your results, if you were able to use that chart?

Forensic Science Student: Yes.

Prosecutor: At this stage Your Honor, I will offer 98 in evidence as a demonstrative aid, please.

Judge: Any objections?

Defense Attorney: No.

Judge: You may use the exhibit.

Prosecutor: Alright, describe for us what is going on in 98, what all of the various markings mean—if you would please.

Forensic Science Student: Sure, so this is my table. On the left here, these are my item numbers going down. And across the top, these are all the markers, the 16 markers that I test for.

Prosecutor: OK, let's talk about the markers, the 16 items that you test for. Some of them across the top are in the form of "D," then a number, "S," then a number. For example, first column on the left there … D8S1179. What does that mean? Why is that written that way?

Forensic Science Student: OK, so first, D8S1179 was the first marker we tested for … "D" stands for DNA, 8 is the chromosome number, which is the location, "S" is single copy, and 1179 is just a number that they assigned when it was discovered.

Prosecutor: Some … Oh no, I'm sorry—go ahead.

Forensic Science Student: There are also other ones that are not in this format, as you can see going across, we have one that is CSF, there is a TH01, and vWA—these are noncoding regions of genes that we look at and they have different names, for example, VWA is the "von Willebrand factor."

Prosecutor: What about amelogenin? What's that?

Forensic Science Student: As I spoke about earlier, this is the sex determining chromosome, the "X X" indicates a female, and "X Y" indicates a male.

Prosecutor: Alright, and you said down the left-hand side, that those are the items of evidence that you tested, right?

Forensic Science Student: Yes.

Prosecutor: Included there is the reagent blank that you talked about, is that right?

Forensic Science Student: Yes, those include all my controls used.

Prosecutor: All of the controls are there too?

Forensic Science Student: Yes, I also have a substrate control here.

Prosecutor: What's that mean, a substrate control?

Forensic Science Student: It was taken from the T-shirt to determine if there was any background or trace DNA on the T-shirt, which I concluded that there was not.

Prosecutor: OK, it was taken from what part of the T-shirt?

Forensic Science Student: Close to where the possible bloodstains were found.

Prosecutor: But outside those stains?

Forensic Science Student: Yes.

Prosecutor: Alright, and what about the numbers inside the chart, if we look at, let's take again for example D8S1179. There is a pair of numbers underneath that, in that column, what are those numbers about?

Forensic Science Student: These are the short tandem repeats we were talking about, the number of repeats. Monica Thompson, at D8, has a 12 comma 12—so that means that she inherited a 12 from her mom and a 12 from her dad. Adam Jones at that marker is a 13 comma 15, so he has two different repeats, he inherited one from his mom and one from his dad, and they were different. And this allows us to tell the difference between two individuals. And we look at these, not only at this marker, but all the way across.

Prosecutor: What does each number mean? 12 means what—in the context of the D8 marker under the Monica Jones buccal … I'm sorry, Monica Thompson buccal swab. What does 12 mean?

Forensic Science Student: It's the number of repeats you're seeing at that marker.

Prosecutor: Those boxcars you were talking about before, is that fair?

Forensic Science Student: Yes.

Prosecutor: Some of the locations have more than two numbers, right? For example, let's look at item 63, the buccal swab of Adam Jones and go way out to the D5S818 locus, what's going on there?

Forensic Science Student: Over here we have three numbers—a 10, a 12, and a 13—this is what we call a tri-allele, it's very rare and uncommon to see, but we have seen it in casework before, and it has been documented. It happens for a few different reasons, one of them being a mutation earlier on in development, and clearly in Adam Jones we are seeing this at his D5 marker.

Prosecutor: OK, let's also look, if we could, at item 64, the vaginal swab "EC." "EC" means what?

Forensic Science Student: That's the epithelial cell fraction, the skin cell fraction.

Prosecutor: There are more than two numbers in a lot of those boxes, what's happening there?

Forensic Science Student: Yes, item 64 was a vaginal swab sample, and I performed a differential extraction on, that's why we're seeing "64 EC" and "64 SP," for the epithelial cell fraction and the sperm cell fraction. We're seeing more than two at each marker, or at most markers, because this indicates a mixture because they were completely separated, which the goal of differential extraction is to completely separate, but there may be male epithelial cells in the epithelial cell fraction.

Prosecutor: OK, you can have a seat again, if you would please.

Prosecutor: Alright, given your results here Ms. Forensic Science Student, do you have an opinion to a reasonable degree of scientific certainty, whether the DNA profile that you developed from the sperm fraction of the vaginal swab. Can you tell us your opinion, whether that matches the DNA profile that you developed for the buccal swab of Adam Jones.

Forensic Science Student: The sperm fraction of the vaginal swab, I had one marker that had a third allele, which I marked inconclusive at TPOX—as you can see. So, the major profile detected in that sample is the same as item 63, the reference buccal swab from Adam Jones.

Prosecutor: OK, I guess I need to ask two questions. Buccal swab, what does that mean?

Forensic Science Student: A buccal swab is a swab from the inside of one's cheek.

Prosecutor: OK. And you said something about a major profile, what's that mean?

Forensic Science Student: Yes, a major profile is when you have a mixture and you can determine a major profile in that mixture, when the intensity of some peaks are much greater than the others.

Prosecutor: OK. So, explain to us now what happens at that TPOX location on the sperm fraction of the vaginal swab.

Forensic Science Student: I observed a smaller peak at TPOX, it was significantly less, so I was able to differentiate a major contributor, the 8,10 is from the major, and the smaller peak that I detected fell into my inconclusive range, which is between 50 and 75, so I marked it as inconclusive.

Prosecutor: Other than that location, what can you tell us about whether or not the sperm fraction of the vaginal swab—that profile—matches that of Adam Jones?

Forensic Science Student: It is a match.

Prosecutor: What is the significance of that match? The fact that those two profiles line up like that—what's the significance of that?

Prosecutor: Is there a way you can tell what the significance is, how likely those profiles are in the general population?

Forensic Science Student: Yes, I calculated the probability that you would see that profile in the population and the probability that a random, unrelated individual by chance would possess the same DNA profile as the major DNA profile detected in this sperm cell fraction is approximately 1 in 36.6 quadrillion, US Caucasians; 1 in 5.47 quadrillion, US African Americans; 1 in 616 quadrillion, for CA Hispanics; and 1 in 19 quadrillion for the general Asian population.

Prosecutor: OK. Give us a sense if you could please, of what those numbers mean. I mean, a quadrillion, the numbers you generated … can you give us a feel that we can all understand, about what a quadrillion means?

Forensic Science Student: A quadrillion is a really large number that has 15 zeros after it. To put it in perspective, the world population is 6 billion, so a billion has 9 zeros after it, so if you had 600 million worlds with the same number of people on those worlds—then you would see that profile once. That's how big a quadrillion is … 600 million worlds.

Prosecutor: Thank you. No other questions.

Cross-Examination

Defense Attorney: Good afternoon Ms. Forensic Science Student. You told this jury about certain calculations that you made with respect to the probability associated with this match that you indicated you found on the evidence and the sample provided by my client, Mr. Jones.

Forensic Science Student: Yes.

Defense Attorney: And I think you said there were something like … 200 million worlds … something to that effect … I didn't really get it all. But, it's a big number, right?

Forensic Science Student: Yes.

Defense Attorney: And I suppose the purpose of the up-shot of that testimony was that it is really, really unlikely that it could have come from anybody but my client, correct? That's the point of that number, right?

Forensic Science Student: No, I am not determining where that profile is coming from, I am stating how rare or common that ...

Defense Attorney: Let's be practical about it, the fact is that you give that number, and the suggestion is that it is *exceptionally* unlikely that any other human being in 200 million worlds could have contributed that particular sperm other than my client, Mr. Jones. Isn't that correct?

Forensic Science Student: No, I am stating how uncommon and rare that profile is.

Defense Attorney: Well, right. But, there's an inference that you're asking the jury to draw from that, correct?

Forensic Science Student: It's up to their interpretation.

Defense Attorney: Now, besides the match, that you claim you discovered from your scientific testing, there was also some evidence that didn't match, correct?

Forensic Science Student: Yes.

Defense Attorney: OK, what's the term that you use for an evidence sample that doesn't match the known sample?

Forensic Science Student: When an evidence sample does not match a known sample we exclude, it's an exclusion of the reference sample.

Defense Attorney: The person is excluded, meaning, you can say with utter certainty that that person did not contribute the DNA that you found, correct?

Forensic Science Student: Yes, that's correct.

Defense Attorney: Alright, and in fact with respect to ... if I could, may I borrow your laser pointer?

Forensic Science Student: Yes.

Defense Attorney: I'm going to point this bloodstain A from the T-shirt, you indicate that at D8 the genotype was 11,12—correct?

Forensic Science Student: Yes.

Defense Attorney: And with respect to Mr. Adam Jones, it was 13,15—correct?

Forensic Science Student: Yes.

Defense Attorney: But with Monica Thompson, she's a 12,12—right?

Forensic Science Student: Yes.

Defense Attorney: And the bloodstain was 11,12?

Forensic Science Student: Yes.

Defense Attorney: So essentially the difference of one number—12,12 versus 11,12—means that there's no way that she contributed that blood to that bloodstain, correct?

Forensic Science Student: Yes.

Defense Attorney: Right, one of those numbers out of all … those numbers, if one of those numbers is not accurate … if one of those numbers that you claim that you discovered in your testing … is incorrect, then all those other numbers, 112 quadrillion … quintillion … mean absolutely nothing, and it's zero, right?

Forensic Science Student: No, that's not correct.

Defense Attorney: Well, wait a minute. The fact is, that if one of those numbers is wrong on your testing, you associate with the evidence sample, if you're not accurate, if it's a 12,12 … instead of an 11,12 … then theoretically my client should be excluded from that evidence, correct?

Forensic Science Student: Are you referring to two different samples right now?

Defense Attorney: No, I'm saying … yes, I am talking about the evidence sample versus the known sample. If one of those numbers, across that board, 15 or 16 regions times 2, 32—if one of those numbers doesn't match my client's excluded, correct?

Forensic Science Student: The way we make exclusion, for example when we are looking at two single-source profiles, one difference between those two profiles is an exclusion … but, when you're looking at a mixture more interpretation goes into making an exclusion.

Defense Attorney: Well, OK, let's talk about mixtures. How long have you been doing this now?

Forensic Science Student: Approximately one year.

Defense Attorney: Approximately one year, and how many samples have you done?

Forensic Science Student: Sixty.

Defense Attorney: Sixty … sixty samples. My client is looking at life in prison and you've done sixty samples. Are you familiar with the Butler book?

Forensic Science Student: Yes, I am.

Defense Attorney: OK. And are you familiar, and I'm going to ask you agree or disagree with this particular statement: "Mixtures arise when two or more individuals contribute to the sample being tested. Mixtures can be challenging to detect and interpret without extensive experience and careful training."

Prosecutor: Objection … Your Honor.

Judge: Let's hear the question first and then I will rule on the objection. Go ahead Mr. Defense Attorney.

Defense Attorney: "Mixtures can be challenging to detect and interpret without extensive experience and careful training." Do you agree or disagree with that particular statement?

Forensic Science Student: I agree.

Prosecutor: An objection is forthcoming.

Judge: Objection is for foundation, overruled.

Defense Attorney: Now, as I indicated, if one of those numbers is wrong, if you're inaccurate on one of those numbers, in your testing ... then my client should be excluded, correct?

Forensic Science Student: When you're comparing single-source samples that is the case.

Defense Attorney: Well, wait a minute, the fact is you came in here notwithstanding the fact that was a mixture ... and testified that there was a major donor. Now, am I wrong in my understanding, that if you find a major contributor, then you treat it like a single-source sample, isn't that correct?

Forensic Science Student: That is correct.

Defense Attorney: So, the fact is that we're treating it like a single-source sample for your interpretation. So, again, the question is, if you get one of those numbers wrong, my client is excluded ... and if you're wrong, he spends the rest of his life in prison because of your mistake, correct?

Forensic Science Student: If the jury finds him guilty, yes.

Defense Attorney: Now let's review some of the process that you ... tell the jury exactly ... you've heard the term "DNA fingerprinting" before, correct?

Forensic Science Student: Yes.

Defense Attorney: OK ... and you know how fingerprinting works, right?

Forensic Science Student: Yes.

Defense Attorney: OK, you press down on the fingerprint, and you compare it against a latent print, and you take a magnifying glass, with your eyes, and you look at both sides to see if they match, correct?

Forensic Science Student: I haven't actually performed that, or have experience with that, but that is my understanding.

Defense Attorney: OK, did you actually compare the genetic DNA that you found, did you look at it with your eye and make a comparison to see if the DNA was the same?

Forensic Science Student: Using an electropherogram, yes I did.

Defense Attorney: Well ... no, no, no, no ... Did you actually look at the DNA to compare?

Forensic Science Student: The way we visualize DNA using an electropherogram, I did.

Defense Attorney: Whelp, alright, why do we just take a step back and say how this electropherogram business works, OK?

Forensic Science Student: OK.

Defense Attorney: I think you alluded to the 3130?

Forensic Science Student: Yes.

Defense Attorney: That's a machine, correct?

Forensic Science Student: Yes. That's an instrument we use during the last step of the DNA analysis process.

Defense Attorney: OK, so, you mix up this batch of DNA in the lab, and then you amplify it by putting it in this thermal cycler, so you make a billion copies of the DNA … and then you take a little bit of that mixture and you put it in this machine, correct?

Forensic Science Student: Yes.

Defense Attorney: And this machine sucks a little bit of the liquid out and sends it up a tube, correct?

Forensic Science Student: Yes, that's correct.

Defense Attorney: And then when it goes up this tube, eventually it gets sucked past this little glass window in the tube, right?

Forensic Science Student: It passes by a window that has a camera at it.

Defense Attorney: Right. How big is this window?

Forensic Science Student: It's …

Defense Attorney: Is it as big as that window over there?

Forensic Science Student: No, it's fairly small.

Defense Attorney: Fairly small? Like, as in, maybe a millimeter? Two millimeters?

Forensic Science Student: It would be less than a square centimeter.

Defense Attorney: OK, can you see the DNA whizzing by?

Forensic Science Student: The instrument visualizes the DNA passing by the window.

Defense Attorney: Wait a minute, the instrument doesn't have eyes. What do you mean the instrument visualizes it?

Forensic Science Student: Using the camera-like device that I spoke about.

Defense Attorney: Well the fact is, there's a laser beam that fires at this window and supposedly, it excites this fluorescent tag that's been attached to the DNA, when you were mixing it up in the lab, right?

Forensic Science Student: Yes, that's correct.

Defense Attorney: And then this window supposedly interprets this flashing light and tells you what the DNA profile is, right?

Forensic Science Student: The instrument is able to detect and visualize dyes that are attached to the DNA during the amplification process, and as the DNA passes by the detection window, it is excited by a laser, and the instrument is able to detect the different colors that are passing by that window.

Defense Attorney: Now how do you know that this even works?

Forensic Science Student: The instrument and the protocol have been validated in our lab, and many other laboratories across the country.

Defense Attorney: OK, let me ask you this. What's an allele call?

Forensic Science Student: An allele call is … an example of one would be any of the numbers on this chart. We detect the number of repeats.

Defense Attorney: Well *you* don't detect anything! The machine puts out a thing called an electropherogram, which is nothing more than a thing with peaks and marks on it. And then you look at that, and you use your judgment and decide … well, maybe that's a number on the thing, or it's something else, right?

Forensic Science Student: Like I said, the test and method have been validated and found to be accurate.

Defense Attorney: What's pull-up?

Forensic Science Student: Pull-up is something that occurs in the electropherogram, due to overlap of the dyes …

Defense Attorney: It looks like a peak though; it looks like a bump on the electropherogram, right?

Forensic Science Student: It is a peak that is observed in one color that originated in another color.

Defense Attorney: Whelp, regardless of where you say it originated, it's a peak, right? I mean this is what we're talking about. Why don't we—to give the jury some perspective—why don't we put one of these electropherograms up and you can tell them all about it.

Forensic Science Student: Sure.

Defense Attorney: Let me show what's been marked as Defendant's K for identification. Do you recognize that?

Forensic Science Student: Yes, I do.

Defense Attorney: That's a page from your report, is it not?

Forensic Science Student: Yes, it's page 56 of my report.

Defense Attorney: And does it fairly and accurately show page 56?

Forensic Science Student: Yes, it does.

Defense Attorney: OK. I'll offer Defendant's K for identification into the evidence.

Prosecutor: No objections.

Judge: OK. Admitted into evidence.

Prosecutor: 56, Mr. Defense Attorney?

Defense Attorney: Yes.

Defense Attorney: Now, if you could, could you tell the jury what this is along here, what is that? This line here, this squiggly line all along the bottom.

Forensic Science Student: That is data that is collected by the instrument, and we call it the baseline.

Defense Attorney: The baseline, correct?

Forensic Science Student: Um huh.

Defense Attorney: And then at some point the baseline goes up, right?

Forensic Science Student: Yes.

Defense Attorney: And those are called peaks, correct?

Forensic Science Student: Yes.

Defense Attorney: And when you see these peaks, there's something about them that supposedly tells you that there's DNA there, a particular allele, right? There's some information that you're supposed to glean from that?

Forensic Science Student: The instrument is detecting something at that space, but, like I said, there's overlap between the dyes. And what you're actually seeing here is overlap from orange into the yellow, which is consistent with the size standard.

Defense Attorney: What would an allele look like? Up and down, right? The same thing, a peak?

Forensic Science Student: An actual peak from a DNA would have a different shape to it.

Defense Attorney: Well, what's this business here (referring to the edits made on the electropherogram)?

Forensic Science Student: So, those two peaks at 300.00 and 339.92 they were called because they fell into the bins. The bins are ...

Defense Attorney: Well let's just stop right there. They were "called," meaning the machine identified them as alleles, correct? The software, the computer program that you rely on to do this. That program said, no there's some DNA here—that's an allele.

Forensic Science Student: The software detected a peak there, but it did not detect an allele. Both were marked OL, for "off ladder"... we use a ladder to determine ...

Defense Attorney: Well who marked it OL?

Forensic Science Student: The software did.

Defense Attorney: OK. And what did you do?

Forensic Science Student: I made the marking of PUO, which stands for "pull-up orange." And also, marked it as removed with the diagonal line through it.

Defense Attorney: And essentially what you did was, you edited out that thing which you determined might not be an allele, correct?

Forensic Science Student: I did edit out these two off ladder calls; it is part of the interpretation process.

Defense Attorney: But the fact is, that you have no way of actually knowing what that is, with your own eyes, you have to rely on some computer software to suggest to you what it might be, but you actually can't know for certain what that is.

Forensic Science Student: That is not correct. I could process the sample and interpret the sample without the software; it would just require a little more work. Using the ladders that we also ran ...

Defense Attorney: My client is on trial for his life, so I think maybe a little more work would be what you owe him.

Forensic Science Student: The software is set up so that it accurately sizes all of the alleles, and we set up the software to the right specifications so that every sample is analyzed the same way, and is validated.

Defense Attorney: OK, let me ask you this, as long as we're on the subject, that you set up the software the same way … if you could bear with me for a minute … tell the jury, what's a sizing standard?

Forensic Science Student: The size standard is run in the orange dye, that we just saw was being pulled-up into the yellow, and it is used to account for the variations from sample to sample, and run to run, because the fragments of DNA migrate through the capillary and it can vary slightly due to temperature variations in the room, so this accounts for every sample.

Defense Attorney: And so that sizing standard is pretty important, correct?

Forensic Science Student: Yes it is.

Defense Attorney: And in fact you cannot get an accurate result from a DNA test if the sizing standard is off, correct? Because if the sizing standard is off, what its doing is it's telling you that a 16 could be a 15, if the standard isn't accurate, correct? It throws the whole interpretation off.

Forensic Science Student: No, that's not correct. I think you're referring to the ladder. If the ladder was off then all of the alleles would not be called correctly.

Defense Attorney: Well the sizing standard is still going to indicate whether or not a peak is truly a peak, correct?

Forensic Science Student: No, the sizing standard does not determine if a peak is truly a peak.

Defense Attorney: OK, well what does the sizing standard do?

Forensic Science Student: As I stated, it accounts for temperature variation through the run.

Defense Attorney: Well, let me show you what has been marked as Defendant's L for identification. Do you recognize that?

Forensic Science Student: Yes I do.

Defense Attorney: What is that?

Forensic Science Student: It's page 52 of my report marked with my initials.

Defense Attorney: OK. And is that an accurate depiction of page 52?

Forensic Science Student: Yes, it is.

Defense Attorney: OK, and what happened with the sizing standard that you ran on that particular run? What happened?

Forensic Science Student: It sized according to standard.

Defense Attorney: OK, why did the machine not write in there 450 at the end?

Forensic Science Student: That was just a printing issue.

Defense Attorney: A printing issue? Were there any other printing issues on your electropherogram that would jeopardize my client's liberty for the next 25 years?

Forensic Science Student: No, the label that was not on this size standard was the 450 peak and the peak is still observed there, it's just that the label for that peak was cut off.

Defense Attorney: Now this process, besides the electropherogram, you use what's called a PCR process, correct?

Forensic Science Student: Yes, that's correct.

Defense Attorney: And it's polymerase chain reaction, correct?

Forensic Science Student: Yes.

Defense Attorney: And the polymerase chain reaction involves a catalyst that's derived from *Taq* polymerase, some organism that grows in hot springs, in volcanic springs, correct?

Forensic Science Student: Yes, that's correct.

Defense Attorney: OK, and it's sensitive to variations in heat, correct? Temperature?

Forensic Science Student: Yes.

Defense Attorney: OK, and what it does is it makes DNA, under the right conditions, essentially go wild, right? It just completely, copies itself over and over again, every time you heat it up the DNA copies itself, you cool it down, you heat it up and so it's 1, 2, 4, 8, 16, 32, 64, 128 … until you get 28 cycles, correct? That's a billion copies of DNA, right?

Forensic Science Student: That is a billion copies of DNA. The *Taq* though aids in the reaction by allowing it … the reaction won't start without a heat hold step, the whole reaction is heated to a very high temperature, for an 11-minute hold, and …

Defense Attorney: That denatures the DNA, right?

Forensic Science Student: It's denatured at the first step of the thermal cycling, I'm referring to the heat activation step of the *Taq*.

Defense Attorney: Well, regardless, the fact is that, it causes tiny, tiny, tiny amounts of DNA to become a lot of DNA, right?

Forensic Science Student: It aids in that process, yes.

Defense Attorney: Well that's the purpose of it, because you want to run a lot of DNA through that genetic analyzer with the window, and the laser beam, and the light, and the fluorescence, right?

Forensic Science Student: Yes.

Defense Attorney: You want to run a lot of that through there. So, if you start out with a little, you have to copy a lot, correct?

Forensic Science Student: Yes.

Defense Attorney: And, as a matter of fact, if one tiny, tiny, tiny, tiny bit of DNA, from some source other than the sample, manages to find its way in there and contaminate the sample, that tiny, tiny, tiny amount of DNA ends up in the sample that is run through the genetic analyzer, correct?

Forensic Science Student: Yes, that's correct.

Defense Attorney: It gets copied as well. Contamination is a serious issue with polymerase chain reaction, PCR process, isn't it?

Forensic Science Student: It is, but when you have such a small amount of DNA—which we will refer to as "trace DNA"—it will be at much less of a concentration, those peaks in the electropherogram will be very small compared to the actual sample that we are amplifying.

Defense Attorney: Well the fact is, Mr. Prosecutor asked you about positive controls and negative controls, all of which are designed to make sure that there's no contamination, correct?

Forensic Science Student: Yes, that is correct.

Defense Attorney: And there are certain protocols that you are supposed to follow, like not having the two samples, the evidence sample and the known samples, together, isn't that correct?

Forensic Science Student: Yes, that is correct. In our protocol there is one step during quantitation that we do process those samples together.

Defense Attorney: And as a matter of fact, in this particular case, those two samples existed together on the same tray at the same time, the known sample of DNA from my client, and the suspect's sample from the vaginal swab, isn't that correct?

Forensic Science Student: At which step are you referring to?

Defense Attorney: Whelp, I'm going to refer you to your organic extraction worksheet. Are you familiar with that?

Forensic Science Student: Your Honor, may I refer to my notes?

Judge: You may.

Forensic Science Student: Do you have the page number?

Defense Attorney: I'm going to wrap up, I don't have any further questions for this witness.

Critique of Student's Performance on the Stand

Defense Attorney Comments: I thought you did a very nice job. You stood your ground, which is good, that's exactly what you should do. I thought I was appropriately obnoxious, but not too over the top. You stood your ground very well. The only real criticism that I have is with—and this is just a matter of practice—you tend to concentrate a lot on the person that is examining you, so even on the direct, you really were fixed heavily on Mr. Prosecutor (he's a dashing young fellow—it's to be expected), but the fact is you have to bring the jury in, alright. The whole idea is that you're having a conversation and you're bringing them in—and you have to do that with your eyes. But otherwise, I thought you did a very nice job, your demeanor was appropriate, you were completely unflappable … maybe you smile a little bit too much—which that's okay, but you have to maintain a certain level of seriousness this is serious business. When someone says, hey my client's life is on the line …

Prosecutor: Someone's not going to say that in a real trial, they'll be shut down.

Judge: They'd be in trouble if they do.

Prosecutor: A lot of what he [the Defense Attorney] did would get shut down. I'm not defending you, this is an exercise, you have to defend yourself up there. What he said about eye contact is true, I'm standing over here (near the juror box) on purpose to give you the chance to glance over there a little bit more—work on that a little bit. A couple of things I noticed … a lot of um's and uh's, early on, but they disappeared about halfway through the direct … they were there at first … it's a discomfort thing and you seemed to get more comfortable up there as time went by. Wait for a ruling on objections, I'm screaming about foundation because he had, you have to say this book is authoritative before you can quote from it, OK … the judge overruled my objection, but I was hoping he would sustain it, and then you get say, no that's not authoritative.

Judge: In a real situation that probably would have happened, but had you been a real firefight.

Prosecutor: You answered the question before the judge made a ruling, I'm hoping for a ruling that says you don't have to in that form … but you've already answered the question, and the answer is out there. So, just wait for those rulings. We talked about compound questions, he [the Defense Attorney] had some doozies in there, I mean he had this question where the machine was doing this and you were looking at that … 12 parts to it … and you just answered it. Some of them you tried to break them down and answer all the parts, toward the end Defense Attorney was doing that. I would just say Mr. Defense Attorney, or counselor, there are several questions in there (normally the Prosecutor would be up demanding that he break it down, but if your Prosecutor is sleeping at the switch), I would just say something like, there are several questions in there, which would you like me to answer—and just sort of protect yourself that way. Your role is not to make conclusions about his specific guy, he was asking you about his client was going to go to prison for life, and you gave an answer—it depends on what the jury finds— I would claim that I know nothing about that, all I know is I analyzed evidence, I don't know what's at stake here, I really don't know those kinds of details—keep it away from his specific client, because you're really not talking about his specific client, you're talking about a piece of evidence. Good job otherwise, I thought.

Mock Trial #2

Defense Attorney: Your Honor, at this time the People call Forensic Scientist Student.

Judge: Okay Mr. Defense Attorney, please proceed with your case.

Defense Attorney: Could you please state your name for the jury, please?

Forensic Scientist Student: Forensic Scientist Student.

Defense Attorney: Ms. Forensic Scientist Student, where are you employed?

Forensic Scientist Student: I am employed at the ___ Police Department, Criminalistics Laboratory.

Defense Attorney: In what capacity, what do you do there?

Forensic Scientist Student: I am a Criminalist within the Forensic Biology Unit.

Defense Attorney: If you could please, tell the court and the jury, what are your duties, what do you do as a Criminalist in the biological sciences?

Forensic Scientist Student: As a Criminalist, I examine evidence for biological material. If biological material is identified, I will perform DNA analysis testing on that item.

Defense Attorney: Can I just stop you right there … you indicated you perform DNA testing on evidence. Tell the jury please, (1) what is DNA, and (2) what kind of tests you perform on this DNA?

Forensic Scientist Student: DNA is deoxyribonucleic acid, and it's a molecule that is found in every cell of the body—in the nucleus—except for red blood cell, red blood cells do not contain nuclei. And it's the genetic information that is passed on from one generation to the next, so the way a person obtains his or her DNA is from their parents; they get half from their mother and half from their father. And it's a very long molecule that has two strands, so it's a double-stranded molecule, and it's unique to each individual (except for identical twins).

Defense Attorney: And specifically, this "DNA" that's found in biological materials, what sort of "tests" do you perform?

Forensic Scientist Student: If biological material is detected from the item, I will first try to remove that DNA from the item, and that's called an extraction. And once we remove the DNA, what we want to obtain is a DNA profile for that item …

Defense Attorney: Now if you could, these are terms that people may not be familiar with, tell the jury what is a DNA profile?

Forensic Scientist Student: DNA as I mentioned is a very long molecule, and for the most part, it is the same in every individual, but there are certain locations on the DNA that differ between individuals … and these locations are what makes us different. So, with a DNA profile, we are looking at these specific locations—that we call STRs—and we are trying to determine the variations, what makes people different within these markers … and the entire makeup of all of these markers, is what is known as a DNA profile.

Defense Attorney: And once you have obtained a DNA profile, from the DNA within a particular item of evidence, what, if anything, do you do?

Forensic Scientist Student: Once the DNA profile is obtained from an evidence item, I will then compare it to a reference sample, a sample that came from a person—and is from a known source. And I will compare the two profiles.

Defense Attorney: To see if they match?

Forensic Scientist Student: To see if there is an inclusion or exclusion.

Defense Attorney: Now with respect to this DNA testing, this work that you do at the lab, do you have any particular education or training that allows you to do this work for the ___ Crime Lab?

Forensic Scientist Student: Yes, I do.

Defense Attorney: Okay, what is that?

Forensic Scientist Student: I received my Bachelor's of Science degree in Biology, with a concentration in systems physiology, and two minors, chemistry and justice studies, all obtained from San Jose State University. I also received in-house training at my laboratory, and I've attended several training courses in DNA analysis with CCI, which is the California Criminalistics Institute. And I have also attended a 17-week DNA academy at NERFI, which is the Northeast Regional Forensic Institute. And after having obtained my degree from San Jose University, I had worked as an intern at another laboratory performing the DNA analysis steps that I had performed on this case, and I also worked at that other laboratory, as a Laboratory Assistant.

Defense Attorney: Your Honor, at this time I would like to move to have the witness qualified as an expert in DNA testing.

Prosecutor: I object. I don't believe her qualifications are sufficient, given the testimony so far.

Judge: Do you wish to conduct voir dire on the witness, or do you wish that I rule on your objection from this point?

Prosecutor: I would like a ruling on my objection.

Judge: Approach the bench please.

(Communications at the bench that we are not privy to.)

Judge: I do not believe there's been an adequate foundation laid so far. I am going to sustain the objection, and I am not yet persuaded that Ms. Forensic Scientist Student is an expert.

Defense Attorney: Now, Ms. Forensic Scientist Student, if you could please, tell the court and the jury, how long have you been employed with the ___ Crime Lab?

Forensic Scientist Student: I have been employed there since December of 2007.

Defense Attorney: And in connection with your work at the crime lab, approximately how many samples have you tested to develop a DNA profile?

Forensic Scientist Student: Prior to working at the ___ Crime Lab, I have analyzed about 120 samples, prior to working there.

Defense Attorney: Okay, and since working there?

Forensic Scientist Student: Since working there, I have analyzed an additional 60 samples.

Defense Attorney: And with respect to that, was that under the immediate supervision of a forensic scientist with the ___ Crime Lab?

Forensic Scientist Student: No, it was at the 17-week DNA academy at NERFI.

Defense Attorney: Okay, for the purposes of this examination, you have been proficiency tested, correct?

Forensic Scientist Student: That is correct.

Defense Attorney: And did you pass your proficiency testing?

Forensic Scientist Student: I have to backtrack a little bit, I have taken a competency test and I did successfully pass that.

Defense Attorney: And have you been qualified as an expert in other courts in the state of California?

Forensic Scientist Student: Yes.

Judge: Alright Mr. Defense Attorney, the court is satisfied at this point that Ms. Forensic Scientist Student is an expert in the area of DNA forensic analysis—you may proceed with your examination.

Defense Attorney: Now, Ms. Forensic Scientist Student, in connection with your testimony here today, did there come a time when you had occasion to test certain items of evidence that were submitted to the ___ Crime Lab by the ___ Police Department?

Forensic Scientist Student: Yes.

Defense Attorney: And if you could, tell the court and the jury please, what did that evidence consist of?

Forensic Scientist Student: The evidence consisted of two reference samples, one that was identified to have come from Monica Thompson, and another reference sample that was identified to have come from Adam Jones. And two evidence samples, one was a vaginal swab, identified to have been obtained from Monica Thompson. And also a T-shirt with what appears to be bloodstain, obtained from Adam Jones's apartment.

Defense Attorney: Okay, now with respect to those items of evidence, did you ultimately have occasion to perform DNA testing on those items?

Forensic Scientist Student: Yes.

Defense Attorney: Okay, specifically, if you could, tell the jury please, what's actually involved in this DNA testing? Tell them the process, what do you do?

Forensic Scientist Student: DNA testing is a multistep process, and there are four steps. The first step is called an extraction and in this step I hope to remove the DNA from the evidence item. This includes adding all of these chemicals and trying to get the DNA out of the cell and out of the nucleus. Once the DNA is removed and is extracted, that means it is exposed and in its open form. And it's ready to be processed in the next step of DNA analysis, which is quantitation.

Defense Attorney: And what does that involve?

Forensic Scientist Student: Quantitation is a step we use to first determine if the DNA we detected is human DNA, and also estimate how much of that DNA is present in that sample.

Defense Attorney: And what's the next step in the process, after the extraction DNA and determining that it's human, and there's sufficient quantity ... what's the next step?

Forensic Scientist Student: So now we have an estimated amount of how much DNA is present in that sample, so now we want to amplify that DNA, and this is called amplification, so we're making millions and millions of copies, of these certain markers or locations that make us different between individuals. So we are only making many, many copies of those certain markers.

Defense Attorney: And why do you need to make millions of copies of the DNA?

Forensic Scientist Student: Well, the DNA is still present in a small amount, but we want to obtain an accurate DNA profile, and we do so by getting as much DNA as we can.

Defense Attorney: And what's the last step in the process?

Forensic Scientist Student: After we have amplified the DNA we put it through an instrument that will detect the size of fragments. DNA is made up of bases, and they are of different lengths, and these varying lengths are what makes us different from each other, the combination of these different fragment lengths. This instrument, called a genetic analyzer, will detect the different fragment lengths and it will output this information in a form known as an electropherogram.

Defense Attorney: Now, in connection with the evidence samples that were submitted to you, did you in fact perform this DNA testing on the vaginal swab that was submitted to the lab?

Forensic Scientist Student: Yes, I did.

Defense Attorney: Okay, and did you perform this DNA extraction process that you described to the jury?

Forensic Scientist Student: Yes, I did.

Defense Attorney: Okay, and did you perform a particular type of extraction with respect to the vaginal swab.

Forensic Scientist Student: Yes, I did. It's a different extraction; it's called a differential extraction.

Defense Attorney: Why do you perform a differential extraction on the vaginal swab?

Forensic Scientist Student: The vaginal swab is what we call an "intimate sample," so there are what's called epithelial cells—which are skin cells—and there are another type of cells called sperm cells for this sample. So, what we wanted to do is separate the different cells, and obtain two separate DNA profiles: one from the epithelial cell fraction, and the other from the sperm cell fraction.

Defense Attorney: Now the epithelial cells—the skin cells—that presupposes that it came from the person that was actually swabbed?

Forensic Scientist Student: Yes.

Defense Attorney: And with the sperm cells you are looking for who the donor of the sperm cells was?

Forensic Scientist Student: Yes, who the donor of the sperm cells was.

Defense Attorney: How do you go about this process of differential extraction?

Forensic Scientist Student: The evidence item is sampled, we take an actual cutting, it is then placed in a tube and various chemicals are added to break open the epithelial cell. The reason why the sperm cells don't break open at this point is because they are a little hardier, meaning, during this first step only the DNA from the epithelial cells will be released. We actually physically separate the epithelial cell fraction from the sperm cell fraction. We do this by centrifuging the tube and pelleting the sperm at the very bottom of the tube. We then remove the liquid, which contains the epithelial cell DNA and place it in a separate tube. At this point we extract the DNA from the sperm cell pellet. And how we get to the DNA within the sperm cell is by adding an additional chemical, called dithiothreitol (otherwise known as DTT). And what we have at this point are two separate tubes: one with just epithelial cells and the other with just sperm cells.

Defense Attorney: So theoretically, the DNA from the sperm is in the one tube, and the DNA from any epithelial cells is in the other tube?

Forensic Scientist Student: That's correct.

Defense Attorney: And did you perform that test with respect to the vaginal swab?

Forensic Scientist Student: Yes, I did.

Defense Attorney: And were you able to extract DNA in connection with both of those, the epithelial and the sperm cell fraction?

Forensic Scientist Student: Yes I was.

Defense Attorney: And did you quantitate that DNA?

Forensic Scientist Student: Yes, I did.

Defense Attorney: And was it in fact human DNA?

Forensic Scientist Student: Yes it was.

Defense Attorney: And was there sufficient quantity of the sperm DNA to allow for testing?

Forensic Scientist Student: Yes there was.

Defense Attorney: Did you in fact go on to the next step, the amplification process?

Forensic Scientist Student: Yes I did continue the DNA analysis process to the amplification step.

Defense Attorney: Okay, if you could, describe how you actually go about amplifying or copying the DNA.

Forensic Scientist Student: So now the DNA is within the tubes and we know how much DNA is present. The DNA will now be subjected to different chemicals that will help amplify the specific fragments, and this is done by a cycling between high and low temperature, and there are 28 cycles where this occurs … and this all takes place in a thermal cycler, another instrument that we use in the laboratory. At a high temperature the small fragments of DNA will separate, then at lower temperatures even smaller pieces of DNA will sit-down (aneal) on these now separate fragments and they will target just the areas that we want to focus on, just the areas that differ between individuals. Once the small pieces of DNA sit-down (aneal) on the template DNA, the DNA to be amplified, the temperature will again increase and the small pieces of DNA will use the template DNA to create an identical copy. And this process, the heating and cooling, is repeated, and at the end we will have millions and millions of copies of the targeted regions.

Defense Attorney: You indicated that there are targeted regions of DNA. What are those targeted regions called?

Forensic Scientist Student: The targeted regions are STRs.

Defense Attorney: What does STR stand for?

Forensic Scientist Student: STR stands for short tandem repeat.

Defense Attorney: Could you explain to the jury what a short tandem repeat is?

Forensic Scientist Student: Short tandem repeats are the locations that differ between individuals, and as I mentioned before, DNA is made up of four bases: adenine, thymine, guanine, and cytosine (abbreviated A, T, G, and C) … and these four bases will repeat at these certain locations that we are looking at and amplifying. So the number of short tandem repeats, they repeat adjacent to each other, the number of repeats is what differs between individuals. So there can be A-T-C-G, A-T-G-C that can repeat 10 times for one person, and 15 times for another person. So that's where we differ.

Defense Attorney: So you're actually counting the number of times a particular sequence of DNA repeats itself?

Forensic Scientist Student: Yes.

Defense Attorney: Along a certain section of DNA?

Forensic Scientist Student: Along a certain section, that's correct.

Defense Attorney: And in connection with your testing here of the vaginal swab, did you amplify the epithelial fraction of that sample as well as the sperm fraction of that sample?

Forensic Scientist Student: Yes, I did.

Defense Attorney: And did you subject both of those samples to that last testing that you described—the genetic analyzer?

Forensic Scientist Student: Yes, I did.

Defense Attorney: And were you able to develop a DNA profile with respect to both of those items of evidence?

Forensic Scientist Student: Yes, I was.

Defense Attorney: In connection with the testing that you performed, did there come a time when you had occasion to test a certain T-shirt that was submitted to the ___ Crime Lab?

Forensic Scientist Student: Yes.

Defense Attorney: And let me show you what's been marked as People's exhibit #55 for identification; I want to look at that outside of that, do you recognize that?

Forensic Scientist Student: Yes, I do.

Defense Attorney: Okay, and what is that item?

Forensic Scientist Student: This is item 69, and this was the T-shirt that was identified to have been obtained from the apartment of Adam Jones.

Defense Attorney: Okay, and if you could, I'm going to ask you to open that bag up—it's sealed, correct?

Forensic Scientist Student: It is sealed, yes.

Defense Attorney: I want you to open that bag, and if you could, look inside and tell the jury what's inside that bag?

Defense Attorney: What is contained within that item?

Forensic Scientist Student: On this item there appears to be a bloodstain.

Defense Attorney: On the T-shirt? And do you recognize that item as the T-shirt you tested?

Forensic Scientist Student: Yes.

Defense Attorney: And does it appear to be in the same, or substantially the same, condition as it was when you first obtained it from the evidence receiving vault?

Forensic Scientist Student: No. I had sampled the item, so there is a cutting taken from the item.

Defense Attorney: Okay, so there is actually a piece of the cloth that has been cut out of there?

Forensic Scientist Student: That's correct.

Defense Attorney: Other than that, does that appear to be in the same, or substantially the same, condition as it was when you recovered it?

Forensic Scientist Student: Other than that, yes.

Defense Attorney: And the other item contained within the bag?

Forensic Scientist Student: These are the extracts, or the samples, that I generated from this item.

Defense Attorney: And do they appear to be in the same, or substantially the same, condition as they were at the time that you generated them?

Forensic Scientist Student: Yes.

Defense Attorney: Alright, at this time I'll offer People's 55 for identification into the evidence.

Judge: Received into evidence without an objection.

Defense Attorney: Now with respect to People's #55, did there come a time when you actually tested the bloodstained cutting that you got from that item?

Forensic Scientist Student: Yes.

Defense Attorney: And did you subject that to the extraction, quantification, amplification process?

Forensic Scientist Student: Yes.

Defense Attorney: And were you able to develop a DNA profile from the bloodstain contained on the cutting from People's 55?

Forensic Scientist Student: Yes, I was.

Defense Attorney: Now with respect to the other items that were submitted to you, you indicated previously that there were submitted two known samples from individuals?

Forensic Scientist Student: Yes, that's correct.

Defense Attorney: The one sample consisting of what?

Forensic Scientist Student: One sample was identified to be a blood reference from Adam Jones, and the other sample was identified to be a buccal reference obtained from Monica Thompson.

Defense Attorney: Or was it the other way around?

Forensic Scientist Student: No, that's the way…

Defense Attorney: Huh…?

Forensic Scientist Student: Nope, that's the way.

Defense Attorney: And with respect to those items, did you have occasion to subject both of those to this DNA testing that you described?

Forensic Scientist Student: Yes.

Defense Attorney: And were you able to develop a DNA profile from the known sample from Adam Jones?

Forensic Scientist Student: Yes.

Defense Attorney: And were you able to develop a DNA profile from the known sample from Monica Thompson?

Forensic Scientist Student: Yes.

Defense Attorney: Now, with respect to those items … well let me ask you this, in connection with your testing, which items were tested first at the lab?

Forensic Scientist Student: During my testing, the evidence items were tested first.

Defense Attorney: So you do the evidence testing first and after you have developed a profile, you go and test the known samples?

Forensic Scientist Student: That's correct.

Defense Attorney: And did you generate a report detailing your findings with respect to the testing that you performed?

Forensic Scientist Student: That is correct, yes I did.

Defense Attorney: Now let me show you what has been marked as People's exhibit number 56 for identification. Could you tell the court and the jury what that is?

Forensic Scientist Student: That is a page out of the report that I generated.

Defense Attorney: This is a chart indicating your findings from your report.

Forensic Scientist Student: That is correct.

Defense Attorney: And does it fairly and accurately show the findings of the testing that you performed?

Forensic Scientist Student: Yes, it does.

Defense Attorney: And do you believe, or could you tell the jury and the court, would this chart aid you in explaining your testimony to the jury?

Forensic Scientist Student: Yes it will.

Defense Attorney: Your Honor, at this time I would like to offer People's 56 for identification into evidence as People's 56 as a demonstrative aid.

Prosecutor: Objection.

Judge: Alright you may proceed then to use the demonstrative exhibit.

Defense Attorney: Your Honor, I'm going to ask if the witness could be allowed to come off the stand and explain some of her findings to the jury using the chart.

Judge: OK.

Defense Attorney: Now Ms. Forensic Scientist Student, if you could, tell the jury what is that chart? What does it consist of?

Forensic Scientist Student: Here on the left of the chart are the items that I performed the DNA analysis process on. Items 68 and 69 are the two evidence items, you'll see here 68EC, for epithelial fraction, and 68Sp, which is sperm cell fraction, so there are two tubes from item 68. And at the bottom there's the reference samples.

Defense Attorney: And just so that it's clear, those numbers, 65, 64, 63 … those are item numbers that were given to the exhibits or the evidence when it came to the lab, correct?

Forensic Scientist Student: That's correct.

Defense Attorney: Separate from the numbers that we're using here in court?

Forensic Scientist Student: Exactly.

Defense Attorney: Okay, so, 55 was the evidence number given in court here, the T-shirt, what number was that item given in the lab?

Forensic Scientist Student: 55, the T-shirt, was given item number 69 in the laboratory.

Defense Attorney: What was the number?

Forensic Scientist Student: 69.

Defense Attorney: So you have the item number on the left and a description of the item to the right (on the chart), and along the top row there are numbers ... and letters ... that don't really mean a whole lot to me, could you tell the jury what they actually need?

Forensic Scientist Student: These numbers and letters across the top are actually the markers that we are testing when we are performing the DNA analysis process, the amplification step is targeting these markers, and these are the areas that differ between individuals.

Defense Attorney: The different locations on the DNA molecule that you tested?

Forensic Scientist Student: That's correct.

Defense Attorney: What's the first one there?

Forensic Scientist Student: The first one that's listed is D8S1179.

Defense Attorney: What's that stand for? What's that really mean?

Forensic Scientist Student: The "D" stands for DNA, the "8" stands for the chromosome that this marker is found on, the "S" stands for single copy, and "1179" refers to the order in which it was discovered.

Defense Attorney: Now if you could, just stop for a moment ... so we're at this marker, area, location that you tested, and D8S ... whatever it is ... I want you to go down, and if you could, go to the reference sample for Monica Thompson on that chart and there are two numbers shown there, could you just tell the jury what those are?

Forensic Scientist Student: In the lab we use abbreviations, it's called D8 for short, is a reference sample from Monica Thompson, to the right of her name is her DNA profile. At D8, we see a 13 and 14, previously I mentioned short tandem repeats, in repeat sections within these locations, so she has a repeat of 13 on half of her DNA, and a repeat of 14 on the other half.

Defense Attorney: And why are those different?

Forensic Scientist Student: The reason why they're different, as I mentioned before, you get half of your DNA from your mother and the other half from your father, we can't tell which repeat she obtained from whom, but one parent gave her a 13 and the other of 14.

Defense Attorney: Okay, can you have the same number, or are they always different?

Forensic Scientist Student: It can be the same number, for instance, at the location of the D16 she has a 12,12, so she obtained both a 12 repeat from her mother, as well as a 12 repeat from her father.

Defense Attorney: Now, I want you to drop down one row on the chart and refer to the known sample from Mr. Adam Jones, were you able to develop a DNA profile with respect to Adam Jones?

Forensic Scientist Student: That's correct.

Defense Attorney: At that first marker, what was the DNA type that you developed at that location?

Forensic Scientist Student: At the first marker, D8, a 14,15 was seen for Adam Jones.

Defense Attorney: So, his marker at that location is different?

Forensic Scientist Student: That's correct.

Defense Attorney: And, if you could, tell the jury, ultimately, how many of those markers are used in determining if there is a DNA match?

Forensic Scientist Student: Ultimately, we look at every single marker. So, in this case, there are 16 markers that we are looking at, and we determine if it is a match to the unknown DNA profile.

Defense Attorney: Now, with respect to the sperm fraction of the vaginal swab, you were able to develop a DNA profile, correct?

Forensic Scientist Student: That is correct.

Defense Attorney: Did you compare the DNA profile from the sperm fraction against the known sample from Mr. Adam Jones?

Forensic Scientist Student: Yes, I did do the comparison.

Defense Attorney: Were they a match?

Forensic Scientist Student: No, they were not a match.

Defense Attorney: So what's the significance of that?

Forensic Scientist Student: In this case we can exclude Adam Jones as being the donor of the sperm fraction to the vaginal swab.

Defense Attorney: So he did not contribute that, correct?

Forensic Scientist Student: That is correct.

Defense Attorney: Did you have occasion to compare the DNA profile of the victim, Monica Thompson, against the DNA profile that you develop from the bloodstain on the T-shirt?

Forensic Scientist Student: Yes, I did do that comparison.

Defense Attorney: And what was the result of that comparison?

Forensic Scientist Student: The results of that comparison, between the bloodstain on the T-shirt and the reference sample from Monica Thompson, they appeared to be a match with the same DNA profile.

Defense Attorney: So the same DNA profile appears for the victim and from that of the bloodstain on the T-shirt found in the defendant's home?

Forensic Scientist Student: That is correct.

Defense Attorney: Now, if you could, did there come a point in time when you had occasion to calculate—in statistical terms—the frequency, or the likelihood, that an individual chosen at random, would have a

DNA profile that matched that which was found on the evidence sample located in the trash of the defendant's home, specifically the T-shirt?

Forensic Scientist Student: Yes.

Defense Attorney: Please describe the results of that calculation.

Forensic Scientist Student: Your Honor, may I please refer to my report?

Judge: Do you have any objections?

Prosecutor: No objection.

Judge: You may refer to your notes.

Forensic Scientist Student: For the bloodstained cutting from the T-shirt, the statistics that were generated were that a random, unrelated individual, by chance, would possess the same DNA profile as that detected from the bloodstained cutting of the T-shirt is approximately, 1 in 10.4 quintillion for U.S. Caucasians, 1 in 31.9 quintillion for U.S. African Americans, 1 in 765 quintillion for California Hispanics, and 1 in 178 quintillion for the general Asian population.

Defense Attorney: Now why is it that you have different numbers for different populations?

Forensic Scientist Student: These numbers were obtained from a table that contains statistical data, which looks at the frequency of, for instance, a 13 at one of the markers that we are testing. So data was generated by observing how often (aka frequency) this variation, 13, is seen at this particular marker—and within different populations these frequencies can vary. This can be due to the fact that like mates with like, creating variations between populations, but these variations in frequency have been noted and calculated, and the frequencies I used to calculate the statistics previously stated came from the various population data that were generated.

Defense Attorney: Now, just so that I'm clear, the chances of a match, a random match, between the blood on the evidence sample matching the victim Monica Thompson, is what?

Prosecutor: Objection! This is asking the answer Your Honor, come on!

Judge: Overruled.

Forensic Scientist Student: So for the DNA profile obtained from the bloodstained cutting, the probability that a random, unrelated individual, by chance, would possess the same DNA profile as that detected on the T-shirt is approximately, 1 in 10.4 quintillion for U.S. Caucasians, 1 in 31.9 quintillion for U.S. African Americans, 1 in 765 quintillion for California Hispanics, and 1 in 178 quintillion for the general Asian population.

Defense Attorney: I don't have any further questions of this witness.

Judge: Mr. Prosecutor, do you wish to cross-examine this witness?

Prosecutor: Yes, Your Honor.

Prosecutor: Ms. Forensic Scientist Student, I have to tell you, these statistics … they just fascinate me. Can I ask a couple of questions about your background, please? You mentioned that you have a degree from San Jose State, right?

Forensic Scientist Student: That's right.

Prosecutor: And part of your education involved courses in genetics?

Forensic Scientist Student: I did receive a course in general genetics.

Prosecutor: In "general" genetics … Are you familiar with something known as the DNA Advisory Board?

Forensic Scientist Student: Yes, I am.

Prosecutor: What's that?

Forensic Scientist Student: The DNA Advisory Board was a group that was organized—made to last only five years—to set standards for forensic laboratory.

Prosecutor: Basic standards for forensic laboratories, right? They made a bunch of recommendations or guidelines about how forensic laboratory should be run, right?

Forensic Scientist Student: That's right.

Prosecutor: And they made recommendations about how forensic analysts are supposed to be trained, right?

Forensic Scientist Student: That's right.

Prosecutor: Does your lab follow those recommendations?

Forensic Scientist Student: Yes, the lab does.

Prosecutor: Now, is it true the DNA Advisory Board, can we call it DAB for short?

Forensic Scientist Student: Yes.

Prosecutor: Now isn't it true that the DAB requires that you have a specific course in population genetics?

Forensic Scientist Student: No, the DAB requires that there is a course in genetics … I believe …

Prosecutor: You're familiar with this book right? *Forensic DNA Typing*, by Prof. John Butler?

Forensic Scientist Student: Yes, I am.

Prosecutor: You were trained on this, is that right?

Forensic Scientist Student: We refer to that from time-to-time, use it as reference material.

Prosecutor: You were trained using this book, right?

Forensic Scientist Student: I did read some parts of that book.

Prosecutor: During your training at the … what is it called, the Northeast Regional Forensic Institute, they trained you using this book, didn't they?

Forensic Scientist Student: They did obtain some information from that book, but all of my training is not based on the information in that book.

Judge: Ms. Forensic Scientist Student, do you consider that book an authoritative source?

Forensic Scientist Student: No, I do not.

Prosecutor: Well, at this stage in your career you don't have any reason to quibble with anything that Prof. Butler says, do you?

Forensic Scientist Student: There is some information that our lab and I do not agree with.

Prosecutor: Okay, let me ask you this question. I'm not asking you to call this an authority or not, if you could just take a glance at page 602 of Prof. Butler's book for me. Those are the DNA Advisory Board's standards, right? With respect to training of analysts, right?

Forensic Scientist Student: Yes.

Prosecutor: Just take a look at that. Okay, did you have a chance to look at that?

Forensic Scientist Student: Yes.

Prosecutor: Now, it lists genetics twice, doesn't it?

Forensic Scientist Student: It does have genetics in here twice.

Prosecutor: Okay, so it lists a general genetics course and it lists a genetics course that's specific to DNA, doesn't it?

Forensic Scientist Student: It does.

Prosecutor: And you have one genetics course in your background, is that right?

Forensic Scientist Student: Yes.

Prosecutor: Now you gave us a number, what was it … 7-ish quadrillion …

Defense Attorney: I believe it was quintillion.

Prosecutor: My apologies, 1 in 7-ish quintillion for one of the statistics you gave us, right?

Forensic Scientist Student: That's right.

Prosecutor: Everything you gave us was 1 in some-number quintillion depending on which population was involved in your database, right.

Forensic Scientist Student: That's right.

Prosecutor: That's a pretty big number, one in quintillion, isn't it?

Forensic Scientist Student: It is a very big number.

Prosecutor: You're not saying, I take it, that the DNA samples that you analyzed, in this case the bloody shirt, the sample that you analyzed from the bloody shirt, you're not saying that's my client's DNA, are you?

Forensic Scientist Student: That is not what I am saying.

Prosecutor: What are you saying?

Forensic Scientist Student: I'm saying that the probability a random, unrelated individual, by chance, will possess the same DNA profile as that detected on the bloodstained cutting from the shirt is approximately 1 in 10.4 quintillion for U.S. Caucasians, 1 in 31.9 quintillion …

Prosecutor: Well, okay, I heard all that … but you're not saying it's my client's DNA, are you?

Forensic Scientist Student: I'm not saying that.

Prosecutor: In fact, there could be more than one person that has that DNA profile, couldn't there?

Forensic Scientist Student: There's a probability that this profile is seen more than once in these numbers.

Prosecutor: Okay, so there could be a lot of people that have that profile.

Defense Attorney: Objection.

Judge: What's the basis of the objection?

Defense Attorney: Characterization.

Judge: Overruled, you may answer the question.

Prosecutor: There could be a lot of people that have that profile, right?

Forensic Scientist Student: It's very rare, this profile is rare …

Prosecutor: There could be a lot of people that have that profile.

Forensic Scientist Student: In these sized numbers, there could be.

Prosecutor: You're just saying it's really unlikely, right?

Forensic Scientist Student: I'm saying that the probability is unlikely.

Prosecutor: You said that these quintillion numbers are based on unrelated people, right?

Forensic Scientist Student: That's right.

Prosecutor: Do you know anything about my client's family?

Forensic Scientist Student: No I don't.

Prosecutor: Do you know anything about Ms. Thompson, the alleged victim in this case?

Forensic Scientist Student: I do not.

Prosecutor: Do you know whether they're related at all?

Forensic Scientist Student: No, I do not.

Prosecutor: Do you know whether my client has an identical twin?

Forensic Scientist Student: I do not know that information.

Prosecutor: And yet you can still make the statistical calculations without knowing anything about the relationship between these parties?

Forensic Scientist Student: That's correct.

Prosecutor: That's your testimony?

Forensic Scientist Student: Yes, I can.

Prosecutor: Do you know anything about my client's racial or ethnic background?

Forensic Scientist Student: No, I do not.

Prosecutor: And all your databases assume that there's a specific population involved, right?

Forensic Scientist Student: There are four different populations that we test.

Prosecutor: Sure, California Hispanics, African Americans, a couple others, right.

Forensic Scientist Student: That's correct.

Prosecutor: And those all assume a specific population was involved in that data, right?

Forensic Scientist Student: Can you rephrase the question, I'm not …

Prosecutor: Well, if the database is for California Hispanics, that database assumes that everyone contributing to the database was a California Hispanic, right?

Forensic Scientist Student: Yes.

Prosecutor: And for African Americans, for example, that database assumes that everyone contributing to that database was an African American, right?

Forensic Scientist Student: Right.

Prosecutor: Now, without knowing my client's ethnic or racial background at all, you can still make these determinations that he fits into this profile?

Forensic Scientist Student: Yes, they're based on statistical numbers.

Prosecutor: Statistics, again—okay! How big are the databases that you use? Well, let me back up a second here. Let's take a look at these two documents, these are Defendant's KKK and JJJ—for identification. Can you tell us what KKK and JJJ are?

Forensic Scientist Student: These are the articles where we obtain the data we use to generate our statistics.

Prosecutor: OK, so these statistics and these databases that you are talking about, the numbers for statistics are in those articles?

Forensic Scientist Student: Yes, these two articles.

Prosecutor: Those are the two articles that your lab uses to generate the statistics?

Forensic Scientist Student: Yes.

Prosecutor: And how many people were in the databases involved in KKK and JJJ?

Forensic Scientist Student: There were approximately 200 individuals that were sampled for these databases.

Prosecutor: 200!

Forensic Scientist Student: Approximately.

Prosecutor: How many people live in ___?

Forensic Scientist Student: I don't know that number off the top …

Prosecutor: 600,000-ish … would you quibble with me about that?

Forensic Scientist Student: Probably a little more, but …

Prosecutor: How many live in California, about 15 million?

Forensic Scientist Student: I can't tell you an exact number.

Prosecutor: Millions!

Forensic Scientist Student: Millions.

Prosecutor: About 300 million in the United States?

Forensic Scientist Student: I don't know that exact number either …

Prosecutor: Still, lots of millions, right?

Forensic Scientist Student: In the millions, I would agree.

Prosecutor: And your database involves 200 people?

Forensic Scientist Student: Approximately 200, yes.

Prosecutor: How old were you in the year 2000? Were you in high school, junior high school?

Forensic Scientist Student: I just graduated high school in 2000.

Prosecutor: Okay, so you remember the 2000 election.

Forensic Scientist Student: Yes.

Prosecutor: President Bush, now, former President Bush and Al Gore, remember that?

Forensic Scientist Student: I do remember that.

Prosecutor: Remember how the state of Florida changed hands three times within the space of one night?

Forensic Scientist Student: I don't know the exact details for that ...

Prosecutor: Remember how the news media in Florida went to Bush, then it went to Gore, then it went to Bush ... then nobody knew for months, remember that?

Forensic Scientist Student: That was an issue in that election, yes.

Prosecutor: The news media, their exit polling involves exactly the same type of statistics that you use in DNA analysis, don't they?

Forensic Scientist Student: No, it does not.

Prosecutor: Why not?

Forensic Scientist Student: The type of testing that we are doing it's not a survey, we're looking at genetic markers, we can't ask somebody ... "What do you think you have at the marker D8? What do you think you have at D21"... so, we don't know what they have, and they don't know what they, themselves, have.

Prosecutor: But in both cases, the news media polling and your analysis, you're taking a sample from a larger population and extrapolating as to what would happen in the rest of the population, right?

Forensic Scientist Student: In those terms, yes.

Prosecutor: How many people do the news media use to make their predication?

Forensic Scientist Student: I can't tell you that number ...

Prosecutor: They use about 1,200, don't they? In those kinds of polling samples, don't they?

Forensic Scientist Student: Possibly.

Prosecutor: And you use 200!

Forensic Scientist Student: Approximately 200.

Prosecutor: What's a sufficient sample size, in your database, given the specific locations on the DNA molecule that you look at?

Forensic Scientist Student: A sufficient sample size was created by expert statisticians who agree that a size of approximately 200 people is a sample, is sufficient to create the estimates/numbers that we are looking at.

Prosecutor: This multiple quintillion number that you gave us a little while ago, how did you arrive at that number?

Forensic Scientist Student: For the statistics that I generated for this DNA profile, we perform what is called a Random Match Probability. And on my chart I showed you that there are different variations at each marker, so we take the frequency of those variations at one marker, and we multiply it by the frequency of the variations seen at the next marker ... and we do this for all 13 markers, and that's how we generated the random match probability.

(Displays chart from report on the projector screen.)

Prosecutor: This is the chart that came from your report, right?

(Shows Forensic Scientist Student her name/initials.)

Forensic Scientist Student: Yes.

Prosecutor: That's the chart that you prepared in connection with this case, right?

Forensic Scientist Student: That is the chart I prepared.

Prosecutor: And it shows for each particular location involved, it shows the likelihood of that combination of alleles appearing in the California Hispanic population, for example, or the general Asian population—right?

Forensic Scientist Student: That's right.

Prosecutor: And what do you do with those?

Forensic Scientist Student: On the California Hispanic side, those are the frequencies, the percentage of how often we would see this combination of, for example 15,17 at the D3 loci (which is the marker that we are testing) ... that's the frequency that we will see that combination in the population. So what we do is multiply the frequencies all along the loci and that's how we come up with the estimated frequency for this entire DNA profile seen in a population.

Prosecutor: And that number, way down at the bottom, say under California Hispanic, 7.6555 etc. E+20 ... that's the 7.6 quintillion number that you mentioned earlier, is that right?

Forensic Scientist Student: That's right.

Prosecutor: Is there some formula that you use to try and figure out from the genotype, the alleles on the left, to get to the number at the bottom? For example, California Hispanic, do you use some formula for that?

Forensic Scientist Student: There is a formula that we use to generate those numbers.

Prosecutor: Well, where's that formula come from?

Forensic Scientist Student: It's called the Hardy-Weinberg equilibrium formula.

Prosecutor: Okay, if we have time, we'll chat about the Hardy-Weinberg equilibrium formula. But, let me show you this first ...

(Puts the NRC II Recommendation 4.1, Random Match Probabilities, formulas for homozygote and heterozygote on the projector screen.)

Prosecutor: Take a look at those ... those are the formulas that you use to determine the number under, for example California Hispanic, the probability of a particular set of alleles at one location, the probability that that set of allele would occur at that location ... is that right?

Forensic Scientist Student: One of the formulas is the one we use.

Prosecutor: Which one?

Forensic Scientist Student: The homozygote formula, and for the heterozygote we do not include the "1-theta."

Prosecutor: Really, are you sure about that?

Forensic Scientist Student: I am almost sure ...

Prosecutor: Let me ask you this, if you're not sure, let me ask you to take a look at page 506 of Prof. Butler's book, correct me if I'm wrong, but you use in your lab the National Research Council Recommendation 4.1 in arriving at those calculations, right?

Forensic Scientist Student: Yes, we use the homozygote formula, under 4.1 from the NRC. And for the heterozygote formula, we use the 2PiPj.

Prosecutor: Well Prof. Butler indicates that the NRC recommendation is to use the formula I have on the board, doesn't it?

Forensic Scientist Student: I believe he does agree with that.

Prosecutor: He agrees with what?

Forensic Scientist Student: To use those two formulas.

Prosecutor: To use these two, right?

Forensic Scientist Student: Yeah.

Prosecutor: And he indicates that both of those are recommended by the NRC 4.1, right?

Forensic Scientist Student: Right.

Prosecutor: So which formulas do you use, the National Research Council's, or this other formula that you say has no 1-theta, on the heterozygote formula?

Forensic Scientist Student: The difference between the heterozygote formula that you have up there ...

Prosecutor: Which formula do you use?

Judge: Just answer the question.

Forensic Scientist Student: The 2PiPj formula.

Prosecutor: Not the one that Prof. Butler says is the one that the NRC recommends, is that right?

Forensic Scientist Student: That's right.

Prosecutor: Alright, now this whole thing that we have been talking about, where you're multiplying together probabilities across the different locations, that's called the product rule, right?

Forensic Scientist Student: Yes, that's the formula we use.

Prosecutor: You have to make several assumptions before you can use the product rule, right?

Forensic Scientist Student: Yes we do.

Prosecutor: What are those assumptions?

Forensic Scientist Student: The assumptions are that there is an infinite population ...

Prosecutor: An infinite population!?

Prosecutor: Okay, let me break them down for you. There are two assumptions you have to make, they're called independence assumptions, right?

Forensic Scientist Student: That is another assumption, yes.

Prosecutor: One of those independence assumptions is called linkage equilibrium, right?

Forensic Scientist Student: Right.

Prosecutor: What's that?

Forensic Scientist Student: The linkage equilibrium refers to how the different markers are linked, or not linked, we don't want them to be linked. So, for instance, there are two markers that are on the same chromosome (chromosome 5) but they are far enough apart on the chromosome that they are not linked when they are being passed down to the next generation. So they are independently linked, so the markers aren't passed down with each other, they are passed separately, the information at one marker is independent of what the other marker is doing and how it's being passed down.

Prosecutor: And that has to do with the physical location of marker/locus on the chromosomes, right?

Forensic Scientist Student: Yes.

Prosecutor: What's the other type of independence?

Forensic Scientist Student: That these markers are mutually exclusive events, either one occurs over the other.

Prosecutor: Okay, this is where I wanted to get into Hardy-Weinberg equilibrium, isn't that the other independence that you need to have before you can apply before the product rule?

Forensic Scientist Student: There are assumptions under Hardy-Weinberg that need to be met before you apply the product rule.

Prosecutor: Such as, as you said a minute ago, an infinite population, right?

Forensic Scientist Student: Right.

Prosecutor: Which we don't have.

Forensic Scientist Student: There is an infinite population of these markers.

Prosecutor: That's referring to the population of the earth, isn't it?

Forensic Scientist Student: For the infinite population?

Prosecutor: Yeah.

Forensic Scientist Student: No.

Prosecutor: Okay, let me ask you this. Is any population infinite?

Forensic Scientist Student: No.

Prosecutor: So then, by definition, you can't have an infinite population, right?

Forensic Scientist Student: I would say so.

Prosecutor: Okay, you would say that you cannot have an infinite population? Yes, or no? Well, let me put it this way, it's impossible to have an infinite population, right?

Forensic Scientist Student: Right.

Prosecutor: Hardy-Weinberg also assumes that there are no restrictions on mating between individuals, right?

Forensic Scientist Student: That's right.

Prosecutor: Well that's not true either, is it?

Forensic Scientist Student: It is true in a sense that people are not mating based on attributes such as, a 13,14 at marker D8.

Prosecutor: But society puts restrictions on mating all the time, doesn't it? Some groups only mate within themselves, right?

Forensic Scientist Student: That's right.

Prosecutor: So, somehow, we've got restrictions on mating all over the planet, don't we?

Forensic Scientist Student: In some sense, yes.

Prosecutor: The Hardy-Weinberg equilibrium assumes there are no mutations in the population over time, right?

Forensic Scientist Student: That's right.

Prosecutor: And that's not true either, is it?

Forensic Scientist Student: Mutations are rare.

Prosecutor: They happen …

Forensic Scientist Student: They do happen, yes.

Prosecutor: But Hardy-Weinberg requires that there be no mutations, right?

Forensic Scientist Student: That's right.

Prosecutor: Hardy-Weinberg equilibrium requires that there be no immigration or emigration from one location to another, right?

Forensic Scientist Student: That's right.

Prosecutor: And we know that's not true. Because there is immigration and emigration routinely around the world, isn't there?

Forensic Scientist Student: That's right.

Prosecutor: And among populations to …

Forensic Scientist Student: Yes.

Prosecutor: So those assumptions by Hardy-Weinberg don't really exist, right?

Forensic Scientist Student: The type of testing that we are doing …

Prosecutor: Those assumptions don't really exist, right.

Forensic Scientist Student: Right.

Prosecutor: So Hardy-Weinberg equilibrium doesn't exist, right?

Forensic Scientist Student: That's not right.

Prosecutor: Well, if the assumptions that it is based on are false, isn't the entire concept false?

Forensic Scientist Student: Not for the type of testing that we are performing.

Prosecutor: Well you just told me a minute ago that you had to have Hardy-Weinberg equilibrium in order for your product rule to work, right?

Forensic Scientist Student: Right.

Prosecutor: And now we have established that the assumptions of Hardy-Weinberg are wrong, right?

Forensic Scientist Student: No, not for the type of testing that we are performing.

Prosecutor: So what you told us before was a mistake? You don't need Hardy-Weinberg equilibrium for the type of testing you are performing ...

Forensic Scientist Student: No, I did not say that...

Prosecutor: Okay, this is a good place to let you off!

(*Applause.*)

Prosecutor: Are you alright?

Forensic Scientist Student: Yes!

Prosecutor: What happened up here?

(*Puts NRC II, Recommendation 4.1 up on the projector, from J. Butler,* Forensic DNA Typing, 2nd ed., *page 506.*)

Prosecutor: What happened with that? I didn't do that to you, I did not do that to you!

Forensic Scientist Student: Ummmm ...

Prosecutor: I didn't do that to you, somebody else did.

Forensic Scientist Student: Really...?

Prosecutor: Nobody here ... Butler's wrong!

Forensic Scientist Student: Ahhhhh.

Prosecutor: Whoever put that chart in the book got it wrong. He's wrong on the random match probabilities, he's wrong on the conditional match probabilities, the other formulas are wrong too. But, you did not bite, if you had bitten on those you'd been doing calculations up there, and you would've gotten that all wrong. They only would've been theta off, right, they wouldn't have been that far off, but they would've been wrong, and I would've been wondering why your computer got it wrong. So you were very wise not to bite on that.

Forensic Scientist Student: Okay.

Prosecutor: The lesson to be learned there is, you've already learned it, obviously, is don't let some defense lawyer hand you something, don't buy it hook, line, and sinker. You might have asked for this (NRC II), because they got it right—they wrote it! So that's the lesson to be learned there, just because a defense attorney hands you something doesn't mean it's right. A defense attorney could look at Butler, think he's right, crunch the numbers (which you would have done, if you had bitten on it), and they'd think you got it wrong. I think you did very well. There's very little I have to say. This statistics stuff you should really bone up on because many cases have DNA, and the defendant is cooked over here—he's got the bloody shirt from the dead victim in his garbage can and he's in big trouble ... and all the lawyer has to go back to are the statistics, because the science is so good and your lab has procedures that make it so clean ... I thought you handled yourself very well, I didn't notice any real slip-ups.

Defense Attorney: I also thought you did a great job. Your demeanor was excellent, very appropriate, and very professional. I thought your explanations were good, not overly scientific and very understandable. I think with time, when you become more relaxed, people are going to like you a lot, in terms of the way you present ... you have a nice smile, you come across appropriately and confident in your conclusions, you're solid with the science as far as I can tell. You stumbled a little bit on the STRs, you've got to explain it, you can fall into a trap ... it's like a box car ... well, no, it's not really anything like a box car ... but, how you ultimately do it is going to be up to you, just as long as you can come up with a readily, understandable explanation for what those numbers on the chart mean—because that's really what it's all about. Those numbers mean something to you, they probably mean more to you than to me—in terms of the science, but to the jury, it's a combination, as long as they feel that it's accurate then that's fine. If they have some sense of what it is you're actually measuring, then that's going to increase their comfort level, because what happens, invariably, particularly with any kind of scientific testimony, once somebody loses it, and they're not really following what you're saying, because it's over their head, they tend to shut down a little bit, and they wave the expert witness off.

I thought you did a nice job, you stumbled a little bit on the stats, but, it's clearly the hardest part to explain, but otherwise, I thought you did an excellent job!

Forensic Scientist Student: Thank you.

Prosecutor: Actually, if I could make two more comments. Eye contact, you were very good on the eye contact on the direct, but then on the cross, I stood way over here (away from the juror box), and any defense attorney would do the same to keep you from looking at the jury. You were sporadic in looking at the jury during the cross. Definitely any answer of any length, you want to speak to them, not to the defense attorney. In my mind there's a happy medium, I'm asking mostly leading yes/no questions, and you can't at every turn look at the jury to answer yes or no.

For both of you, in the future a defense attorney may ask you about the loci names that do not start with "D8...," some of the loci are within genes. Be sure to bone up on their location within the genes and the actual genes' names. And be sure to be clear about the fact that those locations are not able to tell us anything about those actual genes (noncoding regions).

References

American Society for Training and Development (ASTD). (2012). 2012 State of the Industry. Retrieved May 28, 2013, http://www.astd.org/Publications/Research-Reports/2012/2012-State-of-the-Industry.

American Society of Crime Laboratory Directors (ASCLD). (2007). ASCLD Resolution 07-0422-02. Retrieved May 2013 from http://www.ascld.org.

Becker, W. S., Dale, W., and Pavur Jr., E. J. (2010). Forensic science in transition: Critical leadership challenges. *Forensic Science Policy and Management* 1(4): 214–223.

Cascio, W. F., and Boudreau, John W. (2008). *Investing in People: Financial Impact of Human Resource Initiatives.* Upper Saddle River, NJ: Society for Human Resource Management.

Cornell University Law School. (n.d.). 28 CFR Part 28. Retrieved May 27, 2013, from http://www.law.cornell.edu/cfr/text/28/28.

Dale, W. M., and Becker, W. S. (2005). Managing intellectual capital. *Forensic Science Communications* 7(4).

Dale, W. M., and Becker, W. S. (2007). *The Crime Scene: How Forensic Science Works.* New York: Kaplan.

Deming, W. E. (1986). *Out of Crisis.* Cambridge: Massachussetts Institute of Technology.

Federal Bureau of Investigation. (2013). FBI Quality Assurance. Retrieved from http://www.fbi.gov/about-us/lab/biometric-analysis/codis/codis_quality.

Internal Revenue Service (IRS). (2013). IRS Publication 15a. Retrieved August 13, 2013, from http://www.irs.gov/pub/irs-pdf/p15a.pdf.

ISO/IEC 17025. (2005). General requirements for the competence of testing and calibration laboratories. Switzerland: ISO.

Kirk, P. L., and Thornton, J. I. (ed.) (1953/1974). *Crime Investigation*, 2nd ed. New York: John Wiley & Sons.

Maryland v. King, 12-207 (U. S. Supreme Court June 3, 2013).

National Academy of Sciences (NAS). (2009). *Strengthening Forensic Science in the United States: A Path Forward.* Washington, D.C.: National Academy Press.

National Institute of Justice (NIJ). (2004). Education and Training in Forensic Science.

U.S. Department of Labor. (2013). Natural Sciences Managers. Retrieved May 30, 2013, from: http://www.onetonline.org.

U.S. General Services Administration. (2013). GSA Per Diem Rates. Retrieved May 27, 2013, from http://www.gsa.gov/portal/content/104877?utm_source = OGP&utm_medium = print-radio&utm_term = perdiem&utm_campaign = shortcuts.

University at Albany. (2013a). Biology Master of Science in Forensic Biology. Retrieved May 29, 2103, from http://www.albany.edu/graduatebulletin/biology_master_science_forensic_biology.htm.

University at Albany. (2013b). Department of Chemistry Faculty Research. Retrieved August 17, 2013, http://www.albany.edu/chemistry/research.shtml.

University at Albany. (2013c). Forensic Biology M.S. Retrieved August 17, 2013, http://www.albany.edu/biology/4_bio_fmb-about.shtml.

Appendix 4A

Instructor: George Carmody, Ph.D.

Course: Population Statistics & Forensic DNA Analysis

Slide 1:

Dr. Carmody introduces himself and mentions his personal Web site.

Slide 2:

This 4-day course will cover probability statistics and population genetics. One of the important concepts that you will need to understand and know is that probability itself has certain conditions or assumptions, whenever you calculate a probability there are assumptions being made in order to be able to perform that calculation. When we use examples, such as: flipping coins, tossing dice, or drawing cards from a deck ... the assumptions are pretty inherent and understandable, and you do not have to be explicit about them and that's one of the reasons we use them for teaching purposes. We are making assumptions when we are flipping a coin: that it's a balanced coin, it has a head and a tail, the person that flipped the coin is doing so in an honest way, and so forth. All of these assumptions are pretty explicit and you do not have to belabor what they are. In the case of our (forensic) calculations, it is not inherently obvious what those assumptions are. When we generate statistics such as the random match probability (RMP), what that means and what the assumptions are when we do that calculation need to be explicit and known, as well as clearly understood. We are going to be spending some time addressing the fact that it is very easy to misrepresent, or misinterpret what these numbers are ... to say that they mean such-and-such, when in fact they do not. This is an important aspect of probability, knowing that there are certain associated assumptions we need to be aware of.

We will also cover hypothesis testing. In order to be able to perform these calculations (random match probability), it is important to establish that a couple of things hold true regarding the genetic data, namely, that there is independence of the two alleles at a locus. The two alleles that are inherited at a locus, one from the mother and the other from the father, are independent of one another. An important consequence of this is that we can multiply the probabilities of those two things, because they are independent events. If we multiply the probability of each of those events by the other, we can get a measure of the joint probability, or both of those things co-occurring in an individual. But first, we have to establish that they are independent, and it's not altogether clear—when you look at genetic data in human populations—that, in fact, the two alleles at every locus would be independent of one another. There have been sets of tests conducted, which test the hypothesis as to whether the two alleles at a locus are independent. We give a name to the independence of two alleles at every locus, the Hardy-Weinberg equilibrium. It's important that you understand what it means for our calculations.

Slide 3:

Approximately 60% of DNA casework involves sexual assaults. Typically the analyst is looking at the sperm fraction from a vaginal swab, which has been transferred by the perpetrator of that crime (in the general scenario). Transfer evidence ties someone to the victim, the victim to a crime scene, the victim to a suspect, and so forth. The NRC II is a report that came out in 1996, and this group of experts made some specific recommendations for the forensic community. We are going to go through nine of them that address statistical questions. When we do these calculations certain correction factors (theta)/conditional formulas are used. They are not easy to explain. In other instances we're not trying to give a number about a random match probability, but about the probability that this person—who's been charged with a crime, whose DNA genotype matches the crime scene DNA—not a random person, would match the crime scene DNA. Other instances call for the probability of whether this person's brother, or this person's father, or son, half-brother, first cousin ... might match the evidence and have an identical genotype profile. These would be conditional probabilities based on other assumptions as to who we are looking at; it is not the random match probability anymore. We will be getting into some statistical aspects of mixture calculations.

Slide 4:

We'll also discuss paternity calculations and likelihood ratios in general, which is a way of taking two probabilities and dividing one by the other. When it is applied to paternity calculations it is called a Paternity Index, sometimes referred to as PI. And it is really just a ratio of two probabilities, but one of the interesting things that occurs when we divide one probability by another probability is that we no longer have a probability. We can add probabilities under certain circumstances, we can subtract, we can multiply, and when we do any of those three arithmetic operations, the result is a probability. But, when we divide we no longer have a probability, it is then called (under certain circumstances) a likelihood ratio—it's an odds form of two probabilities. We are going to spend a considerable amount of time on misinterpretation of the random match probability, and what it does or does not mean. Many crime labs use a program called PopStats. A lot of what I have to say will be relatable to the PopStats program and what the PopStats program does. In addition, there are some labs that have developed their own software for these same purposes.

Slide 5:

We will also extend paternity calculations into what is known as kinship calculations. Where, for example, a child goes missing and remains are found. We need to establish whether this is in fact the child that went missing and we don't have a direct reference sample. These would be kinship calculations, and the question is slightly different than that being asked with paternity indices. These calculations are also used for mass disaster identifications. Mass disaster identifications get into partial profiles issues. We are also going to talk about presenting statistics in court and tactics used by the defense.

Slide 6:

Human identity testing is used to match suspects to evidence or victims to evidence. It is also used in paternity testing to identify the father, the father might be a missing person, or the mother or child might be a missing person. What's important is that having someone's DNA does not, in and of itself, mean we can identify who that person is. In order to identify the person we need to have something we are comparing the unknown DNA to, perhaps family members or a direct reference sample (personal effect of the victim's). There can be various missing person situations that arise in the course of our work. Another application of human identity testing is disaster identifications, where often we are trying to match pieces from a person that were fragmented during the disaster (e.g., plane crashes, terrorist attacks, bombings). Where we're trying to associate pieces and determine whether they belong to the same person/victim. We will also talk about convicted offender DNA databases because these have facilitated the solving of a significant number of cases that otherwise would have gone unsolved, but they present some interesting issues regarding statistics.

Slide 7:

Human genome facts: Our genome is interspersed throughout with repeats that look as though at one point, evolutionarily, they were transposable elements. We still have some in our genome—*Alu* sequences, for example—that still show some movement, it is very rare, but there are some polymorphisms for *Alu* insertions that different groups, biogeographically around the world, have insertions in various places in the genome, where other people don't. But the majority of these elements are no longer transposing, but still present.

A significant portion of our DNA is transcribed into RNA, but this RNA is typically not messenger RNA. It is all kinds of interesting classes of RNA; we are discovering more each year, many we do not yet understand.

Only a small proportion of our genome codes for protein sequences, which means, if we randomly looked at a portion of our DNA it would most likely not be from a coding region. It would not be DNA that is significantly changing the physiology of ourselves, it is not likely to show any phenotypic effect.

The microsatellites we use in forensics are part of a small portion of our genome known as Simple Sequence Repeats, which represent approximately 3% of the human genome. We are interested in tandem, simple sequence repeats, meaning they occur in clusters and are connected together in a head-to-tail orientation.

Slide 8:

If we are going to identify people, and do so by finding differences between people, we will have to look at those parts of the DNA that differ from one person to another. And those areas are called polymorphic DNA, as opposed to monomorphic. 99.9% of our genome is the same among all people. If we took just a random sequence of DNA and compared that sequence from one person to another, we would all be identical. Thus, these results would not discriminate between one person or another. In order to discriminate, we have to look specifically at the elite fraction of our DNA that is different—polymorphic DNA. These regions are not necessarily heterozygous; there is a difference between heterozygous and polymorphic. Polymorphic is an idea that comes from taking a group of people—let's say a sample of 100 people—and comparing their DNA for a specific region. And if that DNA is identical in everyone that we sampled, we say it is monomorphic, and it's not going to be a candidate for discrimination. In the case of polymorphic regions (a very small minority of the genome) there are differences from one person to another. We look specifically at these regions.

There are a number of different kinds of polymorphisms. The ones that may come to mind first are base pair substitutions, which we call SNPs, single nucleotide polymorphisms; these are due to an error during replication. They have a fairly high density, approximately 1 in 1,000 bases shows a SNP polymorphism, although not uniformly. Sometimes we get clustering. Their disadvantage, in terms of forensic identification, is that they have just two alleles. With two alleles at a particular position, there will only be three possible genotypes. For example, an A or a G at that site on the DNA (one strand). The site can be homozygous for the G or homozygous for the A; or we can have a heterozygote, where one chromosome has the A and the other the G (in a homologous pair). Again, only three different genotypes, which means we are very limited (in terms of that polymorphic site) of being able to identify people. When using a bi-allelic polymorphism, like a SNP locus, in order to get unique identification we're going to need a large number of these loci. In fact, when people look at the discriminating power of SNPs, a general conclusion is that approximately six SNP loci are needed to equal the discriminating power of just one STR locus. However, SNPs can be used successfully for paternity tests. Often with paternity tests, sufficient quantity and good quality DNA is submitted for analysis. With these resources we can run a whole battery of SNPs. There are commercial kits available that look at 96, 128, and so forth, allowing for good discrimination. We can also use SNPs on highly degraded DNA because we are looking at a single base pair difference. This technique suffers from the fact that it does not have good discriminating power per locus; furthermore, SNPs are very difficult to sort out with mixture samples.

Insertions/deletions (aka "indels") can be large or small, again these suffer from the fact that they are bi-allelic (example: *Alu* polymorphisms), meaning there are only two variants and only three genotypes, and thus, many people will have identical genotypes.

Minisatellites: Previously in the field, RFLPs were used, which are minisatellites (typically 9 bp to 36 bp). These consist of large stretches of DNA containing tandem repeats of large core repeats. This technique had good discriminating power; but, it was tedious, labor intensive, used radioactivity, and required a large quantity of high quality DNA … often hard to come by in forensic casework.

Microsatellites have the advantage of using the polymerase chain reaction (PCR), allowing for the use of exquisitely small amounts of DNA. Short tandem repeats (STRs) are beneficial because they have many alleles (as opposed to only two as discussed previously), but they have a relatively high mutation rate. The mutation rate noted on the slide is 1 per 1,000 bp; it may be as high as 1 in 500, or 1 in 300 for some loci. Two things can happen with a high mutation rate. First, we might expect that what gets passed on from a parent to a child may have undergone mutation, so there might be instances, where at a specific genetic locus, the parent and child do not possess the same allele—even though they are the biological parent. The other effect of mutation rate is that mutations can happen within the clone of cells that each individual is made of. Each of us started out as a single cell, underwent numerous mitotic divisions, leading to all the cells of our body. If during any one of those DNA replication events a mutation occurred, changing the number of core repeats, the result would be somatic mosaicism. In situations where we are analyzing blood, for instance, we're looking at white blood cells. White blood cells have a number of different origins in our body. They can come from the spleen and various locations of bone marrow. If any one of these locations has a mutation that makes it different from the rest of the bone marrow, the total population of white blood cells under analysis may show a polymorphism, which would present as a three allele pattern.

The estimation of mutation rates, which can be found at STRbase (http://www.cstl.nist.gov/strbase/), comes from looking at parent to child generations. Looking at multiple parent–child pairs (where there is certainty about the parent), it is possible to estimate the mutation rate as a frequency, the numerator becomes how many of those parent–child pairs are discordant. But there can be mutations that don't call themselves to our attention; some may be masked, and thus the estimated mutation rate will always be an underestimate.

Slide 9:

STRs have discrete alleles, meaning one base pair resolution. STRs are abundant in the genome so there are many that can be used; and they are highly discriminating. This is a list of the loci that are used. These are the core 13; there are now two additional loci at D2S1338 and D19S433.

Slide 10:

Here are the 15 loci. The core CODIS loci are in yellow. A couple of things to point out here. First, most of the loci are on different chromosomes. We know that during meiosis the two alleles at a locus segregate independently from one chromosome to another, and this is known as independent assortment. That is what Mendel found in the 1850s. So it is no surprise that what is inherited at the D8 locus is independent of, and not correlated with, the alleles inherited at D7, or TH01, or vWA, or D21, and so on. When looking through a pedigree, there should be independence between each of these loci. Thus, any calculations that we do are going to be based on the assumption that what happens at each of these loci is independent of what is present at each of the other loci. There are two exceptions though. The first is D5 and CSF. They are both on chromosome 5, and not only are they on the same chromosome, but they are also on the same arm of the chromosome (q arm). In fact, when we measure the recombination rate between them, it is approximately 20%. Within a pedigree, there is not going to be random segregation of these two loci. So, within a family they will show an association. However, if we take a sample of people from a population, and we look to see whether among these unrelated people there is a correlation in genotypes at D5 and CSF, what's found empirically is that there is no pattern of correlation. That is, at a population level, we say the genotypes at these two loci are in linkage equilibrium.

This also holds true for TPOX and D2. They are also on the same chromosome, and as a consequence, in theory, they could be correlated with one another; but again, in terms of the overall population they are not. Interestingly, TPOX and D2 are far enough apart: one loci is on the p arm and one loci is on the q arm, therefore, there is a large amount of DNA separating those two loci. Meaning, there is going to be recombination occurring between these two, so in fact, even within a pedigree we do not see a statistical correlation between TPOX and D2.

The second point that I would like to make here is in regard to the amelogenin locus. The amelogenin locus is amplified and analyzed using the same principles. We have two primers that bind to the flanking regions of the locus. However, the amelogenin locus is not a tandem repeat and it is not an STR locus. It is a single copy locus. It is a coding region and within the amelogenin locus is a protein product. Here we have an example of a monomorphic locus. Monomorphic, meaning that when we analyze the amelogenin product between these two primers virtually all X chromosomes are the same; they all show 106 bp. On the Y chromosome they are also monomorphic but they show 112 bp between the two primers. So, there's an insertion/deletion difference at the amelogenin locus on the X versus the Y chromosome, and this is how we can type a person in terms of whether they are XY (male) or XX (female).

Slide 11:

I want to put the emphasis of this workshop on the concepts, logic, and ideas. There is not going to be as much emphasis on equations, formulas, and algebra. However, there will be sufficient equations, formulas, and algebra to meet most people's appetite.

Slide 12:

Let's look at transfer evidence. Edmond Locard (1877–1966) is one of the first people who would be called a forensic scientist. He worked for the police department in Lyon, France. He published widely in forensic science; in fact he published (what he called) an encyclopedia of forensic science where he tried to give a philosophical framework for what we are doing in terms of forensic science. He had this idea we now call the "Locard exchange principle."

Slide 13:

Locard said, "Whenever two objects come in contact with one another, there is a transfer of some molecules from one object to another." He was thinking at the time of things like hair and fibers; he was thinking of soil and of those kinds of macromolecules that could be transferred. He was *not* thinking of DNA or even serological typing. But the same idea holds when we are using DNA. With DNA there is a transfer of evidence. If we can uniquely identify the source of that DNA, we can often then say that, yes, this person had to have come in contact with that person through this transfer evidence. You can use DNA to make that association.

Slide 14:

When we make this sort of association, there are three things that can happen in terms of a lab result. The lab results from the sample comparison can be that the results show the DNA patterns are different. The pattern from the crime scene sample that belongs to the culprit does not match that which was obtained from the submitted reference sample. The person that provided the reference sample is not the person who committed this crime. In this case we would have an exclusion. When we have an exclusion we do not make calculations. It is an exclusion; we know that these two samples came from different people and that in and of itself answers the question. With DNA we have very high discriminating capacity and we would exclude almost every-one but the person who left their DNA at the crime scene.

A second result can be inconclusive. It could be a situation where the crime scene sample, in particular, may be degraded or contaminated with inhibitors, where ultimately we do not get a reliable profile from the crime scene sample. Typically from the reference sample that is not an issue. Usually, if the reference sample were degraded or contaminated for some reason, we could go back and obtain another sample from that person. The reference samples are usually well taken care of. They were collected properly and then stored properly (not exposed to the elements), before they were submitted to the lab for analyses. However, for the forensic samples, we have no control over storage conditions, exposure to the elements and insulted by environmental factors, or contaminated by inhibitors (e.g., indigo dye, etc.); there can be all kinds of things that have gone wrong. When the result is inconclusive, all we can say is that there is no decision. We cannot exclude and we cannot include. Again, when we get an inconclusive result, there are no numbers associated with that result.

The last situation is the situation that we are going to be spending almost all of our time on. And that is where we have extracted the DNA, amplified it, compared, and essentially they are the same genotype. I say "essentially," meaning that they are the same genotype at every locus we could interpret (if not all loci amplified well). In this situation, we have to come up with an estimate for how likely it is to have seen that match just by coincidence. If this person left their DNA at the crime scene, if this person committed that crime, essentially what we are doing is analyzing two samples from the same person. I know that humans are not error free, but almost certainly we are going to get a match. And the question then becomes, what is the probability that just by shear fortuitous coincidence we would find a match like this of DNA coming from two different people. Well, that's where random match probability comes in. Because what we are now interested in calculating is the frequency that we would see this particular crime scene DNA profile in the general population. This means that we have to try to estimate the frequency of that particular genotype that was found in the crime scene sample. I want to make this point very explicit: it is in the *crime scene sample*. The question here is what's the probability if we chose a person at random and analyzed their DNA, that they would match the DNA profile from the crime scene. It is not the probability if we chose a person at random would they match the suspect. There's an important distinction to be made here. This number that we're calculating—the random match probability—is the estimate of the frequency of the profile, is about the *crime scene profile*, and about the questioned specimen. It is not who else could match the suspect and it is not who else could have the suspect's profile; it is about the crime scene sample. Because from that crime scene sample, in the best of circumstances, we get a nice single-source, high-quality, full-length, 13-loci profile—but it is not uncommon that when we look at the questioned sample we are unable to get all 13 loci. Maybe we can only get 11, maybe there are 2 that are inconclusive (e.g., below threshold). So in this case, if we were to look at the reference sample where we have the full 13 loci, and you have 11 loci on the crime scene sample, and those 11 loci match that same 11 loci on the crime scene sample (the other two on the crime scene sample cannot be used) … and suppose we said, well 11 loci match and I am pretty sure that if I had those other two loci on the crime scene sample, they too would match the reference sample, so I am going to give the random match probability for all 13 loci. Now, I am sure you realize that is incorrect. With the reference profile we are going to get the full complement; the random match for having that full complement of loci is not what the evidence is. The evidence is what the evidence is, or in this case, only 11 loci. So, we're limited; the number that we calculate is based on the limitation of that questioned crime scene sample.

Another situation where things could get complicated is when the crime scene sample is a mixture, there is another person in there. It might be major/minor, but there may be two loci where we cannot distinguish a single profile. Even if we could say I can see every one of the alleles that my reference sample has present in this mixture—another thing that would be incorrect would be to say that well all of his alleles are in that mixture, so I am going to calculate the random match probability for a single source reference profile, because they could not be eliminated from the mixture. Again, that would be incorrect. Because, in fact, that is not what the evidence is. We are trying to give the court some information about how rare it is, that if we chose a person they would match that crime scene sample. If it is a mixture, there is going to be more than one person that could match that crime scene sample. So giving the random match probability on the reference sample would be incorrect. We have to be careful about that. We have to estimate the frequency of the crime scene profile, and not the reference profile, and the estimated frequency is based on the limitations of the crime scene profile.

Another thing I wanted to point out is this word "estimate." Whenever we try to estimate the frequency of a particular DNA profile, it is always going to be an estimate. We do not know what the actual frequency is for any profile. The only way we would be able to establish what the actual frequency is, the real, true, correct frequency for a profile, would be to sample every individual in the entire world. You can image that it is never going to be feasible to get the DNA profile of every single person in the world. Even if we came up with huge amounts of money, instruments, consumables, and analysts to do this, by the time we finished some of those people would have died and some new people would have been born, and so it is really never going to be practical and feasible to have genotyped every person in the world. So that means that we have to estimate the frequency. The estimate is actually quite precise. It is based on a model and theory for how genes and variants occur in populations and how randomly they have come together, and so forth. We are going to have to estimate the frequency based on samples. As you will see, this is what statistics is all about. Statistics tries to estimate the probabilities that get used in probability theory or in population genetics theory. We take data samples to be able to estimate the probabilities (or frequencies) that we are going to use. And so these estimates are not a guess; they are a reliable way of estimating the frequency.

Slide 15:

To just summarize this, our interpretation and the numbers that we come up with are about that questioned sample; it is about that crime scene sample. What is the probability if we chose a person at random they would match the crime scene profile, whatever the limitations of that crime scene profile are? So, the known matches the questioned—that is what the evidence is. The question we are asking is who else could match that questioned profile. Who else could not be eliminated from matching this questioned sample? Taking into account there can be partial profiles or mixtures. Again, we cannot use the reference profile to give an estimate of the frequency. One of the reference articles that was provided is by Jonathan Koehler [1]. It is a very interesting article. I strongly recommend that you spend some time during your training to read this article, because he tediously went through court transcripts where DNA was presented and has excerpted examples where forensic analysts misrepresented or exaggerated the value of the DNA evidence. And you will see in there many of the things that I am going to talk about, examples of the various fallacies, mistakes, and misinterpretations.

Slide 16:

Many labs use PopStats (other software is available) to estimate the frequency of the match to forensic evidence, not the suspect. A question that comes up is who is included in the suspect population. Does the suspect population include only people like the suspect, and by that I mean coming from the same racial group or coming from the same neighborhood (geographically)? Who is in the suspect population? In many cases, if the suspect did not commit the crime, than the true culprit we know nothing about. There may be cases where the victim can give some testimony about the nature of the suspect and maybe characterize the suspect. But in general, the suspect population is unknown in terms of who the real culprit might be. We typically calculate the frequencies of these genotypes on the various populations that are available in PopStats. Many labs are using the FBI databases; there is a Caucasian database, an African American database, and two Hispanic databases (depending on which section of the country you are in). These are the four major databases that most profile frequencies are based on. Depending on the policy of your lab, you might provide all of these estimates (one for each database), or what many labs do is report the most conservative estimate.

Slide 17:

Let me give you an example of a case that occurred in Burlington, Vermont. The case is known as *Vermont vs. Passino*, 1991. The suspect's name was Albert

Passino. It was an FBI case using RFLP, and the suspect was accused of having sexually assaulted and murdered a woman near Burlington. His DNA profile matched the crime scene profile; it was vaginal swab evidence. He matched the vaginal swab, and the defense that was made was that Mr. Passino had a somewhat unusual family background. It was pointed out by the defense that his paternal grandparents were Italian, but his maternal grandfather was Native American, and he belonged to a group of Native Americans named Abenaki. His maternal grandmother was half French and half Native American and the defense argued that the numbers given by the FBI databases (based on the FBI Caucasian, African-American, and Hispanic databases) were actually irrelevant because the only pertinent number that should be given at trial would be from a database of people that had exactly the same background as Mr. Passino. And in fact, this came up as an appeal, and there was an exchange of letters in *The American Journal of Human Genetics* (a very prestigious journal), and it was pointed out by British forensic scientist Ian Evett and a population geneticist Bruce Weir, that this argument was completely specious, because what you would calculate if you had a database of people completely identical to Mr. Passino is the probability of finding his profile in a group of people that had the same background as Mr. Passino, which would only be correct *if* you were to assume that the real suspect had to be somebody who shared this exact same background. When in fact, there was no evidence as to what the true culprit's background was. So the correct argument in an estimate coming from these databases is the best approximation that we have for a random, alternative male having committed this crime in the state of Vermont. The defense's approach turned out to be a completely bogus argument that does not hold, and the court ultimately agreed on that. So, which group do you use for the database? Most jurisdictions either do one of two things: they either calculate on all the databases that we have and present those statistics, or they do that and then present only the most conservative.

Slide 18:

To estimate the genotype frequency, the first thing we do is estimate the frequency at each locus. To do that we evoke an idea that is called the Hardy-Weinberg equilibrium. I want to point out to you that the idea of Hardy-Weinberg is preposterously simple. It is the simplest model we have. The Hardy-Weinberg equilibrium essentially means that the two alleles you inherited at each locus are uncorrelated with one another. That is all that it means. If I told you one of the alleles at D3, and then asked you to guess what the other allele was, the fact that I gave you previous information regarding one allele will not change or influence your guess for what the other allele might be—there's no correlation between the two alleles. We call it the Hardy-Weinberg equilibrium because two people, Hardy and Weinberg, published (separately) on this idea more than 100 years ago (1908). It is very simple:

the two alleles that come together to form the genotype at every locus, to a very close approximation, can be treated as though they are completely independent of one another. The chance of getting one and the chance of getting the other are strictly the frequency we would have for those in the general population.

Slide 19:

I wanted to point out at this juncture, that we actually use three genetic models in forensic applications of DNA. The one I have mentioned previously during our discussion of transfer evidence is mitosis. Mitosis means that all of us are a clone of identical cells. So, if you look at our blood cells, our epithelial cells, sperm cells, hair root cells, whatever the biological evidence might be, cells that originate from one person will have an identical genotype, barring mutations.

The second genetic model is meiosis. We have a model for the relationship between parent and child. We know, going back to Mendel, that if a locus is heterozygous there are two different variants present; these variants are going to segregate during meiosis and only one of the two will be passed on to the offspring with a 50/50 probability. We can use this model to calculate things such as exclusion probabilities, paternity indices, kinship coefficients, and so forth. We use this model as a basis. These two models are based on cellular behavior. Mitosis describes how one cell divides and the daughter cell is related to the parental cell. Meiosis is the hereditary connection between one organismal generation to another.

The third model that we are using is this Hardy-Weinberg law. It is just one of three models. I'm trying to dispel you from the notion that, oh my goodness, we are using this model of what is going on and it is a theoretical model, and because it is a model we have to be worried about the fact that it does not apply to the real world. I want to show that in fact it does. It is only one of three models that we use. It is saying if we know the frequencies of alleles at a locus, we can estimate the frequencies of genotypes, because there is a connection between genotype frequencies and allele frequencies. I think the reason that people are more worried over this particular model (Hardy-Weinberg), than with either of the other two models, is that for both of those models (mitosis and meiosis) we can imagine an easy physical basis for them. Hardy-Weinberg is more abstract, you cannot "see" it. Not even with a microscope.

Slide 20:

Let us use an example here of a locus where there are just two alleles. There are two alleles, so there can be three genotypes. We could have homozygote for one allele, or homozygote for the other allele, or heterozygous. What Hardy-Weinberg law says is that these genotypes came about by the random collision of male and female gametes. Let's say the male is A1 and A2, and that the female is the same, A1 and A2. If we knew the frequencies of these variants, we could then calculate the frequency that they would collide. In order to have the genotype A1 A1, the offspring must have inherited an A1 from the mother and that same allele, A1, from the father. There is only one way to get this genotype: the same allele had to be chosen twice, once from the population of female gametes and again from the population of male gametes. The same with the other homozygote, A2 A2—there is only one way that it can come about. However, the heterozygote can come about in two ways, and there is no genetic reason for discriminating between the two possibilities— either way the result is still heterozygous (genetically identical).

If the frequency of the A1 allele was some number, say 30%, then the other allele, A2, must be 70%. In this case they have to equal 100% because there are only two of them. Using this information, we could calculate what the frequencies are for all of those collisions happening.

If p_1 is the frequency of allele A1 in the population, then the probability that this allele will collide with itself at random will be p_1^2. The same holds true for the other homozygous. If p_2 represents the frequency of allele A2, then the probability that this allele will collide with itself at random will be p_2^2. But for the heterozygote we have to take into account that it can come about in two ways, and the genotype frequency will be $2p_1p_2$, where the 2 indicates that this particular genotype can come about in either of two ways. This is not necessary for the homozygotes because they can only come about in one way. If there were three alleles at this locus there would be another column and another row to the Punnett square, both labeled "A3," and it would become a 9-celled Punnett square. Even with this expansion of alleles, the same pattern and predictions would hold, regardless of how many alleles you have. At STR loci you can have 12, 18, or 24 alleles and it will lead to a humongous Punnett square.

Slide 21:

So, again, we do this at every locus. The more common the alleles at a locus, the more common are the possible genotypes at that locus. In other words, if you have common alleles, you will see more of that genotype than if you had rare alleles (depends on the frequencies). So now we have the frequency at each locus (13 or 15 loci), and now we can assume there is independence across loci—in order to calculate the frequencies at each locus we had to assume there was independence between alleles—and now we will have to assume that the genotypes at each locus do not influence one another. If we can make that assumption then we can multiply the frequency of those genotypes together. That lack of association, that lack of correlation, that independence between loci is given the term "linkage equilibrium." This is a very important idea; in order to be able to multiply two probabilities together and to interpret the number that results, we can only do that when the two things we are multiplying together are independent of one another. Multiplying two independent numbers together is called using the product rule. The result interpretation is the probability that both this *and* that occurred. That both the genotypes are at D3 and D7, the probability for having that joint combination is calculated by multiplying the two probabilities together.

The NRC II Committee pointed out that real human populations do not fit perfectly to Hardy-Weinberg equilibrium predictions. They deviate a little bit, that is, if you think about it, human populations do not mate randomly, very close to random, but what we have in human populations is what is called, among human population genetics, "positive assortative mating." You *tend* to get (this is by no means exclusive) people mating who are more like one another genetically and phenotypically than two random people in a population. So, it's not uncommon that we choose our mates based on commonalities, maybe religious background, linguistic background, social background (in terms of years of education or socioeconomic background); there tends to be correlation between people mating. This means that the alleles that are coming together are not completely random and the deviation from randomness can be encapsulated in a number that is called "theta." This theta correction is a way of measuring the deviation from the perfect Hardy-Weinberg equilibrium. This means that with positive assortative mating there's a slight increase in the probability that the two alleles that come together in an individual, because the two parents tended to be correlated with one another to a slight degree, that's there's going to be a slight excess of homozygotes. It's more likely the two alleles coming together will be derived from a common ancestor. Ultimately, the probability of having the same alleles coming together to form a homozygote will be higher than Hardy-Weinberg would predict. This increase we call the "theta correction factor."

[1] Koehler, Jonathan, J. 1993. Error and Exaggeration in the Presentation of DNA Evidence at Trial (1993). *Jurimetrics Journal* 34: 21. http://ssrn.com/abstract = 1432065.

Slide 21 (continued):

The NRC II also recommended using a minimum allele frequency, and the number they suggested is 5/2N. They also recommended that we calculate a confidence interval. These are done by PopStats and the NRC II recommended that these numbers be available, particularly the confidence interval, which gives a range within which we estimate that the real frequency resides, let's say 99.9% of the time. When we quote a number of 1 in a trillion, how precisely do we know that it is actually 1 in a trillion? Is it really different from 1 in 1.1 trillion, is it really different from 1 in 110 billion, how different is it? Is it different from 1 in 1,000, or a septillion? What kind of range do we associate that number to be relevant given the relative sizes of our databases? The NRC II pointed out that the confidence interval that we have to keep in mind is approximately a 10-fold one on either side of the number we quote as the random match probability.

Slide 22:

Just to remind you, the Nation Research Council Report II can be found online. It is rather convenient having it on the Web, and one thing that is rather convenient is that you can do a word search for terms such as "mitochondrial frequencies," or "Y chromosome," and the word search will allow you to view all of the relevant sections very quickly.

Slide 23:

An earlier version, NRC I, came out in 1992; there were some differences in the recommendations. I'm going to highlight two of them that I think you need to be mindful of. One of them is how to treat mixtures and the other is how to treat a cold hit in a database search, in terms of whether you should modify the random match probability or not.

Slide 24:

This is the correction formula that NRC II recommended, as well as the theta values. For the homozygote frequency, if we remove $p(1 - p)\theta$ from the equation, that leaves just p^2, which is pure Hardy-Weinberg, simply the frequency of that allele squared gives the estimate of the frequency at that locus. NRC II is saying that because of the slight amount of positive assortative mating (increasing the probability that the two alleles coming together are from a common ancestor) will add this positive amount $p(1 - p)\theta$ to p^2. $p(1 - p)\theta$ has to be a positive number, the smallest it can be is zero, a theta of zero essentially means you have perfect Hardy-Weinberg. If theta is zero the additional term, $p(1 - p)\theta$, drops out entirely. If, however, theta takes on some positive value then in fact the term $p(1 - p)\theta$ will be some positive number. It may be fairly small and in general it is. This positive theta will increase the frequency of homozygotes. What the NRC II said was that, yes, the homozygotes will be increased by this process of nonrandom mating that occurs in human populations, but that means if the homozygote frequency is higher in real populations then the heterozygous frequency must be lower. In order to increase the homozygous frequency, you must lower the heterozygous frequency—the sum of the two must equal one. NRC II said to be conservative, let's just leave the heterozygous estimates at the values you would use if it were perfect Hardy-Weinberg. So, this number $2p_ip_j$ is going to be conservative, higher than the frequency would be for real heterozygotes in the population.

Slide 25:

The minimum allele frequency being 5/2N, where N is the number of people in the database that we are using. The 2N comes about because we are looking at human beings, which have diploid, autosomal loci. With N number of people in a database, there are 2N for the number of copies of a gene. 5/2N is giving us the 99% upper-confidence interval. It is a very conservative upper bound for the frequency of an allele that has not been seen in our databases.

The confidence interval, this is based on empirical studies, and those empirical studies suggest that if we quote a number, 1 in a billion, that is our best estimate based on the knowledge that we have. But we know that this is based on a sample of people, and all we can say is that 99% of the time it will fall within a 10-fold range. When we quote a number of 1 in a billion, the range will be 1 in 10 billion (more rare) to 1 in 100 million (more common).

Slide 26:

Here I use the metaphor of shooting at a target and trying to hit the cross-hairs, but what I am trying to portray is the technical difference between precision and accuracy. The difficulty that we have with these two words is that they are used colloquially as though they are interchangeable and mean the same thing; this is not *technically* correct. When used with statistics, these two words mean very different things, and it is possible to have one without the other. There are four possible combinations and I tried to portray that as the scatter you might expect to get when shooting at a target. In the two upper cases, the shots are quite scattered around the crosshairs; meaning, that if you were to take another shot, your ability to predict where the next shot might land is quite unknown. There is very poor reliability, what you might expect for a novice; for every shot that is taken there is a lot of variability. Whereas the lower two examples are tight clusters, what you might expect to see if a person had practiced and knew what they were doing. The same holds true with analytical techniques. When using your procedure, several iterations of the same sample would give gravely different estimates, as portrayed in the upper two examples. It tells you that there is great imprecision in your data. That is, there's some uncontrolled variation that needs to be adjusted/scrutinized and made consistent. Precision is defined as how close replicates are to one another. The lower two panels portray very good precision. On the lower right, you have an example where every shot is landing very close to a previous shot, and if you were to try to predict where the next shot would land, it would be reliable to say that it is likely to land in the grouping of previous shots. The same is true for the lower left panel. But the other thing that needs to be taken into consideration when determining these estimates is how close your estimates are to the correct (true) values, and the true values may not be reflected by the precision.

Again, both of the lower panels have very good precision, but the one on the left does not have good accuracy. It is not giving us the correct answer, or in this case, the bull's eye. Typically the way we would adjust our system's output to look like the panel on the lower right is to calibrate the system using known standards. For many crime labs this means using NIST (National Institute of Standards and Technology) standards. The standards have been sequenced many times and the correct, exact alleles are known. Without this calibration, it is possible to get reliable and precise results that are inaccurate. Bringing the precision and accuracy together is often referred to as validation, which ensures reliable, correct results. Now you can understand why it is so important for labs to have both precision and accuracy.

Slide 27:

How do we come by these numbers used for the allele frequency differences? This is a typical genotypic array, vWA data. It is data taken from a sample of 129 people and they were genotyped for all 13 CODIS loci (not just this one locus). But for vWA, this is a very concise way of summarizing the genotypic data at this locus. To read this half matrix, the 9 means there were 9 people of the 129 tested that possessed a 14,14 homozygous genotype at vWA. All the homozygote individuals from this sample would be along the diagonal, and all others are the heterozygous combinations. This half matrix illustrates a few things. The first being that for most of the STR loci we look at, they are, sort of, normally distributed, in the sense that the majority of the frequencies occur in the intermediate allele sizes. As we get to smaller and larger alleles, they tend to be rarer. The second thing that it illustrates is that even with a sample of 129 people there were a number of genotypes that were never seen. That is not to say that those genotypes do not exist. They almost certainly do exist, they might be rare, but when we take a sample of 129 people, some of those genotypes are just not going to turn up. Using this genotypic data we can extract and calculate the allele frequencies. The way we do that is by using a technique called "gene counting." And we can show statistically that it is the most reliable technique as it uses all of the data. It is the best estimate for allele frequencies, and we do this by counting the number of times that each of these alleles appears in these 129 people. As we mentioned previously, if we have 129 people, that means we are looking at 2×129, or 258 alleles (because these are autosomal, diploid loci). Then in order to estimate the frequency of the 14 alleles, we first determine how many copies we are looking at. Then determine how many of those 258 were 14 alleles. If we look at the half matrix, all of the 14 alleles are in the first column on the left. All of these individuals have at least one copy of the 14 alleles. The only exception being the first number, 9, which is the count of 14,14 homozygotes, so ultimately there are 18 copies of the 14 alleles. If we add up the number of copies of the 14 alleles present in this genotypic data set, we would have: $18 + 3 + 19 + 23 + 6 + 6 + 0 = 75$.

$$f(14) = 75/258 = 0.291$$

Let's now do the 17 alleles, as the other allele calculations are a bit different from the 14, in that you have to count across the 17 row, as well as down the 17 column. Again, keep in mind to count the homozygous allele twice. So, we have $23 + 1 + 14 + 18 + 10 + 3 + 3 = 72$.

$$f(14) = 72/258 = 0.279$$

And that is how the frequencies for these alleles are derived. These are actual data; I am using this as an example to demonstrate what was done in all of our FBI databases and what occurs in PopStats. In fact, any database that we may encounter for STRs, the allele frequencies are determined in exactly this same way (typically using computers). The logic behind this method is very direct, it is strictly gene counting. In terms of assumptions, the biggest assumption is that when we record a genotype as homozygote, that it really truly is a homozygote, and not an allelic dropout or a null allele.

Slide 28:

To generalize this concept, we have alleles A_1 through A_k. n_1 through n_k are the number of occurrences of those alleles in a particular sample, and those numbers add up to 2N, where N is the number of people in your database. So that's the way in which we generate the numbers that are seen in the allele frequency tables. When we look at the PopStats numbers, typically those samples are on the order of 150, 200, maybe 250 people. It is very common to get questions about this on the stand. Because the way this is often played out in court is that you quote an unimaginably small number and during the cross-examination the line of questioning will lead to something along these lines:

Defense: In order to estimate a number like 1 in a trillion, you must have had a very large sample. I would think you would need at least 100,000 people to get a number like that.

You: No, we didn't have 100,000 people.

Defense: So you must have had at least 10,000 people.

You: No, we didn't have 10,000.

Defense: Well, you must have had at least 1,000.

You: No, we didn't have 1,000.

Defense: Please tell the court how many people were in the database that was used.

You: The Caucasian FBI database has approximately 180 individuals.

Defense: 180 people? Could you repeat that for the jury, please?

You: The Caucasian FBI database has approximately 180 individuals.

Defense: You're telling me, that by looking at 180 people, somehow, by some process that eludes me, you were able to extrapolate up to 1 in a trillion, is that even possible?

Now, intuitively, many people think, yeah, how could one look at a mere 180 people and somehow spin that, by some mystical process, and generate a number of 1 in a trillion—it doesn't make any sense. Well, I think the counterargument to that would be to explain that a sample of 180 people is perfectly adequate to give us sufficient precision we need to generate this kind of estimate. In any area of statistics, the sample size is dependent on the level of precision needed for the application. An important thing to remember about sample size is that when we use larger and larger samples, our results are no more accurate. The size of the sample has nothing to do with accuracy of the result. What the size does change is the precision of your estimate. With increased sample size there is less variation in results between multiple samples.

Slide 29:

With a 13-loci profile there are 26 pieces of information, and each of these 26 alleles has an associated frequency. We then multiply the 26 allele frequencies together, and any loci where there is a heterozygote we multiply by 2, and the homozygous loci get a theta correction factor. To do this we are using the product rule, multiplying these independent things together to get an overall estimate of the frequency for this full genotype profile. Each of the frequencies is a number less than 1. When we multiply numbers less than 1 together the number gets smaller, and smaller, and smaller. That's how the power of discrimination of each locus comes into play. Just to point out, the majority of people are heterozygous at a locus, and the heterozygosity at these loci is in the range of 80% to 90%. The theta correction factor is only going to be applied for those loci where there's a homozygote. In your casework you will see it is much more common to see a profile that is completely heterozygous than it is to see a profile that has 8 or 10 homozygous loci. As an aside, I am homozygous at 6 of the 15 loci.

Slide 30:

This is my profile. When we multiply all the allele frequencies together, add in the 2s for heterozygotes, and the theta correction for homozygous locus, the number we get is a really, really small number. We deliberately express this number as 1 over XXXXX. Our minds are not good at comprehending decimals, particularly these very small decimal numbers; it is difficult to communicate those. So we deliberately change those into a format where we use whole numbers, say 1 in 3.6 billion, for example.

We also have my Y-STR profile. Males have one Y chromosome, thus the single allele portrayed—a haplotype. These are not inherited independently from one another; these are inherited together as a unit. As an aside, males that have XYY essentially have two Y chromosomes, but remember both of these Y chromosomes originated from the single Y chromosome of the father, so these XYY individuals do not have two different Y-STR haplotypes; the haplotypes of the two Y chromosomes would be identical (barring mutation). With Y-STRs you cannot multiply the frequency of one allele times the frequency of all other alleles to determine the frequency of the haplotype. That is because the haplotype is inherited as a unit, a package deal, they don't segregate, they're not independent of one another. The way we estimate the frequency is that we look up the frequency of that total haplotype, the configuration as a whole. The numbers are typically on the order of 1 in 500 to 1 in 1,500.

Slide 31:

Let's discuss human genetic variation. There is an article I would recommend; the lead author is Barbujani [2]. This article was an interesting attempt to look at human variation across the world, and they did this by taking a large number of samples from around the world, and all of those samples were analyzed for a large number of genetic loci. Of the loci that were examined, some were STR loci, others were protein-coding loci, and others still were serological loci. With this information the authors calculated heterozygosity, which for a genetic locus means the fraction of people in your samples who are heterozygous at that locus. They performed an analysis of variance, or in other words, what's the pattern of variation that is seen. The first thing they looked at was "total heterozygosity." Meaning that they use all of the data from all of the populations, regardless of its originating location in the world, and then analyzed it as if it were one big sample. They could also sort the data set according to continental area. As an aside, the samples were collected from indigenous peoples, not from those that may have immigrated, the authors were looking for inherent differences. When they calculated the heterozygosity of the continental groups (roughly racial groups) the heterozygosity decreased; the allelic frequencies are a little different between continental areas. Next they calculated the heterozygosity within each individual sample to get an average heterozygosity per population. When they did this the heterozygosity again decreased (lower than both the total and continental heterozygosity). From these data the authors concluded that most of the genetic variation found worldwide is found in every population. By using different populations in our casework calculations we are essentially taking into account the variation between total and continental (racial group) heterozygosity. The actual genetic variations between populations, within the same continental group, are very small, inconsequential even (e.g., all the countries of Europe). These results argue that we need not have separate allele frequency estimates for each local crime scene. In addition, our different databases do not take into account the 5% of variation between populations within racial groups, and the argument there is that the theta correction factor accounts for this. And since 1997 there have been additional, more extensive studies, and their findings corroborate Barbujani's initial findings. Again, just a reminder that these percentages are the averages across all loci. At each of the individual loci the percentages could vary a little, but the overall picture remains the same.

Slide 32:

Elementary probability theory is a way of quantifying uncertainty. We can restrict the unlikely events and then proceed to quantify what we do not know. We can restrict the possibilities and then give values as to how likely something is. This ability to calculate such things is actually a more recent invention, only about 400 years ago were people able to figure out how to do this. I would also like to say that all probability is conditional, with certain assumptions built into them. For example, we can calculate the probability of event A, given that event B has already occurred, written as $P(A/B)$. The information, event B, changes the probability of event A.

Slide 33:

There are three axioms to probability theory. A probability theorist makes certain assumptions and then determines probabilities based on those assumptions. They do not worry about whether the assumptions are true, and if there is a probability, then such and such follows from these axioms that I can assume are true. There are three probability axioms, and all probability theory can be developed from these. The first is that a probability is never a negative value. For the next, the Greek letter omega is used to indicate all the possible outcomes of a certain event. The probability that the resulting outcome is one of the outcomes represented by omega is equal to one. The third assumption is a little trickier. It says that if I wanted to know the probability that event 1 or event 2 occurred, I can calculate that by adding the individual probabilities together. But there's a restriction here: the two events must be mutually exclusive. They cannot occur at the same time; it has to be one or the other, it can't be both. In our case, this is especially true for genotypes.

Slide 34:

From those axioms, it follows that a probability has to be on the interval of 0 to 1. We know that the frequency estimate for our alleles falls in this interval, and we know that when we multiply numbers that are less than 1 together the resulting probability will get smaller and smaller (power of discrimination). It also follows that the probability of everything other than event 1 is 1 minus the complement of that event; and you'll see where we used this with mixtures and with probability of inclusion/exclusion. We also know the probability of event 1 or event 2 is equal to the sum of those two probabilities (if they are mutually exclusive). If, however, they are not mutually exclusive, then we have to include an additional term that takes into account the overlap of these two events when they co-occur, and subtract that term because we do not want to count this overlap area twice. This situation is typically not encountered when determining the probabilities of genotypes.

Slide 35:

There are two views of looking at probabilities, philosophically. The first one is most intuitive, the "frequentist." I can measure the probability by doing the same thing a large number of times. For example, determining how often you get heads when flipping a coin, by actually doing just that and recording the outcomes. The more trials I perform the closer the observed value gets to the predicted probability, in the case of a coin, 50%.

Opposed to that, there is another way of thinking about probability where there is subjectivity to it. This is called a "Bayesian" approach, named after the Rev. Thomas Bayes, who in 1763 had the idea that probabilities are going to depend on each of our unique experiences and so it might be different from one person to another (a subjective opinion). This may even be true in the courtroom where the jury tends to believe one witness over another, for example. However, depending on the question at hand, both approaches can have useful insights.

Slide 36:

The independence of events means that you can multiply the two together. But, if they are not independent then the equation becomes more complicated. Fortunately for us, we do not have to worry about the non-independence situation as all of the alleles at all of the loci have been shown to be independent of one another.

I wanted to talk about a case, *The State of California vs. Collins*, 1968. It has been widely written about in the probability literature and it exemplifies how *not* to use probability in courtrooms.

Slide 37:

This case occurred in the San Pedro area of California. An elderly woman was returning home after completing her shopping and was pulling a small trolley cart containing her groceries. The elderly woman passed an alley, when a woman pushed her down, stole her purse, the woman ran to a get-away car, and the car sped off. One of the principle witnesses was a man whose house was very close to this alley who was outside at the time of the crime and he testified during the trial. This is one of the first cases where probability theory was used in a criminal trial. The prosecution hired a probability expert. The expert presented the probabilities of the physical characteristics reported for the alleged suspects. The probability expert was then asked to report the overall, joint probability for all of these characteristics being true, keeping in mind that all of these things were true of Mr. and Mrs. Collins (the alleged suspects). The probability expert testified to the jury that if you multiply all of these characteristic probabilities together you get a probability of 1 in 12 million. With this, Mr. and Mrs. Collins were found guilty. The case, however, was appealed and the guilty verdict was reversed. The reasoning for the reversal, regarding the statistics, was that these physical characteristics that were used were mere hearsay, there is no empirical foundation. But the court's second point was that by multiplying these probabilities together the expert was assuming that each of these characteristics are independent of one another. If, however, these characteristics are not independent, then the number generated does not really mean anything. This is a classic example of an incorrect application of probability.

Slide 38:

How many genotypes are at a locus? This can easily be calculated if I told you the number of alleles at that locus. If there are K alleles, K has to be an integer, some whole number. If there are K alleles, then you can be homozygous for each one. In order to be heterozygous you have to have two alleles that are different from one another. So there are K possibilities for the first allele, but since the second allele must be different, there are K − 1 possibilities for the second allele. And we divide the second term by 2, because the order of the alleles does not matter (e.g., 15,20 is the same as 20,15). Now we just add these two terms together. This involves some algebra; in order to add them we have to get them over a common denominator, and ultimately it boils down to $(K^2 + K)/2$. When performing these calculations you'll note that as the number of alleles increases the number of genotypes increases significantly, in a nonlinear fashion, it is actually quadratic.

Slide 39:

Answers to the equation discussed in slide 38, for values of K 2 through 6.

Slide 40:

If you were to graph these results, genotypes versus alleles (K), the graph will be a parabola (on the slide I cheated a little with half a circle).

Slide 41:

Let's apply this to the genetic loci that you work with. These calculations have been performed based on the FBI's Caucasian databases. These numbers do not mean that all of the possible genotypes at a locus are equally frequent. So, for example, any genotype at D3 does not have a 1 in 55 chance. More alleles means more possible genotypes, equals higher discriminating power.

Slide 42:

Additional loci results, and since all these loci are independent from one another, we can multiply the possible genotypes together to get the total number of genotypes you would expect to be able to discriminate at these 15 loci in Caucasian populations. That number is 460 septillion genotypes. Let's put that in perspective. The world population is roughly 7.0×10^9. This is telling us that the number of possible genotypes is exceedingly larger (17 orders of magnitude) than the number of people in the world. This can be interpreted as most of these possible genotypes do not exist in the world, there are not enough people. At most, with no identical twins, the largest number of genotypes we could have is $\sim 7.0 \times 10^9$. Another line of thought might be how many people have ever existed on the earth. Physical anthropologists have gone through and figured this out, and they conclude it is in the range of 10 to 20 times the current world population.

Slide 43:

Even 20 times the current world population, 140×10^9, and yet this has really very little effect; most possible genotypes have still never even existed.

Some population geneticists in the forensic field argue that when calculating the random match probability we know that the genotype profile developed from the evidentiary sample exists somewhere in the world, and this should be your assumption. This assumption will severely restrict the possible genotypes to those currently seen in the human population of the world. This calculation is called the conditional probability, and it boils down to what is the probability that you would see this particular profile again given that you have already seen it once. PopStats will calculate this for you. It will make your reported statistics a little more common but not a lot.

Slide 44:

Here are some big number names, just in case you ever wanted to impress your friends.

Slide 45:

I kept going …

Slide 46:

For 13 loci, you can calculate the most common and the most rare profiles, using the most common and least common allele frequency at each locus, respectively. For 15 loci the number would be even more rare. I think on average that each locus adds at least a power of 10, if not more. These are hypothetical, but they bound the range you can get with the random match probability. Keep in mind that as the denominator gets larger the overall number gets smaller; we are dealing with really tiny numbers here.

[2] Barbujani, G., A. Magagni, E. Minch, and L. Cavalli-Sforza. 1997. An apportionment of human DNA diversity. *PNAS* 94:4516–4519.

Slide 47:

Where I want to go next is how to measure discrimination at a locus. This is not something that you would typically do because most labs use commercially available kits and the R&D scientists at those companies have made these calculations and choices. In general, the more alleles you have at a locus the more discriminating power you have. The other factor at a locus that plays into the discriminating power is how evenly the allele frequencies are distributed. The maximum discrimination at a locus comes about when you have an evenly balanced distribution of allele frequencies (e.g., 10 alleles all with frequencies of 10%). A good measure of the power of discrimination at a locus is the heterozygosity. The heterozygosity is the fraction of people that would be expected to be heterozygous. You can calculate the homozygosity much more easily (far fewer possibilities, equal to the number of alleles present at that locus), then subtract from one to obtain the heterozygosity. To find the homozygosity, you would square each of the individual allele frequencies and then sum those estimates to get the homozygosity for that locus.

Slide 48:

If you were to now subtract the homozygosity from one you would obtain the heterozygosity for that locus; since, if a person is not homozygous at a locus they must be heterozygous.

Slide 49:

Here are the number of observed alleles and their respective heterozygosities for the loci we work with. Again, to obtain these numbers I use the FBI's Caucasian database. For each database the number would vary *slightly*. A population geneticist would say the higher the heterozygosity the higher the genetic diversity at that locus (the greater the number of possibilities). The higher the heterozygosity the higher the discriminating power you would expect from that locus.

Slide 50:

Everything else being equivalent, which one of these loci would you choose to add to an STR kit? You would calculate the heterozygosity for each of these loci and then pick the one with the highest. Just by looking at these examples you can probably already guess that locus #1 is the best choice, as it has the most even distribution of allele frequencies.

Slide 51:

I go through the arithmetic here. Keep in mind this is a population phenomenon and is not strictly a factor of the molecular biology of the locus. After performing the calculations it is clear that we would choose locus #1, all else being equal.

Slide 52:

In conclusion, more alleles are better, and even frequencies of those alleles are better as well. You can also measure the discriminating power directly, called the PD, the probability of discrimination.

Slide 53:

The probability of discrimination is calculated similarly to the heterozygosity, in that it is easier to calculate the probability of a match and then subtract it from one. So, if we chose two people at random, what is the probability that they would have the same genotype at a particular locus? What if they were both homozygous for the same allele? And along those same lines, what if they were both heterozygous for the same two alleles? Do this for all the possible allele combinations and this would give you the probability of a match between two random people at a locus.

Slide 54:

Here is what that would look like in comparison to the heterozygosity. PD is a measure of how discriminating that particular locus is. Let's look at CSF1PO: If you chose two people at random and looked at their genotypes at that locus there is an 89% chance that you would discriminate between those two people—they would have different genotypes. That also means there would be an 11% chance that they would be identical. Keep in mind that when two people's genotypes at a locus match, it does not mean they are related. Let's look at TPOX: 80% of the time their genotypes will vary; however, 20% of the time they will be identical—that's 1 in 5. Also note that the heterozygosity closely corresponds to the probability of discrimination: you would get the same discriminating power ranking of loci using either of these calculations. I have ranked the highest three in order: D18, FGA, D21.

Slide 55:

Seeing the kinds of numbers that are generated from PopStats most people think to themselves, that's a number that's very close to zero, that's pretty rare, a pretty unlikely probability. What we do instead is that we express that number to the jury as a ratio of two whole numbers. Whole numbers go back to counting, and counting is a very natural thing for us—1, 2, 3.... Even though they are the same number arithmetically, the second one is communicated more effectively. This number can be explained as the probability that the profile found at the crime scene would match a person at random. If you subtracted the random match probability from one, you get the probability that we can exclude someone as having left that sample at the crime scene, as they don't match. Again, expressing this as a percentage of 100 is something that people are much more familiar with.

Slide 56:

Numerical conversion error, the mistake comes in the belief that if the frequency of a something is 1 in some number N, that you will not see it until you look N number of times. This is simply not true. You could see it the first time you looked, or you could not see it at all. The average is 1 in N. I think where the mistake comes from is that people imagine a finite group of people (let's say 1 million) and they imagine all 1 million people are in a stadium and someone has a winning ticket. Now it is easiest to imagine that in order to find the winning ticket we allow everyone to come through the exit doors and as they leave we check their ticket, and eventually we will come across the winning ticket. This is called sampling *without* replacement. However, this is not what is going on. We are sampling *with* replacement. Using the same imaginary scenario, 1 winning ticket among 1 million people in a stadium, we check their ticket at the exit, but, if they do not have the winning ticket they are asked to go back into the stadium, so the population of people holding tickets always remains at a constant 1 million. We are not whittling our way down to the winner. And if you do the calculations you'll see that over one-third of the time you will not find the winning ticket.

Slide 57:

The easiest way to do this arithmetically is to use a Poisson distribution. Again, the 1 in a million is an average. If you were to look for the winning ticket 1 million times, what are the chances you would never find it, the chance you would find it once, or the chance you would find it more than once? This applies when n is relatively large, p is relatively small, and the product of those is 1.

Slide 58:

This slide sums us what we discussed with the stadium and the winning ticket analogy. Another place that I have seen this misapplied is determining what the probability is that two siblings have the same genetic profile. And not surprisingly, it comes out to be more common than the random match probability. If they have the same parents, there are at most four possible alleles at each locus and there are a limited number of combinations that the offspring could be. The number works out to be something like 1 in 2 million (about), and the fallacy comes in when someone says, no one has that many siblings (of the same sex) so it is impossible for them to have the same profile. This does not follow. Now, I will agree it is *unlikely* but not impossible. For example, there have been cases where potential hits have been made in databases at 12 loci (for example) and the offender and the person already in the database are brothers.

Slide 59:

Another way of looking at the indeterminacy in a system is called "odds." An odds is just a ratio of two probabilities. As I mentioned earlier, when you divide one probability by another probability, you no longer have a probability. A probability is conveniently located on a scale from 0 to 1, so when you quote a probability you immediately have a sense of that number. But when you divide one probability by another this no longer holds true. There is no bound, and the number can get infinitely large; however, it cannot go below zero (bounded on lower end).

First I want to point out that odds and probabilities are just two ways of looking at the same thing. The odds here is going to be the probability that the event does not occur (person does not have that genotype), compared to the probability that the event does occur (person does have genotype). It is a ratio of these two things; it is no longer a probability. But, if I gave you the odds, could you calculate the probability from that? It is possible. With some algebra you get the final equation in blue. This type of equation is used when calculating the paternity index.

Slide 60:

Here's a word question. We've seen the genotype once, how many people would we have to sample before we have a 50% chance of seeing that genotype again? Many people might think that we need to look at 100 people. The chance of not seeing it is 0.99. Then we solve the next equation for N. When you do that, N = 69. Again, not 100! In other words, by the time you look at 69 people, you have a greater than 50% chance of seeing the 1/100 genotype.

The take-home is that we can expect to see that genotype before we get to the number in the denominator.

When you say 1 in a million, you in fact expect to see it well before you reach a million. The point I'm trying to make is that when you say 1 in a million it does not mean that you have to wait until you reach one million to find what you are looking for. Another fallacy associated with number statements like this is that once you have sampled one million people you are guaranteed to have seen it. This does not follow either, because again, we are sampling with replacement.

Slide 61:

How many people do we need to sample in order to ensure that there is a 99% chance of seeing it? And by solving the equation for not seeing 0.01% of the time, you'll find that we have to perform a significant amount of oversampling, a sample size of 459. And again, this is because we are sampling with replacement. We can never get to 100%. This scales up, just like before, to 1 in 4,590,000—again, very nonintuitive.

Slide 62:

I am going to derive an equation where the resulting product is very interesting and can be very useful in forensic science (and it has a long history of being used in forensic science). I want to point out again that all probabilities are conditional. This first line reads as: What's the probability that event A occurred, given that we had knowledge about event B? I would also like to point out that the opposite equation, the probability of event B, given that we have knowledge about event A is not equal. This rearrangement of the equation is called "transposing the conditional." When this is done the resulting two equations are typically not the same. This type of mistake can be made with the random match probability, sometimes called the prosecutor's fallacy. We are going to be deriving Bayes' theorem in the odds form.

Slide 63:

Now I am going to replace the probability of event B with the complement (B with a bar over top). If we divide the lower two equations by each other, the probability of event A (nonconditional) will cancel out leaving us with a ratio of two odds. This is called Bayes' theorem in the odds form.

Slide 64:

These three components have names. The center component is known as the likelihood ratio (LR), the right-most component is known as the prior odds, and the left-most component the posterior odds. This is saying that if we had some way of determining the prior odds (the probability that even B occurred versus the probability that event B did not occur), then we were given some new information that could be incorporated into the likelihood ratio, such as how event A influenced event B and B's complement. By multiplying those two together we could solve for the posterior odds.

Slide 65:

Now we are going to incorporate some values that have forensic meaning. In this case "guilt" means the person in question committed the act and left their DNA at the crime scene. For transfer evidence the likelihood ratio portion of the equation is usually a very large number. The numerator of the likelihood ratio component is the probability that the DNA evidence matches the suspect's given that he committed the crime. So, the forensic analyst is essentially comparing DNA from the same person. The probability of this event should be relatively close to 1. The denominator is saying that the suspect's DNA does not match the DNA found at the scene, and this would be the random match probability. Let's use one in a million. This would be verbally stated as "it is a million times more likely that this DNA match would be seen if the suspect had committed the crime than if a random person had committed the crime." This is sometimes called the "weight of the evidence." Remember that we can never discuss our answers in terms of the posterior odds, and that is because we need the prior odds in addition to the random match probability, and only the jury can determine the prior odds.

Slide 66:

Just to make my point clear, I have placed the three components in parenthesis with their corresponding names below. It is important to keep in mind that the LR is just that, a ratio, and not a probability. In addition to that, it exists on a scale of zero to infinity. And the two events (hypotheses) in question have to be mutually exclusive.

Slide 67:

Just another way to think about this...

Slide 68:

The LR can range from zero to infinity. When the LR equals one, the two hypotheses being tested are equally likely. When the LR is greater than one, which it most often is with DNA evidence, the numerator hypothesis is more likely than the denominator hypothesis.

Slide 69:

Some verbal equivalents for these LR numbers, this table is taken from a book by Evett and Weir [3].

Slide 70:

Since DNA evidence most often exceeds these numbers, Evett later published a revised table [4].

Slide 71:

Let's talk about statistics in general; up until this point we have been talking about probability. Statistics is a way of taking data and generating probabilities. Statistics are applied when trying to make a decision based on limited information; we never have perfect, complete information. I joke that statistics "is never having to say you're certain." In statistics we have a question that we're interested in and to answer this question we collect samples. Typically, the question or decision deals with a large group and we cannot examine the entire population in question, exhaustively, to know for sure. In forensics we are trying to establish a reasonably accurate estimate of the probability of the frequency of a genotype. The information from the samples (in our case allele frequencies) allows us to make inferences about the larger unit and make some decisions about it. Sampling in statistics is critical. How to sample, what those sample can tell us, is there a bias in the sample, and do we have to correct for certain things are all questions to be asked. These questions can be addressed by taking replicate samples and determining the sampling variance. Almost all of statistics is based on taking a random sample.

Slide 72:

These are some examples of questions that might be asked where statistics might be applied. The take-home here is that the sample size depends on what the question is and how precisely we need to know the answer.

Slide 73:

Much of statistics is based on assuming that you have a random sample. Random samples for human populations are very difficult to obtain. Something that is often done is the collection of "convenience" samples. There is a third way of sampling that typically does not make it into forensic-type applications and it is known as a "judgment sample." These are used by pharmaceutical companies during drug trials, where they don't want just a random sample of people. You most likely want equal representation of males and females, with dispersion over the age range, and essentially you are arranging your sample given what you already know. This type of sampling is also used with museum collections.

It is important when sampling to ask yourself: What is the question? And how much imprecision is allowable? Keep in mind that the accuracy of the sample is not determined by the size; with a larger sample you would expect there to be less variation (more precision).

Slide 74:

Hypothesis testing is a paradigm that goes back to the 1920s. It is called the Neyman-Pearson model of hypothesis testing. We are testing two things: (1) whether the populations these samples were taken from are in the Hardy-Weinberg equilibrium, and (2) whether the populations the samples were taken from are in linkage equilibrium. We want to know these two pieces of information because we want to use the product rule.

Now we can see when it is set up in this fashion, there are two ways that you can make a correct decision and two ways in which we can make an incorrect decision. The first of these is called a type I error (alpha), where the hypothesis is rejected but actually is true. There are also type II errors (beta), where the hypothesis is accepted but is actually not true. We want to know the specificity of our test, and we call this the power of the test, and we find this by subtracting beta from one.

Slide 75:

The first question we ask is if the observed numbers fit what the Hardy-Weinberg theory would predict. We can calculate the expected numbers for each of these genotypic categories, collect a sample, and then compare the observed to the predicted numbers. If they are close we conclude that they are consistent with one another. The classic way of doing this is to use the chi-square test.

Slide 76:

The chi-square test is known as the "goodness of fit" test. The problem we encounter when we try to apply this type of a test to the genotypic data that we deal with is that we have so many genotypic categories. The kinds of statistics that were done on the databases we use are based on resampling methods.

Slide 77:

Reasons why these "complicated" statistical tests are necessary for our databases.

Slide 78:

There have been a series of tests performed on the databases to ensure that they are in Hardy-Weinberg, and one of those is called "bootstrapping." Let's say we have 200 people in a sample and we are going to use this sample to determine allele frequencies at a locus. We could use the counting method, or we could use bootstrapping. Bootstrapping can tell us how much variation we would see in another sample (for the thing that we are calculating) without actually taking another sample. We take the initial sample and we treat it as if it were the population we are interested in and we resample from it *with replacement*. We then compare the numbers obtained from the resampling to the initial observations. We then repeat this procedure n number of times. This is often done with computers now, very quickly and cheaply. From this we can develop a distribution around any one particular allele frequency (in our case) and then determine a 95% confidence interval for that distribution. This statistical technique was first suggested by Bradley Efron (1973) and it is a very widely used statistical technique.

[3] Evett, I. W., and B. S. Weir. 1998. *Interpreting DNA Evidence: Statistical Genetics for Forensic Scientists*. Sunderland, MA: Sinauer Associates, p. 226.

[4] Evett, I. W. et al. 2000. *Science & Justice* 40:233–239.

Slide 78 (continued):

It gets its name from the expression "pull yourself up by your bootstraps," which is an impossible thing. This application might seem impossible too, sampling over and over again to generate more data. There are also some older techniques that have been used on our databases and I want to introduce them just so that you are familiar with their names.

Slide 79:

An older technique, known as jackknifing, was popular before the time of computer power. One at a time we would eliminate an observation from the data set. For example, if our data set contains 200 observations of allele frequency, we would perform the appropriate calculations and then we would eliminate an observation leaving us with 199. We would then perform the same calculations over again generating a second table of allele frequencies (slightly different from the first). We would then return this observation to the data set, and remove another (different) observation and perform the calculations again. So, in essence, we would generate 200 subsample allele frequency tables, each with 199 observations. Again, we could use the distribution of that data to put it in context by looking at the variation surrounding the variable we initially wanted to measure. The value in performing either the bootstrapping or jackknifing approach is that we make no assumptions about the distribution. We can have a normal distribution, or a bi-modal distribution, or even skewed distributions—it does not require that we have an asymptotic (aka normal) distribution. In other words, we resample by leaving one observation out of the original N observations to create N subsamples, each of size N – 1. This technique was first proposed by John Tukey in 1953.

Now I'm going to get into permutation tests, which were actually used on the FBI databases. Using an example with five people's genotypes, I can determine whether the population these people were selected from is in the Hardy-Weinberg equilibrium, just by shuffling the five people.

Slide 80:

We are going to permute the original sample, which will generate a new genotypic distribution. Typically this needs to be done 400 times (which can be done easily with computers). There are no assumptions made about the shape of the distribution, and this technique is widely used in many areas of statistics, not just forensics.

Slide 81:

Exercise for class: Each student receives five blank index cards. They write the genotypes "AA" on three of them, and "aa" on two of them. They then tear the cards in half (separating the two alleles) and randomly shuffle them together (to simulate random mating). When finished they will randomly place the 10 halves into 5 pairs (5 new individuals). As per the slide, after doing this, there are only three possible combinations of cards: no heterozygotes, two heterozygotes, or three heterozygotes. We can then determine the observed allele frequencies and compare them to the precalculated expected Hardy-Weinberg frequencies. Using this information, one can determine whether the sampled population was likely in Hardy-Weinberg equilibrium.

Slide 82:

Genotypic array (just like the vWA data), if we were to perform a chi-square test (which in practice we would not because N is not large enough), but if we did, we would find that sample #1 (no heterozygotes present) was rejected because it had a probability of occurrence that was less than 5%. It would be more valid to come to this conclusion using a permutation test on samples such as these than to use the chi-square test. We can imagine that these might be samples of 150 to 180 people, where there are 20 alleles at a locus, and so forth, so there are a lot of genotypic combinations, but the logic works in the same way. The computer would permute these samples to give an estimate of what the probability is that we would see a sample like the one that was obtained (that's in the database, in PopStats), to determine if this sample is consistent with a sample that is in Hardy-Weinberg equilibrium, and the results are, yes, it is.

Slide 83:

I have an example here of how quickly it can get complicated. This is a sample with 10 individuals and 3 potential alleles at a particular locus. Ultimately, the point I want to make is that the FBI databases have been shown to be in Hardy-Weinberg equilibrium, and even more so with the application of the theta correction factor.

Slide 84:

I have some references to software that perform these types of tests. I believe all of the data in PopStats was analyzed using the first reference, DNA type.

Slide 85:

Let's get into why the NRC II recommends that we use a minimum allele frequency of 5/2N. I would like to start out by saying that it is a fairly general problem, where we would like to estimate the frequency of something we have never seen before. So, if we take a sample of 1,000 and we don't see the "thing" we imagine exists, what can we say about its frequency? A frequency of zero may not be correct. The thing may be so rare that we would not see it in a sample of 1,000. But, we can model the upper confidence level of the frequency of something that did not show up in a sample of a certain size.

In 1992 Bruce Weir suggested that we could use this approach to determine a minimum allele frequency for alleles we did not see when sampling for the databases, where alpha (α) is the significance level, which we typically set to 0.05 or 5%, and 2N where N is the number of individuals we have sampled, and 2N is the number of copies of the gene observed. So, for example, let's say we have looked at 200 people, or 400 copies of a particular locus. We have never seen a particular allele (maybe an off-ladder variant) but it turns up in a case. It is not present in our databases so we apply this formula. Doing so, we can calculate the 95% upper confidence level of that allele frequency, even though it has never been seen before. When calculated, the answer is very close to 3/2N. This formula is also used for mitochondrial DNA as well as Y-haplotype estimates. A few years later, Dr. Weir and colleagues published another paper where they took into account that in forensics when we see a mutation at a genetic loci it is almost always a jump of a single core repeat (e.g., a 14 allele becomes a 15). To account for this, they incorporated a new term C, where C is the number of alleles that have actually been seen. So, we can imagine that if there are more alleles at a particular locus, then there are more opportunities for mutations to generate alleles that have not been seen before. The NRC II looked at this, and they decided to simplify it by suggesting 5/2N, where 5 is more conservative than 3, meaning greater than 95% CI, closer to 99% (have not actually calculated it out). PopStats applies this when an allele is entered that is not present in the databases or has been seen less than five times.

Slide 86:
    As the database gets larger, you can use lower minimum allele frequency estimates. One of the features of using larger databases is that we can calculate rarer allele frequencies/rarer genotype profiles.

Slide 87:
    Examples for each of the three methods, note that the Budowle method is with eight alleles at the locus (a little low for STRs).

Slide 88:
    Here there are 16 alleles at the locus, and we can see that in this case the Budowle method is more conservative; however, labs that are using PopStats use the 5/2N approach.

Slide 89:
    Another question regarding databases that comes up is the question of minimum size. There is not a single number answer to that question, like 119, but instead you have to consider what the database is being used for and how the data will be applied. For our application we need to keep in mind that the number of alleles at a particular locus are within an intermediate

range. There are currently no loci with as many as 50 or as few as 5, so there are some boundaries. We want our sample to be large enough that we are seeing all of the common alleles. In population genetics, an allele that is present in 5% or more of the population is considered a common allele. So, when determining the sample size, we want it to be large enough to ensure we see common alleles at least a few times but not so large that we see every conceivable allele—that is why we have the conservative minimum allele frequency estimate of 5/2N. If we have STR loci with 5 to 15 common alleles, then a database of 120 to 150 individuals is adequate to give us the required precision we need for STR profiles.

There are often issues that come up regarding offender databases that now, at the national level, have several million entries. The question that comes up regarding "cold hits" is what kind of discrimination do we need as databases get larger.

Slide 90:

As the size of the databases gets larger, the number of comparisons that we are making between people goes up exponentially.

Slide 91:

As the offender databases grow in size, there have been studies conducted comparing the individuals contained within, and when that was done high-order matches were found. Out of the 13 CODIS loci, there have been 12, 11, and 10 loci matches. Subsequently, these matches were determined to be among brothers. In later years, 13 loci matches have been found between brothers in the databases. There have been some very interesting articles on this subject published in the *LA Times* by Jason Felch.

Slide 92:

Moving away from random match probabilities, to finding matches among relatives; PopStats allows you to calculate this, it's called the relatives calculation. We will be calculating conditional probabilities for a specific genotype between people with a given degree of relatedness (e.g., full siblings, half siblings, or parent–offspring). Relatedness refers to a common ancestor, the further those two people are from the common ancestor the less their chance of inheriting the same alleles. The relationship that has the highest probability of possessing identical genotypes is siblings (which is higher than a parent–child relationship). In order to perform these calculations we need to know the specific genotype and the degree of relatedness.

Slide 93:

These formulas were developed in the late 1930s by Charles Cotterman. He developed an algorithm to determine the amount of genetic sharing between any two people within a pedigree.

This formula calculates the chance that full siblings have an identical genotype. For example, at a locus the genotype is 14,14 and the allele frequency is 0.10. The chance that full siblings would share this homozygous genotype is 1 in 3. If the alleles are more common, then the chance of sharing increases. On the slide I have used 1/4 per locus, this would be true if both parents were heterozygous.

Slide 94:

If both parents are heterozygous at a locus, then there are four possible offspring combinations (barring any mutations).

Slide 95:

Across the top, there are four possible genotypes for the first child, and along the side there are four possibilities for the second child, and these two events are independent of one another. Of those 16 combinations there are four instances where both children have the identical genotype. Now let's suppose that one of the parents is homozygous. That will limit the possible genetic combinations for offspring, leading to only two genotypic possibilities. But we also have to consider both parents being homozygous; that will mean that all of their offspring are identical at that locus. If we were to average all of these scenarios together, the average of full siblings having an identical genotype at a locus is 1 in 3.

Slide 96:

The leftmost column where I have used 1/3 most accurately reflects what we might observe in real life, we can see for 15 loci it is more than 14 million. But again, as we discussed earlier, just because people do not have 14 million siblings that does not mean this will never be seen; it just means that it is rare. The formulas are available in NRC II. This was for full siblings.

Slide 97:

Now let's do half-siblings. The measure of relatedness is how many meiosis events separate the two individuals, or in other words how many meioses have occurred going back to their common ancestor. The more meiotic events that separate them, the less likely it is that they share genetic components. Half-siblings share one parent; the probability of half-siblings having an identical genotype is 1 in 18 (homozygotes). With the parent–child relationship there is an obligate sharing; there has to be at least one allele at each locus that is common to both. However, the relationship between full siblings has a higher probability of having identical genotypes, but two siblings could also not share any common alleles (i.e., completely different genotypes), especially if both parents are heterozygous. We will also find that the sharing of one allele at a locus is not that different than what you would expect between random people.

Slide 98:

First cousins, still using the 14,14 genotype with a 10% allele frequency, and using the NRC II formulas, the probability of first cousins having an identical genotype is approximately 1 in 31.

Slide 99:

Some labs actually generate these numbers for each case so that they are available upon request. Keep in mind that these are conditional probabilities and to calculate them we need a specific genotype and a defined degree of relatedness; and the highest probability of sharing identical genotypes is among full siblings.

Slide 100:

It is also important to keep in mind that this is a different question than kinship. With kinship we have two profiles, which are different from one another but with *some* allele sharing. Now the question becomes what is the probability these two people would share this number of alleles if they were full siblings (for example). We will discuss kinship later on in the course. Keep in mind that PopStats can calculate both of these for you.

Slide 101:

At what point does the random match probability get so small that we can say with reasonable certainty that, yes, the profile at the crime scene and the reference sample that was analyzed are both from the same person. This is called the source attribution statement. In the NRC II there is a section on "uniqueness."

Slide 102:

Imagine that we have a genotype and we have calculated the random match probability. The exclusion probability is 1 minus that RMP number. The chance of not seeing that profile when we looked for it in N number of people is $(1 - P)^N$. Then we have to consider what risk we are willing to take in terms of making a type I error. It is up to us to decide the significance value, alpha. For example if we want to be 99% sure of not making a mistake we would set alpha to 0.01.

Slide 103:

There are three variables, and they have been constrained so that they no longer act independently, and by using this equation we are trying to set certain values for alpha and N, leaving P free to vary.

Slide 104:

Looking at some actual values, down the left column we have increasing population sizes of N, and along the top we have increasing values of alpha. This chart represents cut-off values, for example, using the last N (approximate population of the world), and we want to be 0.9999% certain, then we would need a random match probability that is less than 1 in 6.5 $\times 10^{13}$. Then we can say with a specific degree of certainty that the source of a particular profile is a specific individual. Some labs use this approach; some labs choose to report the random match probability—it is completely up to your lab.

Slide 105:

These are some possible statements that I am aware of in Canada.

Slide 106:

This is a statement of David Stoney, a well-known trace analyst. It is like when you are a child in grade school and everyone makes snowflake cutouts and the teacher says there are no two snowflakes that are identical.

Slide 107:

I cannot emphasize enough how important it is for you to know about this report, as many jurisdictions are following the guidelines from the NRC II. If asked in court any questions about why your lab follows a certain procedure regarding statistics, you can cite the NRC II. And it is not just that the guidelines are published in a book, but the NRC II is a highly esteemed committee. Dr. James Crow (a very distinguished individual and a member of the National Academy of Sciences) put together a group of population geneticists that had no connection to the prosecution or the defense. There were also statisticians and forensic scientists, as well as legal professionals on the committee. Virtually all the members of NRC are also members of NAS. The report holds a great deal of weight. It is written from a completely unbiased point of view, and the committee approached the issues from a strictly academic perspective. Now, I'm not saying that no committee is infallible, because that is certainly not the case. But just that this is a very important document. It is also not a document that you read like a novel; it has great organization to allow for quicker referencing. It has a very useful executive summary that I would suggest you read. Being familiar with the report and your lab's implementation of the recommendations will help to assist you with any line of questioning you may encounter in court.

Slide 108:

There are nine recommendations that I would really like to hammer home during this course. The first being correction factors for homozygotes. Empirical data suggests that 0.01 sufficiently corrects in most parts of the modern world. For native populations it is increased to 0.03. By not applying the same correction factor to heterozygotes we are, in fact, being more conservative.

Slide 109:

These are the number of populations that were used in the empirical studies to determine theta.

Slide 110:

These values are calculated per locus, because each locus is a sample of what is happening at this level of genetic differentiation and substructuring within populations. When the values are negative that simply means that there was an excess of heterozygotes, when compared to Hardy-Weinberg expectations. These are most likely to be sampling effects. We then take these values per locus and we average across all 13 CODIS loci. If we look across the populations at all loci, nearly none of them even comes close to 0.01, the exception being Native American populations.

Slide 111:

The remaining CODIS loci, again, the same repeats itself. When we take the average we can see that using a theta value of 0.01 is very conservative for all populations tested, except the Native American populations, and that is why we use 0.03. Just a reminder, these values are for North America.

Slide 112:

Let's look at European populations. Again the application of a theta of 0.01 is conservative.

Slide 113:

And among Latin American populations, the average is still well below 0.01.

Slide 114:

The conclusion from these studies is that the empirical data supports the recommendation that a theta correction of 0.01 is conservative.

Slide 115:

NRC II, equation 4.1 with the application of theta will make it more common. There are additional formulas, 4.10a and 4.10b, and they are modeling something slightly different. They are calculating the probability of finding that same profile in the *same* subpopulation that the accused originates from— even when we cannot define what the subpopulation is. This formula enriches the database with the very profile that we are trying to estimate the frequency of. PopStats allows us to do this, and this is called the conditional random match probability. The condition being, given that we have already seen this profile once, what is the probability that we would see this profile a second time? Having seen this profile once it suggests that maybe those alleles are a bit more common in the subpopulation they originated from, and so this formula enriches the database with those alleles and then performs the calculation. These formulas are a little more conservative and there are several jurisdictions throughout the United States and the world that use them exclusively.

Slide 116:

This is the model these formulas are based on. We know that in real populations there is substructuring (indicated by circles). Formula 4.1 is used to determine the frequencies among the entire general population, whereas formulas 4.10a and 4.10b are used to determine the frequencies within specific subpopulations (i.e., within a circle).

Slide 117:

The second NRC II recommendation is to *not* include error rates in these calculations. They suggest this for several reasons: (1) it is almost impossible to measure the error rate, and (2) is there such a thing as an error rate that we can apply to all casework (no two cases are the same). They suggest that we retain a portion of the sample being tested, and we do so at the earliest possible juncture. In this way, if anyone ever questions whether a mistake was made, there is still a sample remaining to analyze a second time. Although in some cases this may not be possible. In those cases, it is suggested to at least keep some of the extracted DNA. Instead of incorporating an overall error rate into the calculations, we examine each of the analysis steps separately utilizing controls.

Slide 118:

On the other hand, you want to be careful about stating that your error is zero.

Slide 119:

The NRC II's third recommendation is not to use the "ceiling principle." This is an idea that goes back to the NRC I report (1992), and the very early days of DNA. At this time the statistics were performed in a very cautious manner; looking back, we now know they were overly cautious. This ceiling principle said that we would look up a particular allele frequency (let's say D3:12) in all of the databases, and we would use the most common frequency found. We would do this for each allele at every loci. So we end up mixing and matching, so to speak, generating the frequency of a hybrid profile. Using this approach we would never use an allele frequency less than 10%. However, the report also stated that as more data became available and additional populations were examined, then the 10% should be relaxed to 5%. Many people felt very strongly about this idea, on both sides of the argument. When the second NRC committee met it answered this hotly debated topic with the 5/2N recommendation. I would recommend that you take some time and learn the options that are available in your lab's PopStats installation or equivalent. I would also recommend that you have a feel for the size of each of the databases and their origins.

They also addressed the fact that these databases had been created from the sampling of FBI recruits (recommendation #4). Sociologically, this is not a perfect sampling of the demographics of the United States. The NRC said that "convenience sampling," as it is known, is okay.

The fifth recommendation is to provide a confidence interval. Now they do not say that we have to include this in our report. But that we make clear to anyone who uses this data (as jurors are doing), that there is imprecision. This imprecision is due in part to the database size but also the inherent variation within human populations. But keep in mind that the databases we use are adequate in size for the purposes they are being used for. And even if you made the databases 10 times larger, it really would not change the level of imprecision. The 10-fold recommendation is based on empirical studies (data contained within NRC II publication).

Slide 120:

The NRC II's sixth recommendation is that the database size should be several hundred. They were not exactly specific. What does *several* hundred mean? It most assuredly means more than one hundred, but does it mean more than two hundred? The DNA Advisory Board says that for STRs a database of 120 to 150 is okay.

The seventh recommendation addresses what to do if we do not have data for a particular population (a particular group of Native Americans, for instance). They say that we should use data from a database that is as close, anthropologically, as possible and to quote several numbers. This will demonstrate to the jury that no matter which database we use the 13-15 loci profiles are rare.

Slide 121:

OmniPop can be downloaded from www.STRbase.com. This spreadsheet uses macros that use population data that has been published in peer-reviewed journals, and based on the entered profile, it will report a RMP (from each of the available database) in the form of a histogram. You can even change the value of theta.

Slide 122:

This shows the origins of the populations that are the data behind the spreadsheet. In OmniPop there is a reference section that tells you about each of the databases used. This program has been validated, but you are on your own if you use it. The creator of this program has put it together as a hobby.

Slide 123:

Recommendation number 8 says to calculate the conditional frequency of related individuals when it is relevant to a case. For instance, if there is a question about the possibility that a brother is the actual culprit.

Slide 124:

Background: Labs submit profiles from crime scene samples in hopes of getting a hit. When the profile is uploaded it gets searched against local, state, and national databases. Sometimes you get a hit in the offender database— "cold hit." NRC II says that when we get a hit we should multiply the RMP by the number of people in the database of the hit (NP).

Slide 125:

Currently, there is not complete consensus among the forensic community on how to interpret mixtures. We are going to touch on several issues that arise when interpreting mixtures.

Slide 126:

When interpreting mixtures there are two main steps. Step one, eliminate the artifacts (such as stutter peaks, -A, pull-up, and spikes), followed by interpretation. Whenever possible, we should try to make our interpretation of the mixture based solely on the mixture alone, meaning before looking at reference samples.

Slide 127:

The types of samples where we can find mixtures.

Slide 128:

How to identify whether we have a mixture. There are more than three alleles at several loci. Several loci are necessary because there have been instances reported where single individuals have three alleles at a locus (tri-allelic). When these are encountered they are used to determine a match, but they are not used in the generation of statistics—there is no way to determine the probability of a tri-allele.

Slide 129:

Here is an example of a common two-person mixture. If all of the loci have four or less alleles we can usually conclude that we have a two-person mixture. The exception would be people who are related to one another. And this is not to say that it is not possible by combining three "random" people. If we have a locus with four alleles, we may want to start there to determine the potential mixing weights. If at one locus we determine there is a 3:1 ratio of contributors to this mixture that the ratio needs to hold true, *roughly*, at all other loci. Sometimes with mixtures all we can say is that a particular individual cannot be excluded as having contributed.

Slide 130:

I would say there are three ways we diagnose a mixture: (1) by the number of alleles at each locus, (2) peak height imbalance, and (3) stutter peaks being higher than our validation study suggests they should be.

Slide 131:

To simplify, either we can account for the alleles in a mixture sample or we cannot.

Slide 132:

Ladd et al. [5] break it down into four groups: First we are only able to make a qualitative statement, "cannot exclude." Many would argue that this statement needs to be qualified. For example, we only have a few loci, the loci are complex with 6 alleles. We may want to include some details clarifying that we could not exclude based on this limited amount of information. We are not getting good discrimination and a large portion of the population could also not be excluded from this mixture sample. Ultimately, we do not want to misrepresent the evidence to the jury, or allow/enable them to incorrectly misinterpret what we say.

The second approach is to deconvolute the mixture with major/minor peak heights, sometimes called "single sourcing" the contributors (differential extraction helps when applicable). The third is the probability of exclusion; the probability of inclusion and exclusion add up to one for mixtures. The purpose of the probability of exclusion lends weight to the fact that we were *unable* to exclude this person from the mixture. It is not necessary to calculate a probability if we did exclude an individual from having contributed to the mixture sample.

Last is the likelihood ratio approach. PopStats will allow us to calculate both of these last two. Using the likelihood ratio we have to make assumptions based on how many people are believed to be included in the mixture. People argue that the likelihood ratio allows us to take into account more of the information (such as peak heights).

Slide 133:

There have been rare instances of chimerism, which is different than somatic mosaicism. Somatic mosaicism is when some of your tissues possess a different genotypic profile, for instance, some men have shown a different profile in their spermatozoa. Chimerism is a similar situation, but these individuals have more than one genotype in various parts of their body, depending on how the chimerism came about. For instance, if blood was drawn and analyzed it would appear as a mixture sample (with chimeric bone marrow cells).

First, each of the peaks has to meet your lab/s criteria for a peak (threshold, morphology, etc.) to ensure we are not dealing with artifacts. There are several computer programs that have been developed to assist analysts with mixture interpretation.

Slide 134:

Least squares deconvolution: This method only works with two-person mixtures and it works out all possible combinations of alleles given those two people. The program calculates the mass ratio to explain the peak heights at a particular locus; it then does that at each locus. It then determines which mass ratio would best explain the entire profile of data. This program is available online from Dr. Wang. This is an aid that helps the analyst.

Slide 135:

Another program is the Linear Mixture Analysis designed by Dr. Mark Perlin. There have been several others developed as well.

Slide 136:

Many in the community feel we should try and avoid mixture interpretation through deconvolution. If we are unable to do so, we go with an exclusion probability or, if there are reasonable peak heights, perhaps a likelihood ratio. But again, this is all dependent on your particular lab's protocols.

Slide 137:

With the exclusion probability we assume Hardy-Weinberg, but we do not apply a theta correction factor, although there is a variant formula available in PopStats that will allow us to do so.

Slide 138:

Exclusion probability: If we have three alleles at a locus, there are six possible combinations of genotypes. We would calculate the Hardy-Weinberg probability for all six and then we would add them together and that becomes, for that locus, the probability of inclusion, that is, the fraction of the population that we would include at that locus. It is not saying that they all have to be there, but that is the fraction that is included at that locus.

Four alleles, same way, but we get more possible genotypes (a total of 10). PopStats will perform these calculations; even if you have 6 or 8 alleles, PopStats will still calculate it for us.

Slide 139:

If we have two alleles, we add up the frequency of those two alleles and then square the result; that number is equal to the sum of all possible genotypes that could not be excluded. Again, all done in PopStats, but always remember it is possible to calculate by hand.

Slide 140:

Using the likelihood ratio approach, we are calculating the middle term, and we are calculating the probability of seeing this mixture under the prosecutor's hypothesis (H1, numerator) and the defense's hypothesis (H2, denominator). There are some labs using this approach, but in general it is restricted to two-person mixtures.

Slide 141:

There are certain assumptions that are made: the independence of alleles and loci, and theta is not a significant issue. Next, it may cause you some pause when I say we must assume that all contributors are of the same racial group. But the reason I say that is because we need to obtain our allele frequencies to perform the calculation from somewhere. Theoretically we could take alleles from multiple databases to account for different scenarios but that would lead to a large number of calculations. Another statistically feasible possibility is to use a ceiling principle by taking the most common allele frequency from each of the databases and use that in the calculation, giving us a conservative estimate for that mixture sample. We also make the assumption that all contributors to the mixture are unrelated to one another; they are random. Now we can all imagine cases where we cannot necessarily make that assumption. We also assume that there is no allelic drop-out. There are other models that can be used when allelic drop-out is thought to have occurred. These calculations will also not account for peak height intensity differences (too close to determine major/minor). Last, clearly defined hypotheses must be present.

Slide 142:

The likelihood ratio gives you a "better" number, but it is a trade-off because those numbers are the result of the assumptions just discussed.

Slide 143:

Three allele scenario: For the probability of inclusion we are calculating the possibility of all of these genotypes, even though in a mixture all of them would not be present. This calculation does not mean we have to assume all possible combinations are present. But if we had a person that possessed an allele other than these three, they would be eliminated as having possibly contributed to the mixture. At some point to use this calculation we have to assume that we are "seeing" everything that is there (no low-level, no drop-out, etc.). Any contributor to this mixture must possess at least one of these alleles.

[5] Ladd, C., H. C. Lee, N. Yang, and F. R. Bieber. 2001. Interpretation of complex forensic DNA mixtures. *Croatian Medical Journal* 42(3): 244–246.

Slide 144:

Be careful about remaining objective and try to make your decisions and calculations before looking at the reference samples. What I'm saying is, when at all possible, try to interpret mixtures and make your conclusions before looking at the references. This may be the only way to remain completely unbiased.

Slide 145:

Determine all possible suspect genotypes that could not be eliminated, add up the frequencies of those alleles to get "big P"; if you then square that number it will give you the sum of all the homozygotes and heterozygotes included in this mixture sample. This is done for each and every locus, an inclusion for every locus. You then multiply those inclusions together locus by locus to get the CPI (combined probability of inclusion). This number represents the fraction of the population that you would expect would not be excluded from this mixture, and this particular suspect is included in this elite fraction of the world population that could not be excluded. You could then subtract this very small number from one to represent it as a percentage.

Slide 146:
The same holds true for a four-allele locus.

Slide 147:
CPE (combined probability of exclusion): Multiply all of the inclusions at each locus together, and then subtract that number from one and that gives us the CPE. Different labs choose to express this number to the jury in different ways, wording for effective communication (still all the same number with the same meaning).

Slide 148:
In some cases where we can deconvolute the mixture, maybe at 12 of the 15 loci, and the remaining loci are somewhat ambiguous, some labs might declare the three ambiguous loci as inconclusive (not use them in the calculation) and then proceed with a single-source calculation for the remaining loci. Another possibility is to use more definitive hypotheses. By that I mean for certain intimate samples you may be able to safely assume that particular profiles should be seen, and thusly, subtract them from the mixture.

Slide 149:
In an article by Gill et al. [6], the word "unrestricted" is used to mean that we are not using information from peak heights. Maybe it is not clear which peaks go with which, and maybe shared alleles are not clear, and so forth. By using this approach we are not going to restrict ourselves to certain allele combinations. For example, if there are three alleles we are going to assume that any possible combination of those alleles having come from two people is plausible.

Slide 150:
Let us assume this is an intimate sample and the victim is part of the mixture. The prosecution would assume this is a two-person mixture and after the victim's alleles are accounted for, that leaves two alleles that are attributable to the suspect (almost like a single source).

Slide 151:
What we will calculate in this approach is a likelihood ratio, where the numerator is the probability of seeing that evidence from the prosecution's perspective (the victim and the assailant), which has a probability of one. In the denominator is the probability that a random person could explain the remaining two alleles being contributed to the mixture. The number in the denominator is going to be less than one. When that is

divided into the numerator the resulting number will be greater than one (at this locus).

Slide 152:

Let's take another scenario where there are three alleles present but the victim is homozygous.

Slide 153:

The reasoning is very similar to the last example, if you assume a two-person mixture, when the victim's alleles are accounted for that leaves only two alleles for the suspect.

Slide 154:

And again it is one over the probability of a random person, like the random match probability.

Slide 155:

Three alleles; this is where it gets a little more interesting.

Slide 156:

In this case the prosecutor's hypothesis will not change, and the probability in the numerator will remain one. However, the defense's hypothesis will want to argue for more possibilities given that this combination of alleles allows for a heterozygous contributor to be masked.

Slide 157:

There are three possible genotypes to explain the evidence now. The two heterozygous possibilities are masked by the victim's two alleles (potentially).

Slide 158:

With those three genotypes, their corresponding Hardy-Weinberg frequencies will be added together (because it is one of these three possibilities, it cannot be all three; it is either one genotype or another [they are mutually exclusive]), and that number goes in the denominator.

Slide 159:

With this formula you can see that it is in the defense's interest to invoke as many contributors as possible. They may even try to pull in stutter peaks as actual contributors. By doing this they increase the size of the denominator, and in doing so decrease the probability (making it less incriminating, evidence has less weight [e.g., 1 in 500]).

Slide 160:

Now let's talk about two cases where the victim is not in the mixture (or we do not know whether the victim is in the mixture). In other words, we do not have a reference sample to attribute the additional alleles to (someone else is in there and we do not know who they are). I just want to show you that the algebra does get complicated but that PopStats is available to help you. Using likelihood ratios you can even take into account the possibility of allelic drop-out, which, with the current approaches is not easily handled.

Slide 161:
Let's look at this case with four alleles and two contributors.

Slide 162:
The suspect is heterozygous and matches two of the alleles, and there are two unknown alleles. If you make the assumption there are two contributors to this mixture sample, then the two remaining unknown alleles belong to the other. However, the defense is going to argue that there are a number of genotypic explanations for this combination of alleles. Remember, additional possible contributors in the denominator are in their favor.

Slide 163:
For the prosecutor's hypothesis of two contributors, one being the suspect and the other an unknown random person, we will have the Hardy-Weinberg expression in the numerator.

Slide 164:
Now in the denominator, along the top we have the various possible heterozygotes using the four allele set. If you assume there are two contributors, and you have four alleles at that locus, then everyone must be heterozygous. The combinations that would explain the presence of these four alleles at this locus are all along the diagonal. For instance, if one individual had A_3A_4, then the other contributor must have A_1A_2, and so on. There are a total of six combinations that could explain the given data set.

Slide 165:
Again, these are the six possible pairwise combinations from the previous slide. Here are the associated Hardy-Weinberg terms with the frequencies of each of the alleles, as well as two 2's since both contributors have to be heterozygous. Keep in mind that there are two ways in which these allele combinations could come about, having come from two people.

Slide 166:
The numerator is the prosecution's hypothesis, while the bottom is the defense's hypothesis with two random people and all six allelic combinations. Then this fraction reduces to simplified terms.

Slide 167:
With three alleles (and still not using peak height information) there are going to be many additional possible allele combinations in the denominator, and this is even true for the numerator. The prosecutor has to take into account possibilities of allele sharing with the third allele unaccounted for.

Slide 168:

The prosecution would acknowledge that the suspect is present in the mixture, but then they also have to account for the other remaining allele, and take into account the possibility of allelic sharing. In Hardy-Weinberg terms you will have the homozygous frequency, as well as the heterozygote with one shared allele, and the heterozygote with the other shared allele = numerator.

Slide 169:

Now for the denominator, there are many possibilities, including homozygotes and sharing (remember, we are still not using peak height information), and all the associated Hardy-Weinberg terms.

Slide 170:

Denominator continued, carried over onto another slide. Ultimately, PopStats can assist us with this calculation. But still, by looking at the resulting formula we can see that the numerator is still larger than the denominator, resulting in a rather weighty LR. Again, just to emphasize, in criminal cases we are only able to calculate the middle term (the LR). We cannot say anything about the posterior odds; that is for the jury to decide.

[6] Gill, P., C. H. Brenner, J. S. Buckelton, A. Carracedo, M. Krawczak, W. R. Mayr, et al. 2006. DNA commission of the International Society for Forensic Genetics: Recommendations on the interpretation of mixtures. *Forensic Science International* 160:90–101.

Slide 171:

Moving on to paternity and other associated calculations, such as missing persons, pedigree evidence, and disaster identification.

Slide 172:

DNA is very useful for several reasons, but it is really attractive because no other evidence has a hereditary component.

Slide 173:

We use mitosis to assist us in transfer evidence analysis. We use meiosis in paternity and missing person cases, and we exploit this pattern (Mendelian inheritance) in meiosis where there is a 50% transmission probability of codominant alleles.

Slide 174:

A classic paternity question is one in which we have three genotypes that are not identical. These are usually civil cases in which the evidence has been collected, handled, and stored appropriately so that degradation is not an issue. Also bear in mind that the court's decision in a civil litigation is not made based on "reasonable doubt" but on a "preponderance of the evidence."

In the majority of paternity cases the validity of the mother–child biological relationship is not an issue and not the relation being challenged. In classic paternity cases it is a question of who is the biological father.

Slide 175:

Given the three genotypes, we know which of the child's alleles must have come from the father, otherwise known as the obligate paternal alleles. Using this information we can exclude any male that does not possess the obligate allele. We can then calculate the exclusion probability for all of the genotypes in the population that do not contain the obligate allele, and thus cannot be the father of the child. If we did not have the mother's genotype to help us determine the obligate allele, we would have to modify our calculation to allow the father to be homozygous for each allele or heterozygous (given that the child is heterozygous). Under these circumstances there would be a much larger fraction of the population that could potentially be the father. Ultimately, we will get more power if we have the mother to help determine the father's obligate alleles and then perform the calculations accordingly.

Another approach is to calculate a paternity index (PI), and the PI is a LR, as it is a ratio of two probabilities. Some people have argued that the PI uses more of the available information, such as the genotype of the "tested man." If, for example, the potential father is homozygous for the obligate allele at a given locus then he is going to be twice as likely to have passed on that allele than if he were heterozygous at that locus.

Slide 176:

This calculation is very similar to the mixture calculations, although I stress this is the case if the pedigree relationships are true and in Hardy-Weinberg equilibrium.

Slide 177:

This is the formula that is used, and again you are calculating the LR or the middle term. The prosecutor's hypothesis (numerator) is that the alleged father is in fact the biological father, and the defense's hypothesis (denominator) is that the father is a random man not excluded (i.e., relatives). With this calculation you often see the prosecutor's fallacy where they transpose the conditional.

Slide 178:

Again, the PI is the ratio of two probabilities, meaning it is no longer a probability; where the numerator assumes paternity and the denominator assumes random man.

Slide 179:

These are two mutually exclusive, competing hypotheses that are both trying to explain the data in mutually exclusive ways.

Slide 180:

Just to emphasize what happens, if the two parents are heterozygous there are a number of genotypic possibilities for offspring given Mendelian segregation.

Slide 181:

This matrix represents the two siblings depicted in the previous slide. Here 2 means that both siblings are genotypically identical, 0 means they share no common alleles, and 1 means that there is one allele that is common to the two siblings. These are known as the phi coefficients, and for siblings $\phi_0 = 25\%$, $\phi_1 = 50\%$, and $\phi_2 = 25\%$.

Slide 182:

Many labs practice the rule that you must be able to exclude a male as being the father at two loci, at least—again this is based on the obligate allele.

Slide 183:

This is the most common pattern that is found, where both parents are heterozygous. I think it is clear that in this example the C allele is obligate. So we would calculate, using Hardy-Weinberg expectations, all of the genotypes that could contain the C allele, and that will give us the exclusion and inclusion calculations for that locus.

Slide 184:

Here it is represented algebraically. I think you can see that C is common to each of these terms, with the first being the homozygote and the rest various heterozygote combinations. The simplified formula is below and this is what PopStats uses to make these calculations. Remember that these calculations are performed at every locus.

Slide 185:

The exclusion calculation is one minus the inclusion calculation. Again, I have simplified the formula.

Slide 186:

When this calculation is performed over multiple loci, you multiply the inclusion probability at each locus, and then subtract that very small number from one to obtain the exclusion probability.

Slide 187:

Let's look at the LR approach. First, we have the Hardy-Weinberg terms for each of the parent's genotypes. Then there are the Mendelian ratios of passing that genetic information to their offspring. Now we multiply those four probabilities together, this will give us the expression that will be the numerator for the PI. As an aside, if the father was homozygous for C that would change the Hardy-Weinberg expression as well as the Mendelian transmission probability, which would essentially be one. These changes will make the numerator twice as large.

Slide 188:

Now for the denominator, the Hardy-Weinberg terms remain the same for the parents, but we also have to take into account the possibility that the C allele was passed on by a random man.

Slide 189:

The LR is called the paternity index when applied in a paternity case.

Slide 190:

The LR is all about the evidence. The evidence does not influence the hypotheses.

Slide 191:

Another way to think about it is how much support the evidence has from hypothesis #1 relative to hypothesis #2.

Slide 192:

One nice thing about the LR is that it often zeros in on the heart of the argument.

Slide 193:

A recap with Bayes' formula.

Slide 194:

It becomes more complicated when the mother and father share alleles.

Slide 195:

There are 15 possible combinations of genotypes for a paternity trio.

Slide 196:

Here are the eight where ultimately the PI ends up being 1 over 2 times the obligate paternal allele. These are all cases where the father is a heterozygote.

Slide 197:

Then there are four cases where the father is a homozygote. The PI ends up being one over the obligate paternal allele.

Slide 198:

The remaining three cases are cases where we are unable to determine the obligate paternal allele. In the denominator we essentially end up with "or" terms: it is either this allele *or* the other, which are mutually exclusive so we add those probabilities together.

Slide 199:

Keep in mind the combined paternity index is not a probability. Be careful not to confuse this acronym with CPI from mixtures, or combined probability of inclusion.

Slide 200:

An example of what the numbers can mean.

Slide 201:

Suppose we could calculate the posterior odds (often in criminal cases we cannot). We can only do that when we can put a number to the prior odds. Using the posterior odds we can calculate the POP. The POP (probability of paternity) is equal to the posterior odds divided by one plus the posterior odds.

Slide 202:

If we can calculate posterior odds, here is a summation of POPs.

Slide 203:

Another application of this approach is missing persons. What if Dad has gone missing? All of the formulas and algebra remain the same, but the question has changed.

Slide 204:

What if Mom goes missing? The same holds true. Except in these cases the question is not whether the alleged parent is in fact the biological parent of the child, but whether the remains (or other forensic evidence) is that of the missing parent. For these calculations we assume that the parents are in fact the biological parents.

Slide 205:

If remains have been found that are believed to potentially be the missing mother, we have this pedigree: we do not know the mother's genotype. Let me preface this with the statement that direct references are the best means of identification, but if they are unavailable, then this can be helpful. So, getting back to the pedigree, using this example the numerator will be the same as before.

Slide 206:

The only difference in the denominator is that we are looking at the obligate maternal allele (in this case). Many of the terms cancel out and it reduces to this simplified formula.

Slide 207:

Now if the child in this pedigree has gone missing …

Slide 208:

… the difference being that the denominator will be a slight bit different. Now we cannot assume that either of the parents are the source of obligate alleles. In the numerator we will assume that these two people are the biological parents. In the denominator, however, these are three random people (so to speak). This formula reduces to something quite different.

Slide 209:

This is sometimes referred to as the "parentage calculation." From the perspective of the remains, we are trying to establish the parents of the deceased child.

Slide 210:

The exclusion probability is only used with a first-degree relationship (parent and child). Otherwise, we have to use LR calculations comparing two alternative hypotheses.

Slide 211:

First we require a genetic connection. Often in times of emotional distress, unrelated individuals want to offer their DNA to help with an identification (e.g., spouses, step-relations, relatives by marriage, etc.), even though there is no genetic link between these individuals. In addition, the degree of relatedness between two people is the number of meiotic events between them.

Slide 212:

In pedigrees, full siblings have the highest degree of relatedness. The sharing between first cousins is "almost" indistinguishable from unrelated individuals. If the family possesses a rare allele, it makes identification much easier. The sharing of common alleles has less identification value than if the alleles were rare in the general population (maybe 1% to 2%).

Slide 213:

I previously mentioned the name Charles Cotterman. He was a graduate student at Ohio State University when he worked all of this out. In identity by descent, two people share the same allele because they inherited it from a common ancestor. However, we cannot measure this. We can never know that in fact this is the case and that they do not possess this allele merely by chance, or identical by state, meaning they have the same number of repeats (in our case). Even though this idea of identity by descent is hypothetical and cannot be measured, it allows us to make predictions about allele sharing between related individuals, which allows us to conduct kinship analysis.

Slide 214:

These represent the seven possibilities we could get when looking at two people at one locus. Among these relationships the two individuals can share all alleles, share one allele, or share no alleles. As a reminder, all of these combinations are possible among full siblings.

Slide 215:

We looked at this pattern of sharing among siblings when we discussed the phi coefficients.

Slide 216:

These are the result of identity by descent, not identity by state.

Slide 217:

These methods were published in 1954, again, long before we were using DNA for forensic identifications. This is an identity matrix that is the result of complete sharing, if two people share two alleles that are identical by descent. What this matrix is saying is that we do not expect two people to share in any other arrangement other than along the diagonal. These matrices are most useful to us because they result in equations. There are three matrices in total: 2 alleles, 1 allele (Slide 218), and 0 alleles (Slide 219).

Slide 220:

Using the sharing phi coefficients, we can work out the pattern we would expect to see of these combinations of genotypes between any two people. It comes down to these following equations. Now, I know they look daunting, and you are saying to yourself, "This is why I went into biology, to avoid such equations." I know it may look like rocket science, but if you want to calculate the probability that you would see that predicted combination if you had a sibling, you can insert the phi coefficient for that particular relationship, and it will give you the LR. There are various software programs and spreadsheets that will do these calculations for you and they will tell you what the LR is. And ultimately, it boils down to the rarer the alleles, the higher the LR will be.

Slide 221:

Here is a list of several programs that are available for free.

Slide 222:

There are also several commercially available programs.

Slide 223:

These are some average LRs that we might expect to see based on 15-loci identifications. For example, if we are trying to identify someone and we have references from both parents, we can expect a LR in the neighborhood of 3 million. If, however, only one parent is available we might think that the LR would be half as powerful. But, this is *not* the case. In fact, the strength of the LR is weaker than 50%. And given *only* this information, we may not even come to the conclusion that this is the child of this particular parent. One common rule of thumb when trying to identify people indirectly is that we try to get at least two close relatives.

Slide 224:

These are some pictures that I have excerpted from a book [7]. This shows us the LR patterns we would expect to get on a log-rhythmic scale (e.g., 5 on the scale is equal to $10^5 = 100,000$). These patterns are for 15-loci identifications. The solid line is for related people, and the dotted line is for unrelated people. This shows us that a large percentage of the time we are able to distinguish between full siblings and purported siblings (nonrelated people). Ideally, we would like for the two curves to have no overlap. In order to achieve this we could add more loci. How many loci, you ask? According to the calculations, we would need approximately 40 loci (with the discriminating power of the CODIS loci) for complete separation. To separate out full siblings it is thought that it is best to have a LR threshold of at least 1,000.

Slide 225:

These curves are for half-siblings. With less sharing between these people, it becomes harder to distinguish between related and nonrelated individuals.

Slide 226:

And last, first cousins. Distinguishing between related persons is possible but improbable, as first cousins and random people have equal amounts of sharing.

Slide 227:

We can think of the random match probability in three ways: (1) an attempt to estimate the frequency of a particular profile in the population. The issue we run into here is that the frequency we get is often smaller than 1, over the world's population—and people (jurors included) have a hard time wrapping their head around this number. It does not seem feasible. There are some labs in the world that cap the number and will just state that the statistic is below this cap. (2) Chance that a random person would have that genotype, a probability. (3) Chance if defendant did not leave his DNA he would match the crime scene DNA. These are three correct ways of thinking about what the random match probability means.

Slide 228:

When we quote the random match probability, it is *not*: (1) the chance that someone else is guilty. (2) It is also not the chance that someone else left the bloodstain (or other evidence). (3) Nor is it the chance of the defendant not being guilty. And last, (4) it is not the chance that someone else would have that genotype. With this last one, be careful with the use of the word "someone." To be correct, "someone" has to mean a random, unrelated individual.

[7] Buckleton, J. S., J. M. Triggs, and S. J. Walsh. 2005. *Forensic DNA Evidence Interpretation*. Boca Raton, FL: CRC Press, 2005.

Slide 228 (continued):

Often many of these mistakes are made when people are trying to make the stats more clear/understandable for the jury.

Slide 229:

This is called the prosecutor's fallacy because there is a tendency for prosecutors to believe this is what the random match probability actually means, but it is a misinterpretation. The error comes about by transposing the conditional. Instead of looking at the probability of the evidence given the hypothesis, you are looking at the probability of the hypothesis given the evidence.

Slide 230:

Another mistake that we may see in the courtroom is the defense attorney's fallacy. The fallacy often revolves around a group of people with the same genotype having the same prior odds for having committed the crime. Another probable place that we see this error is with mixtures. We must be very careful and cautious. Be prepared and well versed in these common errors so that you do not commit them yourself, or verbally agree when an attorney does so. These are very easy errors to make, especially when speaking and you don't have the leisure of writing the words down and reviewing them for correctness.

Slide 231:

When presenting statistics in court, here are a few pieces of advice I would like to offer: (1) Keep it simple. It will help your credibility if you keep your testimony understandable to all who are listening. You want to come across as well versed, knowledgeable, and trustworthy. (2) I like to try to come up with vivid metaphors to help others understand the points I am trying to make. For instance, it can be hard for people to understand one in a trillion. Most people do not encounter numbers in the trillions in their everyday lives, so it can be hard to fathom. But you may want to stay away from games of chance (e.g., cards of a deck, flipping coins, etc.). It may inadvertently portray the idea to the jury that guilt or innocence is almost like a game of chance, and that is certainly not what we are trying to convey.

Also when testifying it is important, and effective, to answer and make eye contact with the jury, even though the attorneys are the ones who asked you the questions. Be sure that you come across as a human being to the jury. But, be careful. Realize that your demeanor is being observed even before you come to the stand. You want to be sure that you are seen as someone who is taking this seriously. You are a professional, a knowledgeable expert. Remember that it is not just what you say, but your body language and how you are dressed. Also be sure to be completely prepared, and that you have reviewed the case and your notes. As we all know, a considerable amount of time can pass between the time that you examined the evidence and when the case goes to trial. You will also want to be careful to control your demeanor when answering questions for the prosecution and the defense. You will want your demeanor to remain the same. You do not want to come across as favoring one side or the other.

Another thing that I found helpful is to pause for a few seconds before answering the question.

Slide 232:

Here is a list of some of the questions you are likely to encounter regarding statistics. One of the most popular—so be prepared—is in regard to the size of the database. Many people have a hard time understanding how we generate such powerful numbers using databases that contain 150 people. Many people also ask why we do not use offender databases to calculate allele frequency. We have these very large databases that contain millions of people. It would seem logical to many people that these would be very useful for this purpose, and they would be. However, there is legislation that prohibits the offender databases for use in science. So, although it would be great to ask a lot of interesting statistical questions using these databases; it is not allowed by law.

Just keep in mind that the databases are of adequate size, and they have been scrutinized. We are following the NRC II's recommendations (in terms of size). So, for the purposes of the application that we are using these databases for, they are perfectly adequate in size.

You will also get questions about the fact that you do not have a database for the specific racial or ethnic group that the defendant is associated with. But remember that the differences between databases is not that great, so even if you were to get a database for the specific background of the defendant, the reported statistics would not change markedly, and the profile will still be rare. Also, if the defendant did not commit said crime, then we have no reason to believe that the actual culprit is from the same specific background as the defendant. This often comes up in urban areas where you have large ethnic neighborhoods, such as in New York City. Along these lines, you will also get questions about population substructure.

Questions regarding "relatives" and the random match probability are common. You cannot answer this directly. Yes, it will be more common in a relative, but you cannot give a number for a relative unless you have the specific degree of relatedness (e.g., sibling, half-sibling, first cousin, etc.).

The Hardy-Weinberg assumptions come up as questions. Many of these assumptions are not met in the real world. All of the assumptions in some way are invalid; however, when you take samples of populations you cannot statistically detect differences from the Hardy-Weinberg equilibrium, and therefore we do not reject the model of the Hardy-Weinberg equilibrium.

The same holds true for linkage equilibrium. Believe it or not, there are populations where correlations have been shown to exist for genes on different alleles. But for our loci of interest, it has been tested and correlations have not been detected on a population level, even for those on the same chromosome.

Slide 233:

Ideally, I would like to convey my thoughts on presenting statistical evidence in court: keep it simple. The people of the court will be better able to digest, understand, and retain what you have presented if you do so, and thus, associate the appropriate weight to this invaluable evidence.

ISO Accreditation Implementation

5

A Framework to Implement a Quality Service

HAROLD PEEL AND MURRAY MALCOLM

This chapter is written by Dr. Harold Peel (former director of the Royal Canadian Mounted Police Laboratory) and quality subject-matter expert Murray Malcolm. Peel and Malcolm have many combined years of experience implementing and auditing many public and private service laboratories worldwide. Their well-known text on this subject, Introduction to Accreditation for Forensic Labs, is referenced by many laboratories operating in accordance with ISO/IEC 17025 and the Standards Council of Canada, ASCLD/LAB International, and Forensic Quality Services, and is used to sustain accreditation in many forensic laboratories (Malcolm and Peel, 2005).

Background: International Organization for Standardization (ISO) and Accrediting Bodies

The International Organization for Standardization, commonly known as ISO (http://www.iso.org/), is a federation of national standardization bodies from over 110 countries around the world (International Organization for Standardization, 2013). Based in Switzerland, its mission is essentially to promote the development of standardization to facilitate international exchange of goods and services. International committees prepare standards for ISO, which are in turn supported by many technical committees from ISO membership countries.

These international standards cover a vast range of topics to facilitate standardization in manufacturing and international trade and services, such as laboratory testing. ISO 9001 *Quality Management Systems Requirements* (ISO 9001, 2000) is the internationally recognized accepted quality management standard, which is widely used throughout the world for companies and agencies that provide manufactured goods or supply services. The standard ISO/IEC 17025 (2005) *General Requirements for the Competence of Testing and Calibration Laboratories* (ISO/IEC 17025, 2005) is accepted worldwide as the primary document that recognizes technical competence, as well as quality management.

All elements of ISO 9001 are included in the management portion of the standard ISO/IEC 17025(2005). A big part of a quality system can be stated as, "Say what you do, and do what you say."

However, there is a big difference between ISO 9001 *certification* and ISO/IEC 17025 *accreditation*, the latter requiring the laboratory's technical and scientific competence be assessed by a team of qualified scientists. Qualifications and capabilities of personnel, scientific validity of test and calibration procedures, and proficiency testing are examples of what is assessed in terms of compliance with the standard and the laboratory's own procedures.

In addition to ISO, there are several international committees that supply information that may be useful to a laboratory seeking and maintaining accreditation. One of the main committees is ILAC (International Laboratory Accreditation Cooperation). Its guidance and technical documents are available on its Web site http://www.ilac.org/ (International Laboratory Accreditation Cooperation, 2013). One of the most pertinent is the guide for forensic labs, ILAC G-19:2002 (ILAC Guide 19, 2002), but there are several others. You are well advised to consult them.

Accrediting Bodies

Who accredits an accrediting body? Who can accredit to ISO/IEC 17025? ISO has a demanding standard and audit for accrediting bodies to meet before they can be recognized internationally. There can be many organizations (government sponsored or independent) within a country capable of being recognized as offering accreditation to ISO standards. Many are qualified to *audit* an organization for ISO 9001 for certification. Fewer are recognized to *assess* laboratories for ISO/IEC 17025 for accreditation, and still fewer who list forensic laboratories in their scope of accreditations. It is important for the laboratory seeking accreditation to be aware it is speaking with an accreditation body (AB) that can meet its requirements. In the United States accrediting bodies that are recognized as competent to accredit forensic laboratories include ASCLD/LAB International (American Society of Crime Laboratory Directors/Laboratory Accreditation Committee; http://www.ascld-lab.org/), ANSI-ASQ/FQS (National Accreditation Board/Forensic Quality Services; www.forquality.org/) and A2LA (American Association for Laboratory Accreditation; www.a2la.org/). In Canada and Australia, the accreditation bodies include, respectively, the SCC (Standards Council of Canada; www.scc.ca) and NATA (National Association of Testing Authorities; www.nata.asn.au).

It should be clear that all sorts of scientific specialties, such as forensic sciences, can be accredited under ISO/IEC 17025, but because the standard has to be written rather generically to cover all specialties, its elements are sometimes a poor fit for a given specialty. To counter this problem, an AB is permitted to apply amplification documents that address the unique features of certain scientific specialties. All the requirements of ISO/IEC 17025 must still be met, but the amplification documents may add requirements and clarifications so that ISO/IEC 17025 better fits different specialities. ILAC Guide 19:2002–*Guidelines for Forensic Laboratories*, which describes the scope of work conducted, some terminology, and some suggestions for operational procedures common to forensic laboratories, has been accepted by ABs offering accreditation specifically for forensic laboratories. Check the ABs listed earlier for their amplification documents.

Why Consider Accreditation? Advantages and Some Considerations

Advantages

In some places, the law requires that forensic laboratories be accredited. If that is not the case in your jurisdiction, you as a manager have to ask why would your lab voluntarily take on the task of becoming accredited. It's going to cost time and money, and not just a one-time-only expenditure, either. These costs will continue as long as you choose to maintain your lab's accreditation status.

Some of the benefits that are generally cited are increased confidence of personnel in their work, improved control of operations, increased credibility with customers (i.e., police and courts), and savings of time and money. This latter point may sound contradictory but it has often been found that a close look at administrative and technical procedures in terms of quality (as demanded by the accreditation process) can yield increased efficiencies and effectiveness. The lab's customers should see improved liaison, and have a better understanding and increased public confidence in your laboratory's services. In the courtroom, the evidence provided by an accredited laboratory is usually considered more accurate and reliable than that from a nonaccredited laboratory. As a result of looking at procedures from a quality system perspective, there is usually a reduction in repeated tests, fewer errors are committed, and fewer reports have to be recalled because of mistakes or weak procedures. Furthermore, accreditation can be a real source of pride of accomplishment for staff, and this pride often leads to improved morale, as they see they have the same accreditation status as their peers, both national and international.

The 2009 report by the National Research Council, *Strengthening Forensic Science in the United States: A Path Forward* (NAS, 2009), was a wake-up call for everyone working in crime laboratories, and brings out the importance of quality and consistency in forensic technologies. For all of these reasons, virtually all forensic laboratories throughout the world are accredited or considering the accreditation process.

But Consider

As the legendary fighter of oil-well fires Red Adair allegedly said: "We can do it fast; we can do it cheap; we can do it well. Pick any two." That about sums up lab accreditation as well as anything.

Accreditation using qualified scrutiny by an outside credible third party offers added assurance and credibility. Quality is no accident and has to be carefully planned for and maintained with a constant effort for improvement. It does cost time and money, particularly in the initial phases of preparation and implementation. If your lab is already operating with quality processes in mind, there may be little change to meet the requirements of the standard. The ISO standard arises from the notion of best professional practice, with some common sense thrown in. The preparation phase should not become a lot of change just for the sake of change, massing up piles of paper that ought to have been left in the form of trees. Accreditation does not necessarily demand any change in your laboratory's practice, but if your procedures (managerial and technical) are not up to an assessment by a qualified team of assessors who are forensic scientists, then changes can be expected.

Most important, it is crucial that laboratory management be fully committed to the laboratory becoming accredited. In addition to the ongoing commitment of time and money to quality assurance activities, you will note that there are five or six specific elements in the standard that are addressed directly to lab management. These elements require the involvement of top management in the details of communication and review. Most lab managers would take on these tasks just because its good management practice. But you are also required to do them in order to comply with ISO/IEC 17025. The specific elements will be considered later in this chapter, but for now, the lab manager should be aware that the activities connected to accreditation cannot be delegated completely to a quality manager. Accreditation to ISO/IEC 17025 is definitely a hands-on process.

You may hear some opposition to accreditation. It is a common accusation, for example, that accreditation requires huge amounts of documentation, much of it useless. Documentation *is* a crucial part of the process and is often the most difficult part of setting up your quality system in terms of time. Procedures (managerial, administrative, and technical) must be written (paper or electronic) in a clear and concise detail that will not cripple the intended activity. If your lab does not have such documentation, you will certainly have to create it. But the lab manager needs to be clear: the standard does not demand overdocumentation. The manager must be vigilant to ensure the quality system created remains as lean as possible.

As well, some individual specialists may express concern that accreditation is an unwarranted intrusion into their professional domain. However, an understanding manager can resolve this, as it is hard to deny that a review by a qualified peer assessor is entirely consistent with best professional and scientific practice.

Because it involves considerable staff time and there are fees paid to the accrediting body, the costs for laboratory accreditation are highest in the initial preparation and implementation phases. Depending on the starting point and situation, some labs or agencies may need 10% to 15% of the budget on quality assurance. Once the quality system is accredited, the manager can expect these costs to drop somewhat.

Terminology

To more clearly understand the accreditation process, the lab manager is well advised to become familiar with the terminology used in the following outline and comment of the standard ISO/IEC 17025. Many of the official definitions are contained in ISO Guide 2:2004 (*Standardization and related activities—General vocabulary*) and ISO 9000:2005 (*Quality management systems—Fundamentals and vocabulary*) (ISO 9000: 2005, 2013). These documents can be purchased from ISO or national standardization agencies. As some of the *ISO* terminology can be rather complex, we have tried to interpret a more simple meaning for the purposes of this chapter.

accreditation: The recognition by an objective third party that a lab is competent to carry out certain named tests or examinations.

standard: A document containing specifications, requirements, or rules that have to be met. In this chapter, it usually means the document ISO/IEC 17025. (There is some risk of confusion here since it is common to refer to a pure chemical compound used to set or calibrate a measuring instrument as a standard. In the ISO world, the pure chemical is referred to as a reference material. The process of using such a reference material to set a measuring instrument would not be called "calibration." That term would be reserved for the metrologically sound procedure by which a measuring instrument, such as a balance, is linked to a national or international reference, such as the International Kilogram. The use of a pure chemical compound to set a measuring instrument would be referred to as "standardization," possibly "verification" in some contexts.)

standardization: The idea that "we all do it the same way." At different levels of use it can mean using the same method, meeting the same specifications, or complying with the requirements of ISO/IEC 17025.

quality: This word is something like "art" (hard to define, but recognized when it is there). ISO has a complicated definition, but for the forensic laboratory think of quality as "reliability" or "accuracy."

quality control (QC): All of the technical, bench-level things a competent analyst/examiner does to make sure that the test results she obtains are reliable. These things would certainly include the routine use of control materials, charting the control results, doing the stats on them, and interpreting trends in the data. But the idea can be widened to include calibration checks on balances, for example, checks of wavelength calibration in spectrophotometers, monitoring volumes dispensed by auto-samplers, and so on.

quality assurance (QA): Refers to the reliability of test results, too, but with a broader meaning that encompasses all the QC measures used, and in addition includes all the other activities, whether technical or administrative, that a lab performs in order to ensure reliability of its test results. So this would include the training program that is in place. It would include practices such as having a second analyst review the analytical work of the first before the test report is sent to the customer. The procedures by which the lab provides reagents of the proper purity for analysis would be included; so would the procedures of detecting and correcting errors. And so on.

quality management: Everything a laboratory does to lay out its policy with respect to quality of test results and to put those policies into action. It will include QC, QA, planning, setting objectives, making improvements, and so forth.

quality system: The organizational structure, procedures, and processes that the laboratory uses to make quality management happen. (ISO/IEC 17025 uses the term management system, which is also known as quality management system [QMS].)

quality policy: The broad statement of the overall direction that a laboratory intends to take regarding quality in its operations. Typically, this will be stated by top management in the quality manual.

quality objectives: Something sought or aimed for which relates to quality. (A quality objective would be a stated goal of management to accomplish something specific with respect to the quality of the laboratory's operation. There may be several quality objectives, but it is crucial that these objectives must be measurable.)

quality manual: The standard (ISO/IEC 17025) requires that every accredited lab have a quality manual, in which the lab's quality policy and objectives are stated, and the quality system (see earlier) is described. No particular format is prescribed. For now, the lab manager can think of it as a sort of map describing the operation of the lab and the documents needed in that operation.

should/shall: These terms are used in the QA world specifically to indicate what is optional and what is mandatory in the standard. "Should" indicates a suggestion or a recommendation, but the laboratory is free to follow the suggestion or not, as it chooses. The word "may" carries the same meaning. This word only appears in NOTES in ISO/IEC 17025, not in the text of the elements themselves. On the other hand, the word "shall" indicates that there is no option; it is mandatory to do as instructed. The words "required" or "requirement" are often used to convey this same idea. (But be warned: Some accrediting bodies and some auditors may interpret a "should" as a "shall," so be sure to check it out.)

policy/procedure: The standard uses these two terms extensively; several elements require that the lab have documented both policy and procedure(s). The manager will certainly have some knowledge of both. It is important to understand that they are quite different. As noted earlier, a policy is a statement of the overall direction or thrust an organization takes with respect to a stated issue. Policy can often be stated in a sentence or two. By word count, there are nine clauses in the standard that require a statement of policy. They are shown in Table 5.1.

By contrast, a procedure is a detailed description of how a policy is put into action. Typically it says what is done, who does it, when and where it is done, if those are important, and sometimes how it is done. A policy might give rise to several procedures. Again using a simple word count, there are 33 clauses in the standard that require a procedure. These are listed in Table 5.2. Depending upon the exact nature of the lab's work, some of these may not apply. However, the majority of labs, including forensic labs, will certainly need procedures for most of the clauses.

Table 5.1   Mandatory Written Policies

ISO 17025 Clause Number	Description
The standard requires a policy statement in nine subject areas. A lab may have additional policies, to meet organizational needs, but the following nine are the minimum.	
4.1.5c	Protecting customers' information
4.1.5d	Avoiding activities that decrease confidence
4.2.2	Quality
4.4.1	Review of contracts
4.6.1	Purchasing
4.8	Resolving complaints
4.9.1	Handling NC
4.11.1	CA
5.2.2	Training

Table 5.2   Mandatory Written Procedures

4.1.5c	Protecting customers' information
4.1.5d	Avoiding activities that decrease confidence
4.3.1	Document control
4.3.2.2	Document review/available where needed
4.3.3.3	Amending docs by hand
4.3.3.4	Changes to docs in electronic systems
4.4.1	Review of contracts
4.6.1	Purchasing
4.8	Resolving complaints
4.9.1	Handling NC
4.11.1	CA
4.13.1.1	Records
4.13.1.4	Electronic records
4.14.1	Internal audit
4.15.1	Management review
5.2.2	Training
5.3.5	Special housekeeping
5.4.5.2	Validation
5.4.6.1	Estimate of uncertainty (calibration)
5.4.6.2	Estimate of uncertainty (testing)
5.4.7.2	Protecting electronic data
5.5.6	Use of equipment
5.5.10	Intermediate checks—equipment calibration
5.5.11	Updating correction factors
5.6.1	Calibration of equipment
5.6.3.1	Calibration of reference standards
5.6.3.3	Intermediate checks—ref. stds.
5.6.3.4	Handling, etc., of reference standards
5.7.1	Sampling
5.7.3	Recording sampling data
5.8.1	Receipt, etc., of test items
5.8.4	Avoiding loss/damage of test items
5.9.1	QC monitoring

Procedures may be required for the unmarked clauses (*) as well but that has to be decided for each individual laboratory. If the lab has a DNA section, for example, or a trace analysis section, or a firearms section that conducts analyses for gunshot residue, procedures will certainly be needed for special housekeeping (5.3.5). The manager will need to use judgment concerning the remaining clauses. Check for any amplifications that may be applied by your accrediting body.

ISO/IEC 17025 (2005): Outline and Comment

To fully understand the following comments, a copy of ISO/IEC 17025:2005 should be available. When you flip through ISO/IEC 17025:2005, you will note immediately that it is divided into two major sections: Section 4, which covers management or administrative elements, and section 5, which covers scientific and technical requirements. We have tried to focus on the key parts of these elements, so the lab manager has a clear overview, uncluttered by fine detail. In addition, there are some areas in which the standard lists several separate but related clauses. In these instances, we suggest that it may be more efficient for the lab to consider the separate clauses as a cluster and, possibly, deal with them all in a single process.

Outline of the Managerial and Technical Requirements

Management Requirements (Section 4)	Technical Requirements (Section 5)
4.1 Organization	5.1 General
4.2 Management system	5.2 Personnel
4.3 Document control	5.3 Accommodation and environmental conditions
4.4 Review of requests, tenders and contracts	5.4 Test (and calibration) methods and method validation
4.5 Subcontracting of tests (and calibrations)	5.5 Equipment
4.6 Purchasing services and supplies	5.6 Measurement traceability
4.7 Service to the customer	5.7 Sampling
4.8 Complaints	5.8 Handling of test (and calibration) items
4.9 Controlling of non-conforming testing (and/or calibration work)	5.9 Assuring the quality of test (7 calibration) results
4.10 Improvement	5.10 Reporting the results
4.11 Corrective action	
4.12 Preventive action	
4.13 Control of records	
4.14 Internal audits	
4.15 Management reviews	

Section 4

Organization (4.1)

This introductory requirement defines the structure of the laboratory within which the quality management system is built. It is made up of four major requirements: being legally identifiable, accepting responsibility to meet the requirements of the standard ISO/IEC 17025, implementing a management system at all facilities (permanent, satellite, temporary, mobile) of the laboratory, and clarifying any activities that may have potential conflict of interest, particularly if part of a larger organization. In addition this clause contains a list of 11 required subclauses of specific items related to such things as responsibilities and authorities of managerial and technical managers, customer confidentiality, backup personnel, communication within the laboratory, a defined organizational structure, job descriptions, and the appointment of a quality manager. The lab manager is well advised to take an active role in considering what has to be done to comply with these clauses since they impinge directly on the structure of the organization. As noted earlier, the standard has several elements that are directed specifically at lab management. Clause 4.1.6, concerning communication, is one of these. To understand the full content of this first requirement, this part of the standard should be closely studied as well as appropriate amplification documents from the selected accrediting body, which may have supplemental requirements.

There are two clusters that include elements from 4.1. The first might be called the "communication cluster." It is made up of clauses 4.1.5k, 4.1.6, and 4.2.4. They refer to communication processes of several types that the manager is responsible for organizing and implementing.

The second might be called the "conflict of interest cluster." It is made up of 4.1.5b, 4.1.5c, and 4.1.5d (i.e., undo influence, confidentiality, improper activities). It may be useful to think of these as a unit because it may be possible to cover all three requirements with a single signed agreement by the staff. Note that 4.1.4 is a conflict of interest clause as well but its focus is at the organizational level rather than at the personal level.

Management System (4.2)

This requirement includes seven clauses that demand a lot of work and organization. Again, several of these clauses are addressed directly to the lab manager. To begin, a management system must be established and fully described in a quality manual regarding all policies, systems, procedures, and objectives of assuring the quality of the laboratory's results. The management system has to be relative to the scope of tests of the lab. The manager needs to recognize that the lab is not required to create policies and procedures for things the lab does not do. Now, this may seem painfully obvious, but it can be interpreted as authorizing the lab not to overdocument and amass stacks of useless paper. Just keep it simple! Staff who are working in the management system need to be made aware of, and understand, the content of the management system.

You, as lab manager, need to attend very closely to clause 4.2.2. It is stated as your responsibility to approve and issue a definitive quality policy statement. Typically these statements can be brief but must include the following five elements: (a) management's commitment of quality to customers, (b) statement of the lab's standard of service, (c) relation of the management system to quality, (d) familiarity with, and use by staff of documentation related to quality, and (e) compliance to the standard.

Clause 4.2.2e and 4.2.3 form part of the continuous improvement cluster. As noted earlier, it may be advantageous to consider the concept of continuous improvement as expressed in these clauses, as well as in 4.10 and 4.12, and create a unified process that complies with them all. Other clauses in 4.2 note the importance of meeting the service needs (i.e., casework) of customers, specific content of the quality manual, roles and responsibilities of personnel, and preserving its integrity during any modifications. Writing a quality manual is a big job, one that you will certainly delegate to key members of staff, but which you as manager would be wise to stay closely connected with.

Document Control (4.3)

In 4.2 (management system) and 4.3 (document control), there are several clauses addressing the broad topic of documentation. It is a central aspect of the standard and is often one of the more difficult parts to initially address, as well as being a topic on which some laboratories are weak. Documentation can be paper, or electronic, or a combination of the two and must be readily understandable and available where needed. Furthermore, the standard interprets the word "document" very broadly, including manuals and procedures, but also drawings, tables, and software (Note 4.3.1). But what documentation does the standard require?

One can imagine a hierarchy of quality management system (QMS) documents, with the quality manual (QM) at the top.

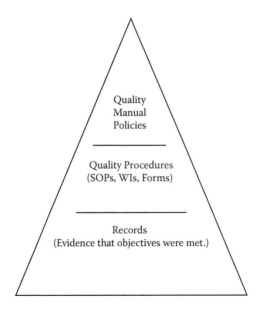

In 4.2.2, the standard lays out the requirement for a QM. There is no official format for a QM, but, as 4.2.2 notes, there are some statements of policy and standards of service that must be included in it. Some laboratories put only statements of policy in the QM, quite rigorously segregating all procedures to separate documents called "procedures," or "protocols," or "standard operating procedures (SOPs)." The net result is a QM in which is stated all the lab's policies (lab manager's input here), with references to all the procedures and SOPs by which those policies are put into action. The QM is like an index or a map. When that is done, the QM will be quite a brief document, possibly a couple of dozen pages.

Immediately below the QM in the documents hierarchy are procedures (SOPs, detailed work instructions). The rule of thumb is that the laboratory must have an authorized document describing how to carry out every procedure in the lab that could affect the reliability of a test result. There would necessarily be an SOP for conducting the management review, for example, and a procedure for ordering supplies, and another one for handling exhibits from crime scenes, and so on. Of course there would be a procedure for each test or examination the lab conducts, and one for proper operation of every piece of equipment.

Below the SOPs, one might list work instructions. One common interpretation of the term "work instruction" is that of a very concise, usually step by step, abbreviation drawn from an SOP that is too long to be easily and conveniently used at the bench. Worksheets and forms might also be listed in this group. And at the bottom of the hierarchy are all the records that arise from carrying out all the procedures. Records are so important that the standard devotes all of section 4.13 to their proper handling.

This produces an impressive list of documents, which leads to the second part of the documentation system: document control. Each of these documents has to be controlled, which means that someone (often the quality manager) has to make sure that documents are readily available where they are needed at the work site, that only the current version of each is available, and that there is no chance that an obsolete version could be used inadvertently. Document control also requires that certain information be included on all controlled documents, that they be approved for use by an appropriate authority, and that they be reviewed periodically and revised if necessary to keep them current. (If writing the lab's documents was a large task, controlling them afterward is at least as large.) Although excellent document control can be done in manual all-paper systems, there are also several commercial data systems available that work extremely well.

We mentioned earlier a criticism that has been leveled at accreditation generally, and accreditation to ISO/IEC 17025 specifically, namely, that the process leads to overdocumentation. This is so important to the diligent lab manager that we offer some additional comment. It is true that laboratories may create excessive documentation. This may happen because of a mistaken assumption that certain documents are demanded by the standard. Sometimes an auditor has demanded them without justification. At worst, documents may just be written with the intention of mere compliance. The standard does not require useless documentation. It specifies a QMS that is *appropriate to the lab's scope of activities.* The lab manager plays a key role in determining what is appropriate. And you must make the decision; you cannot count on external auditors to make it for you. As a general rule, an auditor will review whatever documents the lab submits, assessing only whether those documents comply with the standard. (If the lab has submitted a lot of extraneous material, the auditors will likely ignore it.) Too much documentation is not a non-conformity, however, so the auditor has nothing to say about it. But it can bog down the operation of the lab and be an impediment during an audit when conflicting points are found. It can be described as a Goldilocks situation—not too little documentation, not too much, but just the right amount.

Contract Review (4.4)

The standard describes the review of contracts that must take place. This is a "shall" statement, so it is mandatory, but this element can be a bit confusing for public sector forensic laboratories. The lab manager is well advised to give this element serious thought. The language of the standard speaks in terms of a "contract" existing between the laboratory and its customers. Of course, the contract for forensic laboratories is the understanding between the police departments and your lab to have certain examinations performed. This understanding may not be a written contract as such but simply provided in a "statement of services." Remember, however, that ISO/IEC 17025:2005 encompasses all sorts of labs and sometimes the fit with a forensic lab operation may be less than perfect. The standard states that such a contract must exist and that the lab must have a policy to review it. Your lab needs a procedure governing how you decide whether you have the resources and expertise to address the customer's request. Your procedure should indicate how targets for turnaround time on results are negotiated with the customer. All of these factors may be covered in a statement of services developed by your laboratory in consultation with its police customers. This section brings out important considerations regarding available resources and the lab's capability to do the tests/examinations, liaison when changing service lines, and record keeping.

Subcontracting (4.5)

If some of the work under the lab's normal scope has to be subcontracted to another part of the organization or to an outside agency, then there is a responsibility to ensure the subcontractor is competent. Such situations can arise when casework backlogs occur, temporary problems have developed, or outside expertise is needed. The customer is to be made aware of situations where subcontracting is done. If subcontractors are used, they must be listed in a register along with complete records. (However, if subcontracting is not a part of the lab's operations, it can be clearly stated in the QMS.)

Purchasing (4.6)

The lab's policy and procedures for selecting and purchasing services and supplies have to be documented. Although the standard says this applies to those supplies/services that affect the quality of the test samples, it is usually easier to write the procedures to include everything. The standard requires that your lab ensure that reagents, equipment, and so on are suitable for the purpose for which you intend to use them and not used before they are verified. To show that the purchasing process is a controlled procedure, there must be clear details defining who approves and signs purchase orders before they are sent out, and that they are examined on receipt. (Such approval may require a *technical* evaluation of the service or supply item, if appropriate.) Finally, a list of suppliers of those reagents and services, which are deemed as critical to the tests/examination results, is maintained along with records of appropriate evaluations.

Customer Service (4.7)

At first glance, the elements included within the customer service requirement may not seem to be of highest order, given all the other complex issues the forensic lab encounters. However, in the context of demonstrating that a quality service is in place, the manager knows that matters related to cooperation; good relationship; and service to the police, courts, and public are important. Such things as reasonable accessibility to the laboratory (with appropriate security and confidentiality), communication, and customer feedback are included. Addressing this requirement links nicely to the requirement under management review (4.15).

Complaints (4.8)

Although the complaints requirement of only two sentences may seem like a minor topic included under management requirements, it would be a mistake to assume, as a consequence, that it is not very important. It is in a cluster of three related elements dealing with mistakes, errors, and things gone wrong, namely, 4.8, 4.9, and 4.11. We will expand on this later. For clause 4.8, simply stated, the requirement is to have policy and procedure in place to address, resolve, and record complaints. Since the phrase "received from customers or other parties" is used in the standard, complaints from both external and internal sources must be considered. Besides clarifying the complaint, the procedure should identify the individual(s) responsible for investigating the complaints, correcting any problems, and contacting the customer or the employee who raised the complaint in the first place. All that information forms part of the complaints record. A first step could be to develop a procedure to determine the seriousness or merit of the complaint, who is to handle it, and how to proceed in its resolution.

The lab's immediate goal—and one of the main points of your complaints procedure—must be to correct the problem. Once the problem is fixed, that could conceivably end the matter. But common sense (and the spirit of the standard) would dictate that, if it is possible to fix the problem in a way that prevents the problem happening again, that is what should be done. This connects logically with your lab's procedure for dealing with non-conformity, as we will see in the next section.

Control of Non-Conforming Work (4.9)

Control of non-conforming work is the second element in the "NC–CA (non-conformance–corrective action) cluster." Non-conforming work can mean a test result or a laboratory report that is inaccurate, not following your own procedures, or not meeting the standards of quality that you have stated. But there is much more to interpreting this term as the definition of non-conformity from ISO 9001 is "nonfulfillment of a requirement." The key idea here is that something has gone wrong—possibly serious, possibly not so serious—and the clause requires the lab to have a written policy and procedures to follow whenever something does go wrong, meaning there will be a statement of policy in the quality manual, and you will have procedures for addressing non-conformances. These procedures will, among other things, identify who has the authority to stop testing, to recall reports already issued, to order that necessary changes to lab procedures be implemented, and to order that testing resume once the problem has been fixed.

You can see how the complaints procedure can be one way of identifying potential NC. Imagine it like this. Somebody has complained to your lab, triggering your complaints procedure. The complaint may have merit or it may not. If it has merit, it must be identified as a NC, and as soon as that happens, your NC procedure should kick in. Obviously, fielding complaints is not the only way to identify NC, but it is one of the ways. When the procedure for dealing with non-conformance shows that the NC could occur again or the lab's own policies and procedures are not being followed, corrective action procedures (4.11) have to be put into action.

Continuous Improvement (4.10)

Continuous improvement in a short clause seems almost like a break in the discussion around complaints (4.8) and non-conforming work (4.9). This is not a "policy-and-procedure" element, so your lab is not required to make a policy statement in your quality manual nor are you required to write a procedure covering continuous improvement (CI) to comply with this element. However, there is a strong streak of redundancy in this section because you have already seen CI previously with two clauses that speak to continuous improvement as a requirement, that is, in the statements of quality (4.2.2e), and evidence of commitment to continually improve the management system and its effectiveness (4.2.3). We noted that these clauses were particularly addressed to the lab manager. As noted earlier, it might be to your advantage to think about them as a cluster.

About all this requirement (4.10) contributes is to state a few specific tools you are expected to use in your CI efforts. When you consider the overall tone of ISO/IEC 17025, it appears to consider CI the key to an effective management system. The seven tools are quality policy, quality objectives, audits, corrective actions, preventive actions, management reviews, and analysis of data. Your lab must be able to demonstrate that it is taking action to facilitate CI through the use of these tools.

Since policy and procedures are not required by this element, an audit cannot, strictly speaking, ask for them. What the team can ask for, however, is "evidence of compliance." And you need to consider what evidence you have at hand. On the technical side could there be improvements in accuracy and sensitivity, or perhaps efficiencies in examinations, tests, and handling crime scene materials? There may be the belief that lab results are already sufficiently accurate, understandable, and timely to meet the needs of customers, so what is the point of getting faster and more accurate if customers do not need it? Perhaps you need to find out if your customers really are completely satisfied with your service. It is unusual in a forensic laboratory where turnaround time for test results was not an issue. These are questions that the lab manager must focus on.

Corrective Action (4.11)

Corrective action is the third element in the NC–CA cluster. It requires a policy statement in the quality manual, and a procedure (possibly more than one) for corrective actions (CAs). There are four specific elements required within the corrective action process:

1. To identify the root cause of the problem (cause analysis) and eliminate it so that the problem never happens again. This may not be a simple and quick process and it may take days, or even weeks, to complete. For that reason alone, a lab should be cautious to trigger its CA procedure when it is not necessary.
2. To select an action that meets the seriousness of the problem. As some complaints and non-conformances are more serious than others and it is recognized that some problems are more grievous than others, careful judgment is applied to determine the optimum

corrective action so the problem is eliminated and should not happen again. The standard does set a parameter here to say that the action applied shall be appropriate to the magnitude and the risk of the problem. In other words, you don't have to use overkill.

3. Following the implementation of the CA, to monitor the results to ensure they were effective. Your corrective action procedure would logically include this step, and the CA record would naturally show that the monitoring had been carried out. The lab can set up whatever monitoring effort it considers appropriate, but it must be shown that every action has been checked for effectiveness.

4. To conduct additional internal audits as soon as possible if there was a non-conformance identified with the laboratory not following its own policies and procedures, or with the standard, or if there is serious risk to the lab's service.

It is important to distinguish between the corrections or fixes you made using the procedure for non-conformances (4.9.1c) and the formal CA procedure being described here. Many (probably most) of the NCs that are flagged are usually comparatively minor occurrences. They would be fixed, you would keep a record of the NC and the correction, and you would get on with your lab's work. As mentioned before, there are really only two situations in which the standard states that your NC procedure would have to lead to the corrective action procedure:

1. if it appeared that the non-conformance is likely to recur, or
2. if your initial investigation of the NC showed that your lab may not have been following its own policies and procedures

If the procedure for non-conforming work is written well, it will reliably distinguish major incidents from minor ones. That means that only major incidents are directed to the corrective action procedure, where larger amounts of lab resources (i.e., money and time) become focused on fixing the problem. Minor issues will be dealt with swiftly and simply.

Because lab management would logically want to know how the system is behaving, the manager should encourage lab staff to flag NC every time one appears or is even suspected. It will also be useful if the lab manager can be sure that the procedures used do not trigger the formal CA procedure unnecessarily.

In the aforementioned cluster of requirements (4.8 complaints, 4.9 non-conforming work, and 4.11 corrective actions), it is easy to see the requirements as a reasonably coherent whole, with logical connections. However, by looking at these issues together, the laboratory can avoid creating several independent procedures—possibly overlapping, possibly redundant and wasteful.

No lab wants to be stuck in a quagmire of documents. Given the importance and complex relationship of these requirements, an approach is offered at the end of this chapter using a flow chart to understand the interrelationship.

Preventive Action (4.12)

Preventive action is described as a proactive process that anticipates problems before they develop. An ISO-based management system is always striving for improvement and this requirement calls for the lab to have a means to identify potential sources of non-conformities. Procedures for non-conformance and corrective action deal with problems that have already occurred, whereas preventive action tries to anticipate the problem and prevent its occurrence before it happens.

An example of a preventive action might be your monitoring of turnaround times (TATs) for reports. Let's assume you have set a TAT target of 10 working days. Let's also assume that your normal TAT fluctuates around 5 working days. If you see TAT beginning to increase—up to 6 days, then 7 days—as a manager, you might choose to take preventive action. Sometimes it is useful simply to think of things your lab has already done to improve some part of its operations such as exhibit reception and control, anticipating end-of-life for critical equipment, scouting out backup suppliers for reagents/materials for critical tests, anticipating staff retirements, and so on. Often, those improvements can be interpreted as ways of preventing NC. They would likely count as preventive actions if they were documented properly. Preventive actions might also arise from monitoring critical points and performance measurements of your total operations. Occasional staff meetings to scout out potential problems or make improvements, involving all levels of administrative and technical activities, are often useful for identifying preventive actions as well.

Records (4.13)

Aligned with the control of documents (4.3), the control of records is a major part of the quality management system. Unlike some earlier clauses, records control is not an activity that the lab manager is likely to have much contact with day to day. But it is crucial that the manager be involved in setting up the procedures in the first place.

The standard requires you to have procedures describing how your laboratory identifies, collects, indexes, accesses, files, stores, maintains, and disposes of records. Records have to be legible, retrievable, and stored in a protected and secure environment. If records are stored on the fifth floor, and only the director's administrative assistant has a key, it may be hard to argue that they are readily retrievable. On this point, you will recognize that the key thing is that records have to be readily retrievable by those who have a need to access them and not necessarily every staff member. And on the question of secure storage, you will probably want to take advantage of the fact that as a forensic laboratory, your entire facility is probably a limited-access facility and, obviously, any records within its perimeter of your lab are stored with some degree of security, without your taking any special measures. This does not discount that some records (e.g., personnel, training) are held more securely.

The term "records" includes all the different types of records found in a laboratory: technical records of examinations and analyses (discussed further later), quality records (non-conformance, corrective action, complaints, internal audits, and management reviews), and operational records (purchasing, security). You will have records of instrument maintenance and calibration, records of staff training, records of proficiency testing, and so on. Making a list of the various types of records you have in your lab will likely total at least four types of records and possibly more, depending upon how you classify records in your lab. When writing the procedures include the usual actions of how, who, where, and when, as appropriate. Unless the retention time and disposal procedure of your records are already covered in the policy of your parent organization or in defined legal requirements, you have to determine and state them in the control procedures. (You are certainly entitled to retain records indefinitely, if you wish, but if that's your practice, document it.)

The standard elaborates on the term "technical records," also known as the case file, and refers to the notes, readings, instrument printouts, chain of custody record, uncertainty estimates (if appropriate), and interpretation of results that the lab gathers in a given case. Similarly, the term "quality records" includes a range of specific records relevant to the test or examination such as those for equipment maintenance, temperature monitoring, verification of balances, calibration of mass spectrometers, analysis of control materials, and so on. Some of this information has to be included in, or at least referenced from, the technical record in order to make it complete. The technical file must be complete in the sense that it has to accurately record everything that was done on the case: who did it, when it was done, what the results were, how they were interpreted, and what conclusions were drawn.

In order to link a given case file to the related quality control activities going on at the time the case was analyzed, you have to retain both types of records for the same time period. (These are the types of questions that can arise in court testimony.) Theoretically, the file should contain enough information to permit repeating the analysis and certainly enough to permit an independent, competent scientist to assess completely the original work. Also the standard calls for details on the manner in which a mistake on a record is corrected. There is no room for correction fluid, erasers, sticky notes, or temporary labels.

Be sure to check the amplification documents provided by your AB for more detailed requirements.

Internal Audits (4.14)

A couple of things are said about auditors: "They come in after the battle and stab the wounded" and "If it moves—train it; if it doesn't move—calibrate it; if it is not written down—it didn't happen." Whether all that is true or not, some of your staff members will have to become auditors. An internal audit (IA) must occur to verify that the quality management system (both management/administration and technical areas) is functioning properly and is in compliance both with the lab's own policies and procedures, and with ISO/IEC 17025. There is no option on this. But as lab manager, you should be aware that the IA is one of the most powerful and useful tools available to you to keep your quality system on track.

There must be written policy and procedures along with a plan and audit schedule. The audit process is implemented, keeping appropriate records of any findings and resulting corrective actions. You may choose to do an audit of all elements at once, or conduct an audit of different sections/units throughout the year or different elements of the management system at different times. That is up to you. You have to decide the persons who are qualified to participate in the audit, recognizing they must be trained for the task, and are preferably not directly connected to the work area being audited. In short, you have to be satisfied that your internal auditors are capable of providing you with an objective and competent result.

A complete internal audit (i.e., all elements of the management system, including testing activities) is usually conducted once a year as a matter of routine and more often if necessary. (Some forensic amplifications require annual audits as a minimum, with all documentation retained for at least one accreditation cycle.) A couple of reasons that additional internal audit may be needed: perhaps you have had a wheel come off in one of your analyses or a training-related problem has occurred and you want to ensure that everything has been properly fixed; or a new process has been implemented and you, as the manager, want to check to make sure it is working as well as expected. In serious findings, the customer may be notified. Finally there is a follow-up audit to ensure the effectiveness of any corrective actions.

In the preparation for your initial accreditation assessment from your accreditation body, you will find that internal audits are a very powerful tool for identifying things that still have to be done. That process might be called a "gap audit." The audits are also an effective way of helping your staff come to grips with the details of the standard because you will enlist them to work with you on audit teams. There is no better way to understand ISO/IEC 17025 than to figure out how it applies in a colleague's section. The process encourages the culture change that is necessary in some labs as they become accustomed to the idea of somebody looking over their shoulder.

Management Review (4.15)

The management review element is written mainly for the lab manager. And in keeping with the idea of clusters used earlier in this chapter, management review (MR) might be called the mother of all clusters, because it addresses directly or indirectly essentially all the other elements of the standard. Here is what is involved.

The standard requires that management periodically review the QMS and testing activities to "ensure their continuing suitability and effectiveness and to introduce necessary changes or improvements" (4.15.1). This might be paraphrased as "Take a hard look at the whole lab operation, and ask yourself a couple of key questions: Is everything we're doing suitable and effective, and is there anything we can improve?" The element then provides a bullet list of 11 individual items that must be considered in the MR. This list should be considered the bare minimum as most labs add their own items to the list. There are three NOTES in this element (and recall our earlier statement that NOTES are not mandatory, merely suggestions). NOTE 1, however, says that it is typical for the MR to be conducted annually. The lab manager would be wise to simply schedule the MR annually and be done with it, as it is a powerful and versatile management tool, and any argument that it should be done less frequently is almost certainly a waste of breath. Records of the review are made with subsequent actions addressed appropriate to their seriousness.

Section 5

In this area of technical requirements, it is important to know there are many forensic-based amplifications that have been made by ILAC Guide 19 and the forensic accrediting bodies (Table 5.3).

Table 5.3 ISO/IEC Technical Requirements

5.1	General
5.2	Personnel
5.3	Accommodation and environmental conditions
5.4	Test (and calibration) methods and method validation
5.5	Equipment
5.6	Measurement traceability
5.7	Sampling
5.8	Handling of test (and calibration) items
5.9	Assuring the quality of test (7 calibration) results
5.10	Reporting the results

General (5.1)

This introduction simply lists the important factors that affect the correctness and reliability of tests (and examinations), such as personnel, laboratory facility, methodology, equipment, traceability (of measurements and critical materials), sampling, and handling (casework) items. It also provides notice that uncertainty of measurement is going to be an important factor in the elements to follow.

Personnel (5.2)

Management is responsible to make sure personnel are competent and duly authorized to do their assigned work such as conducting particular tests and examinations or other specific activities. Naturally, education, training, experience, and demonstrated ability of individuals are the main factors by which the laboratory determines the competence of its staff. An individual's training record will contain copies of diplomas and degrees, as well as records of any other professional development courses (internal/external training) that he or she has taken. There will be records of whatever on-the-job or understudy training the individual had to complete, along with any tests of competence such as written exams, mock trials, or practical tests at the bench. All this must be documented, and when the training is completed a formal statement is included and signed by the appropriate person authorizing the trainee to take on specific lab work. Such competency testing is required for each discipline and for each independent test or examination process done by the individual. Do not assume that demonstrated competency in the use of one method assures competency in the use of an unrelated method.

Policy for training goals and professional development needs, which lead to procedures for identifying and implementing training programs, must be set and evaluated by laboratory management. While writing the required policy and procedure, ensure that training needs are formally included. (Although it is not a requirement, perhaps this can be part of a yearly performance review.) Current job descriptions must be in place. Assume they should be signed off, as there are many amplifications made by ILAC Guide 19 and the various accrediting bodies that have become supplemental requirements (such as training for court presentation; retraining/maintenance of personnel). These sources should be consulted.

Accommodations and Environmental Conditions (5.3)

To meet this requirement, the forensic laboratory must have a facility in which the tests and examinations can be conducted in an environment conducive to achieving good results. The important thing is not to have situations that may invalidate or affect the quality of the results. The nature of work conducted in forensic laboratories involves trace materials, high risk of cross contamination and decomposition, as well as a high level of security, for which environmental details are important. There are many amplifications on this element made by ILAC and the accrediting bodies that have become supplemental requirements.

We suggest that you categorize all the tests and examinations you do in your lab as to their operating and environmental requirements. Go through the list item by item to determine if there are environmental conditions that have to be controlled in order for this test to be done properly. What about temperature? Humidity? Vibration? Noise? Dust? Power and light supply? High purity water? As with several other points, it is often useful to reverse these questions. That is, rather than ask "Does the temperature of this freezer have to be controlled?" ask "What happens to stored items if the temperature in this freezer rises to room temperature?" If the answer to any of these queries is that changes in the particular condition would interfere with a test, or cause deleterious changes to samples, you must control the condition. The quality manual or procedure should include those conditions that are important to achieving accurate and reliable results. Environmental conditions that are deemed as significant have to be controlled, monitored, and recorded.

Controlling access to the lab is required. Again, this requirement will not be news to most forensic scientists, as no doubt security measures are already in place in your lab. Evidence storage areas require particular attention. You will decide who is to have access to what areas within your lab. Check your records for the distribution of keys/cards. The security policy covers such things as visitors, police investigators, trades people, after-hours security, and emergency calls. This is a good time for you to review exactly what is needed and to document the appropriate procedures.

Document the procedures you have in place to maintain and clean the laboratory. This can include the cleaning frequency, use of contracted outside cleaners, and details for specific areas of the lab. If certain areas are to be cleaned only by lab staff, specify such. Although safety requirements are not specifically mentioned in ISO/IEC 17025, accreditation bodies will often cover this in their amplification documents as well as matters of health and safety.

Test Methods and Validation (5.4)

The test methods and validation technical requirement is extremely important and somewhat complicated. As the standard deals with labs of all types, including both testing and calibration labs, the language may seem a little fuzzy. Keep in mind that we are discussing accreditation for a (forensic) testing laboratory, and not a calibration laboratory, although the calibration of breath test instruments may touch on the latter. Again there are several amplifications to the standard to make it applicable to the forensic specialty area. There are seven clauses in test method/method calibration.

General (5.4.1)   The thrust here is that there are written instructions (methods, SOPs, procedures, work instructions—whatever you like) available for all analyses and examinations, for all the instruments used in those examinations, and for other activities such as the handling and storage of casework samples. The SOPs must be written in enough detail that a trained analyst can correctly follow the method as well as a peer scientist who may be technically assessing the method for accreditation. As these are part of the quality document system, they will be current and available. (The phrase "readily available" appears again in this clause, and it means the SOP ought to be at the bench or beside the instrument at which the instructions will be carried out.) Also the document control system will state who has authorized the use of the SOP.

Selection of Methods (5.4.2)   The standard states that the methods used will meet the needs of the customer. For this to apply to a forensic laboratory, appropriate methods taken from professionally accepted publications can be followed. But most important to know is that they must have first been validated in your laboratory before being used on casework. Here is where a number of amplifications are applied: required validation (with records), a procedure for infrequently performed tests, and verification of standard materials/reagents.

Laboratory Developed Methods (5.4.3)   If your lab develops its own methods of analysis or examination, there will need to be written policy and procedure that ensures the development is a planned activity, conducted by qualified persons who are equipped with adequate resources. The validation and approval processes are very important here.

Non-Standard Methods (5.4.4)   The wording in this clause may be a little confusing for the forensic laboratory. Keep in mind that the term "standard method" in ISO/IEC 1025 relates to official methods (like AOAC or ASTM methods), but these types of methods are not common in forensics. However, the essence of this clause makes clear all the detailed workup with the 11 items that are to be part of any method of analysis or examination in use.

Validation (5.4.5)   Method validation is the collection of objective evidence that a certain method of analysis actually does what you claim it does. It was a main concern that was identified in the 2009 NRC report *Strengthening Forensic Science in the United States*. It is precisely the question that has been behind many of the attacks on the reliability of certain forensic examinations in recent years. This is so important that we chose to set aside a detailed discussion of validation in the forensic context at the end of this chapter.

Uncertainty of Measurement (5.4.6)   Estimation of uncertainty of measurement is a very important point in ISO/IEC 17025 and requires a procedure. For testing laboratories, all quantitative methods must include the consideration of estimate of uncertainty, as required in the standard. The concept of uncertainty of measurement does not apply to qualitative methods. (It might be a good idea to state this clearly in laboratory policy.) The standard does not explain how to estimate the uncertainty except to say that all critical factors, which can affect the result, are to be considered.

As a first approximation, it is suggested to derive the standard deviation (SD) from all the critical measurement data. For example, if you run the same control material, batch after batch, you obviously have some replicate data from which you can calculate an SD. You can use that number to estimate a confidence interval (95% is common) for the measured results of your case samples. This is not metrologically rigorous, however, it is a useful and practical way to make a reasonable estimate of the uncertainty of those measurements. The Guidelines of ILAC Guide 19 can be helpful for sorting out this subject.

Control of Data (5.4.7)   The control of data clause concerns calculations, the transfer of data, security, and validity of software. The simplest way for checking calculations and data transfer may be to have a second person (as an independent reviewer) do the check, and then initial and date the case file. The manner of controlling electronic data is also covered here and must be documented. If you are using commercial software, you can generally assume it has been validated. On the other hand, if you have written software routines in-house, such as spreadsheets that perform calculations or databases that search for case-related information, these must be documented with a record to demonstrate that the programs are, in fact, doing what they are intended. Feeding in dummy data to make sure you get the correct output is one obvious way of doing this.

Equipment (5.5)

Equipment and instruments must be at hand that are capable of performing the work your laboratory offers in its scope of services. These must be properly maintained and each instrument used in casework must be calibrated before they are used in casework. There must be safeguards in place to prevent unauthorized use of equipment and software. These elements apply not only to large pieces of equipment but to smaller items like pipettes if they play a critical role in the quality of the test result. If you have to use "outside" equipment for your work, the same requirements for calibration and validation must be followed. All this has to be described in a procedure, and of course, records will demonstrate these actions. As in the earlier requirements, records will show that the operators of the equipment and instruments are successfully trained and authorized by the appropriate person. The operating instructions (SOPs) must be easily available for the operator to use.

An inventory list is required, along with eight specific items of information for maintenance records for equipment and software critical to the determination of the result. (This suggests an inventory list and a logbook, or a database for equipment records.) Such items as the method and frequency of calibration and preventative maintenance are not specified, but they will have to have written procedures that can meet the accepted criteria of the scientific community and/or the equipment manufacturers. When something goes wrong in the calibration or maintenance areas, the non-conformity/corrective action procedures kick in. Identify the individual(s) who are authorized to stop testing, to recall reports, to order the necessary repairs, and order that testing can resume once the problem has been fixed. Unreliable or out-of-service equipment must be clearly labeled as such. (Aside from being an easy pick for auditors, there can be no mistake by staff that a particular piece of equipment is unsuitable for casework.)

Equipment that is critical to the quality of the result and requires calibration is labeled as to the status and appropriate dates of calibration. (A balance or pipettor are good examples.)

If the equipment in your quality system has been out of your direct control for whatever reason (borrowed or used by someone who is not under your management system), the status of calibration and function must be verified before using it again. For that equipment where regular intermediate calibration checks are needed, a defined procedure is required. (The idea is that you use the intermediate check to let you know whether an instrument's calibration has drifted, for whatever reason.)

In regard to safeguarding of equipment, actions such as limiting access to certain lab areas only to specified people, using password protection on instruments and software, placing seals on certain adjustments, and applying the write-protection on calculations and methods in certain instrument-control software may be applied. The forensic amplifications in ILAC Guide 19 deal with maintenance issues and checks for general equipment and other such items as microscopes, volumetric equipment, and other various measuring instruments.

Measurement Traceability (5.6)

The importance of instrument calibration is emphasized again in this requirement. Such calibration shall be done before use in casework. There shall be a documented program of traceability to the International System of Units (SI) for any measurements and calibrations done on critical equipment that requires calibration. ("Critical" meaning it has impact on the accuracy and validity of the test result, such as a laboratory balance and weights, thermometers, or micropipettes.) Traceability to international standards must be done, if it is possible to do so. As traceability is a vital element in calibration laboratories, this clause tends to get a bit turgid for most testing labs. The standard does give some brief clarification for testing laboratories (5.6.2.2), but perhaps the most useful strategy is to follow all the clauses in this require-ment that can be applied to a testing laboratory, no matter whether they are identified in the standard as applying to calibration labs. The required characteristics of an acceptable calibration laboratory and the content of the calibration certificate are specified. Basically, this translates to using a cali-bration source (laboratory) such as the National Institute of Standards and Technology (NIST), or one that is officially accredited to ISO/IEC 17025, for such reference standards as primary weights, thermometers, pipettes, and timers. The measurement traceability policy of the accrediting body with whom you are working should be consulted.

An important part of the forensic laboratory is the various collections of reference standards or materials. The laboratory should possess its own certi-fied reference materials for any tests that it conducts, such as for drugs, glass, or DNA, where available. If no certified reference materials exist, such as for paint, glass, ammunition, or fibers, a complete record of the source material is the best you can do to demonstrate that you have traceable control over the materials you are using as reference materials. Procedures for handling and storage of reference and standard materials are required, which give some assurance as to the integrity of the material.

There are important amplifications for forensic laboratories in ILAC Guide 19 and in the supplemental requirements of the accrediting bodies.

Sampling (5.7)

The concept of sampling can apply at several points in a laboratory opera-tion. If your laboratory is responsible for collecting or gathering evidence at a crime scene, sampling will almost certainly be an issue. Once inside the laboratory, sampling can be included in the procedures for testing or exam-ining crime scene materials. This requirement requires that you have formal sampling plans for all such situations and disciplines.

Aside from the examples of off-site collection, it may be that, in some cases, the customer will submit large quantities of such materials as drugs, soils, questioned documents, and clothing, and scientists will be required to take representative samples of these materials for analysis. This process, too, must be governed by a documented sampling plan. Often the labora-tory does not control the sampling procedure at the scene, as the selection and collection is done by scenes of crime officers. As well, forensic samples are often far from ideal. However, you can still work within the spirit of the standard by documenting the limitations placed upon your analyses and by the nature of the samples that were received, by keeping the cus-tomer (crime scene officer) advised of the problems. The forensic training and laboratory procedures for testing and examining materials should be sufficiently rugged to work with the various types and conditions of crime scene samples. (Being proactive and as a preventive action, an investigators "guide" for preferred exhibit submission could be prepared.)

Handling of Test Items (5.8)

All the requirements for receipt, storage, and handling samples in your laboratory, which you probably do already, are described here. This applies to all exhibit lockers, refrigerators, drying rooms, areas for searching/examining/testing—in fact, everywhere crime samples are handled. Also, the procedure for returning or disposing of samples has to be carefully written so there is a complete chain of custody record.

The requirement for clearly identifying and labeling crime scene samples throughout their time in the laboratory is totally compatible with good forensic practice. Samples that do not match the description given on the request or case submission forms are noted in the case file. (It is highly recommended that the laboratory write out exhibit acceptance criteria for each section.) The laboratory's responsibility for the preservation and integrity of samples is emphasized. If as part of the quality process certain samples have to be refrigerated or frozen, monitoring records are kept of temperatures of the refrigerator or freezer. Further, the thermocouple or thermometer used for monitoring has to be calibrated and traceable.

Scheduled monitoring is useful to ensure there have been no equipment failures or electrical interruptions, during which the samples could be altered or destroyed. It is important to clearly state the procedures used in your laboratory by putting in just the relevant details. Your criteria for storage temperatures (precise or a narrow range) will be described in your procedure and will determine the type of (calibrated) thermometer used.

These are general comments, but the requirements on sample handling are, to some extent, specific to each forensic discipline. Forensic amplifications stated in ILAC Guide 19 deal with chain-of-custody and exhibit storage, as well as other supplemental requirements by some of the accrediting bodies. The latter can include requirements such as specific details of continuity, exhibit security in times of temporary absence of the examiner, recording of latent prints, identification of subdivided samples, and many others. For these reasons, consult any amplification documents of the accrediting body that apply to your laboratory.

Assuring the Quality of Test Results (5.9)

Quality control procedures must be used to monitor the validity of the laboratory's results. The emphasis on quantitative measurements suggests using statistical procedures, such as control charts with statistically determined control limits so that trends can be detected. For monitoring qualitative methods, the use of positive and negative controls would be expected, if that is possible. Five monitoring methods are listed that are suggested to be part of the plan and review: use of reference materials, proficiency testing, rep-licate testing, retesting on the same sample, and correlation using different types of methods.

The results of quality control records are analyzed with planned actions (non-conformance) taken in situations that are seen to fall outside the labora-tory's established criteria for results. The terms "planned" action and "estab-lished" or predefined are important, as they must be written into the quality documents. ILAC Guide 19 and the accrediting bodies include many other required clauses that apply to forensic laboratories, including 10 other means of monitoring performance and to demonstrate that a test or examination is under control.

Proficiency testing assumes a much higher profile in forensic laboratories than the standard suggests. As participation in proficiency testing programs is mandatory in many specialty areas, the pertinent amplification documents will provide details such as which tests, who has to do them, how frequently are they done, and the test supplier. The laboratory's procedure for proficiency testing is obviously a very delicate matter, especially when there is a failed test. The situation of a failed test has to be carefully thought out, planned into the quality documentation. Poor results point to the mistakes on the part of the individual scientist or examiner, or with the method. Depending on the cause, corrective actions may involve a suspension; complete or reme-dial retraining, followed by competency tests; or complete revalidation of the method. On the other hand, good proficiency test (PT) results are excellent indicators of test reliability, and using those results to hand out attaboys is important. Also a procedure for regularly monitoring the court testimony of each examiner/scientist is required.

Reporting Results (5.10)

All the information that is expected to be in your laboratory report is listed with this requirement, along with obvious statements related to accuracy, clarity, and objectivity. The omission of any of the listed items will need a valid reason, which must be stated in the procedure for generating reports. Do not just leave out items without explanation. The report procedure will also state in what manner the reports are prepared and provided to the cus-tomer (mail, fax, electronic means).

Where the interpretation of test results, or the assessment of the signifi-cance of certain findings, is the whole point of the testing exercise, as in foren-sic laboratories, the basis for opinions in the report has to be documented. It may not have to appear in the test report itself and is usually sufficient for such documentation to be contained in (or referenced from) the case file. (If your examiners provide opinion on test results over the phone, for example, make sure the essence of those conversations is recorded.) When something is found to be in doubt or error in a report already sent, and it is necessary to issue an amended report, the new report must contain a clear statement that it *is* an amended report and that it replaces the one issued originally.

Finally, there are some supplemental requirements by ILAC Guide 19 and the accrediting bodies that apply to forensic laboratories.

Preparation and Implementation

The steps to becoming accredited are stated quite briefly, along with some suggestions for preparing a documentation system and some detail for addressing the requirements for validation. A more complete guide—*Introduction to Accreditation for Forensic Laboratories*—is available.

First and foremost, you, as the lab manager, and any managers senior to you in your organization must be fully supportive and take the lead in terms of commitment and resource support. Then the hard work of making sure that the laboratory operation covers every applicable requirement in ISO/IEC 17025 must be tackled. Do not presume that you can ignore difficult requirements, as you will be audited to every element in the standard. Once you have your quality system fully operating and under control, you apply formally to the accreditation body you have chosen to work with. As mentioned before, it is a very good idea to have made contact with them early, so that any required amplifications are addressed. Fees are paid and all your documentation is supplied to your accrediting body.

After reviewing your application materials for completeness, the accreditation body will review all documentation and arrange (with your concurrence) for a team comprising a lead assessor and technical assessors, along with proposed dates for the initial assessment. Depending on the size and complexity of the laboratory, the on-site assessment visit can take a number of days. At completion of the visit, the team leader will provide the laboratory with an audit report containing a list of the items that need to be addressed. Once your laboratory has provided satisfactory responses to the audit findings within a specified period of time, you can expect to receive a certificate of accreditation.

Getting Started

If senior management has decided to seriously consider accreditation, someone (QA manager perhaps) will have to determine what has to be done. Compare the policies, procedures, and activities currently used in the laboratory with the managerial and technical requirements of ISO/IEC 17025 and any applicable amplifications. Depending on your familiarity with the standard(s), you could conduct a gap analysis yourself or hire a consultant to do one for you. It is at this point the amount of effort and cost of the accreditation process should start to become clear. An implementation plan is developed that includes what has to be done, who can be assigned to the project, required training, time lines, and estimated costs. A checklist can be very useful for this. Always keep the management and staff in the loop of information, familiarization, and progress.

The Documentation System

Lay out the hierarchy of your lab's quality documents. Determine a consistent format for the quality system manual, procedures, work instructions, forms, and records. Develop clear policy and seek input from the personnel who are doing the various jobs in your lab, such as the clerks, the chemists, and the cleaners. There can be many revisions of documentation before you are satisfied. This is likely the most demanding part of the implementation process.

The documents that comprise the quality system can comprise the following (however named):

1. Quality manual—(Stated in brief) a general description of the management system, laboratory policies and objectives, and specific references to other essential documents, such as the procedures and process control documents.
2. Quality procedures—Include standard operating procedures (SOPs), for both administrative and technical procedures, which provide details of who, what, when, and where. Closely linked are work instructions, which are even more detailed (e.g., specific technical methods and instructions for the operation and maintenance of specific pieces of equipment). Because any forms your lab uses are really abbreviated instructions, they must be part of the quality document system as well.
3. Process control documents—Similar or the same as procedures and include training, proficiency testing, and internal audit.
4. Records—Support the overall documentation system and demonstrate that all of the quality procedures are actually being followed.

It is useful to think of the quality manual as your lab's most senior document, at the top of a pyramid as shown earlier.

Relationship of Non-Conformances (NCs) and Corrective Actions (CAs)

When you are writing your complaints, NC and CA procedures, you might find the flow chart in Figure 5.1 helpful. See also the description of the clauses given earlier. This process takes the position that every legitimate complaint

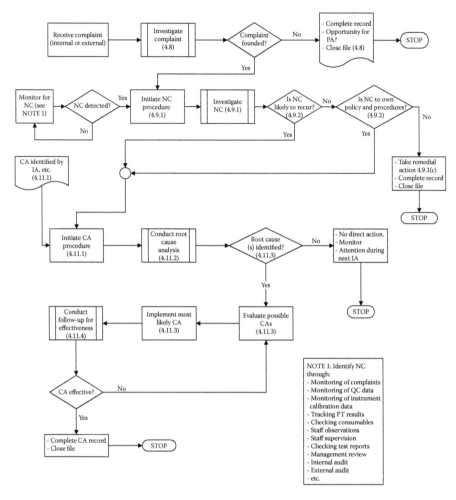

Figure 5.1 Non-conformance corrective action procedure.

is—pretty much by definition—a non-conformity. It may be serious, or not, but sorting that out is what the NC procedure is for. Unfounded complaints are not NCs in this chart but they are still solved and documented, so they can be used as ways to improve customer relations and monitored for possible opportunities for preventive action.

You will see that, in the upper left of the flow chart, there is a simple loop that implies that there is a continuous effort being made within the organization to detect NCs. NOTE 1 lists only some of the more important ways that NC might be detected. For the NC–CA process to work effectively, there must be a continuing effort by everybody in the laboratory to detect NCs. Everybody should be empowered to flag NCs whenever they think they have found one, large or small, serious or trivial. This vigilance should apply in every activity in which people are involved. In those situations where the decision point in the flow chart shows there has been no root cause clearly identified, the best approach may be to monitor the issue and include it in the next internal audit, but do not make random changes in the hopes that something clicks.

Validation

Method validation is a large topic in forensic science, and in some specialties it is an uncomfortable topic. However, ISO/IEC 17025:2005 is quite clear: All the methods you use to analyze crime scene samples or exhibits must be validated before they are used. So let's look at some of the issues that this requirement raises and that were not dealt with in a lot of detail in the amplification documents.

To begin with, it helps to be clear about what method validation entails. Fundamentally, validation is the evidence that a given analytical or examination method actually does what you claim it does. Please understand that we are talking about hard data here: documented, objective evidence that was obtained in your laboratory, preferably, or with some limitations, in someone else's. Statements of belief, wishful thinking, or testimonials that "we have done this examination this way for 20 years" do not constitute validation data.

You have seen that ISO/IEC 17025:2005 refers to a spectrum of method types, including standard methods and lab-developed methods. These differ in the amount of validation data your lab has to generate for itself. For example, if your lab uses a standard method (and here we mean a standard method, such as might be published by ASTM or a similar body), much of the validation of that method has already been done in collaborative studies by a number of recognized labs. Your lab is entitled to rely on its objective evidence, as long as you apply the standard method exactly as it was published. Your lab would have to generate a relatively small amount of data internally to confirm, or verify, that you are actually able to make the standard method work successfully in your organization.

If your lab modified a standard method significantly, you would lose claim to the published validation evidence and would, therefore, have to generate more of that evidence within your own lab. There can be endless debate over what constitutes a significant modification, but you should recognize that the greater the deviation from the standard method, the less you are able to rely on published validation evidence, and the more you will be expected to generate that evidence within your own lab.

In the case in which you are not going to use a standard method but are intending to use a method published from a peer-reviewed scientific journal (e.g., *Journal of Analytical Toxicology*), you have to supply a lot more validation data from your own lab. Such a method certainly has been validated to some degree but not to the extent that a standard method has. The method is considered to be an unofficial method and validation in your lab is required.

At the other end of the scale would be a method that you develop from first scientific principles within your own lab. This is probably more common in forensic science than other testing laboratories, because of the nature and condition of forensic samples. Such a method has obviously not been validated by any other laboratories; and it has not been published in the literature. You have simply developed the method to meet a need in your particular circumstances. (By the way, it is quite all right to do this. ISO/IEC 17025:2005 merely singles out such methods because they have to be handled a little differently.) As you might expect from the continuum suggested earlier, all the validation evidence has to be supplied by your lab. When you look at the details of the standard, we think you will see that the items listed can be understood most easily in the context of a quantitative chemical analysis. So, let's use the quantification of ethanol in whole human blood as an example.

To begin with, you will have the new method written out so everybody can follow it. You will check out the instruments you plan to use, making sure that they are working according to manufacturer's specifications. You will secure a supply of certified ethanol standard and prepare suitable dilutions for use. The balance, the dilutor, and the pipettors you use will all have been calibrated so that measurements made with them are traceable to a national or international standard. By the way, ethanol is an unusual drug in that it is available as a reference material from NIST.

The validation work would consist mostly of preparing a set of standards, covering 0 to 500 milligrams percent ethanol, for example, analyzing them and plotting the results. You can think of the calibration curve as objective evidence that your ethanol method actually does what you claim it does. Is a single calibration curve all you need to validate the method? Probably not. You will need to know how well results can be replicated run to run and day to day and to record the stats that show this. In so doing, you will have repeated the calibration curve a number of times. You will have calculated how precise the method is; you will have assessed the linearity of the curve; you will have determined the limit of detection (LOD) and limit of quantitation (LOQ).

We expect you would also need evidence of the effect of the matrix, for example. That is, does it matter whether the calibration standards are prepared in water or human blood? How do blanks behave in this method? Do blood samples that are known to contain no ethanol actually give zero signal? And so on.

In a forensic application, it might be useful to know if the method gives reliable results for ethanol in serum, or in urine, or in vitreous fluid, as well as in whole blood. Of course, you cannot simply assume that it works with those fluids; you have to run it and collect the objective data. And what of decomposed samples? What about other volatile compounds besides ethanol that might be in the samples? Do they interfere? The list of questions can go on. Our point is to illustrate the sort of objective evidence that you would have to collect to show that your ethanol method is valid. This also illustrates that validation may be an ongoing process in which you expand, through objective evidence, the circumstances under which you *know* the method works (or does not). For example, you might choose to limit the application to samples of whole blood only. In that case, you would never have to collect evidence of your method's behavior with serum, plasma, or urine. This sort of limit is alluded to in the standard.

The preceding discussion deals with validation of a method you developed in your lab—a conventional, quantitative, chemical analysis. There are comparatively few of those, however, in a forensic lab. What about less conventional examinations? How can they be validated? What about qualitative chemical analyses, such as the identification of illicit drugs, or the detection of fire accelerants, or the chemical identification of cosmetics and lubricants? Validation evidence in these situations is quite straightforward. Many of the technical items that you would cover for a quantitative analysis (mentioned earlier) would also apply in qualitative analyses. For example, you would still be making sure instruments were properly calibrated; you would still be considering possible interferences; you would still be exploring matrix effects. Limit of detection might still be an issue. There may be other points you need to consider, as well.

What about less conventional examinations? Consider a method such as comparing a bullet with a given firearm. Your lab claims that your method of examination is capable of determining whether a specific bullet was fired from a certain firearm. How do you validate this method? Almost none of the points listed in the earlier example apply here. There is no standard reference material; there are probably no measuring instruments to be calibrated; questions such as linearity and interfering substances are practically meaningless. There are several other common forensic examinations that present similar problems: handwriting comparison, tool mark examinations, physical matches, and so on. With methods of this sort, you have a limited number of factors that you can use to provide the objective evidence that these methods actually do what you claim they do. Here is what we think is possible.

You can gather the published work—all the scientific papers, for example—that supports your method of examination. Prudence would demand that your literature search would include publications that are critical of your chosen method as well, if there are any. You can show that your examiners are properly trained and tested. You can show that they all follow a detailed, written examination protocol. You can show that they peer review one another's work. You can show that they all successfully perform proficiency tests. And that is about all there is. Of this short list, we consider proficiency testing the most powerful indicator of method validity; and because there is so little other validation evidence available for these examinations, this may be a reason to increase the frequency of proficiency testing in these areas. This is something for your lab to decide.

References

ILAC Guide 19. (2002). *Guidelines for Forensic Laboratories.* Australia: ILAC.

International Laboratory Accreditation Cooperation (ILAC). (2013). http://www.ilac.org.

International Organization for Standardization (ISO). (2013). http://www.iso.org.

ISO 9000: 2005 Quality Management Systems—Fundamentals and vocabulary. (2013). Retrieved from http://www.iso.org.

ISO 9001. (2000, December 15). Quality management systems requirements. Switzerland.

ISO/IEC 17025. (2005). General requirements for the competence of testing and calibration laboratories. Switzerland: ISO.

Malcolm, M., and Peel, H. (2005). *Introduction to Accreditation for Forensic Labs,* version 2.0.

National Academy of Sciences (NAS). (2009). *Strengthening Forensic Science in the United States: A Path Forward.* Washington, DC: National Academies Press.

Writing Policies and Procedures

6

Industrial laboratories, clinical laboratories, and even consulting laboratories find it necessary to conserve time and investment by using the shortest, most efficient, and best standardized methods possible in order to operate efficiently. If the police laboratory is to earn its way, it also must standardize its procedures to cope with the large number of cases that require or should receive its attentions without at the same time being so costly as to defeat its own ends.

P. L. Kirk, *Crime Investigation, Physical Evidence and the Police Laboratory*

When things go wrong in a laboratory one does not have to wait long to hear they were not following procedures, there was no defined procedure, or we need training for that procedure to assure competence. Laboratories have progressed from no accreditation to compliance with the American Society of Crime Laboratory Directors/Laboratory Accreditation Board (ASCLD/LAB) formed in 1982 by the American Society of Crime Laboratory Directors (ASCLD), now called the legacy program, and presently are transitioning to operate in accordance with the ISO/IEC 17025: 2005 International Standard requirements. At the heart of these programs are written policies and procedures that are thoroughly discussed in Chapter 5: ISO/IEC 17025: 2005. It is also possible to perform a procedure with excellent outcomes and use no written procedure. Although this is not preferred or common, there may be several steps of a procedure that have never been put in writing. Many laboratories' procedures are a collection of ASCLD/LAB procedures that have been modified to fit the ISO/IEC 17025 standard. Some laboratories have also benchmarked with other laboratories for best practices and modified others' procedures to fit the processes in their laboratory. All these methods are acceptable and they work. There is also a distinctive difference between administrative support procedures and scientific procedures, which we discuss later in the text. Last, well-written procedures provide the foundation for the training lesson plan. Training lesson plan learning objectives, curricula materials, assessment, and competency measures all develop from the well-written procedures.

However, when things do go wrong, and they will, an auditor external from the laboratory perhaps from the internal investigative unit from the parent agency or from an external regulatory body will not be concerned with the history of the procedures in question. The auditor will be concerned with present conditions and will follow these steps:

1. The auditor will perform a desk audit of the written procedure in an attempt to identify all associated personnel, policies, procedures, controlled documents, data, and controls associated with the task.
2. Next the auditor will develop a process flow chart (PFC) to provide a visual representation of all procedure steps identified in the desk audit.
3. Last, the auditor will interview and observe personnel when they are performing the procedures (surveillance audit) to confirm and verify compliance with all written procedure steps.

As an alternative to revising an existing procedure for improvement, it is at times preferable to start with a blank-white-board approach. The procedure must be aligned with the intent of the ISO clause and describe how *your laboratory* operates in accordance with the specific clause in the standard.

Procedures should also clearly identify non-conformances. Non-conformances to customer requirements should not be relied upon for detection on technical review but identified and remedied by the primary scientist performing the work. The definition of non-conformance(s) should also be defined for each step in the procedure. If personnel have difficulty defining a non-conformance to the procedure, then ask: What outcomes would initiate a reanalysis? The answer is a non-conformance.

Lexicon

The first step in the development of any procedure is the understanding and use of a standardized lexicon or common vocabulary of terms. Policies and procedures for training, operations, communications, and all quality management activities are dependent upon the proper and consistent use of terms. The efficiency and effectiveness of communication and the quality management system are greatly improved when staff understand and use the proper terms. Our discussion of procedure development depends upon the following terms defined in ISO 9000 (International Organization of Standardization, 2013).

Following are some of the basic terms from this standard we will use in this discussion:

Audit (3.9.1)—Systematic, independent, and documented process for obtaining audit evidence and evaluating it objectively to determine the extent to which the audit criteria are fulfilled.

Corrective action (3.6.5)—Action to eliminate the cause of a detected non-conformity or other undesirable situation.

Effectiveness (3.2.14)—Extent to which planned activities are realized and planned results achieved.

Efficiency (3.2.15)—Relationship between result achieved and resources used.

Information (3.7.1)—Meaningful data.

Non-conformity (3.6.2)—Nonfulfillment of a requirement.

Policy (3.2.4)—Overall intentions and direction of an organization (3.3.1) with regard to quality (3.1.1) as formally expressed by top management (3.2.7).

Preventive action (3.6.4)—Action to eliminate the cause of a potential non-conformity or other undesirable situation.

Procedure (3.4.5)—Specified way to carry out an activity or a process (3.4.1). Note 1: Procedures can be documented or not. Note 2: When a procedure is documented, the term "written procedure" is frequently used. The document (3.7.2) that contains a procedure is called a "procedure document."

Process (3.4.1)—Set of interrelated or interacting activities, which transforms inputs into outputs.

Product (3.4.2)—Result of a process (3.4.1). Note 1: There are four generic product categories, as follows: services, software, hardware, processed materials.

Quality assurance (3.2.11)—Part of quality management focused on providing confidence that quality requirements will be fulfilled.

Quality control (3.2.10)—Part of quality management focused on fulfilling quality requirements.

Requirement (3.1.2)—Need or expectation that is stated, generally implied, or obligatory.

National scientific oversight bodies have sounded the alarm and provided guidance to establish and enforce standardization of forensic processes and procedures. In 2005 the U.S. Congress passed the Science, State, Justice, Commerce and Related Agencies Appropriations Act of 2006 authorizing the National Academy of Sciences (NAS) to create an independent body to evaluate forensic sciences (NAS, 2009). The NAS report was the result of many years of advocacy from the forensic professional organizations working with their locally elected representatives. The NAS assembled an esteemed group of professionals who interviewed a diverse group of scientists, legal experts, and leaders from the scientific academic community who interviewed forensic practitioners from local, state, federal agencies, and the academic community. The NAS report stated the need to improve the overall quality of forensic services resulting in 13 recommendations to improve forensic services.

NAS recommendations either directly or indirectly refer to the standardization of best practices for the delivery of forensic services:

Recommendation 1 calls for a newly created federal agency entitled the National Institute of Forensic Science that will "establish and enforce *best practices* [my emphasis] for forensic science professionals and laboratories."

Recommendation 8 states "Forensic laboratories should establish routine *quality assurance and quality control procedures* [my emphasis] to ensure the accuracy of forensic analyses and the work of forensic practitioners."

The NAS report also cited Federal Bureau of Investigation (2013) quality assurance standards for DNA laboratories and the ISO/IEC 17025:2005 International Standard (section 5.4.4) (ISO/IEC 17025, 2005) specifying the process to be followed for validation of scientific methods. Inherent in these scientific and business procedures are quality controls to ensure results are within established customer requirements for approval or rejection of results.

Scientific Procedure versus Administrative Procedure

We would be remiss by not distinguishing the differences and similarities between a scientific procedure used in laboratory analyses as compared to administrative procedures used for support functions and the total performance of the quality management system designed for continual improvement. The scientific applied research procedures grounded in hypothesis testing, rigorous statistical analyses for type A and type B errors, and uncertainty measurement budgets should be clearly understood and used by forensic laboratories if the research method is to be performed in their laboratory by their staff. Most scientific procedures in use by forensic practitioners are methods that have been researched and validated by other researchers and are validated for use by forensic practitioners in their laboratories. Forensic laboratories are now performing more research, and publishing and validating customized procedures for use in case analyses. Laboratories operating in accordance with ISO/IEC 17025 standards are required to perform procedure validation with their staff, facilities, and equipment. The NAS report cites the ISO/IEC 17025:2005 Standard, section 5.4, Test and Calibration Methods and Method Validation and provides a generic guide for the scientific method.

An effective procedure audit tool can be designed to perform an interrogatory "crosswalk" between ISO/IEC 17025 mandatory policies and procedures, and scientific or administrative methods. Table 6.1 is an auditor

Table 6.1   ISO/IEC 17025 Clause 5.4.4: Non-Standard Method Audit Checklist

ISO/IEC 17025 5.4.4 Non-Standard Method Requirement	ISO/IEC 17025 Written Policy Requirement	ISO/IEC 17025 Written Procedure Requirement	Question	Y/N	Comments
Appropriate Identification	4.3.1 Document control 4.3.2.2 Document review	4.3.1 Document control 4.3.2.2 Document review	Is there a clearly written policy and procedure with controls for: 4.3.1 Document control? 4.3.2.2 Document review?		
Scope	4.1.5c Protecting customers' information 4.2.2 Quality	4.1.5c Protecting customer's information	Is there a clearly written policy and procedure with controls for: 4.1.5c Protection of customer's information?		
Description of item being tested	4.4.1 Review of contracts	4.4.1 Review of contracts	Is there a clearly written procedure with controls for: 4.4.1 Review of contracts?		
Parameters and or quantities or ranges to be determined	4.4.1 Review of contracts	4.4.1 Review of contracts	Is there a clearly written policy and procedure with controls for: 4.4.1 Review of contracts?		
Apparatus and equipment, including technical performance requirements		5.4.5.2 Validation	Is there a clearly written procedure with controls for: 5.4.5.2 Validation?		
Reference standards and reference materials required	4.6.1 Purchasing	4.4.1 Review of contracts 4.6.1 Purchasing 5.6.3.1 Calibration of reference standards 5.6.3.4 Handling of reference standards	4.4.1 Is there a clearly written policy for purchasing of standards? Is there a clearly written procedure with controls for: 4.6.1 Purchasing of standards? 5.6.3.1 Calibration of standards? 5.6.3.4 Handling of reference standards?		
Environmental conditions required and any stabilization period needed		5.3.5 Accommodations and environmental conditions	Is there a clearly written procedure with controls for: 5.3.5 Accommodations and environmental conditions?		

(Continued)

Table 6.1   ISO/IEC 17025 Clause 5.4.4: Non-Standard Method Audit Checklist (*Continued*)

ISO/IEC 17025 5.4.4 Non-Standard Method Requirement	ISO/IEC 17025 Written Policy Requirement	ISO/IEC 17025 Written Procedure Requirement	Question	Y/N	Comments
Description of the procedure			Is there a clearly written procedure with controls for: 5.4.5.2 Validation?		
Affixing of identification marks, handling, transporting, storing and preparation of items		5.7.1 Sampling 5.7.3 Recording sampling data 5.8.1 Receipt of test items 5.8.4 Avoiding loss of test items	Is there a clearly written procedure with controls for: 5.7.1 Sampling? 5.7.3 Recording of sampling data? 5.8.1 Receipt of test items? 5.8.4 Avoiding loss of test items?		
Checks to be made before the work is started	5.2.2 Training	5.2.2 Training 5.4.5.2 Validation	Is there a clearly written policy and procedure with controls for: 5.2.2 Training? Is there a clearly written procedure with controls for: 5.4.5.2 Validation?		
Checks that the equipment is working properly		5.5.5 Use of equipment 5.6.1 Calibration of equipment 5.6.3.3 Intermediate checks and reference standards	Is there a clearly written procedure with controls for: 5.5.5 Use of equipment? 5.6.1 Calibration of equipment? 5.6.3.3 Intermediate checks and reference standards?		
Calibration and adjustment of the equipment before each use		5.6.1 Calibration of equipment	Is there a clearly written procedure with controls for: 5.6.1 Calibration of equipment?		

Method of recording the observations and results	4.3.1 Document control 4.3.2.2 Document review 4.3.3 Amending documents by hand 4.3.3.4 Changes to documents in electronic systems 5.7.3 Recording sampling data		Is there a clearly written procedure with controls for: 4.3.1 Document control? 4.3.2.2 Document review? 4.3.3 Amending documents by hand? 4.3.3.4 Changes to documents in electronic systems? 5.7.3 Recording sampling data?
Safety measures to be observed	Federal Occupation Safety and Health Administration regulations State and local safety regulations (HazCom, PPE)	Federal Occupation Safety and Health Administration regulations State and local safety regulations	Is there a clearly written policy and procedure with controls for: Federal Occupation Safety and Health Administration regulations? State and local safety regulations?
Criteria and/or requirements for approval/ rejection	4.2.2 Quality 4.8 Resolving complaints 4.9.1 Handling non-conformances 4.11.1 Corrective action	5.9.1 QC monitoring	Is there a clearly written policy with controls for: 4.2.2 Quality? 4.8 Resolving complaints? 4.9.1 Handling non-conformances? 4.11.1 Corrective action? Is there a clearly written procedure with controls for: 5.9.1 QC monitoring?
Uncertainty or the procedure for estimating uncertainty		5.4.6.1 Estimate of uncertainty (calibration) 5.4.6.2 Estimate of uncertainty (testing)	Is there a clearly written procedure with controls for: 5.4.6.1 Estimate of uncertainty (calibration)? 5.4.6.2 Estimate of uncertainty (testing)?

checklist that correlates requirements for the ISO/IEC 17025—5.4.4 scientific procedure with the mandatory ISO/IEC 17025 policies and procedures listed in the ISO chapter. This checklist is the minimum and can be expanded upon with additional policies and procedures if management has determined there is unique customer or regulatory requirements. For example, there are several Federal Department of Labor, Occupational, Safety and Health Administration (OSHA) safety regulations directly applicable to forensic laboratories. Hazard communications and personal protective equipment (29 CFR 1910) are examples that apply to all forensic laboratories (Occupational Safety and Health Administration, 2013).

Instructions on How to Develop Procedures

Readers are also encouraged to seek additional instruction on how to prepare effective procedures and their use for the development of training programs for new personnel and audit teams. Specific training for the development of procedures for procedural writing teams often leads to the formation of first-party auditing team training lesson plans and specific procedure training for bench personnel to competency.

The development of written procedures incorporates eight main steps:

1. Desk audit
2. Observe procedures being used
3. Interview staff using procedure
4. Develop process flow chart
5. Verbally articulate process flow chart
6. Transcribe verbal articulation to text
7. Add laboratory management performance model (LMPM) metrics
8. Training program if competency affects reported results or opinions

Desk Audit

The desk audit is most commonly performed off-site and is an exercise to identify and understand documents for policy (why), procedure (who does what, when, where, and how), and any supporting controlled documents, records, and data. The main operative word is "who." Procedures are performed by people who are empowered by top management with responsibilities and authority to perform a specific task.

The desk audit will collect all existing policies, procedures, controlled documents, records, and data related to the procedure in question. The desk audit should provide the audit or procedure writing team a foundation for understanding the purpose of the procedure and how it is performed.

Observe Procedures Being Used

The observation of the procedure or a surveillance audit provides the auditor or procedure writing team the opportunity to observe the procedure being performed first hand. Observations are compared to existing policies and procedures to confirm the procedure is being followed as written. It is often the case that changes have been made to improve the procedure but may not have been incorporated in writing.

Interview Staff Using Procedure

Staff is queried as to their ability to articulate their knowledge, understanding, and application of the procedure. Are the staff aware why they are performing the procedure, and do they have the big picture for who does what, when, where, and how?

Develop Process Flow Chart

The flow chart uses standardized symbols that identify sequential tasks, materials, documents, and decisions needed to provide a visual of a specific procedure (Figure 6.1). More complex flow charts can show linkages to other processes, time, and resources needed for each task and selected LMPM metrics. Information to begin the flow chart is gathered from existing documents and interviews with staff and supervisors. The most important step

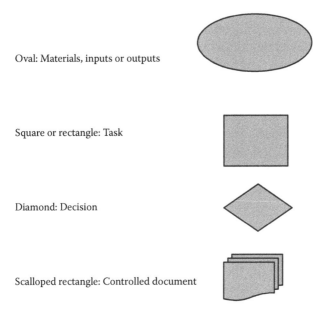

Oval: Materials, inputs or outputs

Square or rectangle: Task

Diamond: Decision

Scalloped rectangle: Controlled document

Figure 6.1 Basic flow chart symbols.

is to observe the procedure from start to finish followed by a comparison of your observations to staff interviews and documents. Do your best to keep this process simple and concise. The flow chart process should identify at a minimum all controlled documents; data collection points; time; costs; nonconformances, rework (go with remediation or no-go with corrective action decisions); and horizontal linkages to other processes, procedures, and regulations. Personnel, by job title, are identified by the step in the process that they perform. Horizontal linkages to other procedures (multisection cases or support services) and vertical linkages to upper-level policies and the laboratory's mission statement and customer requirements ensure the procedure is on target with quality management system goals. A useful adaptation of the flow chart includes scaling of symbol sizes for time or costs, which identify which steps in the process are most costly and timely. For example, the symbol for a specific task is sized at 1″ corresponding to 1 hour. A 2″ square would represent 2 hours. Operational management line leveling procedures indicate no item will cycle through the total process sooner than the timeliest step. Therefore, resources should be applied to the timeliest step in the process to reduce cycle time. Flow charts also provide excellent training aids for new employees learning the process. The flow chart is the foundation of your procedure. The procedure outline and then final descriptive narrative will depend on accuracy and completeness of the flow chart. Ultimately, an internal or external accrediting body auditor will develop their own procedure flow chart for your written procedures mandated by regulations, agency, accrediting body standard, or customer requirements. Remember to keep the flow chart simple and concise. If it becomes visually complex and confusing, then this could be an indication your procedure is too complex and may cause unwarranted remediation, nonconformances, and resulting corrective actions.

Verbally Articulate Process Flow Chart

Perhaps the most challenging and most important task in procedure writing is the concise and articulate written description of the procedure following the PFC. A simple and very effective approach to this critical task is to have one member of the writing team verbally articulate the PFC to the staff that actually performs the task. Any errors in the PFC or misunderstanding on how the procedure is performed will be identified in this step.

Transcribe Verbal Articulation to Text

A scribe will now write the verbal articulation of the procedure on the procedure writing team. The narrative description of the procedure, using active voice, is written after the completion of the PFC (Figure 6.2). One effective way to do this is to verbally articulate a description of the PFC from the beginning

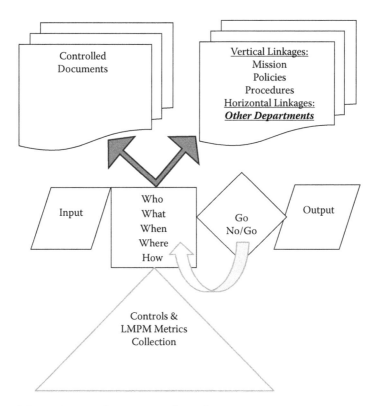

Figure 6.2 Basic procedure process flow chart.

to the end. This does two things: (1) Any redundancies, missing steps, or tasks that do not make sense will be readily apparent. (2) If you cannot "talk" your way through the PFC, then the procedure is not clear and will not be understood by personnel. Do this by yourself, with others on the procedure team, and stakeholders until all steps are concise and clearly described and written. The PFC will be very accurate after several reiterations of this process.

A critical component of the procedure writing process is identification of individuals with writing skills, teaming with subject-matter experts and supervisors, who will be responsible for the writing of all procedures in a clear and consistent manner. This is not an easy task and must be done properly as a team made up of the writers, bench scientists, and supervisors. All will be held accountable to these procedures in future audits, so now is the time to do it right.

It is also very effective for the procedure writing team to be trained as the first audit team. The procedure writing team is best positioned to perform the first audits as they developed the procedures. Writing guidelines for scientists and business are thoroughly discussed in separate works by Hogan (2005) for business writing and Pechenik (2007) for scientific writing. Hogan provides detailed guidance on how to explicitly write clear memoranda, letters, e-mail, and procedures. He emphasized the major mistake that writers make is not including all steps needed in a procedure and or not providing these detailed instructions *when needed* by the readers. Pechenik provides a treasure trove of practical instructions designed for graduate students and research scientists documenting laboratory experiments, writing research papers or posters, and general guidelines for proper scientific writing. The challenge is to combine business and scientific writing skills to provide effective, concise, and practical procedures for the bench scientists, supervisors, support staff, and management.

There are many guidelines for grammar and writing style texts available. Strunk and White's (2000) *The Elements of Style* is one text that should be in everyone's reference library. A consistent format and style are essential for efficient use by all staff. Time is well spent studying basic and advanced protocols for proper grammar, style, sentence structure, and format for business technical writing and scientific publications. We are seeking a unique mix of business technical and scientific writing that will produce a clear, concise and understood procedures that will be *understood and used* for daily analyses and provide the framework for continual improvements. The uniform theme from all writing guides is clarity and conciseness developed from active voice sentence structure *clearly identifying who does what when*.

The most common cause of unclear procedures and related corrective actions are the lack of active voice sentence structure (inappropriate use of passive voice sentence structure) (Table 6.2). It is not clear who is responsible for the task or has the authority and responsibility to make decisions, who being a job title or position (e.g., DNA section supervisor or DNA technical leader). Consistent use of present tense in the active voice will provide the clearest procedure that will be understood and used. The active voice construction consists of subject–verb–object. In passive voice sentence structure the subject is acted upon and the subject is usually unclear or not included. At times the passive structure may be used intentionally not assigning responsibility and authority for a particular outcome. Passive sentence structure has no place in laboratory procedures, as tasks, responsibilities, authorities, and outcome measures must be crystal clear.

Add Laboratory Management Performance Model (LMPM) Metrics

Ideally, procedures should link to the key laboratory performance metrics for customer requirements, costs, capability, cost efficiency, cost effectiveness, performance, and benchmarking (Figures 6.2 and 6.3) for best practice. A collective sum of metrics from all procedures equals the total metrics for the forensic unit (e.g., DNA unit). Staff and supervisors should confirm the procedure is associated with customer requirements. If not, then the procedure may

Table 6.2 Passive versus Active Voice

Passive	Active with Responsibility Assigned
Ensure data from the quantitation step are recorded on form 19b.	The Forensic Scientist III responsible for performing step #3 records all instrumental data generated from instrument ABC123 on form 19b.
A determination is made as to whether the results are acceptable.	The Chemistry Case Review Technical Leader decides if the analytical results from extraction step #6 are within limits of acceptability.
Unacceptable results, as defined in Procedure #12654 Step #21, are monitored for continual improvement.	The DNA Team Leader is responsible for monitoring all non-conformances as defined in Procedure #12654 Step #21, correcting the non-conformance with remediation, or initiating a Corrective Action as per QM Procedure #1299.
Requests for service contracts are accompanied by proper documents.	All Section Chiefs are responsible for including with a Request for Contracted Services (Form Fiscal 103b) three independent quotes for all services over $5,000.
Additional resources can be identified through decreases in nonessential items.	Top management will identify additional resources through the reduction in nonessential services.
Successful completion of the competency will allow her to start work.	If the Forensic Scientist I meets established performance standards, then the Technical Leader for Training recommends to the Unit Chief assignment to supervised casework activities.
Administrative and technical reviews are continually monitored.	All technical personnel are responsible for the initial administrative and technical review for all of their work following Procedure QA1012.
Laboratory-wide preventive actions are designed to prevent high-risk procedures.	All Unit Chiefs are responsible for identifying and monitoring high-risk procedures for non-conformances as per Procedure QA1099.
All Corrective Action Reports need to be completed in a timely manner.	The Quality Assurance Manager is responsible for initiating, monitoring, and completion of all Corrective Reports within 60 days of the Unit Chief verifying a recurring non-conformance as per Procedure QA963.
All e-mails related to case analyses will be retained.	The Forensic Scientist in charge of a case retains all e-mail and hard copy documents verifying communications that affect the case analyses as per Procedure IM#2256.

not be needed and resources can be applied elsewhere more appropriately. The cost of the procedure with personnel time, consumables, contracts, support personnel, and facilities can be measured per unit output and monitored for continual improvement in efficiency and effectiveness. Performance can be measured to determine if capabilities are meeting customer requirements. Last, the procedure using these metrics can be benchmarked with similar procedures and laboratories (private or public). Perhaps the most practical use of the LMPM metrics is to choose one metric of interest for top management and law enforcement customer(s). For example, timeliness or cycle time is a component of the capabilities metrics. Information technology support can

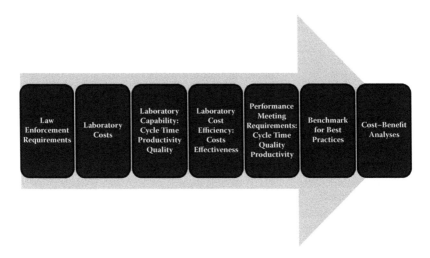

Figure 6.3 LMPM metric categories.

establish data collection points for time integrated with the laboratory information management system at the end of key tasks in the procedure. Similarly, data collection points can be developed for remediation, non-conformances, and reanalysis to gather good and bad quality data metrics.

Training Program If Competency Affects Reported Results or Opinions

Last, the procedure and PFC can be used as a foundation to develop training plans that will ensure competency of personnel. Training plans should develop learning objectives, curricula materials, assessments, and competency tests that confirm personnel perform at the proper standards. Causative factors for all known non-conformances should be identified, measured, and monitored for continual improvement and assurance that the work force is competent.

Following is an example of a Purchasing department procedure that was developed using the above steps starting with the blank-white-board approach. The resulting PFC (Figure 6.4) and the resulting procedure were much clearer and concise than the existing procedure in use that was revised several times over the last several years.

Metro Laboratory
Procedure
4.6.0001 Purchasing
Control Document Number: 4.6.0001-10142012
Approval Date: November 1, 2012
Authority: Chief, Resource Management

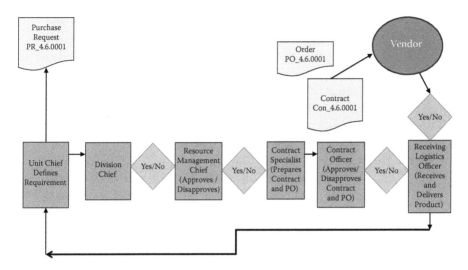

Figure 6.4 Example of purchasing procedure PFC.

1. References
   a. Internal Procedures
      i. 4.6.0002 Competitive and Sole Source Vendor Selection
      ii. 4.6.0003 Receipt of Products
      iii. 4.6.0004 Development and Approval of Annual Budget
   b. External Regulations
      i. ISO/IEC 17025: 2005 International Standard
      ii. Metro City Financial Policy for Vendor Selection
      iii. Metro City Annual Budget Policies and Procedures
2. Laboratory Mission Statement
   Metro Laboratory shall strive to meet our customer requirements through the application of the best science to the best evidence in an efficient, effective, and ethical manner with the highest quality.
3. Policy
   Metro Laboratory shall be diligent in keeping current with state of the art technologies having potential to increase efficiency and effectiveness of services provided to our customers. New technologies may provide greater productivity, higher quality (less non-conformance), increased efficiency (less cost), and decreased cycle times with associated decreased resulting backlogs. *All staff* will continually advise their *Branch Chief* of potential new products for evaluation to increase quality of services provided to our customers.
4. Procedure
   a. All Staff

    i. All staff shall keep current with latest technologies and services that may increase the efficiency and effectiveness, and contribute to the continual improvement of operations in their respective units. Staff shall forward, with detailed descriptions of benefits and a *CD_PR_4.6 (Purchase Request)* to their respective *Unit Chief by 1 June* to be assessed for submission to budget approval and subsequent purchase and evaluation.

  b. Unit Chief

    i. *Unit Chief(s)* shall discuss with staff merits of recommended products and services. Unit Chief will assess potential for increasing effectiveness, efficiency, timeliness, and quality of services and *shall approve or not*, sign, date form Purchase Request (CD_PR_4.6) and if approved submit to the *Chief, Resource Management* by *1 July.*

  c. Chief, Resource Management

    i. *Chief, Resource Management,* shall review the CD_PR_4.6 for accuracy, completeness, and Unit Chief approval. Upon verification of availability of budgeted funds; *approve or not*, sign and date and forward to the *Contract Specialist* as appropriate.

  d. Contract Specialist

    i. The *Contract Specialist* shall review the CD_PR_4.6 for appropriate completeness and appropriate Unit Chief and Resource Management Chief approvals. Upon verification of appropriate approvals, the Contract Specialist will follow appropriate internal/external fiscal policies, procedures, and regulations and decide if the purchase of this product requires a sole source justification or shall be a competitive bid process.

    ii. If a sole source purchase is justified, the Contract Specialist will follow sole source procedures, develop a contract, and *forward to the Contract Officer* for approval and execution.

    iii. If a competitive bid is required, the necessary procedures will be followed to allow competitive bidding by appropriate vendors. Upon completion of the competitive bid process, a contract will be *forwarded to the Contract Officer* for approval and execution.

  e. Contract Officer

    i. The *Contract Officer* shall review, *approve or not*, sign and date all sole source purchases and contracts

(Con_4.6.0001) for accuracy and completeness as per all fiscal policies, procedures, and regulations.

1. Approved Sole source purchase requests and competitive bid contracts shall result in a Purchase Order (PO4.6.0001) approved, dated, signed, and forwarded to successful vendors for purchase of products by August 1.

f. Logistics Officer

   i. The Logistics Officer, upon receipt and before 1 October of the associated funded fiscal year, *will confirm the inventory of the product received is accurate or not* and concurs with associated PO_4.6.0001. Upon verification, the Logistics Officer shall make entry in the Log Book (LB_4.6.0001) the description of the product, invoice number, date, and initials. Any discrepancies or damage will result in the product being returned to the vendor.

  ii. Upon proper receipt, the Logistics Officer, shall affix Property Tag (ID_4.6.0001) for products valued over $500 and shall deliver the product to the associated Unit Chief. Upon delivery, the Unit Chief shall sign and date the Receipt of Product form RE_4.6.0001. The Logistics Officer will maintain completed RE_4.6.0001 forms.

g. Potential Non-Conformances

    i. Purchase not strategically aligned with Mission priorities

   ii. Purchase not strategically aligned with customer requirements

  iii. Purchase does not increase capabilities or performance LMPM metrics

1. Increase productivity
2. Increase quality
3. Decrease cycle time

  iv. Purchase not funded

   v. Incorrect entries or no signatures, dates, approvals on controlled documents

  vi. Controlled documents missing for property valued over $100

 vii. Untimely completion of process steps

1. CD_PR_4.6 Purchase Request
   a. June 1, Unit Chief
   b. July 1, Division Chief
   c. August 1, Resource Management Chief
2. Con_4.6.0001 Contract

     3. PO_4.60001 Purchase Order
     4. Log Book
     a. October 1, Logistics Officer
     5. RE_4.6.0001 Receipt
  viii. Sole Source should be Competitive Bid
    ix. Competitive Bid should be Sole Source
     x. Damaged products received
    xi. Incorrect products received
   xii.   No ID number affixed for property valued over $500

References

Deming, W. E. (1986). *Out of Crisis*. Cambridge, MA: Massachussetts Institute of Technology.

Federal Bureau of Investigation (FBI). (2013). FBI Quality Assurance. Retrieved 2013 from http://www.fbi.gov/about-us/lab/biometric-analysis/codis/codis_quality.

Hogan, R. C. (2005). *Explicit Business Writing: Best Practices for the Twenty-First Century*. Normal, IL: Business Writing Center.

International Organization of Standardization. (2013). ISO 9000: 2005 Quality Management Systems—Fundamentals and vocabulary. Retrieved from http://www.iso.org.

ISO/IEC 17025. (2005). General requirements for the competence of testing and calibration laboratories. Switzerland: ISO.

Kirk, P. L. (1953). *Crime Investigation, Physical Evidence and the Police Laboratory*. New York: Interscience.

National Academy of Sciences (NAS). (2009). *Strengthening Forensic Science in the United States: A Path Forward*. Washington, D.C.: National Academies Press.

Occupational Safety and Health Administration. (2013). Retrieved August 28, 2013, from http://www.osha.gov.

Pechenik, J. A. (2007). *A Short Guide to Writing about Biology* (6th ed.). New York: Pearson/Longman.

Shewart, W. A. (1980). In *Economic Control of Quality and Manufactured Product* (50th Anniversary Commemorative Issue), p. 501. Milwaukee, WI: American Society of Quality.

Strunk Jr., W., and White, E. B. (2000). *The Elements of Style* (4th ed.). Needham Heights, MA: Pearson.

Index

For Product Safety Concerns and Information please contact our EU
representative GPSR@taylorandfrancis.com
Taylor & Francis Verlag GmbH, Kaufingerstraße 24, 80331 München, Germany

www.ingramcontent.com/pod-product-compliance
Ingram Content Group UK Ltd.
Pitfield, Milton Keynes, MK11 3LW, UK
UKHW020933280425
457818UK00031B/696